Scales of Captivity

| Scales of Captivity |

RACIAL CAPITALISM AND THE LATINX CHILD

Mary Pat Brady

Duke University Press   *Durham and London*   2022

© 2022 Duke University Press
All rights reserved
Designed by Courtney Leigh Richardson
Typeset in Portrait by Westchester Publishing Services

Library of Congress Cataloging-in-Publication Data
Names: Brady, Mary Pat, [date] author.
Title: Scales of captivity : racial capitalism and the Latinx child / Mary Pat Brady.
Description: Durham : Duke University Press, 2022. | Includes bibliographical references and index.
Identifiers: LCCN 2021021367 (print)
LCCN 2021021368 (ebook)
ISBN 9781478015314 (hardcover)
ISBN 9781478017936 (paperback)
ISBN 9781478022558 (ebook)
ISBN 9781478092445 (ebook other)
Subjects: LCSH: American literature—Hispanic American authors—History and criticism. | Hispanic Americans in literature. | Children in literature. | Immigrant children—Mexican-American Border Region. | Deportation in literature. | Emigration and immigration in literature. |
BISAC: LITERARY CRITICISM / American / Hispanic & Latino | SOCIAL SCIENCE / Ethnic Studies / American / Hispanic American Studies
Classification: LCC PS153.H56 B733 2022 (print) | LCC PS153.H56 (ebook) | DDC 810.9/868073—dc23
LC record available at https://lccn.loc.gov/2021021367
LC ebook record available at https://lccn.loc.gov/2021021368

Cover art: Betsabeé Romero, *Pendientes de un hilo* (Hanging by a thread). 2019. Silk screen on tin plate. © Betsabeé Romero. Courtesy the artist and Nancy Sever Gallery.

This book is freely available in an open access edition thanks to TOME (Toward an Open Monograph Ecosystem)—a collaboration of the Association of American Universities, the Association of University Presses, and the Association of Research Libraries—and the generous support of the University of Michigan's College of Literature, Science & the Arts and the Provost Office. Learn more at the TOME website, available at: openmonographs.org.

For Kate

and

for Ana Luisa, Rosa, Rafael

with all my love

and

with my boundless gratitude for

teaching me how to feel our belonging

Contents

Acknowledgments ix

INTRODUCTION
The Scalar Lien 1

1   CAPTIVATING TIES
    On Children without Childhoods 37

2   PLAUSIBLE DENIABILITY
    Pursuing the Traces of Captivity 79

3   SUBMERGED CAPTIVITIES
    Moving toward Queer Horizontality 119

4   $N+1$
    Sex and the Hypervisible (Invisible) Migrant 153

5   MISPLACED
    Peopling a Deportation Imaginary 197

    CONCLUSION
    Density's Resistance to Scale 239

    Notes 249   Bibliography 275   Index 293

Acknowledgments

This project emerged in fits and starts as I remembered whispered hisses at conferences, found the figure of the cast-off child repeatedly appearing in disparate Chicana and Latina texts, and struggled to understand the nation's dependence on homophobia for its bordering work, all while trying to raise three young and fabulous kids; care for aging but faraway parents, whose eventual passing would shift how I understood everything; and survive a brush with a fatal disease and its lingering traces. To say, then, that I am indebted to the many folks listed here is only to hint at the numerous friends who have offered support through some really tumultuous times, and it is only to suggest the breadth of my gratitude.

The early stages of this project began in conversations with many extraordinary students, and I am thankful for the chance to learn from Amanda Waldo, Leah Moore, Amelia Samuelu, Adalix Siri, Callie McQuilkin, Thomas Petluck, Jendayi Brooks-Flemister, Sierra Pregosín, Sarah Zumba, Lesle Jimenez, Salvador Herrera, Rosario Majano, Kevin Cruz, Cassy Griff, Margo Cohen Ristorucci, Sydney Lester, and Danielle Terrazas Williams. Rosario, Callie, and Ana Luisa Brady-McCullough also offered significant research assistance as the text evolved. Similarly, a number of graduate students engaged with the questions that shaped this project, and I am so grateful for their scholarship and friendship: Danielle Haque, Joseph Miranda, Nancy Quintanilla, Esmeralda Arrizón-Palomera, Lena Krian, Gilda Posada, Mariana Alarcón, Ariana Vigil, Angela Naimou, Annette Portillo, Belinda Rincón, Breanna Leslie-Skye, Jessica Diaz Rodríguez, Stephen Kim, Jorge Cartoya, Armando García, Oscar Omar Figueredo, Toni Jaudon, Maja Horn, and Melissa Gniadak.

Generous audiences helped hone this project including those at the University of North Texas; Oberlin College; Northwestern University; Indiana

University; Stanford University; the University of California, Riverside; and the University of North Carolina, Chapel Hill. Two groups of listeners bookend this project: at its start I presented a rough version of parts of the project at Princeton, where I benefited especially from the rigorous engagement of Daphne Brooks and Alexandra Vazquez. Near its end, I was fortunate enough to have an audience at the University of California, San Diego, willing to follow the arc of the project, and I am especially grateful to them for their questions and encouragement and to Kirstie Dorr for making the trip possible.

This project received generous support at its inception when I was honored with a Whitney J. Oakes Fellowship from the Humanities Council and the Center for African American Studies at Princeton. When I'd finally reached the finish line, a Rosenthal Advancement of College of Arts and Sciences Women Faculty Award helped me resolve a lingering question. Finally, a TOME award from Cornell University Press supported its publication as an open-access text.

The Picket Family Fund and the College of Arts and Sciences assisted with workshops, research funds, and a subvention. I especially want to thank Caroline Levine, who as a colleague and department chair graciously encouraged this project. Over the years, Roger Gilbert, Wendy Wilcox, Fred Muratori, Marti Dense, Karen Kudej, Kara Peet, and Paula Epps-Cepero have solved small and large conundrums, often without enough thanks or enough time. At Duke University Press, this project has been shepherded by the phenomenal Gisela Fosado, Ale Mejía, and Lisl Hampton. I cannot thank them enough for their patience and efficiency.

An unbelievable number of people generously read versions of the whole manuscript despite its iterative incoherence, and I am so grateful to them for their help: Kate McCullough, Sonnet Retman, José David Saldívar, Patricia Ybarra, Helena María Viramontes, and Alex Vazquez. Kirstie Dorr provided crucial, brilliant feedback at a late stage of the project, and the majestic Richard T. Rodríguez read the manuscript more than once; his extraordinary side notes, questions, comments, and marginalia helped me shape it far more than I can adequately say. An intervention by Laura Harris and Fred Moten transformed the project's through line, and Janet Jakobsen, who listened to my ramblings over the years, provided encouragement at a crucial moment.

Scholarship is collaborative, but writing can be lonely, so I'm deeply grateful for the friendship of many people who also commented on various aspects of this effort: Sonia Saldívar-Hull, Alexandra Vazquez, Michelle Habell-Pallán, Daphne Brooks, Yolanda Padilla, John Alba Cutler, Curtis Marez, Theresa Tensuan, Christina Crosby, Cheryl Finley, Sallie Marston, Joshua Miller, William Orchard, Ariana Vigil, Christopher Pexa, José Muñoz, Shelley Streeby, Deborah

Vargas, Lisa Thompson, and Isaiah Wooden. In Ithaca, I've been especially nurtured and encouraged by Sofia Villenas, Veronica Martínez-Matsuda, and Helena María Viramontes. Their collegiality, friendship, and comments on chapters matter more than they know. So many other friends have given their support for everything from picking up kids to feeding all of us. Their generosity has sustained us across the years. My gratitude to Martha García, Olivia Martínez, Sherri Krams, Jane Weisbin, Charlie Riley, Lisa Fink, Robert Milton, Patrice Jennings, Katie Hascup, Isabel Boggs-Fernández, Zack Boggs, Stacy Snyder, Julia Machlin, and Suki Montgomery Hall.

As my daughter Rosa wisely told me a few years ago, "It takes gumption to write a book!" But it also takes gumption to endure a preoccupied parent whose amorphous thoughts and fragmented attention can be irritating and discouraging. So, for the patience, grace, and love Ana Luisa, Rafael, and Rosa have shown me over the years, I am so very grateful. They've helped me raise this book, and they've cheered me along at every stage. Finally, no words adequately express my gratitude to Kate McCullough. She has made space for the project, listened to me hash out ideas over and over again, and offered extraordinary insights that nudged my thinking along, but most especially she has loved me with friendship, great humor, brilliant meals, splendiferous apple pies, and sparkling kindness. To her I owe my greatest debt.

INTRODUCTION

The Scalar Lien

When the courts declared in 2018 that the Border Patrol and US Immigration and Customs Enforcement (ICE) could no longer separate families seeking asylum in the United States, many thought the practice itself would cease. Few realized that the courts narrowly defined *family*. Only those deemed "immediate"—legal guardians or parents—could count as family. And so, to the shock of refugees but under the radar of an easily bored public media, immigration officials have continued dismembering kin networks, separating grandmothers from their grandchildren, aunts from their nephews, uncles from their nieces, cousins from one another, jailing and detaining them in separate camps, often hundreds, if not thousands, of miles apart from one another. Separated infants and young children are routinely sent to foster homes; if they remain in foster care for six months or more, they can be turned over to US adoption agencies, permanently removed from their birth families, their stories and status absorbed into oblivion. All without their guardian's authorization. Bureaucratic kidnapping.[1]

While such practices certainly exemplify the brutality the United States exerts as part of its system of immigrant deterrence, they also amplify one of the broader sinews holding together the logics of settler colonial and capitalist systems.[2] From its inception as English colonies to the present day, the United States has always relied on dismemberment, beginning with African, Irish, and English children spirited away, kidnapped from their parents by the Virginia Company to work its plantations.[3] It has similarly relied on a practice of shredding affective relations to build and maintain a labor force: not only were indentured and enslaved peoples denied the opportunity to establish permanent kin networks or reliable affective structures, but so, too, were the men recruited from China and Japan in the nineteenth century, as were the men knitted into the Bracero program in the mid-twentieth century.[4] The mass lynching of African Americans and Mexican Americans terrorized people of color for decades and helped keep social relations precarious, as did the institutionalization of segregation, as does its contemporary coefficient, mass incarceration.[5] Similarly, the vision of transforming Indigenous peoples into a new docile labor force entailed deconstructing their social relations by murder and by boarding school.[6] Put differently, the United States has never welcomed a broad, vibrant sociality composed of "families" of color even as such assemblages have developed despite the best practices of a racialized ideology of labor and power.

And if "family separation" has long been at the heart of US racializing labor practices, so, too, has captivity. Of course, the dissolution of kin relations functions within a relay that presumes multiple forms of captivity. The children held in cages along the US-Mexico border, like their grandparents and cousins, must survive not just the "legal violence" of the deportation machine but an economy and history wedded to captivity.[7] The articulation of "freedom" as well as the infrastructure necessary for the unimpeded movement of capital and goods requires constraint, a constraint structured discursively as a threat and a stay, a hedge and a border. While the carceral efforts deployed by the United States have been carefully and brilliantly studied by a number of scholars, the habits of captivity extend beyond the ken of institutionalization, remaining largely adjacent to institutional memories even though the informal captivity practices of Spain, Mexico, and the United States effectively shaped what is now the US Southwest.[8] So, too, life without papers in the twenty-first century must also be understood as a form of captivity, as a flexible enclosure that constrains and delimits socialities just as forced removal and mass deportation have broadened the geometry of captivity seemingly everywhere. Determined to ruthlessly mangle the affective networks that enable social lives to flourish, the US migration system has become the new Virginia Company.

The resurgence of direct attacks on children of color and nonwhite kin networks has been shocking to many because the relevance of captive taking to the maintenance of white supremacy has been partially forgotten, buried in the narrative of racial progress and the teleological accounts of freedom, of equality. Many Latinx writers, artists, and scholars have not, however, forgotten this history, nor have they understood it as either irrelevant or over. Rather, they note the work of ICE and the US Border Patrol, the proliferation of detention centers alongside new methods of constraint, as a reelaboration of a consistent pattern, evidence of the ongoing coloniality of power. Drawing from this repertoire, *Scales of Captivity* argues that if scholars are to come to grips with intensified violence toward migrant peoples, as well as toward people of color more generally, within and at the edges of US geospaces as well as across its spheres of influence, we must study the history that such writers trace as well as the profoundly different conceptions of being in the world that they offer.

Ultimately, the poets, novelists, and artists discussed here open a significant avenue for consideration of the logics behind forced removal and mass deportation. Through their particular attention to captive, cast-off children, they identify, critique, and undermine a fundamental grid structuring the Western imaginary, one of the operative, taken-for-granted principles of the coloniality of power: scale. Not only do they offer this analysis and critique, but they further provide an alternative to scale. In turning to density of connection, they shirk the violence of the scaffold imaginary that scalar thought enforces. And this is necessarily so because the scalar imaginary subtends policies that produce family separation, caged children, mass deportation, and myriad other practices of captivity. Indeed, it is why attention to the captive child is so crucial right now—the child, as currently conceptualized, is scalar force made productive.

In *Scales of Captivity*, I discuss two aspects of scale. Utilizing the conventional understanding of scale as a mechanism to describe spatial-social relations (such as the local, the national, and the transnational, or the body, the family, and the group), I examine how spatial expansion of geo/economic power and reach, or what geographers call *rescaling*, necessarily involves forms of capture and captivity. I draw attention to this crucial dynamic between scale and the production of new methods of containment by tracing the figure of the captive, cast-off child across nearly 150 years of literature written by people who identify as Mexican, Chicana/o/x, and Latinx. I argue that with each wave of spatial rescaling, new variants of capture emerge; economic expansion is predicated on the production of new methods of movement and containment.

Scale is also a powerful epistemological form, neither neutral nor transparent. I take up this aspect of scale as well by showing how it functions as the entrenched logic undergirding the coloniality of power. Parading as a useful, quotidian convention through which the Western imaginary organizes an understanding of spatial and social relations, that is, as the merely logical way to describe being-in-place, scale ultimately operates through processes of comparison and containment, requiring abstraction and homogenization to enact a limiting, hierarchical perception of spatial and social relations. My focus on spatial scaling demonstrates the shaping, capturing force of scale, the way its logic is the sine qua non of colonial power, the force of abstraction through comparison, containment, and homogenization. The writers discussed here draw attention to this aspect of scale through the emergent figure of the cast-off child.

If these writers expose this murkier, virulent, violent aspect of scale, their critical engagement also offers a set of alternatives, a crucial set of approaches to being together and being in place without scale. They enable us to think without scale, to avoid its corrosive, encasing effects. Their turn to what I call *density* and *queer horizontality* reveals not only multiple proximities but also shared vulnerabilities, the shards of obligation both opaque and transparent. This attention to the density of the felt nearby is not a parochial move, nor a narrative mode inhibited by a lack of cosmopolitan sensibilities; rather, it exposes the rich connections that underpin the collective labor of making meaning through relation, and thus worlds more multiple than scalar binaries such as small/large or global/local would permit. So, too, these writers' unruly performative modes—including burlesque and impersonation—alongside their focus on cast-out and cast-off captive children create new possibilities for reparative relations that can counter the understanding of sovereignty animating borders and cages.

To understand the breadth of their intervention and its relation to the many logics that suture together structures of power, I begin with a discussion of the figure of the child as crucial to narratives of freedom, practices of captivity, and processes of racialization. Turning to the figure of the child and the privilege of childhood, I examine these categories' relationship to liberal theories of movement and the manner in which they enable various types of capture and bracketing practices that extend beyond formal carceral structures—an importance that has been lost to much of the current analysis of immigration and civil rights but that these writers have presciently considered. I subsequently offer a discussion of scale as form and heuristic before offering descriptions of the chapters to follow.

In the Beginning

It's worth remarking on the surprising fact that María Amparo Ruiz de Burton, Phillis Wheatley, Olaudah Equiano, Frederick Douglass, and W. E. B. Du Bois all have something in common: their signal meditations begin with a focus on the figure of the child.[9] Writing from different historical moments and with different ends, their combined attention to the child hails our attention. At the very least, their attention to the child highlights the importance of the category, because the category of the child, as a conceptual, scalar practice, is integrally connected to the logics of social life, including governance, force, money, race, work, gender, power, and sexuality.[10] This history reveals that how a child is defined and what is meant by *childhood* have been deeply contested within the Western imaginary. Moreover, the current treatment of child refugees indicates that no settled consensus about what childhood is, entails, or merits has been reached. Rather, who can have access to the protection of childhood remains central to the articulation of racializing economies of governmentality.

The conceptual underpinnings of the liberal nation-state were developed concurrently with and even through the articulation of both an idealized child and childhood as a distinct phase. Sharon Stephens argues that the "emergence" of the nation-state depended on the "hardening" of the child-adult dyad.[11] By this she means that as Thomas Hobbes, John Locke, Jean-Jacques Rousseau, and other political theorists struggled with how to design a government that could be based on the "consent of the governed" rather than the "divine right of kings," they not only attempted to define consent itself but also wrestled with delimiting who could actually consent to be governed.[12] Locke concluded that the right to consent, to exercise political will, requires reason and experience. He defined this right negatively by describing who cannot adequately reason and so participate in a consensual relation to governance. To Locke, children constitute such a perfect class of people who are incapable of consent; children, he argued, lack the reasoning skills, experience, and autonomy necessary to act as a state subject (to vote, legislate, or enter into contracts) free of coercion. They are too easily coerced and too vulnerable to corruption; children's dependence on adults for protection, food, shelter, education, and training is at odds with the independent, autonomous reasoning Locke claimed necessary for citizens of a nation-state.[13] Crucial to Locke's evaluation of the child is his assertion that children are incapable of self-restraint: only those who can exhibit self-restraint, the capacity to curb appetite, to act with rectitude, to think independently, are truly capable of self-governance, of sharing power in a participatory liberal republic. Inherent to this narrative of deficiency, then, is also a claim about development, a linear vision of movement toward some new category of being that is not the child. This developmentalist discourse also entails a nested hierarchy of capacity (staged toward a liberated end: the fully realized rectilinear, autonomous adult). Hence, the category of the child, as a form of scale, and as it evolved from the sixteenth to the nineteenth centuries, finally came to rest on its relationship to lack; the child came to symbolize all those ineligible to claim the right to steer their own social relations or to hold the status of citizen.[14] Put differently, consent was developed as a mechanism to scale the experience of being in place, of being a child, or being an adult, of belonging to a polity.

Of course, as Holly Brewer exhaustively details, the work of defining the child was not left to political theorists alone. British and US politicians wrestled with questions such as at what age a white man could testify in court, serve on a jury, act as a legislator or judge, vote, serve a prison term, or be executed. The resulting legal and civil decisions, Brewer argues, were as instrumental for defining the concepts of a child and of consent within republican governance as any political theory. Colonial leaders such as Pennsylvania governor Robert Hunter Morris put the case this way: "Children do not vote. Why? Because they want prudence, because they have no will of their own. The ignorant and the dependent can be as little trusted with the public interest."[15] John Adams would follow a similar line of argument: "Children . . . have as good Judgment, and as independent Minds as those Men who are wholly destitute of Property."[16] In conflating poverty, or lack of property, and lack of judgment with childhood, Morris and Adams brought together the condition of dependence with the concept of autonomy to establish a boundary around suffrage. By conflating childhood with dependence and a lack of reasoning skills, they also established a powerful trope that continues to flourish.

Novelists also actively developed the figure of the child, weaving it into a long stream of texts that laced the figure into a broader conversation about power. Eighteenth- and nineteenth-century novelists, for example, turned to the orphan as a means to consider relations of governance and consent; children's relationships to their fathers were turned into allegories of the modern nation and its subjects.[17] Stories of parent-child relationships became fictional opportunities to meditate on the various ways the nation could flourish and mediate power among its members. Its usefulness as a category drew in part from its flexibility—the child signals "the promise of autonomy and the reality of dependence," Carolyn Levander notes.[18] Drawing on this tradition, writers as various as Thomas Paine and John Adams repeatedly compared the colonies to a white child whose parent, England, was corrupt and corrupting; they thereby encouraged a nascent nation to identify itself with the image of an Anglo child and to represent itself as such.

By the early nineteenth century, Romantic poets, leaning first on Locke and subsequently Rousseau, further enhanced the category of childhood, according to Robin Bernstein: "William Wordsworth's romantic representation of children as innocent, holy, and able to redeem adults" ultimately wove "childhood and innocence together wholly. Childhood was then understood not as innocent but as innocence itself; not as a symbol of innocence but as its embodiment. The doctrine of original sin receded, replaced by a doctrine of original innocence."[19] Innocence animated childhood after reason and judgment were evacuated from it. In this configuration, childhood became (at least in this fantasy) the zone of the authentic, presocial self of innocence. Innocence stood opposed to reason; experience was distinguished from dependence.

Over the course of three centuries, according to Levander, both political and literary arguments came to depend on child subjects as the means to "represent, naturalize, and, at times, attempt to reconfigure the ground rules of US national belonging."[20] The figure of the child could both mediate belonging and serve as a heuristic for the increasingly racialized narratives suffusing the discourse of suffrage. The heady political work of a seemingly innocuous category such as the child has been effective because, on the one hand, it encourages a faith in a utopian childhood that is demarcated as innocent and outside of, apart from, or protected from the corrosive forces of socialization. On the other hand, depictions of the child have been "shot through with race" so that they are never not embroiled in racializing technologies.[21]

Bernstein explains that "white children became constructed as tender angels while black children were libeled as unfeeling, non-innocent, non-children" because "innocence defined nineteenth century childhood and not vice versa; therefore, as popular culture purged innocence from representations of African American children, the black child was redefined as a nonchild—a 'pickaninny.' . . . Pain divided tender white children from insensate pickaninnies. At stake in this split was fitness for citizenship and inclusion in the category of the child, and, ultimately, the human."[22] On the one hand, a clear cultural practice of racializing childhood established it as the site of innocence. But, on the other hand, as Brewer notes, scores of politicians followed the lead of Thomas Jefferson and John Adams, arguing for the "unfitness" for independence and freedom of nonwhite peoples by figuring them as *perpetual children*: "President Andrew Jackson, for example, justified political authority over native Americans by comparing them to children who lacked reason. . . . President Taft justified American rule over the Philippines . . . by claiming that Filipinos, like women and children, did not have sufficient reason or fitness to choose their own government."[23] In this manner, childhood has been figured into the tropological economy of racialism where protected status becomes a triggering mechanism for forms of capture. Subjugated peoples who cannot claim "innocence" remain perpetual children unable to pass through the phase called childhood. They remain, therefore, perpetually suspect and always available to the carceral economy of freedom.

Childhood ultimately became another scaffold supporting a racialized structure that relies on linking original innocence to whiteness, thereby pinning down "the unmarked status of whiteness."[24] This logic depends on distinguishing "the child" from "childhood," securing childhood as a privileged, innocent, protected phase of life that was racialized as white and establishing a "possessive investment" in childhood.[25] As a category of privilege, childhood marks a life phase that is fleeting; the temporality of heteronormativity earmarks childhood as the period before desire, before responsibility.[26] Marking this temporality is the assumption that the rational adult leaves childhood behind. Inherent to this structure is a tale of development that sustains the possibility of achieving rationality. Such movement *through* childhood, however, has been historically conceptualized as available only to propertied white men. Only they could move from childhood to rational, independent adulthood. The fight for poor white men and any white woman to claim a place in this developmentalist structure was long indeed. For an even longer period, people of color were figured as perpetual children who were nonetheless robbed of their childhood, denied the protection of innocence the label childhood offers as a privilege. In the great interstices between the child and childhood, one could be a child forever but never experience childhood. And for those bent on perpetually reproducing racializing mechanisms, childhood demanded a possessive investment. It deserved protection, a demarcated status, one that could be withheld, stolen, denied.

So it was not for nothing that Wheatley, Equiano, Douglass, Du Bois, and Ruiz de Burton would begin their literary engagements and crucial interventions into political theory by focusing on children and childhood. Intricately bound by the structures of race and writing, childhood functioned as a sort of gateway to freedom through the mid-twentieth century. To insist on an experience of childhood, one that could be narrated and thereby *grown* out of vis-à-vis education and responsibility, was to give evidence of one's capacity to evince autonomy, to inhabit and claim freedom; it was also a distinct challenge to the racializing assumptions that underpinned childhood and the language of liberal subjectivity. These writers and scores of abolitionists and critics of white supremacy who would follow continually rearticulated the significance of protected childhood as part of the project of laying claim to aspirational universal categories such as the human and the citizen.

Working white people wrestled access to childhood from the elite by attacking their assumptions about irrationality and rectitude and insisting that they, too, were capable of independent thought and self-control.[27] They forced laws that provided for education, that prohibited child labor, that expanded the temporal length of the category, and, eventually, pressed by African American activists, grudgingly admitted its cross-racial reach. Nevertheless, the habits and practices of treating everyone under the age of eighteen as equally vulnerable remained unstable. Not only were differential treatments the norm as criminal justice and health care systems were established, but educational structures also served to reinforce and produce distinctions, ranging from Indian boarding schools to the shabbily funded schools for poor children everywhere, but especially for poor children of color. Part and parcel of the civil rights movement, then, was an effort to produce a new concept of childhood, one broad enough to include all children.[28] Yet these efforts were hedged by anxiety and refusal. The agriculture industry, for example, continues to lawfully employ children, just as uneven educational outcomes illustrate the ongoing refusal to adequately educate all students.[29] Most clearly, the disparate treatment of children snared by policing systems reinforces the liberal republic's dependence on a dynamic of inequality. Although children of color have been incrementally granted access to a romantic vision of childhood, complete with some semblance of guarantees to education and health care, such access has been carefully hedged by larger racial projects that produce suspicion and thereby suspend childhood for African American, Latinx, and Indigenous children.

Children without Childhoods

One of the threads that links Latinx writers—whose formal, ideological, and aesthetic projects differ enormously from one another—is their consistent attention to children whose lives have been hedged, bracketed, held in abeyance, and, often, completely enclosed and shackled. If such attention to captive children begins in 1872 with the publication of Ruiz de Burton's *Who Would Have Thought It?*, it also appears in novels that rested in the archives until their belated publication, such as *George Washington Gómez*, as well as those that helped inspire new generations of writers, ultimately becoming the iconic texts of the Chicana/o and Nuyorican movements, such as . . . *Y no se lo tragó la tierra*, *Down These Mean Streets*, and *Nilda*.[30] Of course, this threaded, consistent attention to the constrained child is hardly a coincidence. Not only does it reflect an important aspect of a collective effort to disentangle the logics structuring the US imaginary, but it also signals writers' engagement with the violence of US empire building, the legacies of British and Spanish imperialism, and Mexican histories of complicity with these practices of exploitation, as well as Indigenous Mexican, Chicanx, and Puerto Rican experiences as subjugated peoples.[31]

While such attention to youth loosely links Latinx literature to the canonical British and US novel, contemporary writers such as Helena Viramontes, Manuel Muñoz, and Lorraine López veer away from the historical bildungsroman that figures the child as (Anglo) icon for the nation-state, as emblem of settler sovereignty and liberal governmentality. Their focus on the captive child highlights the racialization of childing (the ongoing construction of people of color as incapable of achieving adulthood) while also illustrating how childhood itself functions as a form of scale. Indeed, concepts such as the child and practices such as racialization work together as conjoined logics of scale showcasing the continuing viability of this relay between denied childhood and impossible adulthood for the political state and for the ongoing efforts to maintain white supremacy within capitalism.

These writers' attention to the variegated forms of submerged captivity reveals how modes of capture anchor articulations of freedom and citizenship and, further, how such modes of capture shift and change as nation-states rescale themselves. That is, with each round of spatial/political expansion, or rescaling of economic and military might, the modalities of captivity change such that the enclosure practices of the seventeenth or nineteenth century look very little like the brackets enclosing young Latinx lives in the twenty-first century. Simply put, if colonial efforts in the Americas began with rounding up England's own poor children and shipping them to Virginia and the Caribbean, their expansion to include the kidnapping of children in Ireland and then across the African continent reveals how much the scalar expansion of capital and empire relies on captivity. By the end of the nineteenth century, captivity included nefarious processes of incorporation such as Indian boarding schools, convict leasing, and sharecropping as the United States extended its (geo)economic reach. By the end of the twentieth century, when national borders had become less crucial to economic scale and the scope of national powers had expanded almost willy-nilly, methods of captivity began to include apparently "voluntary" migration, a face-lift capitalizing on climate change and trade treaties. By the early twenty-first century, after multinational trade pacts fully rescaled markets and recalibrated nation-states into less meaningful economic units, the threat of deportation—omnipresent and sinuous—as well as the very experience of life after forced removal broadened the mechanisms of captivity across the hemisphere. The discussion of child bracketing that follows ultimately reveals how crucial capture is to every successful effort to rescale power.

Yet even as methods of captivity have shifted, one discursive aspect of captivity has not changed—captivity requires forms of witness. Although in many cases witnessing simply serves to reauthorize the state, to indemnify it against its own violent fantasies, these writers remake witnessing, shifting it out of a juridical context and elaborating its potential to repair and heal, to produce connections and acknowledge obligations.[32] Such reparative possibilities entail, however, a different nodal structure, one that does not serve a system of sovereignty requiring a masquerade of rectitude and individuated autonomy, nor one that maintains a system that proclaims freedom by ensuring that only some may enjoy unencumbered movement because others are constrained. Rather, the reparative witnessing that writers elaborate entails connections, acknowledged and shared vulnerabilities, mutual indebtedness, and obligation. This witnessing turns against individuated possession, and it turns against scale—both essential planks of the scaffold imaginary; it emanates from density. Not only do the texts studied here reveal and examine the formal relations among scalar expansion, captivity, and witnessing, but their consideration of the child captive-witness offers an alternative to scale's imposition of the scaffold imaginary as well.

So, when young twenty-first-century refugees approach the US-Mexico border as generations before them have, their horizon of possibilities is already split—a path to childhood lies open at the same time that their access to such childhood is limited by the matrices and land mines of racialization. This splitting is exemplified by the policing practices that justify separating children from their caregivers by categorizing the children, essentially, as objects that have been trafficked; when the parents are accused of felony human trafficking, the children are reconceptualized as captives of their own parents, and the methods of separation and captivity are cast anew.[33] This policy draws on a history of children as captives and of racialized peoples and children as lacking access to the world of adult rationality, and thus a history of children as objects of improper treatment, to justify their policy of separation. When the policy was initially announced, it drew nationwide condemnation as activists and the media drew on the hard-won right of children of color to claim a childhood and to access a romanticized image repertoire of childhood innocence and protection to combat new efforts at subjugation. Partially successful in mitigating some of the brutality of border policing, activists demanded that children, however racialized, could lay claim to childhood. Nonetheless, this clash between competing conceptions of who has access to childhood also reveals another deep contradiction at the heart of the liberal state.

Mobility and Bracketed Lives

When the figure of the child took on new importance as philosophers and novelists began to imagine a world organized not around the sovereign authority of a king but around a form of shared governance by the propertied, the education of elite sons took on a new importance as necessary to widen the ambit of sovereignty and to refine the concepts of both property and contract.[34] Another aspect of the child gained attention too. The movements of a child, a dependent, could be easily constrained, justified as due protection, but what of the child turned unruly adult? Unrestrained movement posed a threat to the propertied elite reliant on constrained bodies to produce their wealth. The figure of the ignorant, willful child disinterested in curbed appetites easily foreshadowed the trouble an unrestrained adult might cause to social stability, which is to say to wealthy property owners. So, just as childhood was figured as a form of privilege, so, too, was mobility, and thus mobility as an expression of freedom appealed, albeit in a contradictory manner, to the liberal imaginary.

Meditations on the capacity of locomotion in Hobbes and Locke especially helped to define what came to be known as the liberal subject. For both, freedom pivots around movement even as, or perhaps especially because, the maintenance of sovereignty increasingly requires more and more modalities to manage, constrain, encourage, and contour movement. The concept of freedom is materialized through mobility, and power is materialized through the ways in which it can regulate and constrain movement. According to Hagar Kotef, "This liberal concept of freedom emerged in tandem with other configurations of movement, wherein movement was constructed as a threat rather than an articulation of liberty."[35] While Hobbes expounded the importance of free movement of capital, goods, and services, he was far less certain that people should be allowed to move without restraint. Hobbes ultimately construed unregulated movement as dangerous, a threat that must be constrained and made real or materialized such that some "subjects appear as free when moving (and oppressed when hindered)." Eventually, the poor, vagabonds, and colonized, racialized subjects, Kotef contends, "were constituted (or rather deconstituted) as unruly subjects whose movement was a problem to be managed. This configuration was the grounds for justifying nonliberal moments—and spaces—within liberal regimes."[36] For the liberal elite to be truly free, hedges and grooves were necessary to constrain the movement of the nonelite. Hobbes's concept of freedom subsequently emerged as intimately bound with a contradictory dynamic, one that requires for its practice the hedging, constraining, and capturing of the movement of most of the inhabitants of a liberal regime. This double play crystallizes in the practices of enclosure, eviction, forced removal, deportation, imprisonment, surveillance, and siege. All of these efforts foreclose movement for some in order to instantiate and seemingly guarantee movement for a few, elite others. Such an understanding of freedom through limitation produced what Kotef calls a "schism, a contrast, between those who can control their movements, and thus rule, and those whose movement is hindered or excessive, and thus cannot."[37] The modern state emerged not only, as Max Weber argues, through its efforts to gain a monopoly on violence but also, as Kotef points out drawing on John Torpey, through its ability to authorize and regulate ways to move.[38] The centrality of movement to liberal subjectivity compels the economies of captivity into the quotidian logics of all subjected to sovereign practices such that "through the production of patterns of movement (statelessness, deportability, enclosures, confinement) different categories of subjectivity are produced. . . . Regimes of movement are integral to the formation of different modes of being."[39] The constraint and bracketing of those denied adulthood, those perpetually deemed the unruly, dependent child, orders movement for everyone else. Ordered movement, configured as liberal freedom corporealized, requires ballast. Private property came to be understood as one of the crucial stabilizers of freedom. For those without property, captivity does the trick.

The Removes of Captivity

As a newly robust concept of childhood began to emerge, redefining the experience for the sons of the British elite, and as the old order of child-rearing was revised to adapt to a changing political economy, nonelite children were redefined by their status as excess. Their capacity to move became an opportunity to exploit. This contrast between an elite few and the broader population reinforced the status, vulnerability, and value of childhood for the elite and reinforced childhood as unavailable to poor people. The distinction is important: for the elite few of the sixteenth, seventeenth, and eighteenth centuries, childhood functioned as a protective embrace, a hedge against vulnerability, and an opportunity for growth. Moreover, it was a stage, a temporally marked platform that young men would leave behind as they acquired the privileges of wealth, power, and property. For the broader population, to be a child was to be permanently assigned the status of *dependent*, incapable of rational thinking, ineligible for transformation. For the broader population, to be a child meant to be ineligible for citizenship; one could not expect to own property or even, practically speaking, to learn to read. Put differently, the systems of enclosure that were articulated through the dynamic of possession and dispossession also entailed a transformation of human relations as scaled into a nested hierarchy reliant on forms of enclosure, which was integral to an understanding of the forms of movement sovereignty would permit. More specifically, childhood was restructured, not as a temporary stage of development, but as a kind of hazard for poor children, who were harvested for the colonial project and nascent industrialization. It is not stretching the analysis too far to suggest that for poor children, childhood and captivity were one and the same.

And children were captives. Tens of thousands of English and Irish children were kidnapped and shipped to the nascent colonies to labor, usually to their deaths.[40] Many millions more were kidnapped from Africa. Forced removal and impressment led to death, and eventually rebellion, as well as new configurations of fugitivity among escapees from English brutality and Native communities willing to welcome them; indentured servitude subsequently served as a palliative to disaggregate Anglo laborers from African laborers and hence refine concepts of movement and captivity still further. In the Spanish Empire, Catholicism, the mission system, and peonage emerged as structures to restrict the movements of Indigenous peoples, while slavery became the major method through which capital and labor were organized and cultures devised in Europe and the Americas.

Given how central regimes of captivity and coerced mobility were to an unfolding discourse of freedom and practice of sovereignty, it should be no real surprise that the first "best seller" in the British American colonies was a captivity narrative.[41] Mary Rowlandson's "The Sovereignty and Goodness of God, Together with the Faithfulness of His Promises Displayed," published in 1682 and republished within the year as "A True History of the Captivity and Restoration of Mrs. Mary Rowlandson," describes Rowlandson's wartime experience of 1675. Printed four times when it was first published (in London and Boston), it was continually circulated and reprinted throughout the colonial era. Credited by scholars as a crucial instance of the development of a nascent colonial literary imagination and, later, of women's writing more generally, Rowlandson's narrative became the iconic US captivity narrative, helping to produce an understanding of Anglo freedom as dependent on the confinement of American Indians.[42] Puritan captivity accounts were lionized in the British colonies and spawned countless imitations even as they served as models for a form of writing that would later be called ethnography and even as they evinced, repeatedly, a certain ambivalence on the part of the white women who related (usually in a mediated fashion) their experiences as prisoners of war.[43]

Embedded in the iconic captivity narrative is a complex economy of recognition and misrecognition in which the "captive" retrospectively testifies to the experience of living within a very different culture. As the captive observes a set of practices drawn from radically different philosophies, she frames and misrecognizes these not as different cultural practices or the articulation of different philosophies but as the habits of the subhuman. She misrecognizes Native homelands as "uncultivated" and "ungoverned."[44] Rowlandson, for example, misrecognizes her own comrades' hostile, murderous actions against Indigenous peoples just as she misrecognizes the Indigenous alliance's own compassionate treatment of her amid the violence of warfare. What is not available in this economy of (mis)recognition is the possibility of open admiration, an acknowledgment of ingenuity, generosity, or compassion, the affective labor of shared sociality. Thus, what Sylvia Wynter calls "transcultural modes of cognition" remained out of reach for Rowlandson, who maintained "the ostensible universally applicable 'natural law,'—a law that imposed a by-nature divide between 'civilized' peoples (as true generic humans who adhered to its Greco-European cultural construct) and those, like the indigenous peoples of the Americas and the Caribbean, who did not."[45]

Read from the perspective of early American literature, Rowlandson's story is one of captivity. Read from the perspective of Indigenous studies, however, a different story of captivity emerges. As Lisa Brooks (Abenaki) astutely notes, "Rowlandson's captivity was not marked by confinement, but rather forced movement through unfamiliar space. Her description of the 'several Removes we had up and down the Wilderness' reflects a discomforting disorientation."[46] She did not know the land that she and her family were attempting to colonize. Moreover, as Brooks explains in her careful study of King Philip's War, Rowlandson's captivity could hardly be said to exemplify captivity as carceral. Rather, the narrative reveals that Rowlandson's experience was just an instance in a wide web of captivity established not by the Nipmuc but by the English, who had laced together numerous carceral spaces in which to hold, imprison, and kill Indigenous peoples as part of their arsenal in a permanent war for control of the territory.

Ultimately, captivity narratives like Rowlandson's and those that followed also served, as Kate Higginson notes, as "*narratives of absolution* strategically mobilized to mask contemporaneous captures of local Indigenous populations."[47] However much one can detect admiration of Indigenous cultures and ambivalence toward Puritan and Anglo cultures in early captivity accounts, the larger effect of the genre was to reinforce the militaristic and violent assault against Indigenous peoples and to underscore their ongoing representation as irrational forces supremely dangerous to Anglo property and prosperity. If Rowlandson's narrative creates what Brooks calls an "uneasy dialectic" in which the Indigenous are "constructed as foreign," it also exemplifies the logic of movement that

Kotef sees as the primal contradiction animating a hidden theme of liberal governmentality: "A contemporary split organized around mobility between (I) the citizen (often as a racialized, classed, ethnically marked, and gendered entity more than a juridical one), as a figure of 'good,' 'purposive,' even 'rational,' and often 'progressive' mobility that should be maximized; and (II) other(ed) groups, whose patterns of movement are both marked and produced as a disruption, a danger, a delinquency."[48] In Rowlandson's account, the unimpeded movement of Indigenous people is counted as "a threat rather than an articulation of [their] liberty," while Rowlandson's hindered movement is accorded the status of oppressive. The captivity narrative reinforces the Hobbesian schema of hedging and bracketing, constraining and denying free movement for all but a few. Rowlandson embroidered this schema with a racializing logic that furthered the creation of a colonial framework and reinforced the budding ideology establishing who got to move and who did not.

This contradictory logic of liberal movement also animates the understanding of the prison in the US imaginary. As Caleb Smith argues, imprisonment has been understood dialectically: one tradition envisions the prisoner as a dehumanized figure, the figure whose unimpeded movement can only be conceptualized as a threat, while a second tradition imagines the prisoner as a figure capable of the necessary self-restraint to reform and move freely. This bifurcated understanding emerged in the century after Rowlandson's narrative appeared and illustrates, as Smith puts it, "the harrowing concept of the human on which the prison rests."[49]

Rowlandson's libelous characterization of Indigenous people thunders across US writing, infiltrating representations of kidnapped Africans and the Mexican residents dispossessed of their status as Mexican citizens after the 1848 Treaty of Guadalupe Hidalgo; it is echoed in the characterization of Asian immigrants as non-Christian, and the ongoing slandering of Indigenous peoples as irrational. Its logics of racialized (im)mobility trundled along through post–Civil War Reconstruction, Jim Crow, and beyond to the late twentieth century, essentially indemnifying the buildup of a mass carceral system. Although the broadening of suffrage chipped away at the exclusionary club established by Hobbes, Locke, Adams, Jefferson, and others, the momentum for a transformed concept of whose movements constituted a threat and whose did not was slowed, nevertheless, by the implacable dependence of liberality on the distinction between a child and an adult, between captivity and mobility. It would creep into the patronizing accounts of the Progressive Era, the Americanization campaigns, and especially the legal opinions of judges who held people's lives in their hands. The racialized narrative of the child that was used to justify captivity, colonization, and depredations against Black and Indigenous peoples remained in force centuries after its development.

Whereas captivity once looked like a very specific set of practices organized especially around chattel slavery, by the early twentieth century multiple other forms of captivity had morphed into myriad forms of bracketing, methods of constraining lives that included, most obviously, mass incarceration. In the literature studied here, however, captivity is treated differently, although the dynamic between respectability and spectacularization remains. The legacy of classic captivity tales animates the work of both Ruiz de Burton and a contemporary writer, Lorraine López, both of whom shadow the captivity tale of Olive Oatman in particular. Yet they, and the other authors studied here, turn captivity sideways, arguing that the United States captured and held Indigenous and Mexican people and resources captive. They further argue that the "victims" of captivity were not always iconic white women celebrated by popular media, such as Rowlandson or Patty Hearst. And, finally, they show how the logic of captivity, its usefulness to the state and especially to the national imaginary, structures and constrains Latinx lives in various ways right up to the current moment when the family separation policy, the rush to put infants and children in different cages from those supplied to their adult companions, became the subject of political outrage and court battles over this treatment of refugees. As the texts explored here show, captivity doesn't need to include iron bars to constrain choices. Being stranded by freeways, abandoned by caregivers, made to migrate, forcibly deported, deprived of historical connections to communities and cultures and life-giving stories all bracket life, hold it captive, constrain possibilities. But as the texts discussed here also show, such experience of violent constraint, of being cast off and cast away, doesn't simply mean loss and death. Instead, by turning to practices of density and queer proximities, these writers refute the logic that splits childhood and children and imagine instead relations linked by reciprocity without sovereignty.

The long development of liberal governmentality clearly depended on the conceptual work of categories such as the child and childhood as much as the empire-building work of Spain, England, and the United States came to depend on material children, deprived of their childhood and harnessed to do the laborious work of extracting resources and planting new economies. Similarly, all three empires depended on hedges and grooves to limit movement for most of their subjects, to contain freedom for an elite (even when proclaimed as available to all). A stunning array of forms of captivity suture the histories of these three empires together, their legacies present not only in mass incarceration but also in the contemporary migration machinery of all three countries, all of which have variously refined their practices of captivity and targeted refugees for new types of enclosures. Yet while these aspects of the emergent modern have been studied (although largely not studied in tandem), far less attention has been given to a crucial conceptual structure that is both a routinized habit of thought and a material practice that lies beneath the work of empire making. It has been essential to the definition of childhood, the logic of captivity, and the making of nations: scale.

Scale and Its Castagories

Scale pervades the form of articulation that names a European longing called America. Yet what is this desire called scale? What work does it do and for whom? Part and parcel of the colonial apparatus that ensnared potatoes, llamas, cacahuetes, cochineal, and on and on into a structure of belonging as owned, even treasured, scale cuts earth, cuts languages, cuts textures of relationality. Then, scale populates, renames, reconceives, possesses, brands, markets, and demeans.

Scale stoked Francisco López de Gómara to ecstatically explain to an audience still hesitant to embrace the categories or especially the authorities bubbling through the ideas called Spain and Spanish that "*the world is only one and not many*."[50] López de Gómara, Hernán Cortés's confessor and apologist, sought to shift away from a plurivocal multiverse to gain a sense of perspectival possession that could enact the terms and architecture for empire and form a monovocal, monofocal universe. He turned to the idea of scale to produce the possibility of empire; scale enables rationalized abstraction (the world is one), transforming and authorizing indistinction and defining possessions claimed and carved and narrated from the ejido to the rancho, from the local to the regional to the hemispheric to the global, the planetary, and beyond. The many belong to the one (a king, a pope), articulated as his, as mappable and mapped, as for sale, a source of tribute and point of pride, articulated within a nested hierarchy, a new geoimaginary. This conceptualization of the world that renders it "only one and not many" is a founding abstraction of the global, initiating the fetishization of separability and individuation, of indistinction amid hierarchies.[51]

Of course, López de Gómara was not the first Spaniard to harness scale for empire. Preceding him by more than a dozen years, the Jesuit theologian Juan Maldonado imagined flying to the moon, where he could visualize the entire surface of the earth as one whole unit. As Jesús Carrillo Castillo explains, Maldonado turned to a "classical topos in order to create a detached view of the world, a fictional vantage point from which to make the world an object of visual scrutiny."[52] From the perspective of the moon, Maldonado envisioned "the earth as a continuously inhabited and fully intelligible surface open to imperial troops and Catholic religious orders," thereby creating "an abstract and strictly theoretical approach" to conceiving the world as one made for empire.[53] From the perspective of the moon, places lose their specificity, and scale emerges fully reliant on fictions of abstraction, homogeneity, containment, and spectacularity. The view from the moon makes possible what geographers call the "scaffold imaginary"— the vision of the world as understandable through a set of nested hierarchies that privilege a vertical plane.[54] Most clearly articulated as the stretch from body to home to city to region to nation to hemisphere, scale names mass and relation, while insisting on the fundamental logic of abstraction, containment, categorization, and comparison folded into a vertical, hierarchical orientation.[55]

Scale, like its workhorse the border, claims its power in part because it functions as metaphor made material, as a rhetorical device and an economic practice, as a register for the selling of socks and the ordering of zoning laws, as the linguistic reservoir for racism and racializing conventions and, ultimately, as both an epistemological and ontological formation.[56] In other words, built into scale is an assumption that the view from the moon offers truth, that the world is one and can be homogenized as such, and that, indeed, the density of the nearby has no transcendent meaning, and certainly no meaning that can't be scaled. Scale underpins the coloniality of power and, as a habit of thought, helps establish and maintain a global order of racialized peoples.

Early in Spain's colonial project, López de Gómara and Maldonado articulated a heuristic structure that would vivify the nascent colonial system, helping to embed it in the emerging colonial violence as perpetual logic itself. Moreover, their claims echo and elaborate the broader effort of early European modernity to insist on the perspective imposed by singularity, to seize the vanishing point that disappears multiplicities. To make the monoworld functional for empire, these and other early modern writers turned to scalar methods that would order and hierarchize relations, compare and contain them. They devised more and more scalar projects, initially by folding descriptions of landmasses into categories that would simultaneously name and discursively homogenize them while also locking them into a structure of comparison. Viewed from the moon, the monoworld could be divided for the pursuits of power, reinforcing verticality and leveraging hierarchy, scooping all into a singularizing accountability through infinite but regulated detail. The seductively explanatory power of scale functions as a heuristic *and* as naturalized phenomena. Scale reinforces an understanding of space and sociality that depends on binaries (e.g., local/global) while romancing the ongoing movement between the small and the large, consistently emplacing sociality within structures of comparison.[57]

This scaling of the world helped create a global order of racialized peoples dispossessed of their relations to their lands, their beliefs, their languages, their socialities.[58]

Spanish colonialists developed an elaborate architecture, the casta system, for naming human relations. Castas held vast legal and political import; they slotted people into a nested hierarchy, creating a scaffolding of peoples abstracted and rationalized into a structure of explanatory difference. Casta logics were marked legally through birth registries.[59] Those designated "of caste" were registered in a book Spaniards called *El libro de color quebrado* (The book of broken color).[60] *Quebrado* can also be translated as "bankrupt," a usage that would have been common in sixteenth-century New Spain; *color quebrado* thereby reinforces an incipient racial capitalism while signaling the relation Spain established between tribute and caste.[61] Castas entailed a process of differentiating peoples by abstracting them into categories aligned with structures of property, thereby materializing as "real" these distinctions and generating a relay between the fictional work of putting people into categories, or *casta*gories, and the recognizably real material demands made by empire. Yet if such castagories offered an aspirational effort to manage and capitalize on sensual relations, they did so by simultaneously homogenizing and differentiating them. Thus, intimacies were intricately categorized such that children were cast through finely tuned division into castagories, while at the same time the intricate, multilingual, complex cultures of kidnapped Africans and colonized Indigenous peoples were homogenized, cast into a kind of named oblivion, into the reductive terms *indio* and *negro*. Such castagories inscribed scaling by disarranging prior social affiliations so that sustainable structures of feeling were narrated against and through nested hierarchies. In this manner, the casta system embedded scale into the quotidian, situating the scale of the body within hierarchal systems of place making, that is, in settler colonial terms of possession, to make real and practical the scaffold imaginary. This elaboration of fictional difference in the name of hierarchy also reinforced Maldonado's view from the moon, because it animated the perspective from *outside*, an apartness that spectacularizes differences while making them manageable and distinct.[62]

Castas begged visualization, a mapping that could make visually explicable complex processes of differentiation and homogenization. Popular and mostly completed during the eighteenth century, casta paintings offered an elaborate and extensive spectacle of social transformation through the visualization of nested hierarchies.[63] They were used to create and illuminate racialized difference, to narrate the meaning of *caste*, or, put differently, to constellate race around sex. They typically depict a woman, a man, and one or more children, each marked or narrated by a visual symbolic that suggests that they are "from"

FIGURE I.1. Eighteenth-century casta painting. Anonymous. From Ilona Katzew, *Casta Painting: Images of Race in Eighteenth-Century Mexico*, 36.

supposedly different "races." These racializing tableaux helped to create a visual grammar of race, sex, and domesticity so that to see race is to know sex. If they typically appeared in sets of sixteen or so to suggest progressions, they also worked to create the concept of a Latinidad in which the visualization of hierarchies was a crucial mechanism for narrating sexualization and racialization as one and the same process.

In their most well-known iterations, they depict grids of trios, a man, woman, and child, each trio elaborately and distinctly garbed, distinguishing them from other trios. Except for the top tier, who may be shown playing instruments, relaxing in elaborate rooms, or viewing their land, the depicted groupings are usually engaged in some form of labor/commerce, and they are always emplaced within an enumerated naming system that identifies each caste, the child, as a "by-product" of the "mixing" of the two adults. The adult figures typically lean toward one another, suggesting desire and care; the paintings thereby casually reinforce their subjects' habits of inclination over European men's supposed habit of rectitude and rationality (symbolized by their portrayal as surveyors and masters of European musical instruments). The presence of children not only naturalizes racialization but reinforces the depiction of women, especially racialized women, as a species governed by maternal and erotic inclinations. As "founding statements of modern representation," casta paintings instrumentalize intimacy as heterosexist and as a mechanism of racialization.[64] Linking the exoticism of intimacy to difference, casta paintings produce race as knowable; they instruct by making race a quotidian materiality, an outcome of the everyday.[65] By scaling cultural difference through the multitude of differentiated garbs and skin tones, casta paintings taught racial difference as cultural difference (marked by clothes, activities, locations) and, through these multiply circulated syllabi, taught Europe to understand race and to find satisfaction in a particularly useful apparatus (scale) that helped render race meaningful, real, natural, and universal.[66] Such efforts helped solidify the idea of a single world, one that could be characterized as having a single, underlying nature or reality but with many cultures. This representational move, according to Arturo Escobar, promoted "the West's ability to arrogate for itself the right to be 'the world,' and to subject all other worlds to its rules."[67] Casta paintings ultimately reinforce the figure of the child as a manifestation of scale and the scaffold imaginary.

Because they situate the heterosexual family as a unit within spaces of consumption and labor, casta paintings also register "families" within scalar structures, including markets of various kinds. They offer an idealization of mixed kinship within the normative family unit, signaling the figuration and castagorization of the child in the name of a scalar project that embedded a nested hierarchy of relations. These paintings similarly work as a modality of dismemberment even as they depict a "family" unit. They divide sociality by establishing who is subject to dismemberment, to analysis, and who is subject to the denial of childhood by way of the ascription of an incapacity for childhood, or inability to have a childhood. Even if these paintings were popular only during the eighteenth century, their visualization of homogenization through differentiation nevertheless cast long shadows.

Castagories helped orient the Spanish Empire and aided in articulating a newly scaled planet as a method of folding the many into one world. Casta paintings helped clarify the newly emerging separation between the observer and the observed as the first principle for what science and ideology would call *objectivity*. This visualization of relations scaled into grids of intelligibility was also important to the effort to produce newly rescaled sovereign imaginaries. The scalar imaginary nurtured its nearest relation, globalization, such that scalar thinking undergirds the intellectual and practical work of empire building just as it mutated into the crucial work of nation building during the nineteenth century.

Scale's utility to empire can also be seen by turning to an obscure speech about an early argument for an infrastructural transformation that would rescale an already powerful but nascent economy. Speaking in 1819 while the United States debated whether to admit Missouri as a slave state, DeWitt Clinton, then governor of New York and the man who propelled the Erie Canal into existence, linked the construction of the canal to the preservation of a union among states:

> A dissolution of the union may therefore be considered the natural death of our free government. And to avert this awful calamity, all local prejudices and geographical distinctions should be discarded, the people should be habituated to frequent intercourse and beneficial intercommunication, and the whole republic ought to be bound together by the golden ties of commerce and the adamantine chains of interest. When the Western Canal is finished and a communication is formed between Lake Michigan and the Illinois River, or between the Ohio and the waters of Lake Erie, the greater part of the United States will form one vast island, susceptible of circumnavigation to the extent of many thousand miles. The most distant parts of the confederacy will then be in a state of approximation, and the distinctions of eastern and western, of southern and northern interests, will be entirely prostrated. To be instrumental in producing so much good, by increasing the stock of human happiness; by establishing the perpetuity of free government, and by extending the empire of improvement, of knowledge, of refinement and of religion, is an ambition worthy of a free people.[68]

Clinton advocates for the creation of a "people" at a national scale, a group that identifies with the national and that emerges out of its production.[69] What should be noted is Clinton's sense of urgency over the production of this national scale. Perceptively suggesting that for the United States in 1819 the national will emerge not through common sociality, nor through a sense of shared responsibility to a communal land, nor through language or ideology, but through technology, transportation, and communications systems and that these will structure the formation of a "people," Clinton calls for shifting the significance of regional scales, by *rescaling* the North through a unitary transportation scheme, through infrastructure that would defeat the South's challenge to Northern supremacy.

Clinton's language reinforces the nested hierarchies of scale (local, regional, national) helping to structure capitalism even as he predicts that the regional would, indeed must, learn, over the course of the nineteenth century, to prostrate itself before the national. Furthermore, his comments neatly anticipate how important the national scale would become to industrial expansion, just as his deployment of the rhetoric of national union, of submission to the national good, anticipates the secessionist conflict. While Clinton also suggests that a national "people" may already be in place—one that can be defined through reference to the discursive—he also implies that the empire of improvement (infrastructure) in the hands of capital would go much further to produce such a "free people." Government-supported capital investment would create the conditions of freedom, a claim long resonant with efforts at intertwining capitalism with nationalism and democracy. And here, in the meshing of the concept of nation with that of people, by creating a category of people comparable to the scale of the national, a project that preoccupied the nineteenth-century intellectual elite across the Americas and that structured the declarations of governors and capitalists such as Clinton, one can see the significance of scale to narratives of nation and identity. Clinton here argues for the usefulness of scale for managing and mitigating dissent even while he might be puzzled by his sought-after national scale's failure to adequately define and structure a homogenized people. Clinton tells us that scaling establishes relations between scales but also, crucially here, entails the consolidation of power and the establishment of affiliations within the order of the scale itself, just as it produces a vision of one's "place" within a scale that must always be transcended. The scalar work of infrastructure makes peoples, creates the condition of possibilities for castagories and for new forms of containment (in Clinton's case, the containment of Southern financial power).

Clinton understood the coercive force of scale and scalar projects' capacity to reshape cultural relations as well as financial ones, and in doing so he was drawing on the already substantial history of rescaling power through captive taking. The kidnapping and forced removal of poor Irish, English, and African children were also mechanisms by which spatial relations were rescaled, power extended, surveillance enhanced, and economic control articulated across a wider swathe of power and space. The process of rescaling was a way to not only transform labor structures everywhere but also to change the narrative about sovereign power and sovereign reach. Forced removal, as a practice of scaling, transformed how people oriented themselves and their relations, creating a structure of loss and producing subjunctive mourning for what could have been. Not surprisingly, the poor, and especially poor children, were most vulnerable to this practice of taking captives and removing them to their deaths. Put differently, rescaling nearly always entails some form of capture, yet the work of captivity is hidden even as everyone from López de Gómara to Clinton to contemporary CEOs celebrates the power of scale and invokes the scaffold imaginary.

Critical geographers such as Sallie Marston have offered a substantial critique of the ideological work that scalar thinking presumes. Marston and her collaborators note the way in which scalar analyses have tended to prioritize large-scale structures. Not surprisingly, "globe talk" implicitly renders as parochial the quotidian practices of social reproduction, from cooking, to sharing an anecdote on a bus, to changing diapers, "thereby eviscerating agency at one end of the hierarchy in favor of such terms as 'global capitalism.'"[70] Such scale talk reinforces what Henri Lefebvre calls "phallic verticality" and a "small-large imaginary" that entails "preconfigured accounts of social life that hierarchize spaces of economy and culture, structure and agency."[71] One can easily see this sensibility in operation given the privileging of global and hemispheric comparisons over the seemingly regional and local, as Marston and her collaborators note: "Hierarchical scale (de)limits practical agency as a necessary outcome of its organization. For once hierarchies are assumed, agency and its 'others'—whether the structural imperatives of accumulation theory or the more dynamic and open-ended sets of relations associated with transnationalism and globalization—are assigned a spatial register in the scaffold imaginary. Invariably, social practice takes a lower rung on the hierarchy, while 'broader forces' such as the juggernaut of globalization, are assigned a greater degree of social and territorial significance."[72] The result is a tendency to direct a "critical gaze toward an 'outside over there' that in turn, hails a 'higher' spatial category."[73] In other words, spatial thinking, but also studies of the world more generally, depends on "prior, static conceptual categories" (nation, region, locale, hemisphere, globe) as a priori explanations in which form determines content.[74] Even as they may critique the logic of property underpinning capital relations, scholars nevertheless recur to Maldonado's view from the moon, presuming the world is one and not many.

Scale's seductive quality is clear. Enormity is scary and threatening, appealing and alluring. Scalar rhetoric, for example, has been used most effectively by anti-immigrant politicians and activists to threaten a social transformation that undermines the power and privilege of white people in general and white men especially. Whether immigrants are described as waves or floods, a scalar affect invokes a force that cannot be withstood.[75] Scale works through multiple analytic strategies as a rhetorical force, as a geographic heuristic, as the apparently neutral, transparent backbone to the logics of capital and empire that would ultimately describe and inscribe more than abstract places.

Scale also draws the attention of literary critics, who see in it a chance to name a critique of the nation form and thereby ensure a call to think and read diasporically, or hemispherically, or transnationally. Inherent to these calls is both a critique of the damage and violence the nation-state did and does and a sense that the nondiasporic, the nonhemispheric, the nontransnational analyses may somehow be too local, hence too narrow-minded, too stuck in the status quo, too enmeshed in "the nation," to effectively capture a liberated imaginary.[76] Such a critique in arguing for radical resistance to US imperialism has often been directed at Chicanx studies as well as African American and Indigenous studies by claiming they fail in a parochial way to understand transnational rubrics and encounters. While this critique of nation-oriented studies has been helpful, it may inadvertently reinforce capitalism's nested hierarchies and size fetishism. Or, as Marston and colleagues note, "A Newtonian worldview continually haunts the calculus of mobilization and resistance," which insists that "global capitalism and imperialism can only be combated by entities operating at a similar scale." Such an insistence "leaves those who are constrained by various 'militant particularisms,' or who are too under-resourced or disorganized to 'scale jump' on the bench when it comes to the zero-sum game of global resistance."[77] Thus, the use of scale to critique the apparently too parochial imaginary of, say, Chicanx studies or African American studies reinforces the violence of scale in the name of scale.[78]

Furthermore, in such a Newtonian worldview, the tide of time moves away from the local, the parochial, and toward the swifter currents of the global, trans, diasporic, and cosmopolitan. The local is surrounded by the eddies of stasis. The local is mired, stuck, out of step with time. This insistence on scalar jumping denigrates the ephemeral, the opaque shrug, the small poem, the devotion to the nearby, the single refusal, the quirky song, the diminutive move, the creative articulation that refuses to be scaled up and rendered "universal" or "transnational," the narrative that stays home and avoids the master. Such attention to the small-large imaginary calibrates narratives about agency only insofar as it can be named through the language of mass mobilization.[79] As Vanessa Agard-Jones argues in her meditation on Michel-Rolph Trouillot, this focus on the world and the planet, or the view from the moon, fails to be sufficiently "attuned to the possibilities" that the body and "the quasi-human agents that constitute it" may compel together.[80] By contrast, Agard-Jones suggests, we recognize the multiple, "material entanglements—be they cellular, chemical, or commercial" that may be engaged with one another at any given time and that disappear within the project of scalar epistemologies.[81]

The view from the moon also fails to understand opacity, density, queer horizontality, social/spatial relations, affective meshes that cannot be narrated via the norms of "family" or "nation" or "region" because they cannot be scaled up. This fetishization of scale, and the scaffold imaginary more generally, repeatedly returns through castagories, and naturalized scalar norms, through the faith that ever more refined and ever grander scales make new legibilities possible. And it is thus in those terms that we see the long fingers of colonial enlightenment continually shaping even our desires to decolonize thinking, to get out from under its weight. Scale hides like a sniper on the moon—emplacing and containing over and over again.

Either World or Situation

The rich critique of scale offered by Marston and others compels us to shift our conception of scale as a fait accompli; it helps us reject the illusion of a monoworld that scale has conjured, so that we can shut our eyes to Maldonado's now-naturalized perspective from the moon. It asks us to understand how sites and events morph, how they exist through dense and changing interactive practices and through the processes by which conditions of possibility for some are conditions of constraint for others.[82] Such an effort demands a shift away from dualistic, hierarchical conceptualizations of relationality: it calls for a new effort, one that leans toward connection. Although Marston and her collaborators urge an effort to "overcome the limits of globalizing ontologies," they admit that doing so will require "sustained attention to the intimate and divergent relations between bodies, objects, orders and spaces, that is to the processes by which assemblages are formed."[83] To think space without scale is to abandon the scaffold imaginary, to imagine relations that don't rely on narrative scaffolds or borders for their definition, their articulation. It is to abandon the romance of family and childhood and give up the nostalgia for the whole and the one.

How, then, to begin to think the textures of connections without relapsing into possession, into emplacement and orientation, into an architecture of explanation that enfolds all form, all narration, all being, into a nested scalar hierarchy? Put differently, how does one read and write knowing the world is many? Undoing the strictures of monoworlding, some would say decolonizing, entails a turn to writers who know the pluriverse, who scrutinize the coloniality of perspective López de Gómara celebrates. To refuse the logic of one world (and the dualist structure it relies on) entails embracing the sense that many worlds coexist together. It is to shift away from what José David Saldívar, drawing on Aníbal Quijano, notes emerges with 1492 and the coloniality of power: the planetary.[84] Fred Moten puts it slightly differently when he writes that the "Atlantic slave trade and settler colonialism (in themselves, which is also to say in the traces of the insistently previous but anoriginal displacements and emplacements they bear) are irreducible conditions of global modernity—that is, of the very idea of the global and the very idea of modernity."[85] Moten's suggestion here is that embedded in the scaling of the nearby and the next door into the "global" are containment, slavery, and the displacement of multimodal ways of being together. The planetary names the global form of modernity that is containment, comparison, and bracketing.

Moten signals this abstraction of land and people together into a scalar project of "emplacement" when he notes, "When being-in-the-world is who you are, and who you are is what you own, and what you own is where and when you are, then what it is to have been taken and to have been made to leave which marks again and again the already inexhaustible vestibule of what is known and lived as the exhausted, is the beginning and the end of the world."[86] So to abandon scale means thinking without not just the coloniality of scale; it also means refusing the idea of a neutral, passive ground from which one claims a sense of self; it is to give up the assumption that the self begins from that which is propertied and can be acquired and scaled.[87] Without scale it may be possible to understand land as "agentive," as Jodi Byrd (Chickasaw) suggests: "There is a possibility that the spirit of the land itself works with an agency of its own on the imagination of settlers, arrivants, and Natives alike, influencing us and actively inflecting which stories we tell and how we tell them."[88] To turn toward a sense of agentive materiality is to engage in an entirely different understanding of relationality; it is to unbuckle scale from connection; it is to make possible dis/objectification without castagories.

Such thinking without scale can also be found in José Esteban Muñoz's theorization of brown relations.[89] For Muñoz, thinking brown shifts us away from the logics of racialization, mired as the language of race especially (but gender and sexuality additionally) is in the scalar metrics of a world that is one and not many, a world that can be abstracted into a scaffold imaginary and assembled within nested hierarchies. For Muñoz, to take brown affiliation seriously may mean to lose the individual per se, to shift from a faith in stability and toward the "swerve of matter" into a brownness that is a "being with, being alongside."[90] To think brown is to think with the density of connection, into a sort of queer horizontality, a queer density textured apart from and without a phallic verticality. Such density leans toward incompleteness; it dips into indebtedness and allows us to relinquish the grounding idea of the whole and the one, to abandon the reverence for rectitude required by the monoworld, or what Adriana Cavarero calls the rectitudinal "geometry of modernity."[91]

The concept of the child has been mobilized to enshrine rectitude. Theorists of the child drew from the earliest of Greco-Roman pedagogies, including Aesop's fables, to train elite children toward rectitude, to produce a developmentalist model that emblematized phallic verticality and that structured markers of the movement toward rectitude within a nested hierarchy. In this way the child came to figure, to serve as an icon, for the logic of scale; it became the face of the scaffold imaginary. Not only is the child the name, the figuration, for a form of scale that works as both metaphor and heuristic; it also relies on nested hierarchies that instantiate norms of "development" toward rectitude and through a process of comparison that unfolds within normative time. This logic of development requires comparison, benchmarks, effectively pitting children against each other, in order to produce the castagorical work that whittles multiplicities of experiences into singularity, normativity, neurotypicality. To have a childhood is to have the capacity to unfold through normative, developmental time into a "properly upright" adult citizen. Those who cannot so unfold, the logic goes, are cast off, hedged and bracketed.

Scales of Captivity examines a group of writers who, if they have not used the specific language of rectitude and inclination, take up the castaway, cast-off child who refuses the conditions rectitude requires; the texts studied here rebuke the emplacements of scale and castagories, unwind the logic of borders, and refuse complicity with a scaffold imaginary in order to imagine being-in-relation, thriving through connection. Not only do they refuse the traffic in bodies that, in the name of rescaled economies and through their false promises, relies on repeatedly shredding the social and sustaining ties and meshworks of relations that enable social beings to flourish, but they also refuse the logic that scalar ideologies deploy. The writers discussed here draw from African American and Indigenous philosophies and traditions, from the hard lessons of organizing and activism against the brutality of the deportation regime, to offer a sophisticated set of theories about how to think about the pluriverse and how to think relationally; by centering the cast-out child, they ask us to start with relational practices of knowledge that do not rely on either the scaffold imaginary or phallic verticality. Rather, they envision relations and connections through a rich sense of the indebtedness that emerges from acknowledging shared vulnerability and forms of interdependence, an understanding that, as Fannie Lou Hamer would have it, none of us are free if we aren't all free.⁹²

Split Off

When Hamer demanded freedom, she refused rectitude and comandeered a different geometry of connection, one not organized around phallic verticality. She insisted on unbracketed movement, without hedges or borders. She redefined freedom away from liberal individuation and autonomy by demanding the sustenance of all as inextricable from the well-being of all. She unbundled children from scale, childhood from captivity. She demanded that we think from debt, from obligation, from inclination. Taken seriously, Hamer's call should rewire academic analyses, because it refuses a functional bifurcation, one that again reinforces the discipline of scale and the logic of the scaffold imaginary. Put differently, the scalar habit of thought tends to lock down how scholars study belonging and belonging together and thereby maintains rectitude against inclination, because scale.

Analyses organized from the moon's vantage point see the world configured as local, regional, and global and tend to take these categories as transparent, neutral, as frameworks for beginning rather than logics that subtend analysis. For example, scholars may take an aspirational approach and focus on relations within a community or nation; this is the approach grouped under the banner of civil rights. The second approach considers how a community or nation is constituted by its limits, that is, by what establishes who can belong to a community or nation; this is the approach demarcated by immigration studies. These two approaches are rarely studied simultaneously. So, for example, scholars who study gay rights or sexual citizenship usually begin from the first perspective by discussing what constitutes the relationship between members of a society, what activities and relations are allowed, encouraged, or prohibited. Scholars studying immigration law and policy, however, take the second approach.⁹³ They study how a nation constitutes itself by creating an outside, a border, a juridical limit that is both geographic and biographical. This bifurcated approach—which considers either how citizenship can or cannot guarantee equality (civil rights) or how outward structures of boundaries (such as immigration) are constructed and reinforced—is untenable for Latinx studies. *Scales of Captivity* therefore examines a set of texts that understand captivity, belonging, and nation making differently. These texts pick apart scale, identifying the violence that scalar practices entail and the methods by which we are inured to the scaffold imaginary. Writers' focus on children, on youth hedged out of childhood, on the methods of captivity, enclosure, and dispossession as they iteratively shift with each project of rescaling from the early nineteenth century into the present, deserves attention, for it reveals a complex technology of the coloniality of power that has largely escaped our notice and continues to encumber our imagination.

Captivity and captivity narratives have typically been studied in a narrow sense even as literary historians have insisted that the captivity narrative itself played a central role not only in US literary history broadly but also, and especially, in the development of literature by white women.[94] Practices of captivity and constraint, however denied or ignored, were crucial to the development of the British colonial system and the later US empire along with its settler colonial imaginary; they helped to establish not only the state's claim to a monopoly on violence but also its claim to a monopoly on movement, on who may leave and who may stay, who may move with impunity and who may not.[95] Yet few studies have highlighted captivity from the other side. Correcting this elision, chapter 1, "Captivating Ties: On Children without Childhood," turns to María Amparo Ruiz de Burton's 1872 novel, *Who Would Have Thought It?*, demonstrating that her portrait of a racialized child held captive by white Northern financiers and abolitionists reveals how practices of captivity, bracketing, and constraint were central to the production and maintenance of sovereignty in general and liberal republican governmentality more specifically. I examine how Ruiz de Burton's novel pursues this problem, showing that in taking aim at the fiction of consent of the governed animating liberal idealism, Ruiz de Burton exposes its underlying quotidian racializing practices and logics and illustrates its crucial reliance on the figure of the constrained and racialized child who is unable to grant consent. This turn to the racialized child, I argue, is both significant and prophetic, announcing the figure as central to any cultural discussion that would seek to engage the experiences of Mexicans and Mexican Americans in the United States over the next 150 years.

While the politics of *Who Would Have Thought It?* have garnered much critical attention, less time has been spent on the novel's formal innovations.[96] Ruiz de Burton drew on the widely circulating captivity genre that had already shaped sentimental fiction, but, more important, she also molded her novel by drawing on a very different repertoire, one that I read as also emerging from captivity: the spectacular, rambunctious display culture of circulated enfreaked and enslaved peoples and the burlesque theater that emerged from that culture. Ruiz de Burton, I argue, mined burlesque for its unruly play with the reveal and impersonation as well as its knowing winks and narrative joking, all of which enable her to dissect the usefulness of captivity to fictions of consent, hedging as it does some people's mobility to enable free association for others. Finally, I demonstrate how Ruiz de Burton's critique of consent and the uses to which the racialized, captive child has been put remains germane today. I do so by examining how immigrant rights activists have deployed both the logic of consent and the figure of the captive child to argue for broader access to forms of enfranchisement within the US polity, even as they, too, like Ruiz de Burton, utilize burlesque forms to contend with and undermine the ongoing demand for varying forms of constraint and captivity. As I show in subsequent chapters, Latinx writers have followed Ruiz de Burton in centering their texts on the figure of the constrained child under duress, thereby putting pressure on propriety's masquerades, on the economies of respectability and authenticity that are interlaced throughout narratives of (white) belonging.

Ruiz de Burton tells a doubled captivity tale, one that follows not simply Lola's captivity but also the capturing of Mexico's and Indigenous nations' resources, a coupling of narratives that illustrates how these resources and people funded the Civil War and rescaled the United States. Her captivity tale makes it clear that practices of capture did not end in 1865, nor did the process of rescaling the nation, as a subsequent set of novels remind us. In chapter 2, "Plausible Deniability: Pursuing the Traces of Captivity," I examine three novels that not only link captivity to scalar practices and highlight its long temporality but also underscore its relationship to systems of labor management. The first novel, *Caballero* by Jovita González and Eve Raleigh, written after the scale of the territorial United States had largely been solidified, returns to the antebellum moment when Anglo settlers invaded Texas and began seizing Tejano ranches, setting off a new enclosure movement and licensing the violent scalar transformation that would leave landholders dead, their families penniless. Yet *Caballero* does not simply tell the story as one of invasion by Anglos; instead, I argue, it locates that invasion within the history of the two-century multinational conflict for control of Texas, a conflict involving the French, Spanish, US, Comanche, and Apache peoples at the very least. *Caballero* makes clear that the ideological formations emerging from this conflict hinged on captivity and were crucial to the development of the abstract fixities necessary for the scaffold imaginary to flourish anew.

This reading of *Caballero* provides a preface to my discussion of two twenty-first-century novels that consider the aftermath of the enclosure movement that shaped contemporary Texas, New Mexico, and Arizona and that offer captivity tales strangely resonant with those of *Who Would Have Thought It?* and *Caballero*. Oscar Casares's *Amigoland* and Lorraine López's *The Gifted Gabaldón*

Sisters also take up the figure of the captive, racialized child instrumentalized for scalar forces. I argue that by staging a captivity narrative as an instance of a senile grump's fantasy life, *Amigoland* comments on captivity's disappearance from historical memory even as it draws crucial parallels between nineteenth-century captivity and twentieth-century labor regimes. Both *Amigoland* and *The Gifted Gabaldón Sisters* change the subject slightly, telling captivity tales that focus on child captives not usually singled out for memorialization; more important, I show how they transform the captivity tale and undo its traditional narrative work. If canonical captivity tales relied on the captive-speaker as an authorizing witness and were subsequently deployed as anti-Indian state propaganda, these two novels unwind that process. Focusing on a Hispano ranching couple who held a Tewa child captive throughout her life and denied her role as her progeny's matriarch, *The Gifted Gabaldón Sisters*, moreover, transforms the function of the witness, challenging its claim to phallic rectitude by inclining the work of witnessing so that it becomes reparative. As I argue, this transformation undoes the phallic verticality that traditional captivity narratives instantiated by pulling down the scaffold imaginary and offering a vision of how contemporary Chicanx might come to terms with our ongoing relations to settler colonial violence amid an ever-expanding deportation regime.[97]

Just as Lorraine López moves beyond the impasse of violent loss toward a reparative witnessing that privileges inclination rather than phallic verticality and market individuation, other writers also underscore inclination as a refuge that rebuffs the logic of containment. As I show in the first two chapters, scalar transformation entails not simply violence but forms of capture that are both material and discursive, ensuring the logic of categorical containment. The scaffold imaginary is structured through these systems of bracketing, but the mechanisms themselves are not particularly stable. The emergence of Fordist systems entailed new processes of rescaling but also new forms of containment, even while these systems transposed the racialized child as productive signifier. Chapter 3, "Submerged Captivities: Moving toward Queer Horizontality," takes up the mechanisms for containment that emerged when canals and railroads were left behind: freeways and highways created new forms of enclosure as they rescaled urban and rural regions and delimited mobility anew. I argue that Helena María Viramontes's *Their Dogs Came with Them* illustrates the coloniality of scalar logic and scalar practices, especially as they are materialized through urban planning and urban policing. The novel offers a searing critique of the scaffold imaginary and the effects of that vision through portraits of kidnapped and captive children who nevertheless find the cracks and faults in the scaffolding that is meant to contain and defeat them. Yet the enclosure of once thriving urban barrios was not the only form of captivity to emerge from new systems of mobility that developed in the second half of the twentieth century. As José Montoya's moving poem "Gabby Took the 99" suggests, captivity can also be stretched out, sinuous and thinned through the figuration of the rural as left behind, left over.[98] This dynamic between the urban and the rural as scalar nodes and predictable steps in the scaffold imaginary, nodes that are temporal and material, also fuels Manuel Muñoz's *The Faith Healer of Olive Avenue*. I argue, however, that Muñoz moves beyond critique to provide instead a vision of situatedness that is not bound by a scalar imaginary; *The Faith Healer of Olive Avenue* offers a queer horizontality that rejects the phallic verticality that scale talk promotes. This queer horizontality acknowledges a different kind of constraint and envisions a tapestry of indebtedness that eclipses and undermines the abstract fixities and castagories enacted by scalar talk. Their works all similarly transform the captive witness, offering forms of reparative inclination, a turning to a density of connection that refuses the lien on our imaginations that the view from the moon extorts.

Chapter 4, "N + 1: Sex and the Hypervisible (Invisible) Migrant," takes up yet another shift in geospatial alignments by examining how the work of neoliberal hemispheric rescaling gained needed momentum from the contemporary anti-immigrant movement that emerged as a homophobic response to an increasingly energized gay rights movement. If previous efforts at rescaling national economies and political reach entailed new rounds of violence and new forms of captivity, the rescaling of the hemisphere at the end of the twentieth century set in motion yet more methods of bracketing lives, in particular the lives of cast-off children. If at the start of the century highways took the place of railways, which took the place of canals, delineating regional scales, eighty years later highways no longer stabilized or articulated scale. Instead, financial institutions found new ways to rescale relations and create wealth; they bypassed traditional forms of infrastructure and initiated new techniques to hobble labor, thereby deflating the gains won by workers over the previous one hundred years. Trade agreements such as the North American Free Trade Agreement (NAFTA) further rescaled the US economy, while dismantling social safety nets, to, in effect, bring structural adjustment programs home to roost in the United States. This complex political and economic transformation simultaneously encouraged flexible, informal labor and dramatically enhanced the surveillance and policing of that labor. If NAFTA tacitly encouraged informal migration to the United States, the subsequent militarization of the border effectively locked people in once they had arrived within its political territories. And, indeed, by forcing people to migrate, the newly rescaled economies of the Northern

Hemisphere effectively turned migration into yet another form of capture. By the end of the twentieth century, the United States was well on its way to creating an entirely new system of captivity even as it relied on an old retainer to service the mechanisms justifying the massive transfer of wealth from social support to incarceration. That is, it relied on sex. Conservative activists were crucial actors in this transformation; they parlayed sex, especially the vision of untethered queer sex, into the required momentum to animate and nurture a new era of anti-immigrant policing. And this new era entailed a new form of capture: the broadening and thickening of juridical borders into deportability.

I place the poetry of Eduardo Corral, Laura Angélica Simón's film *Fear and Learning at Hoover Elementary*, Bettina Restrepo's novel *Illegal*, and Reyna Grande's novel *Across a Hundred Mountains* in the aftermath of this spectacular rupture, a rupture that challenged the explicit work of immigration law to police and maintain white supremacist heterosexuality and to cordon off queer life from the privileges of citizenship. Moreover, I argue that understanding a migration system determined to ruthlessly cleave the affective networks that enable social lives to exist and flourish demands a turn to the imaginary and to the brilliant interventions these literary texts provide. All three texts pursue the relationship between migration and freedom by telling stories that are, in effect, this era's captivity narratives. *Illegal* and *Across a Hundred Mountains* are especially crucial, however, because they portray cast-off female children, thereby defying the dominant portrayal of migrants as primarily men.

While it's clear that the contemporary condition of living in the United States with the looming threat of deportation amounts to a form of containment, a bracketing, it's less common to characterize life after deportation that way. Moreover, rarely do scholars in political theory even question the *right* of the state to remove people, just as few scholars study what life is like for people once they have been exiled, removed, and turned into refugees in the ostensible place of their birth.[99] Far more attention has been paid to the arsenal of tactics the US state utilizes to terrify, snare, cage, and export people, dispossessing them of their livelihoods, belongings, access to friends and lovers and kids.[100] Silence subsequently greets the deportee, and silence helps to sustain the power of the state to act with impunity, to presume absolute power in the name of a shady concept of legality. The failure to tell stories about life after deportation is, in effect, another kind of removal, another kind of disappearance.[101] For these reasons and more, it's crucial to turn to texts that think about the experience of life "after removal." To take on the taken-for-granted—end-of-story—logic of forced removal is to counter the logic of sovereignty and disconnect it from one of its mechanisms for maintaining its power.

In chapter 5, "Misplaced: Peopling a Deportation Imaginary," I discuss three novels written in the wake of a transformed emphasis on removal, each of which considers deportation's wake. Maceo Montoya's *The Deportation of Wopper Barraza*, Malín Alegría's *Sofi Mendoza's Guide to Getting Lost in Mexico*, and Daniel Peña's *Bang* all ask readers to witness the ruthless sociality that deportation produces. I argue that these texts reveal how forced removal kidnaps time and inaugurates a sense of subjunctive mourning; they also demonstrate how even one person's removal is felt broadly among kin and community networks. Forced removal spreads dispossession, containment, and captivity far and wide; not only do the removed feel constrained, but so do those they've left behind and, perhaps, those they've joined. These three novels tell stories of captive and castaway children, youths whose lives have been delimited by the crisis of removal, a crisis that narrates the children's apparent limit. They extend the ongoing story of freedom in the United States, a story predicated on the captivity of people constrained seemingly everywhere. As I argue, taken together, these texts all offer a vision of a different habit of thinking, an understanding that our destinies are bound together. To think past the traffic in unfreedom, the traffic in containment, will be to do conceptual work that thinks densely, without borders, without captives, without scale, without sovereignty.

If one were demarked as a perpetual child as most of the world was by the ruling men of the sixteenth through nineteenth centuries, then one could not actually pass through childhood into adulthood, into the age of reason, to claim the capacity to grant consent to be governed. To seize the narrative of childhood and captivity, then, as the writers discussed in *Scales of Captivity* do, is to refute that tradition and to imagine and conjure a world less structured through the violence of the scaffold imaginary, a world without the possibility of deportability and thus of sovereignty, much less sovereign borders, one created through relations of reciprocity and by a general sense of indebtedness. It is to turn to thinking densely, enmeshed in queer horizontality.

1

CAPTIVATING TIES

On Children without Childhoods

Does it matter that the first novel written by a US Latina centers on a child? This child appears as a fugitive, a captive, an orphan without papers, in María Amparo Ruiz de Burton's snarky and weird 1872 novel, *Who Would Have Thought It?* The child, María Dolores Medina, or Lola, is also figured as a form of stolen property, war booty, and her fictional biography thereby becomes the occasion for a wholesale critique of the US nation-building project even as it functions as a retrenched defense of white supremacy. Bookended by the Mexican-American War and the end of Reconstruction, *Who Would Have Thought It?* argues that the resources and wealth taken from Mexico through that bloody war fueled a transformation in the United States, both economically and culturally. According to the novel, the influx of resources ruthlessly extracted from Indigenous territories transformed the US Northeast from an economy based in subsistence, yeoman agriculture, and small-scale manufacturing into a developing industrial economy in which financial and real estate speculation produced magnificent wealth. For Ruiz de Burton, the Mexican-American War created the conditions that made the Civil War possible; the wealth from the Mexican territories funded the Civil War, a war whose morality she questions as much as she critiques manifest destiny. In bringing together the violence of manifest destiny, speculative capitalism, abolitionism, and economies of racialization, *Who Would Have Thought It?* ties together a set of issues often studied separately. Agreeing with Ulysses S. Grant, the novel sees the links between the Mexican-American War and the Civil War as obvious.[1] What must be revealed, it insists, are the cultural habits and practices that lent moral credibility to manifest destiny and helped ensure the rise of a powerful central government that further calcified the contradictions inherent to liberal social contract theory and the emergence of a new military-industrial-banking class that would usher in a gilded age by deploying extensive new technologies of violence in the name of equality.

By drawing on the display culture made popular through the circulation of so-called enfreaked and enslaved peoples and by utilizing the rambunctious form of burlesque theater, *Who Would Have Thought It?* reveals the tenuous relationship to equality that Mexicans have in the US national imaginary. Crucial to this revelation is Ruiz de Burton's argument that the fiction of "consent of the governed"—celebrated as both enshrining and creating equality—actually functions to dupe most of the US populace into consenting to a farcical democracy that ultimately functions (thrives?) not through consent but through various forms of confinement and captivity.

Perhaps despite itself, in providing the story of a captive, cast-out child, the novel draws attention to the corrupt, violent technologies the United States deployed to rescale itself, technologies that included territorial and capital expansion as well as a reimagination of citizenship.[2] After all, the novel tracks the period in which the United States seized more than half a million square miles from Mexico and from Indigenous peoples, including the Mojave, Navajo, Pima, and Hopi (all territories claimed by Mexico). It also tracks the period in which the United States nationalized immigration management and claimed to homogenize the meaning of citizenship through constitutional amendments. Its portrait of the Norval family further illustrates how this scalar jump led to an enormous change in the national economy. Yet, at every turn, *Who Would Have Thought It?* illustrates how such an extraordinary, transformative process of scalar change depends on multiple forms of captivity and constraint (enslavement, confinement, imprisonment) as well as a series of displacements in which scale's castagories are deftly hidden by the apparently flattening horizontality claimed by the rhetoric of consent. As the novel repeatedly illustrates, the conceit of consent is a scalar ruse, a burlesque of horizontality lubricating a series of nested hierarchies that entangle, among others, cast-out children.

The novel is certainly a racialist romance articulating a distinctly anti-Black, anti-Indigenous narrative. From this malicious platform, Ruiz de Burton offers a critique of the very processes that instantiate the US version of castagories that the novel itself deploys. Through its portrayal of Lola, *Who Would Have Thought It?* examines how the concepts of consent and authenticity work together and thereby excavates the very substructure of US scalar tactics, taking a cudgel to the logics of racialization that inhere in US processes of nation making. Lola functions as a surrogate for the territories the United States seized, a surrogate for stolen resources, kidnapped peoples, and the traffic between ideologies that made such violence possible—including racializing practices such as displaying people of color for entertainment and sale, deprecating non-Anglos as childlike and irrational, and invoking the cultural legacies of Calvinist Puritanism. But as a surrogate, Lola is also, as is the reader, a witness to the coercion and duplicity structured into narratives of equality, democracy, and superiority.

Ruiz de Burton repeatedly turns to the conditional mood (and mode) because the irrealis form is linked so inextricably to revelation. The novelist might have alternately titled her story *What Were They Thinking?* in her suggestion that the discourse of US national superiority is a parody of itself and that its practices have nothing like moral credibility. For her, the revelation to be pondered is the form moral bankruptcy takes: a series of thefts at a grand scale have resulted in a system of confinement linking gender norms, racial superstructures, imprisonment, and captivity. My reading seeks to account for the novel's humor, the nonstop snark, as well as the anger that sutures its innumerable subplots together. I take the narrator's fury seriously, as well as the novel's outrageous parody of sentimental, domestic fiction; its pinioning of the rags-to-riches myth; its mockery of pretense; and its narrative engagement with a readerly presence, in my effort to disentangle some of this very formidable novel's insights from some of its odious ethics.[3]

I explore the novel by studying first the portrayal of Lola as a figure of display. Just as the historical record reports few of the speeches made by displayed people, the novel also keeps Lola silent. Her quietude gives the reader the chance to imagine what Lola might have experienced and felt. This movement between witnessing (Lola) and imagination (reader) upends a set of conventions of captivity and display. I further suggest that the portrayal of Lola as a displayed *child* opens up several avenues for Ruiz de Burton's examination of liberal contract theory's relationship between consent and coercion. If consent functions in a vague way in the novel, as something never really granted or sought, it also works through the text's layered exploration of captivity. I subsequently take up the novel's dance with captivity, suggesting ultimately that Ruiz de Burton sees the US populace as itself captive to an ideology of consent—or, rather, captive to politicians' manipulation of the populace through the apparently leveling theater of consent.

Pulling these strands together, I turn to a formal analysis of the novel to argue that Ruiz de Burton drew on the unusual form of burlesque theater for her dissection of the powerful national mythos that subtends US governmentality. The rambunctious burlesque theater, popular during the mid-nineteenth century, plays with the reveal, the knowing wink. Its gambol between "What were you thinking?" and "Who would have thought it?" provides an unruly opportunity to entrap the powerful with their scurrilous machinations, within the confines of their own discursive maneuvers. Burlesque theater of the 1860s employed song, dance, and multiple, disconnected plots and stories along with extravagant staging to parody cherished myths as well as the corrupt practices of the powerful, particularly their exploitation of dominant institutions to control the lives of most people.[4] As Sonnet Retman notes of burlesque spectacles, "They inhabit that which they mean to critique, using exaggeration, irony, and reversal to reveal the performative dimensions of the object of their scrutiny."[5] Burlesque theater provided Ruiz de Burton with a complex repertoire of forms through which she could illustrate her sense of how people were being duped because, as Retman further notes, burlesques "illumine how the clichéd story of American class ascension—the bootstrap myth—depends upon impersonation, a performative making of the self into the upwardly mobile, white, and male rugged individual."[6]

Finally, I argue that Ruiz de Burton's analysis of the national substructure of belonging through constraint and her use of the burlesque to parody it find a corollary in the national immigration policy continuing to govern the US demos—a national policy most readily pressured by contemporary activists known as DREAMers. Put differently, I suggest that *Who Would Have Thought It?* presciently offers a strategy to undermine the embedded conditions of constraint bedeviling the current moment. For as Ruiz de Burton so fervently argues, the relationship between consent and coercion structures national belonging and animates racialized childhood, just as DREAMers contend today. The complex relationship among childhood, racialization, and liberal notions of consent continues to serve as the substructure of US concepts of belonging today as much as it did in 1872 when *Who Would Have Thought It?* appeared in print.

The Conditional Mood

Mirroring its titular conditional mood, *Who Would Have Thought It?* begins not with an answer to its titular question but with yet another speculative question: "What would the good and proper people of this world do if there were no rogues in it—no social delinquents? The good and proper, I fear, would perish of sheer inanity—of hypochondriac lassitude—or, to say the least, would grow very dull for want of convenient whetstones to sharpen their wits. Rogues are useful."[7] These are the Reverend Mr. Hackwell's words to his companion and friend, Reverend Mr. Hammerhard, as they hurry to meet a train arriving in their New England town. Ruiz de Burton's sarcastic opening declares rogues entertaining, but she also here launches her critique of the "good and proper," of respectable people, and, further, suggests a theory of social formation when Reverend Hackwell goes on to comment that delinquency is a "necessity to good people."[8] This concept of the instrumental work of enmity in producing community, and the critique of social approbation it implies, prepares us for the arrival of the train and the novel's unfolding engagement with concepts of belonging, consent, and propriety's masquerades. It also prepares us for the novel's critique of the dominant production of race, particularly Mexicanity, as a form of roguery and as an outlaw from Anglo whiteness.

The train brings home an adventuring prospector, James Norval, bearing boxes of gold and a child, Lola Medina. The arrival of the girl and the gold sets off a chain of events that the novel pertinaciously follows from its opening in 1857 to its close during Ulysses Grant's presidency. The prospector, Dr. James Norval, had helped Lola sneak away from the Mojave nation, which had apparently adopted her and her mother. While prospecting for gold in the early 1850s, Dr. Norval was asked to treat some wounded Mojave after a skirmish with US troops. He met Lola's mother, Theresa, who told Norval about the gold and jewels she had been collecting over the course of her ten years of captivity; she then dictated a testimonio about her life in captivity and died, having instructed Norval to take the gold and jewels and Lola with him. In exchange for a portion of the gold, she asked Norval to educate Lola and keep her fortune safe until he locates her family in Mexico and returns Lola to them.

The doctor takes Lola's gold to New York and invests it with a banker, instructing the banker to buy Manhattan real estate and to pay into Norval's account a generous portion of the profits earned on the rents and the remaining gold. The Norvals subsequently capitalize on Lola's wealth to enrich themselves and their friends, the Cackles; ultimately, they use part of it to raise battalions for the Union during the Civil War, to build industries serving the war machine, to amass a real estate empire, and to elevate their social standing from upright yeomen farmers to gilded New York power brokers. With so much wealth at stake, the Norvals, not surprisingly, find an easy excuse for not locating Lola's family in Mexico. The doctor conveniently forgets the details given him by her mother and laconically awaits her dictated testimonio, which, unsurprisingly, never arrives. (We later learn that the testimonio ended up in the postal service's dead-letter office.) This gap or loss conveniently keeps Lola confined to the Norvals' home, where they engorge themselves on her gold. It also enshrouds Lola in mystery, effectively rendering her a captive child and orphan with no history. If her first remove was to Mojave country, her second remove was to the Norvals' home.

Lola's removal to New England sets off a firestorm within the Norval family. Lola has a brown complexion, and Dr. Norval's wife, Jemima, objects to welcoming a child of color into her home, despite her claims to abolitionist sympathies. Over the course of the novel, however, Lola's skin color changes, fading unevenly so that for some years she has visible brownish spots until, ultimately, her skin appears white. Lola finally reveals to the astonished Norvals that her skin had been dyed so that she could travel with the Mojave and not arouse suspicion. As Lola's skin transforms and as knowledge of her wealth gets around, she becomes the object of amorous campaigns by two suitors: the treacherous Reverend Mr. Hackwell and the Norvals' son, Julian.

After the novel's initial scenes, Lola mostly fades from view, like her spots, and the real energy of the text centers on Jemima Norval. *Who Would Have Thought It?* then alternates among multiple subplots: it follows the pair of conniving preachers; Jemima's brother, Isaac, a dandy captured during the Battle of Bull Run who struggles to survive in Southern prisons; Jemima's sister, Lavinia, an eccentric spinster who takes up nursing the Union wounded; and two comic soldiers who appear to have stepped off the pages of James Russell Lowell's *Biglow* caricatures.[9] Woven among these subplots are accounts of Jemima, who claims to be a devout abolitionist but whose actions and words make it abundantly clear that her sympathies do not extend to equal rights or freedoms for all. Jemima is hardly the angel of the house; she is an engine of subterfuge and chicanery eager to cheat Lola of her wealth and pursue pleasures prohibited by her Presbyterian tenets. Her duplicitous actions are mirrored by a family of poor farmers, the Cackles, who use Lola's gold to obtain war contracts and congressional and army positions, which they parlay into more defense contracts, thereby growing even wealthier and more powerful. The novel concludes with a seduction romp in which the corrupt preacher, Hackwell, attempts to entrap Lola in marriage so that he can gain her fortune. The effort, of course, fails; Isaac escapes from prison, finds the missing manuscript, and locates Lola's father in Mexico; after a last-ditch effort by Hackwell to force Lola to marry him, Lola and her father escape to Mexico, where Julian eventually arrives to marry her. Meanwhile, Dr. Norval returns from an expedition to Africa, and a stunned Jemima suffers a nervous breakdown. The Cackles and Hackwell continue to enhance their corrupt fortunes and pursue yet more political power.

While not autobiographical in the same sense that Ruiz de Burton's second novel would be, this first novel does draw on the author's experiences to some extent. María Amparo Ruiz de Burton was the granddaughter of a former Spanish governor of Baja California; she married a West Point–trained solder who commanded the US Army's invasion and occupation of Baja California in 1847. This soldier, Henry Burton, rose through the ranks, and Ruiz de Burton accompanied him to the US East Coast, where they mingled with the Northern elite, including Abraham Lincoln, while stationed in Washington and, later, with the defeated Southern elite, including Jefferson Davis, when Burton commanded his prison. Widowed at age thirty-seven in 1869, Ruiz de Burton drew on these experiences of East Coast society. *Who Would Have Thought It?* subtly anticipates the satirical participant-observer ethnographic novels of Zora Neale Hurston and Jovita González of the early twentieth century in its recourse to reportage and documentary, even as it echoes captivity tales still in popular circulation at the time.[10]

If the novel anticipates the ethnography, it also anticipates contemporary critical race theorists because it offers a taxonomy of affective responses to racialization and lays the groundwork for a discussion of the uses to which whiteness can effectively be put. The novel provides a heuristic that understands racialization through a matrix of relations that includes the legacies of Spanish colonialism as well as US chattel slavery and Indian removal and that thus offers a broader set of interpretive opportunities than the more homogenizing Black/white binary typically invoked in canonical nineteenth-century novels. Or as Tereza Szeghi puts it, "Through the misrecognition of a refined and naturally light-skinned Mexicana like Lola, Ruiz de Burton both critiques the rigidity of the black-white racial binary *and* reinforces common associations between whiteness and privilege—thereby molding rather than shattering dominant racial hierarchies to suit her political aims."[11] Yet while the novel loudly trumpets "pure Spanish blood," only by ignoring its engagement with burlesque culture is it possible to claim that it is *not* engaged in an extended critique of the formation of racialization within the United States and its foundational role for US nation making. Put differently, this novel reveals how the production of the liberal subject entails a specifically Anglo white supremacy adumbrated through its claim to an exclusive hold on manifest destiny.

As its opening speculation makes clear, *Who Would Have Thought It?* sets out to ask some difficult questions. Beyond its multivalent suggestion that enmity is entertaining, this opening question, "What would the good and proper people of this world do if there were no rogues in it—no social delinquents?" serves as a clever comment on both the speaker, who turns out to be a rogue, and the novel itself and ultimately as an impish poke at its own readers, who might well seek to avoid perishing from "hypochondriac lassitude" by reading a novel in the first place. This initial question signals the novel's relationship to burlesque theater in particular by ridiculing Northeastern culture through a double play that implicates its own enterprise and audience.

The text's play with astonishment is bitter indeed. The opening question, twinned with the novel's title, signals a stance that undermines the coercive norms of manifest destiny and propriety. It also articulates a stance that it will suggest characterizes the most "authentic" of US citizens as well as the larger national culture. And this stance, the novel shortly makes clear, produced the conditions for the war against Mexico. By the end of the Civil War, Ruiz de Burton considered the Treaty of Guadalupe Hidalgo not a national triumph but a tragedy, not just for herself or for Californios, but for the entire United States. And if her political sensibilities were confused, her sense of the implications of this tragedy was not. Lola's birth in captivity, her mother's abduction and untimely death, and the destruction of Jemima's domestic ideals are signposts for the tragedy's immediate effects, but they also signal the larger destruction the 1848 war wrought in making possible the death machine that was the US Civil War and the rise of an engorged new class of villainous plutocrats.

By tracking the movement of the Norvals (from the California/Arizona region of the Southwest to the East Coast, from rural New England to New York City, to Washington, to Virginia, and back again), Ruiz de Burton effectively narrates the rounds of rescaling of the US economy that occurred through this tumultuous period. The seizure of Mexican and Indigenous territories rescaled the United States geographically and economically. The intensive industrialization of the Northeast to accommodate the Civil War machine further rescaled the economy. And, finally, the Civil War itself, its resolution, and the period of Reconstruction entailed yet another round of rescaling, at every level from the body, to the family, to the region, to the nation. DeWitt Clinton's prophetic vision had been enacted as the wealth of the nation was settled into the narrow geography spanning the Atlantic coast between New York City and Boston.[12]

Each round of rescaling entails processes of violent dispossession, speculation, and profound social transformation, narrated as progress (in the name of enterprise and manifest destiny). The language of progress helped elide the violence of scalar abstraction as places and people were absorbed into (and disappeared by) the abstraction of their relations into a new racial metric with an expanding logic of contracting versions of whiteness and pliable disposability. Along with such rescaling came new narratives proclaiming this scalar shift as a relentless, inevitable transformation. By invoking the conditional mood and underscoring the novel's title with its opening conditional posture, Ruiz de Burton highlights the destabilizing work of this process of rescaling while also challenging its inevitability through a subtle recourse to alternative possibilities signaled by the what-might-have-been.

The turn to the conditional mood also underscores the work of masquerade in organizing social relations within liberal contract theory. Such work, Ruiz de Burton suggests right from the start, depends on a kind of masquerade: "we" all know rogues are useful, especially rogues who masquerade as the precise opposite. The novel's opening sentence twists liberal political theory's vision of an ethical society in which consent, or a fictional social contract among equals, creates the conditions of a polity's existence, rather than legal violence.[13] As Ruiz de Burton cleverly points out, social contract theory may deny roguery even as it acknowledges it as a part of a contractual moral economy. Roguery works in concert with the more presumed concepts of self-assumed obligation in which, as Carole Pateman puts it, individuals are bound by these acts, and power is legitimized through a recourse to the fictional consent of its subjects.[14] The rogue as reverend reinforces the novel's argument that spectacular displays and masquerades are essential to the maintenance of a fiction of consent among equals in liberal democracy. And if rogues are one part of this fiction, "living curiosities" form another, helping to mask the "racial contract" that conditions belonging and materializes scale.[15]

Specters and Living Curiosities

So reviled is Dr. Norval by the "good people" of his hometown, such as Mrs. Cackle and her dear friend Jemima Norval, the doctor's own wife, that when he appears to readers for the first time and simultaneously to his wife and family after many years' absence, Jemima acknowledges his appearance, not with a warm, affectionate greeting, but with alarm, exclaiming, "What upon earth is he bringing now?" Their daughters lightheartedly reply that Norval is bringing home useless specimens such as rocks, bones, and petrified wood, but their mother corrects them: "'I don't mean the boxes in the large wagon. I mean the—the—that—the red shawl,' stammered Mrs. Norval. And now the three other ladies noticed for the first time a figure wrapped in a bright plaid shawl, leaning on the doctor's breast, and around which he tenderly encircled his arm."[16] The tableau astonishes the Norvals into silence, and they stare, not even returning the doctor's greetings: "The meeting with his family, after an absence of four years, would have been cold and restrained enough for the doctor, who had felt nothing but misgivings since he passed Springfield, fearing, like a runaway boy, that even the fact of his return might not get him a pardon. Not a single smile of welcome did he see in the scared faces of his daughters or the stern features of his stately wife." This odd standoff continues until a dog barks, causing "the figure" to scream so that "in her fright she dropped the obnoxious shawl, and then all the ladies saw that what Mrs. Norval's eyes had magnified into a very tall woman was a little girl very black indeed."[17] The narrative, like the shawl, envelops or encloses this young girl, Lola Medina, so that readers meet her physically at the same time the Norval household does. This encounter and revelation are accompanied by a description of the long-standing dynamic between husband and wife; Dr. Norval wriggles with the anxious anticipation of a truant, supporting the portrayal of Jemima as a patronizing tyrant. Typical of tyrants, the paranoid Jemima magnifies the child into an adult, a "very tall woman." Such enhancement of Lola's stature proves prophetic; she will come to occupy a very large part of Jemima's psyche.

This first disruption of visual perception and its counterpoint are followed by a second, subtler shift. The narrative introduces Lola by describing her as "a little girl very black indeed" instead of the more conventional "little black girl." Undoing the typical juxtaposition of skin color with gendered embodiment by inverting the order and splitting "black" from "girl," the narrative alerts us to its interest in disruption and in the perpetuation of disruption. It also builds in a pun—Lola's skin, "very black indeed," was made black through a precise action, a specific deed: it had been *dyed*.

Who Would Have Thought It? thinks a lot about deeds. By the time the novel was written, Ruiz de Burton was embroiled in lawsuits over the deeds to large tracts of land, yet here *indeed* both plays on the use of *deed* as the past participle for a satirical euphemism for *damned*—suggesting the perilous position of any person of color within the confines of Jemima's home (damned—indeed)—and also alerts readers to the way very many deeds (say, those to Lola's real estate empire) will come to matter, just as Lola must suffer from a whole series of Jemima's and Hackwell's misdeeds.[18] But the specific deed, Lola's dyed skin, also points to another complex pun built into the novel. For if Lola's skin was temporarily dyed, how many more died? In this sense, the dyeing or masquerading as dyed brown to conform to the "racial logics premised by US empire," in Alexandra Vazquez's words, is accompanied by dying: innumerable deaths of other bodies.[19] Further, in this disruptive description, the narrator points to the production of race as a performance (because it can be painted on, assumed, as it were) and as a masquerade, a deed, and thus something to be lampooned and examined, studied and anatomized.

The family's realization that the figure is not a tall woman but a small nonwhite child prompts yet another outpouring of racist cant from Norval's daughter, Mattie, who comments, "Goodness! what a specimen!" This "joke" appears to relax the family, and they return the doctor's greetings. As workmen begin unloading the doctor's large boxes, his wife continues the prospecting joke: "'The doctor is not content with bringing four boxes more, full of stones, but now he, I fear, having exhausted the mineral kingdom is about to begin with the animal, and this is our first specimen,' said Mrs. Norval, pointing at the boxes in the hall and at the little girl, who was looking at her with a steady, thoughtful gaze." "The next specimen will be a baboon," added Ruth, "for papa's samples don't improve."[20] With this malignant comment, the family begins to anatomize the child as a specimen, discussing her eyes, lips, and, finally, skin:

> "How black she is!" uttered Mrs. Norval with a slight shiver of disgust.
>
> "I don't think she is so black," said Mattie, taking one of the child's hands and turning it to see the palm of it. "See, the palm of her hand is as white as mine—and a prettier white; for it has such a pretty pink shade to it."
>
> "Drop her hand, Mattie! You don't know what disease she might have," said Mrs. Norval imperiously.[21]

Before they hear Lola speak, or hear her name, Jemima sets the terms of Lola's reception. Deriding her husband's prospecting as well as the child in one swift gesture, she collapses Lola with a collection of rocks. The text has already prepared us for Lola's dehumanization by describing her as "what"; Jemima underscores this dehumanizing, and her daughter shifts the register to a fully, and emblematically, derogatory one by implicitly comparing the girl to a baboon. This overtly racist reaction is underscored when Jemima's sister begins anatomizing and indexing the little girl's features, culminating in Jemima's outraged exhortation against contagion. The group seems to split then into competing alliances, as the Norvals' younger daughter petulantly defends both Lola and her father, until the doctor finally speaks up, apparently in Lola's defense:

> "Isn't she pretty?" exclaimed the doctor, bringing in the last box. "And her disposition is so lovely and affectionate, and she is so grateful and thoughtful for one so young!"
>
> "How old is she? Her face is so black that truly, it baffles all my efforts to guess her age," said Mrs. Norval dryly, interrupting the doctor.
>
> "She is only ten years old, but her history is already more romantic than that of half of the heroines of your trashy novels," answered the doctor.
>
> "She is a prodigy, then—a true emanation of the black art!" said Mrs. Norval, smiling derisively, "if so much is to be told of a child so young."[22]

Jemima continues to alienate the little girl, first invoking ontology and then utilizing temporality by describing Lola as ageless. The conversation suggests the strands of inquiry the novel will pursue when the doctor immediately rebukes Jemima by giving the ten-year-old child a kind of gravitas with a romantic history. He underscores this point by deriding sentimental fiction and thus setting up another of the novel's themes—its ongoing parlays against the sentimental and the melodramatic, forms that the text will simultaneously inhabit and rebuke. Jemima offers a rejoinder that at once returns Lola to the nonhuman as a "prodigy" and an "emanation of the black art." Jemima represents Lola as both a spectacle and a specter, thereby slandering Lola as an object for display and a demon.

The reception given Lola by the Norvals differs very little from that afforded the "living curiosities" that formed a strand of popular entertainment in Europe and the United States during most of the nineteenth century. It is difficult to imagine that Ruiz de Burton did not have salon display practices in mind as the Norvals repeatedly anatomize and index Lola's attributes. Textual evidence also suggests this when Jemima describes Lola as having the effect of transforming men into "Hottentots," and her sister, Lavinia, proclaims Lola an "Aztec."[23] The novel's opening scenes treat Lola as a specimen, a living curiosity, reminding readers of both the display of "freaks" for entertainment and their counterpart, the display of slaves on the auction block. After all, for most of the nineteenth century, an extraordinary pseudoscientific-entertainment industry across Europe and the United States featured "specimens" of human difference.[24]

Circulating across England and the United States throughout the second half of the nineteenth century, for example, were a pair of child captives known as the "Aztec Lilliputians."[25] Brought to the United States and England as young children, they were displayed as remnants or "Descendants and Specimens of the Sacerdotal Caste, (now nearly extinct) of the Ancient Aztec Founders of the Ruined Temples" of Central America. Their handlers claimed these children were found while being worshipped by the adults of an "inbred and degenerate" dwindling race and emphasized the children's diminutive size and distinctively shaped heads.[26] They thereby drew on pseudoscientific forms and language to serve up "science" as entertainment and to shore up and further articulate racial hierarchies (by extending that articulation into the sphere of Latin America).

Drawing from travel iconography, advertisers and illustrators emphasized the children's profiles in order to invite comparison with the illustrations of Aztec and Mayan warriors and gods on altarpieces. By promoting and producing Bartola Velásquez and Máximo Núñez as exotic, contemporary ancestors, Joseph Morris (who had apparently purchased the brother and sister from a Spanish trader who had kidnapped the children from their parents after promising to educate them) created extravaganzas focused on the pair that attracted thousands of people.[27] So celebrated were they that Velásquez and Núñez were even brought before Queen Victoria, President Millard Fillmore, and members of the US Congress as well as the fashionable elite of several capitals; a London newspaper, commenting on their celebrity status, facetiously asked, "Who would not be an Aztec?"[28] As early as 1851, for example, they were brought to the Boston Society of Natural History, according to Thomas Bouvé, where they were "placed upon a table, the members sitting around" while the pair "amused all by their interesting and lively movements."[29] The success of the show led to many sideshow imitations even as the original pair were continually displayed and made the subject of any number of scientific papers and correspondents' letters.

The treatment of Velásquez and Núñez and their reception offer us a sort of mirror of the Norval household's reaction to Lola. The two children were reclaimed as "cute," "sympathetic," and "nonthreatening" over and against the grotesque and monstrous, central tropes in the rhetoric of degeneracy.[30] Just as Dr. Norval represents Lola as precious, the children's exhibitors insisted that they were charming and delightful, linking them to a romantic history. Further reinforcing the parallel between Lola and the children is the plot itself. Lola is similarly petted and respected by one faction, while another faction continually sees her as a threatening and degenerate contagion who must be held in a sort of benevolent captivity in order to further exploit her wealth. Thus, her status as a childish object of curiosity renders her unable to grant consent to the use of her money and enables her guardians, the Norvals, to justify her second captivity. Importantly, the structure of her captivity and her racialization as nonwhite combine to stick her permanently into the category of the child so that if she has traveled far from the Mojave people who cared for her, she has not traveled at all from their shared status (at least to Jemima, the novel's most prominent voice for white supremacist ideology).

But the entertainment industry that grew around displayed people, whether they were marked as freaks or amusements, was not confined to this form alone. Another kind of display culture also arose in the 1850s, one toward which Ruiz de Burton slyly nods. Just as she parodied abolitionist Henry Ward Beecher's love affairs, another of Beecher's activities may well have also helped shape the novel.[31] For while Velásquez and Núñez were circulated across Europe and the United States as curiosities, so were "white slaves." From the early 1850s onward, leading white abolitionists such as Beecher and Charles Sumner circulated recently enslaved girls and young women whom they advertised as "white-looking." Beecher, for example, displayed several young girls, including Sally María Deiggs, whom he called "Pink," before three thousand members of his congregation in an effort to solicit funds to end her slavery. As one reporter described the event, "She was very pretty, of a light complexion, with brown, wavy hair. There was in her face an expression of innocence and gentleness, and a look of sadness too. As she stood there, in her brown frock and little red sack, and Mr. Beecher with his arm thrown protectingly around her, it made a pretty tableau."[32] At another event Beecher presented a young, rescued child named Fanny Lawrence, and accounts again emphasized the child's skin color: "Mr. Beecher carried up into the pulpit a little girl about five years of age, of sweet face, large eyes, light hair, and fair as a lily."[33]

For such abolitionists, the Civil War was necessary to prevent slavery from spreading not just to the newly conquered territories but to the so-called white populace. As Mary Niall Mitchell bluntly puts it, "Instead of a battle for black freedom, the war to end slavery, in Beecher's words, became a means to preserve the freedom and purity of the white race, both of which seemed threatened by slavery. The future of the Union—embodied in a young, unspoiled 'white' girl rather than a black one—was at stake."[34] Such anxiety was stoked by popular novels such as Mary Hayden Green Pike's 1854 *Ida May*, which followed the fate of a young white girl kidnapped from her father, then disguised with soot and sold into slavery.[35] The relay between such a fictive production of paranoia and the shaping of "real" events was so strong that when Sumner displayed Mary Botts, a young child he had reportedly helped to escape captivity, he called her "another Ida May," as did a Worcester, Massachusetts, diarist who went to "the soiree at the Hall" to see her.[36] Similarly, the *New York Daily Times*, commenting on a portrait of Botts as a "real Ida May," also described her as "the young female slave, so white as to defy the acutest judge to detect in her features, complexion, hair, or general appearance, the slightest trace of negro blood."[37]

While Lola Medina never becomes a publicly displayed person, Dr. Norval leverages her presence in a manner that chillingly evokes Beecher's own antics. Beecher frequently displayed young girls before enormous congregations until vast sums, ostensibly to be used to purchase the children's freedom, were collected. So, too, faced with his wife's fury at Lola's presence, Dr. Norval opens one of his boxes to reveal the piles of gold Lola has brought into their economy and, like Beecher, brings together the child's body and the gold:

> Mrs. Norval stood up, uttering a cry of delighted surprise, then, clasping her hands, remained silent, with open mouth and staring eyes, transfixed by her amazement and joy.
>
> "But is it *real* gold?" she whispered hoarsely, after some moments of bewildered silence. . . .
>
> "I think that Lola, instead of being a *burden* to us, will be a great acquisition. Don't you think so?" said the doctor, after his wife had toyed with the gold for some time.[38]

Having exhibited Lola, and indeed having functioned very much as the staged authority orchestrating the appearance and meaning of his own "living curiosity," Dr. Norval, in the privacy of his bedroom with his wife and the boxes of gold, now implicitly acknowledges the larger project of display. Displayed peoples made money for those who displayed them, and display culture was a particularly acute route through which race was articulated and rendered increasingly complex and meaningful as an object of possession and a form of property.[39]

The novel thereby draws Lola into the representational economy of displaying people for entertainment, to raise capital, to produce new articulations or definitions of race, and to create a more refined taxonomy of belonging to such unstable categories as the human and the citizen. Jemima and her daughters immediately know how to respond to a displayed figure. Dr. Norval, who may claim an affection for Lola, also knows how to capitalize on display culture, how to seize the markers of scientific authority and the reins of financial gain. The novel underscores this structure of display by turning Lola into a spectacle for both readers and the Norvals. Lola is never given the opportunity to grant consent to the use of her fortune. She is largely a mute witness to the Norvals' self-aggrandizement. Furthermore, the Norvals closely guard the secret that it is Lola's wealth that seeds their own fortune and that ultimately funds their spectacular display of riches.

The text reinforces and enacts on the narrative level this point by keeping Lola largely shrouded from its readers. She is frequently described but rarely speaks. The narrator doesn't hesitate to enter into the consciousness of a canary but almost never follows Lola's thoughts.[40] Even at the close of her sojourn with the Norvals, she is shrouded from readers, disguised and disappeared on a ship bound for Cuba, having more or less abandoned her wealth in order to flee the menacing Hackwell. In this sense, Jemima's derisive proclamation also turns out to be prophetic: Lola is indeed a specter; that is the role she plays in the novel, and not just formally (she routinely disappears and reappears in the plot; she is without much flesh—whitening into ghostliness as her fortune, to which she has no access, grows). Lola, then, is a touchstone and a symbol rather than a fleshed-out character. Moreover, Lola and her money will haunt Jemima: the specter of Lola departing with her capital (from which Jemima abstracts large sums) haunts her like an ever-present nightmare.

Lola's role as a spectacular figure, a living curiosity, and the textual relation to the nineteenth century's long history of display culture open another avenue for Ruiz de Burton's critique. As Pateman and others have argued, the concept of consent of the governed presumes equality among consenters but also a structure that establishes practices of subordination, because not all people are equal to those who can consent.[41] Charles Mills argues that this structural differentiation emerges as a racial (supremacy) contract.[42] In alluding to a culture of display, Ruiz de Burton signals one of the mechanisms by which equality could be produced for some through a signaling of their difference from others. Humans on display, held before audiences and buyers, orchestrated by "authorities," help naturalize the structure of differentiation that animates Yankee culture, manifest destiny, and the racial contract.

At the end of her debut as spectacle, Lola is finally prompted to speak, and the Norvals marvel when they realize that she speaks English fluently. This fact, rather than normalizing her, only further spectacularizes her and reinforces the relay the servants will subsequently ride between Lola's status as a "brown child" and their racist attitudes toward Black children in general. Put differently, Lola's fluent English, rather than disrupting Jemima's and her daughters' sense of Lola as a curiosity, seems only to enfreak her more.

Just as she points toward the contradictions of US nation formation, Lola also figures the problematics of manifest destiny, which presumed an Anglo right to take possession of territories and abstract the wealth of a continent without obtaining the genuine consent of that continent's inhabitants. As the novel makes persuasively clear, consent at gunpoint hardly counts as meaningful (hence the charade with Hackwell) or indeed authentic. The text's lack of actual interest in Lola, the person, is clearer if she is understood as a necessary signpost and a witness.[43] The novel is in fact more interested in following the money and tracking the transformation that unfolds as the gold grows. This also explains why so much of the plot centers on various aspects of the Civil War (the slaughter of soldiers, the ludicrous military strategies, the corrupt business practices, the bankrupt politics, the heroic nursing, and the suffering of soldiers and prisoners alike). In this, the text offers Lola and her gold as a corrective to the Civil War literature that readers consumed in the previous decade.[44] Lola's gold is the enabling condition for the bloody war, and as such Lola and her mother slip from view—both specters.

The practice of display and the culture of circulating "living curiosities" were part of the processes that helped theorists and politicians produce a notion of state belonging distinct from a feudal and authoritarian construct. Lola might not have recognized herself as kin to either the young children advertised as "Aztec Lilliputians" or the people paraded about because of their fair skin color, but the figure displayed as a specimen before the Norvals, just like children and slaves in general, was cast out from the realm of consent, placed in a castagory at the bottom of the scaffold imaginary.

Child Matters

Scholars have variously described how cultural forms including toys, photographs, novels, and theater further developed the concept of the dependent, racialized child and helped to link the image of the white child to the development of the US national self-imaginary so that it became a vibrant resource for instantiating white supremacy.[45] Sentimental fiction also did crucial work in developing the bourgeois child, in part because the genre took seriously the child's paradoxical status as a symbol of unmediated freedom (innocence) and utter dependence.[46] During the nineteenth century, writers continually utilized the child to sustain a whole series of nation-building projects that were simultaneously racializing projects; that is, they used the child to create a racialized grammar for narrating and naming national belonging and fortification.

Not surprisingly, then, by the time Ruiz de Burton wrote *Who Would Have Thought It?*, childhood had acquired immense affective weight in American culture.[47] If Ruiz de Burton posits Lola Medina as wealthy, she repeatedly underscores Lola's status as a ward so that readers remember that Lola cannot command access to her wealth and indeed does not know of its existence for most of the novel. In the fleeting moments when we see Lola as the plot unrolls, she is always portrayed as feeling her vulnerability and isolation. *Who Would Have Thought It?* engages with the conflation of consent with adulthood on two levels—first, Lola is young and cannot grant consent to the disposition of her vast fortune; and, second, Lola, at least in Jemima's eyes, is nonwhite and is incapable of granting consent, of acting as a subject and citizen, nor can she even access personhood. She can never grow beyond the status of child. To Jemima, Lola is stuck, captive to the condition her racialization has rendered. This status as child also seems to render Lola mute, the foil for the plot. Or, borrowing from Kathryn Bond Stockton, Lola never appears to grow up—she grows *sideways*, figured as the embodiment of the "local"—stuck and contained as a resource.[48]

If Lola's function in the novel is to provoke a taxonomic racial crisis, her appearance as a child also points to the complex question of national belonging opened on the troubled road from the Treaty of Guadalupe Hidalgo to the ratification of the equal protection amendment to the Constitution. If, as Robin Bernstein argues, "childhood *itself*, however, is best understood as a process of surrogation, an endless attempt to find, fashion, and impel substitutes to fill a void caused by the loss of a half-forgotten original," then Lola embodies such a process.[49] She is a surrogate for Mexico's lost territory, lost children, lost resources. And as a surrogate, Lola never belongs; she is never "at home" with the Norvals. Like the stolen Indigenous territories more generally, her wealth engorges the Norvals and the nation, but her presence is never really welcomed or acknowledged as such, nor are her resources acknowledged, despite their centrality to the Norvals' own transformation from middle-class to nascent gilded elite. The novel reminds us many times that New England villagers speculate on the source of the Norvals' wealth and the Norvals themselves actively keep their source of wealth quite hidden.[50] Not only is Lola's presence in their home apparently kept a secret from Jemima's brother, but for the most part Lola is largely kept hidden—only really "seen" within private settings—in the Norvals' garden, at Julian's bedside, and so forth. Ultimately, she is simply absent from much of the novel itself.

It may be coincidental that the most well-known displayed people from Latin America during the nineteenth century were displayed as cute child-relics, yet that figuration undoubtedly reinforced the conflation of people of color with children, with the status of being permanently dependent and infantilized. Lola's portrayal as a child opens up the contradiction of that conflation. The Norvals, after all, utterly depend on Lola; her fortune is the source of their fortune. If Lola is figured as a ward and surrogate for Mexico's lost territories, the Norvals are figured as the very embodiment of US imperialism.

Their outrageous exploitation of Lola's wealth and their mystification of its source perfectly mimic a US culture that jealously guards the source of its wealth so it can be claimed as having resulted not from cupidity (e.g., the extraction of wealth from enslaved African peoples, the dispossession of Native lands, the annexation at gunpoint of a significant portion of Mexico and of Indigenous territories, including Mojave, Comanche, and Navajo lands) but from US (white) superiority.

Lola has been brought into the Norval house because of the complex two-hundred-year interchanges between the Apache nation and the Spanish and Mexican governments, as well as other Native peoples of the region, including the Maricopa, Pima, and Mojave peoples, and eventually the United States. She is a sort of orphaned casualty of this multicentury war.[51] As a child, an orphaned ward, she is fully vulnerable to being taken advantage of, as the Norvals so successfully do. By portraying Lola as a child, Ruiz de Burton exploits the sentimental status assigned to children and reveals the double vision of the child made operational by racialization. On the one hand, the narrator repeatedly figures her as the sentimental, innocent (white and morally superior) child. The scene of her first appearance, the odd pietà in which she rests in Dr. Norval's embrace, underscores this vision. Simultaneously, Jemima's and her servants' reception of Lola signals the other interpretive option—they immediately libel her as nonhuman (a specter). If the narrator shows Lola to be consistently suffering, Jemima treats her viciously, without empathy, as if Lola were insensate to pain, emotional or otherwise.

Childhood, as Ruiz de Burton powerfully shows, is an enormous resource. Drawing from the range of meanings assigned to the category, she lays out the problems attendant to the territories wrested from Mexico and further wrested from the Comanche, Apaches, Mojave, and other nations through even more bloodshed.[52] In offering Lola as a surrogate, first, for indigeneity writ large and, second, for Mexico, Ruiz de Burton underscores how people of color, having been rendered perpetual children in the racial-liberal matrix, can then have their childhood impounded in the name of their own protection or because, as wards, they are incapable of adequately developing the resources a childhood portends. By portraying Lola as both a child and a surrogate, Ruiz de Burton underscores the lack of agency and respect given Mexicanos and Native nations. She also makes it clear through the portrait of such surrogation how a racist and patronizing stance was produced and secured. Dr. Norval may hold Lola to his breast, but he takes her no more seriously as a person or subject than does his more blatantly perfidious wife. For Dr. Norval, Lola is as fungible as her gold and uncut gems.

Captives on Display

By introducing Lola into the narrative as a displayed person with a "romantic history," *Who Would Have Thought It?* reminds us that in the nineteenth century, displayed peoples were very frequently also captive peoples. Yet while Ruiz de Burton embeds a classic captivity narrative within *Who Would Have Thought It?*, she uses that classic narrative to frame Lola's status as a captive, not of the Mojave, but of the Norvals. Locked into her role as a critical witness to the absenting of Mexicans as citizen-subjects in US national discourse and to the manner in which the United States absconded with the wealth and resources of Native nations, Lola brings together two cultural practices: captivity narratives and the display of so-called living curiosities.

Captivity narratives were products of settler colonialism and were used in support of its imperial ambitions, but here Ruiz de Burton represents the Norvals as the kidnappers and suggests further that Lola's various experiences with enclosure find their parallel in other structures of confinement.[53] In other words, Ruiz de Burton gives us the inverse of colonial conquest by representing the captivity account directly *as* colonial conquest, as a technology and result of the US imperial expansion into northern Mexico. What is also interesting is not just that Ruiz de Burton represents captivity but that she also brings the captivity genre to bear on the production of the racialized (and racializing) child through the figure of Lola. Classic captivity narratives do not usually feature children; furthermore, once "freed," captives in these tales don't repeatedly fall into reiterated forms of captivity or enclosure again and again as does Lola. More especially, the captivity narrative, even as a meditation on freedom, did not attune itself to other forms of captivity such as slavery and imprisonment, as does *Who Would Have Thought It?* In bringing together these various forms of confinement (enslavement, imprisonment, captivity, gendered domesticity), along with its vituperative critique of US nation formation, the novel challenges readers to consider the interanimating relations between liberal consent-contract governmentality, with all of its claims to freedom and democracy, and the necessary technologies of punishment and enclosure that function to enforce a fiction of consent. That said, if the novel knits together these forms of confinement, of bracketing and pausing lives, it does not conflate them. Instead, it establishes them as relays.

While, to twenty-first-century readers, the novel's plot could appear farfetched, Ruiz de Burton may well have based her captivity account on the story of Olive Oatman, a woman who lived with the Pipa Aha Macav (the Mojave Nation) for four years after most of her family had been killed in skirmishes with the Yavapai. After the battle, Oatman was initially kept as a laborer for the Yavapai, then traded to the Mojave, who tattooed her chin as a method of communal incorporation and raised her as a member of their nation, not a captive. In 1854 Anglo soldiers forced her to leave the Mojave at gunpoint.[54] Her story was widely publicized in part because of her tattoo. Not coincidentally, the area where the soldiers encountered Oatman was also near a short-lived, but very lucrative, gold mine.

That the plot of the novel has such a vivid historical touchpoint has prodded scholars to note that part of Ruiz de Burton's agitation, and more broadly that of Mexicanos, emerged from the complex relationship that settler colonial ranchers and hacendados had with the Native peoples of northern Mexico before and after the war with the United States.[55] Scholars have tended to focus on the way resentment toward the lack of policing by Mexican state forces encouraged broad and violent relations between Mexican citizen-colonists and other nations, including the Apaches and Comanche. This discussion, however, frequently eclipses the larger history of captivity and war that characterized northern Mexico from Durango to Colorado and from the Atlantic to the Pacific for the two centuries before the Treaty of Guadalupe Hidalgo.[56] It also ignores the history of the Spanish and Mexican governments tacitly (and sometimes actively) encouraging the captivity of Native peoples as forced laborers. As Andrés Reséndez shows, the various systems (both formal and informal) of constrained labor and captivity of Indigenous peoples enabled the expansion and profitability of the cattle industry as well as silver and copper mining into northern Sonora.[57] These systems destroyed kinship networks and century-old affiliative relations among Native peoples; they also functioned as an unnamed war on the Indigenous nations, ultimately provoking a form of regional war and enabling an intensive captive-exchange system involving Mexican settler colonialists as well as networks of Comanche, Apache, Navajo, and other nations.[58] Within this network, enslavement did not look like the chattel slavery practiced by Anglos in the colonial and antebellum periods of the United States; nevertheless, Native peoples and non-Natives were taken from their communities and transported, traded, sold, incorporated into kinship networks, or confined as laborers. Thus, Lola's experience would not have been unique nor isolated; nor would it have been surprising that she and her mother were ultimately knitted into a community structure.

Unlike classic captivity tales, however, *Who Would Have Thought It?* is almost completely silent about Lola's experiences with the Mojave. Theresa's testimonio is never recapitulated for readers. Furthermore, the narrator makes it clear that Lola's and her mother's experiences should remain enshrouded in silence, even shame. Thus, readers learn about Lola's captivity, not from Lola, but from Dr. Norval. So desperate is Lola to keep her history hidden that the perfidious Hackwell bates Lola with threats to publicize it should she refuse to marry him. Lola, Julian, and her father subsequently and energetically work to keep Lola's captivity experiences private and out of the public sphere. This desire to keep Lola's experience a secret could be linked to Oatman's case as well. Shortly after her captivity ended, Oatman turned her experience into a performance piece and traveled the United States describing her life before rapt paying audiences. Reenacting her life with the Mojave and emphasizing her dramatically tattooed chin, she became a living curiosity and the subject of what Margot Mifflin calls a "lurid, best-selling biography" by Royal Stratton that erased her Mormonism and "libeled the caring Mojave Indians who raised her as 'degraded bipeds.'"[59] Ruiz de Burton may well have seen Oatman's efforts to spectacularize her captivity as inappropriate, unbecoming, or unladylike. In this she would have concurred with Oatman's eventual husband, John Fairchild, who before his 1865 marriage to Oatman sought out and then burned every copy of Stratton's *Captivity of the Oatman Girls* that he could find.[60]

Readers thus do not learn any meaningful details about Lola's experience of living with the Mojave from her birth until the age of ten. What does her silence about her experiences achieve? What does it contain? At the fictive-historical level, of course, such silence about captivity and the complex slave/kin network operated by the Comanche, Apaches, and other nations enshrines Lola's experience as unique, exceptional, and unknowable. In such silence, the novel fails to rebut the anti-Native stereotypes trumpeted by Mrs. Cackle at the start of the novel. Furthermore, this approach enhances the claim that captives were tragic victims of brutality rather than active combatants in a massive struggle for control of the region's mineral resources, markets, and trade routes, as was Lola's family (and indeed Ruiz de Burton's). Third, this silence maintains Lola's role as a cipher. Just as we don't learn what life with the Mojave was like, Lola says virtually nothing about life with the Norvals or the nuns.

Such silence flattens Lola's various enclosures (Mojave country, Norval gardens, convent school) into a continuum and underscores Ruiz de Burton's ironic arguments about the way Northern Yankee culture was "barbaric." More broadly, Lola's silence also enables Ruiz de Burton to highlight the parallels between various forms of enclosure, including "Indian" and "Yankee" captivity, Civil War prisons, marriage, and rigid gender norms. While the text roundly makes fun of Lavinia Sprig, Jemima's unmarried sister, it also seriously portrays her experiences as a single woman attempting to help her brother by navigating the machinations of DC corruption. In this effort, Lavinia gives voice to a range of protofeminist ideas about the status of women and the failure of the legal system to provide justice to women, implying that gender norms are enclosures, forms of constraint without end.[61] Like captives, when freed from the confinement of white domesticity, Lavinia is able to articulate an outside to coercive gender norms and voices her own sense of distress over rigid gender expectations, but she finds her release not out in the wilderness with Native peoples but within the hospital as a nurse to wounded soldiers and also in the "wilderness" of DC politics, where she independently works in her brother's interest. As Christopher Castiglia suggests, the captivity narrative was the one genre that authorized women to appear outside of the home, where it could showcase "women's fortitude, cunning, and physical and emotional strength."[62] In this sense, Lavinia, like Lola and Isaac, is dissociated from the domestic turmoil of the Norval home, which in this reverse-captivity plot is the site of savagery and violence. Lavinia's sojourn in Washington begins to provide an imaginative alternative to the domestic tyranny that Jemima enforces, even as Lavinia herself articulates a profound critique of the limitations of her choices.

Another crucial captivity subplot of the novel follows Isaac Sprig, who works as a clerk in Washington, DC. After a brawl with a powerful politician, Sprig is demoted to the dead-letter office, where a buddy gives him Theresa Medina's testimonio to read. Isaac takes it home and shortly thereafter enrolls in the Union army. He is promptly captured and spends the duration of the war as a forgotten prisoner; the same powerful politician who exiled Isaac to the dead-letter office also expunges his name from the prisoner rolls so that he can't be included in any captive exchanges between the warring armies. His papers—like Lola's—go missing. The novel follows both his time in prison and his sister Lavinia's efforts to free him, but Isaac is lost to his family for most of his captivity. When Isaac escapes from prison at the close of the war, his first action is to locate Lola's father in Mexico and then to reunite the father and daughter. So while Lola's gold may have aided her move away from the Mojave only to force her into a new enclosure in New England, Ruiz de Burton circles around this conundrum by paralleling Lola's sojourn in the North to Isaac's in the South before bringing them both "home" to Mexico. This subplot achieves several things, not the least of which is to provide another opportunity to inveigh against Northern chicanery. It also allows Ruiz de Burton to sneakily suture together US imperial energies with the hypocrisy behind white abolitionist campaigns that she contends has structured a broader US culture. Furthermore, it reinforces the link between the two wars, underscoring the role of papers as forms of authority that outline, mediate, and legitimate belonging.

Ultimately, Lola's reticence about her captivity reinforces the same logic that leads her to willingly consider marriage to Hackwell over public exposure of her mother's life as a captive consort. The reason, of course, is consent. As Dr. Norval tells it early in the novel, Lola's mother apparently entered a consensual sexual relationship with a Mojave leader; this kinship relation gave her status and protection. But her apparent consent to this relationship also, the novel implies, permanently severed her from her first husband and birth family. Had Lola treated this relationship as something other than shameful, say, for example, as loving and protective or even pleasurable, then the category of lady would have been even more fully denied her by the Norvals. Put differently, for Lola, captivity and the fiction of consent (however enshrouded) cohere to mystify the coloniality of scale imposed through castagories. Yet according to this logic, as a child Lola would have been absolved of the shame of having granted consent to her kinship relations with the Mojave. This logic enables Ruiz de Burton to portray her as having superior claims to moral purity than the greedy Norvals. Here is a critical knot in Ruiz de Burton's case against US domestic propriety. If she inveighs against the way manifest domesticity props up imperial expansionism, she nevertheless supports the system by portraying Lola as concurring with the mechanisms that trigger gendered shame.

By establishing echoes and relays among these various forms of captivity, Ruiz de Burton's novel highlights a principal issue troubling captivity and troubling the liberal idea of governmentality in which the captivity narrative tradition was born and nurtured. That is, she highlights the very slippery qualities of the doctrine of consent through the relays she produces between captives and narrative forms. Further, in making Lola a child-captive, she particularly underscores the importance of the fiction of consent underpinning social contract theory and democratic governance and the fallacious assumptions holding the concept aloft. That she does so in the shadow of the passage of the Fourteenth Amendment to the Constitution, the equal protection clause, makes her argument all the more troubling in its prescience.

As scholars have shown, captivity narratives were vital for the emergence of a discourse of nationalism in the United States. Written in the shadow of slavery, they highlighted white women's resilience and capacity to escape captivity. They treated captivity as a kind of spectacle, which glowed all the more terrifyingly given the nation's investment in slavery. They also served to underscore the racist libel against men of color, especially since one of the recurring themes of narratives promoting white supremacy has been the claim that men of color threaten white women.[63] Yet the novel comports with the captivity genre obversely. The doctor tells Jemima that the Mojave treated Lola and her mother with care and respect, knitting them into the community structure. However, once captive to the Norvals, Lola is constantly vulnerable to the rogue Hackwell. Further, she is never really knit into the fabric of the Norval family; they prove far less hospitable than the Pipa Aha Macav.

Because the captivity genre became a crucial resource for women writers, who offered some of the first historical romances in which captivity figures prominently, it is not entirely surprising that Ruiz de Burton would turn to such a popular form for her own first novel.[64] In fact, captivity is so pervasive in the novel that it's difficult not to think of the novel as itself a burlesque of captivity. Isaac is a captive; Lola is, of course, but so is Lavinia, as, finally, is Lola's fortune. Lola is the typical example of someone held captive—a white child held captive by an Indian community and then rescued by Anglos. But the true captivity, the novel makes clear, happens only when Lola is taken east to live with the Norvals. Yet Lola does not conform to Castiglia's characterization of women in the captivity genre as figures "who are not simply voiceless and frail items of exchange."[65] To a large extent, Lola appears as voiceless and frail. She does not protest the Norvals' failure to find her father. She does not protest her enclosure in either the house or the convent. She does not protest because she rarely speaks. Lola is properly a commodity who is rarely represented as thinking or choosing or standing up for herself, beyond her refusal of Hackwell. In fact, her function as allegory reveals the structure of captivity energizing the novel: Mexico may be envisioned as a captive; the territories of Native nations are held captive. Read this way, the larger theme of the novel becomes clearer—like the repertoire of the captivity novels and popular narratives from which *Who Would Have Thought It?* draws, the narrator, in Castiglia's words, "mark[s] her distance from the culture."[66] In other words, the apparently obtrusive subplots following Lavinia and Isaac begin to make more sense if we understand them as further examples through which Ruiz de Burton suggests that constraint is the necessary ballast for the liberal freedom white men claim and, further, that constraint masquerades as freedom, such that racial proscriptions disguise themselves as avenues to equality.

"The Imp of the Burlesque"

Most popular literature written during and about the Civil War, as Alice Fahs shows, drew on the conventions of literature shaped during the war against Mexico—these include "dying soldier poems, sensational novels, humorous verse, songs, and patriotic poetry," all of which set the "templates for Civil War literature."[67] Such literature largely focused on individuals' "intense experiences of personal engagement with the war," and, not surprisingly, "the felt tension between the needs of the nation and the needs of individuals became the chief energizing plot device in countless stories and poems."[68] These texts reveled in calls to patriotism and the promotion of a national symbology that would enact the abstract state newly calling for blood. In this context, and despite the mass slaughter, popular literature "explicitly fought against the idea of the mass" and insisted on "individual, personal meanings of the war."[69] For example, one of the most popular forms of poetry across the North and the South focused on the "picket guard"—the lonely and isolated soldier away from his regiment.[70] If the war promoted a new consolidation of the idea of the state and the demos, war literature, Fahs concludes, promoted instead a "new adventurous individualism."[71]

Rather than sounding a patriotic note, *Who Would Have Thought It?* constantly undermines such an affective stance with a refrain that sardonically invokes scale to describe the United States as "the best nation on earth"—a refrain that stands in counterpoint to the plot's unveiling of moral hypocrisy and political corruption. It also stands out against the histories of the war that were published during the war and in its immediate aftermath. These histories largely celebrated the war and, in a melodramatic frame, "created a particular version of imagined nationhood, in which the chief meanings of the war adhered not to the politics of slavery, as Horace Greeley would have it, but to the deeds and sufferings of individuals."[72] Such popular literature also tended to avoid focusing on the effects of the war on the home front, though Louisa May Alcott's *Little Women* (1868) provides an important counterexample.[73] *Who Would Have Thought It?* was also, perhaps, out of step with reading interests in the 1870s. Fahs notes that *Harper's* found room for only two Civil War stories during the entire decade of the 1870s. Not until the late 1880s did new Civil War–related texts begin to be published. Out of step, uninterested in melodrama per se, Ruiz de Burton clearly sought a different literary form for her story, her argument. She found it in burlesque theater, a form that provided her with a dense and varied set of methods to ridicule the habits and attitudes that had enshrined imperialist racism under the banner of manifest destiny and that clothed a pretense of consent and an even more insidious discourse of equality within a structure of stunning inequality. In some sense, the novel's engagement with dominant fictional modes and narrative forms such as the captivity genre, sentimental fiction, and the historical romance shows that these forms are less effective options for enacting a critique since these forms were themselves developed in the service of liberalism. In a dashing stroke of insight, Ruiz de Burton draws instead on display culture and the more radical, though related, form of burlesque theater.[74]

With a narrative voice that often sounds more like Anthony Trollope's satirical accounts of corrupt British parliamentary elections and ministerial maneuverings than that of US writers of the era, such as Harriet Beecher Stowe, Ruiz de Burton makes many stabs at puncturing the inflated myth of a US government characterized by pure democracy and wholesome intentions.[75] *Who Would Have Thought It?* comprises dozens of short chapters, each of which enacts a scene that can be read almost independently, a style that readily lends itself to staging. But *Who Would Have Thought It?* wasn't staged, and there is no apparent record that Ruiz de Burton attempted to have it either serialized or staged. So why write such short, episodic chapters that read like theatrical set pieces? More especially, the chapters often only loosely hold together in a linear manner; the plot unfolds in jerks with repeated disruptions, and the formal conventions of romance, melodrama, and realism do not adequately account for the novel's eccentricities. Burlesque theater, however, does.[76] In an effort to "outsize the narrow representational frames" available to Mexicanos and Californios during the nineteenth century, *Who Would Have Thought It?* repurposes a number of strategies taken from the burgeoning burlesque theater of the mid-nineteenth century.[77]

Shortly after the end of the Civil War, theater impresarios and actors in the United States transformed burlesque comedies into burlesque extravaganzas.[78] Often situated in the theaters attached to "living curiosity museums," these extravaganzas grew increasingly popular and acceptable to middle-class and especially female theater audiences during the 1860s and 1870s with their mocking of power and social norms and their irreverent, lampooning humor. Burlesque shows, or "travesties," turned to Shakespeare as well as Greek and Roman myths, twisting well-known stories and plots into opportunities for irreverent parody. Vividly staged but deploying only a skeletal narrative structure, burlesque travesties offered lavish, appealing sets and costumes, all the while undermining ennobled gods, kings, and princes by placing them in more prosaic settings in order to rail about contemporary issues and make fun of rigid social norms. For example, *Much Ado about a Merchant of Venice*, staged for the first time in 1869, contorted Shakespeare's comedy into an opportunity to inveigh against the extensive corruption plaguing New York City institutions, including its policing system.[79]

Burlesque staging, despite its critiques of raw power, was neither mirthless nor earnest. Instead, deploying puns, ribald innuendoes, popular songs, and dance routines, burlesques joked from beginning to end. Refusing anything that might look like aesthetic coherence, burlesques staged, within a single show, jigs, parodies of the cancan, hornpipe dances, and set pieces drawn from minstrel shows.[80] Similarly, burlesque songs drew on well-known melodies to underline new, joking lyrics about contemporary figures and issues ranging from hair dye to the prim modesty of middle-class norms for women. Burlesque plots were interrupted by processions and parades up to a half hour long; the stories or plots themselves were disconnected from the apparently "gratuitous outbreaks of dancing, or abandoned all together."[81] Burlesque lacked thematic coherence; narrative motion was halting and antilinear and only vaguely gestured toward closure since closure would suggest the sort of containment that this very transgressive form sought to trap into a critique.

As Robert Allen describes it, burlesque "worked by turning meaning inside out. With the pun it exploded the possibility of stable meanings, or in the case of a female performer impersonating a male character dancing a minstrel show jig, it piled too many meanings on top of each other.... Having anesthetized rationality, burlesque gave its stage over to unauthorized impertinence.... When the targets of humor were the venerated, the authorized, the sacrosanct, then laughter became an affirmation of the right of a nobody to question the stature of a somebody."[82] Burlesque theater thereby provided an opportunity to critique normative structures of power and the mannerisms that guarded and guided those enveloped in gilded palaces. And given its interest in impertinence, it is easy to see why burlesque might have provided a helpful model to a recently widowed and very angry Ruiz de Burton.

Part of burlesque's innovation, according to one contemporary observer, Richard Grant White, was its staging of the "monstrously incongruous and unnatural." Burlesque effectively "forces the conventional and the natural together just at the points where they are most remote, and the result is absurdity, monstrosity. Its system is a defiance of system. It is out of *all* keeping.... [B]urlesque casts down all the gods from their pedestals."[83] White was not responding simply to the lampooning of Greek myths or bourgeois niceties but to a new, significant innovation then engaging theatergoers: women were performing most of the roles onstage, including those of men and male gods. The most profitable burlesques featured women in drag, underscoring the apparent incongruity of body to part as well as the "travesty" such cross-dressing seemed to imply and celebrate.[84] Burlesque treated masculinity as a simple caricature of itself, one more aspect of a portrayal of mixed-up roles, categories, and social positions; with this parody, the drag stars onstage also effectively eviscerated the sentimental angel in the wings.[85]

These travesties, more than mere comic entertainments, moved beyond women simply mouthing the words provided them; in putting onstage spectacular ballets and galloping horses carrying the bodies of fallen heroes strapped to their backs, burlesque shifted the burden of signification from a songwriter's or playwright's words to the female form itself. Burlesque performers—including, or perhaps especially, women—directly addressed audiences with winks at their own impudence, drawing audiences into the extravaganza.[86] Moreover, burlesque staged itself as a comment upon itself, joking about its own jokes and satirizing critics of one night's performance with new songs making fun of those critics during the subsequent night's performance. This sense of playing with its own self-narrative, its joking metacommentary, was even signaled by a leading performer, Lydia Thompson, who joked onstage about burlesque's "own awareishness."[87]

Who Would Have Thought It? broadly follows the travails of Lola Medina from her shrouded introduction to New England to her shrouded departure from its shores, yet, like burlesque, the novel's plot is elastic enough to also follow the travails of Lavinia and Isaac Sprig on either side of the war's front lines, the expansion and contraction of Jemima's ethics and passions, the Norval daughters' aggressive engagement with consumer culture, and the Norvals' entanglements with wartime politics and profiteers. Other aspects of the novel suggest the influence of the burlesque form even more clearly: the dependence on puns ("a little girl very black indeed"), the play with drag and impersonation (Lola's dyed skin creates a kind of unsettling incongruity with the repeated proclamations of her pure Spanish blood, even as she is revealed to be a descendant of Austrians as well as Spaniards; as the novel nears a conclusion, Jemima knowingly masquerades as a paragon of virtue), the spoofing of melodramas (Lola rescues the last remaining parakeet; Julian is repeatedly injured), the songs (including triumphant singing at a soldiers' camp and Skaly's crooning to the bemused New York City rats), and the parades (of carriages in Central Park and Wag's prancing horse across Fifth Avenue). Several of the chapters even work as comic set pieces (e.g., the scene around the dinner table joking about Skalywag's names). Put differently, the novel careens from scene to scene with little attention to important details typically dictated by realism or historical romance.[88]

Like burlesque theater, *Who Would Have Thought It?* is highly conscious of itself as a performance and as a critique of the staging, costuming, scripts, and productions of cynical power masquerading as authentic Christian piety and devotion to duty. The novel everywhere employs the strategies of burlesque to critique the nascent myth of class ascension, a romanticized story of young men who pull themselves up by their own bootstraps. Ruiz de Burton stages all of these myths as performances, relying on a set of burlesque strategies that include impersonation and exaggeration. With story after story of comic figures such as the Cackles, who through their cowardice ironically achieve military notoriety and recognition, readers are invited to laugh and sneer at those duped by the theatrics of class ascension, military bravery, and Christian devotion.

Ruiz de Burton is ruthless in her analysis of the seductions of wealth, showing how the rituals of power must be carefully staged and performed even as she details the kind of corrupt business practices and cynical political decisions that caused desperately poor people immense suffering during the Civil War. Her narrator constantly turns to exaggeration and ironic exclamations to scrutinize and satirize the excesses made possible through the exploitation of Lola's wealth. In burlesquing both the rags-to-riches myth and the domestic novel by illustrating in excruciating detail how the Norvals and their friends depend utterly on Lola's wealth, and in showing how their seizure of that wealth entangles them in skeins of corruption, Ruiz de Burton challenges popular plot formulas and social codes that helped to naturalize postwar social relations and produce the narrative scaffolding for the emerging Gilded Age.

If the novel lacks "ennobled gods" per se, *Who Would Have Thought It?* nevertheless lampoons with an "unauthorized impertinence" the secular gods of New England Yankee and Puritan culture, as well as Protestant piety with its feminized expression in sentimental domesticity, and the larger national ideologies of manifest destiny and equality before the law. As Jaime Javier Rodríguez explains, antebellum New England culture was galvanized by an ongoing celebration of Yankee "authenticity"—not simply its historic heritage but its ongoing unmediated enactment of so-called Yankee culture.[89] Such authenticity depended on claims to an "undefiled" Anglo-Saxon language, an ongoing utopian faith in the pastoral, and, in particular, a celebration of the "ordinary" yeoman farmer. The strands of Yankee supremacy—"white ethnicity, social coherence, moral purity"—were sutured together with devotion to isolationism, anti-Catholicism, and a sensibility that melded "New England" to a concept of "authentic American national identity."[90] Such isolationism was held up as the mechanism to protect the purity of Yankee culture and to thereby resist "impurity and change."[91] Yankee history and culture, still heralded at midcentury, "centered on notions of simplicity, authenticity, and independence" and served as the ideological bedrock for "the manifestation of racial destiny."[92] *Who Would Have Thought It?* pillories this romanticized Yankee narrative not only in the sardonic portrayal of the Cackles and Sprigs but also in the interplay between the portraits of Lola and Jemima; the stunning differences between them ultimately enact the novel's ideological critique.

As many critics have noted, the novel signals its parody of Yankee culture at the very start. In one of the text's most studied passages, the two erstwhile parsons repeat Mrs. Cackle's long-winded diatribe against James Norval; only a few paragraphs into the novel, this scene provides a portrait of New England chauvinism with its sweeping antipathy toward all difference, in the name of equality. This speech presages the reception the doctor will receive and establishes a set of terms and attitudes crucial to the novel's burlesque engagement with New England culture:

> [The Norval problems] have their root in the doctor's most unnatural liking of foreigners. That liking was the cause of the doctor's sending his only son Julian to be educated in Europe—as if the best schools on earth were not in New England—and Heaven knows what might have become of Julian if his heroic mother had not sent for him. He might have been a Roman Catholic, for all we know. That liking was also the cause of the doctor's sending Isaac to be a good-for-nothing clerk in sinful Washington, among foreigners, when he could have remained in virtuous New England to be a useful farmer. And finally, impelled by that liking, the doctor betook himself to California, which is yet full of "*natives*." And as a just retribution for such perverse liking, the doctor was well-nigh "roasted by the natives," said the old lady.[93]

In case Cackle's name, derived from a Middle English word meaning "noisy and inconsequent talk," is not signal enough of parody, Cackle herself spouts a whole series of stereotypical beliefs, including the celebration of isolationism, New England supremacy, Yankee authenticity, and the romance of the pastoral.[94] Cackle's comments also make it clear that from the outset the novel intends to conflate Jemima with these Yankee attributes and beliefs. Hackwell partially interrupts these sentiments, however, telling her, "Not by the natives, madam. The people called 'the natives' are mostly of Spanish descent, and are not cannibals. The wild Indians of the Colorado River were doubtless the ones who captured the doctor and tried to make a meal of him."[95] His interruption immediately suggests his own disinclination to embrace all the tenets of Yankee authenticity, as he is willing here to make a historical distinction that acknowledges a Spanish empire but that dislodges the Pipa Aha Macav from their own sovereignty. This moment is also curiously prophetic about his relationship with Jemima—his willingness to quibble and authorize himself predicts his various masquerades. But having already identified himself as a rogue, Hackwell's intervention in the name of "truth" hardly registers as a critique of Yankee hyperbole. So it is not surprising that in their conversation Mrs. Cackle barely acknowledges his correction and continues nattering: "To me they are all alike—Indians, Mexicans, or Californians—they are all horrid.

But my son Beau says that our just laws and smart lawyers will soon *'freeze them out.'* That as soon as we take their lands from them they will never be heard of anymore, and then the Americans, with God's help, will have all the land that was so righteously acquired through a just war and a most liberal payment in money."[96] Invoking the language of manifest destiny, Cackle also deploys the technology of racialization—collectivizing a whole range of historical, cultural, and linguistic differences into a collapsed and homogeneous horridness.

If Mrs. Cackle announces a set of paradigmatic beliefs that the novel will attempt to ridicule into oblivion, the narrator continually reminds readers of the distance between nostalgia for a Puritan past and present conditions. For example, the narrator takes a gratuitous swipe at nationalist orthodoxy by introducing the Norvals' trip to Europe with the comment that it was to occur just after the "anniversary of some great day in New England . . . in which the Pilgrim fathers had done one of their wonderful deeds. They had either embarked, or landed, or burnt a witch, or whipped a woman at the pillory, on just such a day."[97] Cunningly ridiculing the celebrations of the Pilgrims with a list that begins with an almost-nonsensical reference to seemingly prosaic achievements but then juxtaposes them to the less heralded history of misogynist violence, the narrative also makes it clear that the Pilgrims' arrival brought a new violence to the continent. It is a typical burlesque move: disruption through juxtaposition even as it juxtaposes the wealthy US daughter's tour of Europe with the "brave" Pilgrims' effort to flee Europe.

This strategy of juxtaposition is most effectively enacted in the portrayal of Jemima, whom the novel relentlessly burlesques as the (un)angelic mother at the heart of domestic sentimentalism. So distorted is Jemima that she becomes a grotesque parody of her own self-fashioning as the upright angel of the house; ultimately, she is the demented paragon not of New England righteousness and patriotism but of abolitionist racism and Yankee greed. And if the text everywhere betrays a bitter hostility toward the hypocrisy of her abolitionist sentiments, the narrator also makes it clear that Jemima is, ultimately, a product of the culture she has embraced so fully. Tracking her growing erotic desire for Hackwell and her intensifying greed, the narrative notes, "How insidiously that love had crept into her heart! Slowly, stealthily, through the only avenue by which it was accessible—her dark bigotry and her blind prejudices."[98] What the text suggests repeatedly, as this aside implies, is that Jemima is not an exception to Puritan or Yankee morality but an example of it, so much so that Jemima, in giving her greatest praise, even conflates Hackwell with "the old Covenanters."[99]

Not content to ridicule Puritan ideology, Ruiz de Burton also suggests that connected to its bigotry and blind prejudice is greed:

No one could have recognized in this superbly dressed lady the gawky girl the doctor saw for the first time counting the eggs to send to market, nor the rigid Puritan who had scorned the frivolity of lace or a bit of ribbon around her neck. Mrs. Norval looked young for her years. If in earlier life she could have felt the passions to which now she was a constant prey—her ambition, her remorse, her bitter hatred for Lola, her blind love for Hackwell—she might now have been an old, old woman. But the cold selfishness and unloving impassibility of her previous nature had preserved her young, as the ice she used to put around her turkeys to pack them for the Boston market kept those fowls fresh, though she made it a rule to "do her killing" a week before Thanksgiving Day and a week before Christmas.[100]

Comparing Jemima with an old, frozen turkey while also revealing her questionable ethics as a thrifty farmer eager to make a "killing" at the Boston market (by selling less-than-fresh fowl), the text viciously skewers both the young adult and the middle-aged woman she has become. Jemima's apparent lack of passion as a youth had kept her physically and emotionally icy. The sole outlet for an experience of passionate enthusiasm was her faith: "She had had only one passion—her religious bigotry—which had inspired her with a strong hatred towards everything and everybody that was not Presbyterian. She had felt but one ambition—that of saving, saving, saving—putting away more pennies and five- and ten-cent pieces than any of her neighbors. . . . So it was that her soul only warmed into life under the Promethean breath of Hackwell, and it leaped from its lethargy like those lizards imbedded for ages in granite which geologists say resuscitate when brought to the sun and air."[101] Having called her a turkey on ice, the text moves on to suggesting she is a petrified lizard. These swipes at Jemima underscore the limitations of a Puritan ideology but also, more generously, portray a woman damaged, reduced, and limited by it as well. In juxtaposing Jemima to a turkey and a lizard, the novel is also inviting its audience not just to ridicule her but to distance themselves from the calcifying practices that celebrate a Yankee authenticity. This portrait of Yankee thriftiness necessarily contrasts with Jemima's midlife decision to outfit her footmen in Victorian-era livery, showing not only how far she has traveled from her original proclamation of a yeoman ideology of equality but also how much she has embraced the Victorian spectacle of wealth and regal display.

It is in this context that Jemima's repeated espousal of the rhetoric of white supremacy should be studied. *Who Would Have Thought It?* is perhaps less interested in whiteness per se or even in asserting Lola's claim to whiteness (although it does do so repeatedly) than it is in detailing how whiteness emerges as a *function* of a Puritan worldview. By providing such a bitter and cynical portrait of Jemima, by detailing at every turn her racist treatment of Lola, the novel argues that the fetishization of whiteness emerges out of Puritan/Yankee bigotry, isolationism, and selfishness. In this sense, the novel shows how Anglo-Saxonism and its New England variant constructed a concept of whiteness that Lola ultimately disrupts. In becoming white, Lola never becomes a Yankee, never achieves a kind of Puritan access to the Covenant, for her whiteness remains bounded or confined by her Catholicism, by her position as outsider.

The linchpin here is authenticity. Even after Lola's skin has changed colors, Jemima insists on her status as inauthentically "white." For Jemima, Lola cannot transcend what she understands as a degraded category, one that makes access to an authentic white status impossible. Instead, Lola's transformation suggests, to borrow Daphne Brooks's words, a "horrifying taxonomic crisis" that Jemima will struggle to contain.[102] Not surprisingly, then, she both refers to Lola as a "mongrel," echoing one strain of the dominant anti-Mexican discourse of the nineteenth century, and underscores this construction of Mexicanity by linking it to criminality, another technique for sedimenting a racial hierarchy: "'She is a good Mexican, surely, and knows how to put the dagger to the throat,' said Mrs. Norval with a hoarse laugh."[103] Clearly, Lola's skin color disrupts other narratives of what whiteness is, and so Jemima draws from still another repertoire to shore up her argument for Lola's difference. In her position as a guardian of Puritan and Yankee culture and values, Jemima's espousal of such epithets against Lola repeatedly reinforces Ruiz de Burton's portrait of the problems with New England culture and ideologies. Even Jemima's name, a derivative of the Hebrew word for "dove" popularized during the Puritan era, underscores this portrayal of Jemima as a representative of a Puritan worldview that is ultimately corrupt and violent. Her own name mocks and burlesques her attitude and actions.

Whiteness is also structured in the novel as the signpost of respectability. Or at least it is for Jemima. For that reason alone, the novel's burlesquing of Jemima's pretense to propriety and sober Christian virtue troubles the conflation of propertied whiteness with respectability. But it also signals that Yankee authenticity is a far more central gatekeeper to whiteness than is respectability. For if genteel respectability were the key to the door, Lola would have found her welcome. She is continually portrayed as respectable: she speaks French, plays the piano beautifully, greets all with grace, and carefully guards her virtue. She is never conniving or greedy. Thus, just as the novel rebukes the fiction of consent of the governed at the heart of liberal republicanism and argues that people have been bamboozled by it, it takes to task the claims to respectability that have been stitched into the fabric of citizenship from the start.[104]

Julian's response to his mother's diatribe against Lola is instructive here as well: "'Pshaw!' ejaculated Julian, taking his cap and walking towards the door. 'In this instance the simile is bad, for we have appropriated the purse, not she.'"[105] He does not deride the conflation of Mexicanity with thievery but instead suggests that his mother merely misapplies it. This moment implicates Julian in the racial economy that the novel unrelentingly mocks. Ruiz de Burton, at nearly every turn and with virtually every character, makes it a point to illustrate how much self-understanding depends on racialization, on knowing one's castagory. Put differently, virtually every character in the novel makes some sort of disparaging racial comment in a formula in which whiteness is evoked as a metric of authenticity and paradigmatic Yankeeness.

That racialization is so profoundly productive becomes clearest, perhaps, when Julian goes before Abraham Lincoln to defend his honor. Throughout the novel, Julian is lionized as honorable and noble, although he is also subtly ridiculed as the frequently wounded soldier.[106] So it is his position as the plot's stable moral core that makes his route of defense significant. Arguing that he has been convicted without trial, he grumbles to Lincoln, "I wish to have my freedom. If the negroes have it, why shouldn't I? I did not bargain to surrender my freedom to give it to Sambo."[107] In this astounding moment in which Julian invokes a well-worn and derisive term, a number of things become clear. The first, of course, is that Ruiz de Burton here suggests that such a term could be invoked in front of the signer of the Emancipation Proclamation; it subtly reinforces her larger point that the abolitionist effort was not an antiracist effort. Second, Julian makes it clear that the Civil War had not done away with systemic racial hierarchies. And, finally, Julian's argument hinges on the implicit sense that his stature and identity differ from those of African Americans; racialization is the crucial mechanism producing this difference.

This scene with the president also casts light on an earlier conversation. At a moment when Julian and Lola are confessing their love for each other, Lola anguishingly reports that she "could not bear to think that to you, too, I was an object of aversion because my skin was black.... I didn't care whether I was thought black or white by others, I hated to think that you *might* suppose I was Indian or black." In this crucial moment midway through the novel, when Lola finally explains the transformation of her skin color, her larger point is that she fears Julian's attitude toward people of color. He does not dismiss her fear but instead tacitly acknowledges his own prejudice by saying that he already knew she was of "pure Spanish descent."[108] This moment is complex in a number of ways. As Ruiz de Burton undoubtedly knew, the term *pure* held a double meaning in the Victorian era; it referred, for example, to the excrement used to clean leather.[109] Thus, in a burlesque fashion, the text doubles down on purity and underscores the term's imprecision. Julian's understanding of himself depends in part on the production of racial distinctions and the logic of racial metrics. Again, given that he functions as the central hero of the novel— the repeatedly wounded but determined soldier; the loyal son who resists the intrigues of Hackwell—it is clear with such a portrait that the novel is arguing that a racial metric consistently controls New England social relations. No white person rises above it; no one steps out of it. The novel subtly suggests, then, that such a structure produces the culture that slaughtered Native peoples, destroyed much of Mexico, and led to the vast bloodshed of the Civil War.

The novel's mischievous "awareishness" also underscores its relationship to burlesque theater. While the narrative voice is frequently snippy, barking out moral critiques and exasperated expressions of sarcasm aimed at failed ethics (such as the repeated phrase, "best government on earth"), these intrusions also function as winks creating complicity with the readers. Of course, it was not uncommon for nineteenth-century novelists to draw attention to the text itself as a production through a direct address to the audience *as* readers (thereby underscoring the text's status as an object, a book).[110] Nor was it uncommon for writers to play demure with deprecating comments about their own skills. What is interesting about such intrusions in *Who Would Have Thought It?* is that the narrator, like the burlesque star, deploys these intrusions as an opportunity to undermine her own characters rather than to produce sympathy for them or their cause.

This distance supposedly stages the moral perspective of the narrator. For example, while urging readers, "Let us be charitable with [Jemima]," the narrator with an aside comments further, "although she was never known to be so towards any one." Even that stance of high moral ground is immediately undercut when the narrator subsequently warns readers "not to pitch our voices so high as she [Jemima] did at the beginning of her song, for we also may find how difficult it is to maintain such *diapason*."[111] This may well be a comment about self-righteousness, but in burlesque awareishness this comment also functions as a sneaky joke aimed at undercutting writerly ambitions, doubling back to poke at the text's own onslaught of moral raillery against the expropriation of Lola's wealth and the failures of liberal republicanism.

At various points the narrator refers to herself as unambitious and humble.[112] But such comments belie both the audacious stance of the narrator and the scope of the novel (nothing less than massive government corruption and the bankruptcy of treasured national ideologies such as manifest destiny and Yankee supremacy). Such "awareishness" also suggests a certain impudence: at the very point when the plot is about to become a long sensationalist romp and Hackwell will attempt to kidnap Lola, the narrator claims the novel isn't sensational at all. The text uses its own awareishness in a conventional sense, that is, to draw attention to itself as a kind of performance and to place the reader within the plot, within the action of the novel. The narrator then notes, when shifting to Isaac's escape from a Confederate prison, "If Isaac's friends had apparently forgotten him, that is no reason we should forget him, and, since he can't come to us, we must go to him."[113] The narrator jokingly notes the awkward scene change and knows the audience knows it.

Such awareishness underscores the narrator's ambivalent distance from the characters and events of *Who Would Have Thought It?* And it is this distance, this frequent undermining of characters, that shifts the text from a simple satire to a burlesque flouting of the venerated narratives of the nation. Such distance becomes clear at several points in the text. For example, in noting the Cackles' and Lavinia Sprig's earnest efforts as nurses to the war's wounded, the narrator cannot resist adding, "All did their duty—as only ladies brought up as Puritans know how—to the full measure; the gloomier the duty the better accomplished."[114] These narrative asides puncture an overly inflated veneration for an ideology the novel portrays as derisive, mean-spirited, and parochial, while also underscoring the havoc it wreaks on women.

In good burlesque fashion, narrative awareishness ultimately enables the novel to take swipes not just at the characters in the novel but at the audience as well. In a brief harangue about the differences between the solemn politeness of Mexico City taxis and the brusque, dismissive behavior of US taxis, the narrator complains that readers should be grateful when "after cheating and robbing us, and being insolent," taxi drivers "don't apply their whips to our backs, which, I think, the public well deserves for submitting so tamely to all their gross impositions."[115] Such malignant treatment of customers characterizes not just taxis but also the corporate titans and monopolies that force their mandates on a subservient populace, "for in this free country we are the subjects of railroad kings and other princes of monopolies; we obey their wishes and pay our money."[116] Taken together, all of these asides, whether joking or brutal, suggest an intricate relationship between a New England culture that promotes a stoic subservience in the name of equality and a broader structure of exploitation that the novel ultimately excoriates.

Part of burlesque theater's larger joke structure was its play with the reveal: actors in drag revealed that gender is a costume that can be assumed; the gods were revealed as fools; the manners of the elite were revealed as nothing worth revering. So, too, *Who Would Have Thought It?* plays constantly with the reveal. From the slow reveal of Lola's "whiteness," to the revelation of Jemima's secret passions, to the late disclosure that Dr. Norval is alive, to the uncovering of the hypocrisy and corruption of abolitionist Union loyalists, to the allegorical revelation of New England's fiscal indenture to the seized resources of Mexican and Native territories, *Who Would Have Thought It?*, as even its title implies, constantly deploys the structure of the reveal. But what is most interesting about this structure of the reveal is that it frequently fails to be contained. The effects of the revelations overflow the boundaries of the romance plot. And these overflowing revelations dovetail with another aspect of burlesque. If, as Allen argues, burlesque avoids closure and the "imposition of final meaning," the novel also underscores the extent to which closure is an opportunity for containment.[117] Had *Who Would Have Thought It?* ended with reporting the marriages of the Norval children, such closure would have been decidedly unburlesquian.

The final chapter, "Conclusion," does wrap up a great deal of the plot, reassuring the reader that the two Norval daughters will be married and that Julian and Lola will reunite; in that sense, it offers an absolutely conventional ending. But the speech at the end opens the novel back up in a curious way, introducing yet another rhetorical form (so that the novel ultimately includes sermons, letters, telegrams, and comedy sketches) and another avenue for political critique. It opens outward again toward the political and business machinations of the Cackles and their new business partner, Hackwell, and only finally concludes with Beau Cackle reading his most recent political speech to his father. This opening outward to tumultuous politics with its reminder of the ongoing corruption of the Cackles and their ilk undoes the comforting closure seemingly provided by the marriage announcements and returns us to the antics of the rogues signaled by the novel's opening sentence.

Conclusion

This bitter and odd 1872 novel is ultimately engaged in a problem that has compelled immigrant activists for 150 years. The novel's answer to this difficult problem is to reveal the buffoonery of a certain kind of self-righteous bombast and to thereby expose the twofold scandal at the heart of the national machinery. The scandal is of course that the notion of consent among equals within social contract theory ultimately requires forms of ballast; the novel rails against one of them: forms of confinement. Floating the scandal along, the claims to a moral and racial superiority and Yankee authenticity cover over a licentious greed that thrives by supporting the charade of equality and liberal social forms of governmentality. *Who Would Have Thought It?* prods us to acknowledge the extent to which captivity underpins consent and the way this substructure of constraint has been knitted into the fabric of a US imaginary, just as much as consent has been instrumental to the concept of childhood. For it is precisely on these terms that the Obama administration justified its June 2012 monumental shift in deportations and established the Deferred Action for Childhood Arrivals. This policy, generally known as DACA, emerged after years of pressure by activists eager to create a path to citizenship for people in the United States without green cards or visas and to end the broad violence that has transformed the US-Mexico border into a mass grave. As a discretionary program, DACA defers deportation only for people under thirty who were brought to this country as children and who obtained a high school diploma or a GED or served in the military. So far, over 800,000 people have been given DACA status, enabling them to work, obtain driver's licenses, and travel with a bit less fear. This program, established by an administration that by 2010 had begun deporting more than a thousand people a day, was significant.

The push for DACA by organizers and activists pivots on the politics of respectability and the central idea that DREAMers were brought to the United States when they were infants, toddlers, or young children; they therefore cannot be blamed for their informal status. In other words, DREAMers can't be shown to have intended to ignore US immigration policies; that is the definition of consent's relationship to childhood. The implicit point is that they were too young to grant consent to migrating to the United States. In this logic DREAMers are not responsible for their current presence in the United States. Their status in the United States is a result of their having been secreted into the United States, captives chained to a system of labor exploitation. This logic depends on the principle that characterizes childhood by "an almost complete inability to exercise judgment."[118] Circulating across public policy discussions and news articles is the insistence that DREAMers were brought to this country, as President Barack Obama said in framing his announcement of the policy, "through no fault of their own."[119]

Given this framing, it isn't surprising that in the many "undocumented and unafraid" testimonies circulating on social media, performed at public protests, and now collected in anthologies, activists often start their narrative by reiterating how young they were when they were brought to the United States. It is clearly a strategic deployment of the logic of consent, because very few would ever sanction the criminalization this logic of consent explicitly imputes to their parents. Nor would they probably assent to the logic of captivity that helps to secure the concept of consent in this system. The structure linking consent to DACA to criminalization of parents produces an enabling boundary between childhood and adulthood. This boundary then becomes the condition of possibility for a transformed boundary between guardian and child, transitioning into a grotesque status in which DACA youth now have temporary access to rights and guarantees denied their parents as well as their peers who were deported before Obama put the policy in place in 2012. This notion of consent can serve dangerously to reinforce the contemporary consensus of exclusionary mechanisms; parents encourage their children to pursue DACA status because it makes their sons and daughters safer; at the same time, it affirms an intrinsically violent legal structure. The ideological constraints that inhibit Lola Medina and essentially conflate her with the mineral resources seeding the wealth of the Norvals and their friends become the enabling condition for DACA-eligible youth. Their status as children who were unable to grant consent to move to the United States founded Obama's initiative; childhood innocence provided a work-around. And just as Lola was used by the Norvals, corporations are using immigrants and the deportation regime to seed their future wealth. If Lola's wealth came from securing the fruit of her mother's prospecting and her own exploitation of the Mojave nation that held her captive, the contemporary prison industry sees DACA youth and their families as the minerals, the new gold, seeding their own future wealth. One has only to read the shareholder newsletters of organizations like the Geo Group to see how blatantly their CEOs see the deportation regime as providing opportunities for robust growth and revenue.[120]

So, too, for DACA youth, their status as vulnerable is a central aspect of the DACA policy. Under this policy, prosecution and deportation are deferred, not dropped, and that deferral guarantees (or hopes to secure) docility since one of the ground rules for DACA status is that an applicant has avoided confrontations with the police in the first place. It shifts people's status but keeps a structure of vulnerability in place. Consent (figured through the child) has been the productive mechanism to deny rights (locating African Americans, Native Americans, and Latinx, for example, as perpetual children who cannot grow into rational adulthood) as well as to secure them. Ruiz de Burton uses burlesque as an (anti)formal model to register dissent from the flood of US nationalist discourse, to stage a critique of the claim to authenticity made in the name of Yankee superiority, and to show the extent to which the United States, in its claims to equality and to a democracy based on consent of the governed, actually depends on a broad system of exploitation and constraint.

Activists register and protest this DACA imposed vulnerability in multiple ways. Quick to seize on contemporary events, their social media activism suggests the ongoing usefulness of the burlesque form as a mode to create a saturated critique of the systemic violence and contemporary chicanery of US immigration policy. For example, in the weeks following Canadian-born rapper Justin Bieber's 2014 arrest, bloggers circulated critiques highlighting the inequities of enforcement. The uneven logic of prosecution was subjected to relentless spoofing, visually unified by an electric blonde wig that signaled Bieber's bouffant and his status as white. Like the burlesque, these images draw our attention to the claims to authenticity that are embedded in citizenship narratives, just as they suggest the ruses necessary to perform belonging in a context in which what counts as belonging is shifting rapidly. Activists immediately registered the prosecutorial silence around Bieber's immigration status with a new word, *undeportable*, punning on their own uses of the terms *undocumented*, *unafraid*, and *unapologetic*. The Twitter and Facebook spoofing expanded to include other popular forms of caricature, from anime to memes: finally, it circled back to cartoonish repurposing of Bieber. Like Lola, he also had enough gold to prevent deportation.[121] For those who don't, for the twelve million people here in near captivity, impinged on all sides by policing, the burlesque may prove productive but only if it helps us imagine a condition of belonging that does not look like the violently exclusionary citizenship that Ruiz de Burton effectively lampoons. In the Deportable/Undeportable campaign, DREAMers utilized an icon to show the uneven application of the rule of law. Similarly, Ruiz de Burton works to undo the foundations of the law itself and to question the formation of a citizenship now sustained by transforming national borders into international graveyards.

It should be no surprise, although it bears repeating, that burlesque theatricals were first performed in theaters originally built to display captive "living curiosities" such as Bartola Velásquez and Máximo Núñez. And yet mid-nineteenth-century burlesque theater thrived on drawing attention to, engaging, and upending the very "horizon of difference" that the so-called freak shows worked to sediment in scientific and popular imaginaries. At their heart, burlesque theatricals might well have been invested in utilizing "monstrous incongruities" to undermine an unnamed god of myth and legend, a god whose demand for blood sacrifice certainly seemed insatiable by the end of the 1860s. This would be the god that *Who Would Have Thought It?* rails against, and yet the novel also fails to imagine a life without it. This god, whom W. E. B. Du Bois would soon term "the problem of the color line," is simply the drive, paraphrasing Nahum Chandler, to promulgate categorical forms of proscription and subsumption, to instantiate systemic exclusions and hierarchies creating immediate and horrible exploitation and constituting the social and historical forms of order.[122]

The representation of Lola as a brown child, a "specimen" and "specter" whose skin ultimately fades to a "pretty pink," offers another way to make vivid the problem of the color line, another way to identify the castagorical proscription that is the principle and mode of organization of the United States. The traffic between Lola and her gold, the shifting of her meanings from specimen to prize, is not precisely a movement within the system of hierarchy as much as an exposure of that system's dependence on those hierarchies. The novel's titular question is already a form of response or an answer, just as its opening sentence, "What would the good and proper people of this world do if there were no rogues in it—no social delinquents?" indicts this methodical instantiation of a horizon of differential hierarchies driving a charade named by equality and consent.

It may well be, too, that *Who Would Have Thought It?* cannot point a way past this social formation that it so cleverly exposes. That would certainly seem to be the case given its unimaginative resolution to Lola's predicament and its dystopian concluding portrait of cynical business and military men planning their next intricate collusion. Instead, it may well be for current activists and artists who also and perhaps far more vividly experience the sense of inhabiting the seemingly ontological category of rogue, of living outside the status of "good and proper," to do more than burlesque this system, to imagine a way of belonging that thrives not on exclusion or exploitation but on an acknowledgment of shared vulnerability and a commitment to flourishing socialities.

2

PLAUSIBLE DENIABILITY

Pursuing the Traces of Captivity

In 1991 Félix González-Torres put up several billboards depicting unoccupied, unmade beds with just the slightest of indentations where someone might have recently lain. Widely interpreted as a public and evocative engagement with AIDS, these billboards signify loss: lost bodies, lost intimacies, lost caresses; they magnify absences felt and still seen, lingering as monumental and awry. They remain stupendous meditations, preserved now as photographs of photographs on billboards. Calibrated to the devastation that AIDS wrought and continues to wreak, their superb beauty stands as witness to loss and the ineffability of memory.

Whether temporarily installed in New York City or rural New Jersey or suburban Texas, the billboards name the scalar logic that locates intimacy as apart from apparently public and shared space. They seemingly further

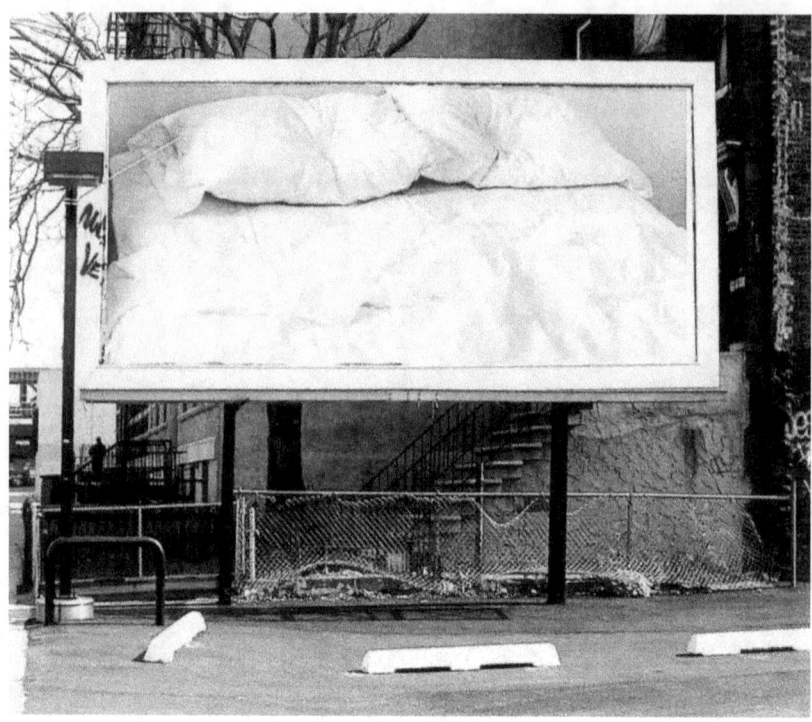

FIGURE 2.1. Unmade bed, intimate traces; billboard by Félix González-Torres. From Félix González-Torres, *Félix González-Torres: Catalogue Raisonne und Katalogredaktion*, 97.

scale by announcing the contrast that scale insists on—the intimate made monumental—yet the disjuncture of this reveal both announces scale's normative labor, even calling attention to the linear temporalities within that scalar contrast, and disrupts it. They invite a return to the folds of memory, perhaps of pleasure, to the covering provided by sleep and the privilege of comfort. These empty beds, unaccompanied by authoritative words, ask us to look and to look past what isn't seen to consider who isn't there but might have been, a riveting visual portrait of subjunctive mourning. They shift us from scaffold to density.

Writing about González-Torres's billboards, bell hooks notes that the "image taunted us with remembered connection. We confront an absence that is also a trace."[1] But what taunts us when connections go unremembered? When does a trace become a taunt? González-Torres's billboards also suggest a palimpsestic way to begin a conversation about another kind of loss that taunts us. By this I mean that those empty beds can also serve as reminders of the legacies of forced labor and captivity that thread through the materiality of mestizaje and the hacendado system of peonage labor. These empty beds signal the complex legacy of a settler colonial fold: people dropped into castagories, stranded on haciendas and ranchos.

This chapter takes up just such a trace—the legacy of captivity—as captive making continued the work not only of warfare and statecraft but also of labor management. The multicaptivity tale that María Amparo Ruiz de Burton tells in *Who Would Have Thought It?* argues that the capturing of people and resources fueled the transformation of the United States into an engine of corruption and consumption. Her story, however, leaves the work of captivity largely in the antebellum era. And, indeed, much of the work of thinking about captivity narratives as central to the nascent US (white) imaginary also leaves them to this period.[2] This habit enables other captivities to go unnoticed and forgotten, untraced by the mainstream story of the end of chattel slavery, the settlement of the West, the emergence of Jim Crow, and the US surge to claim imperial world power. Forgetting captivity also enables the work that captivity did to further produce the postbellum nation-state to remain unremarked.

Captivity narratives typically signaled the state's corollary claim to a monopoly on violence while building the foundation for the state's claim to hold a monopoly on movement, to determine who may leave, who may stay, who can move with impunity, and who may not move.[3] The texts discussed here draw on, rewrite, and open up the captivity narrative, focusing on its memorialization in history, a half-remembering that often covers over its connections to the violent workings of the state and liberal social contract theory. Jovita González and Eve Raleigh in *Caballero* (1996), Oscar Casares in *Amigoland* (2009), and Lorraine López in *The Gifted Gabaldón Sisters* (2008) each revisit the captivity tale, albeit in different guises and to different ends. *Caballero* locates the story of southwestern captivity in the multinational conflicts between political economies over control of northern Mexico and illustrates the ideological formations that sharpened the abstract fixities laced into a scaffold imaginary. *Amigoland* also revisits this history, tightening its angles and changing the story of typical "victimization." Like *Amigoland*, *The Gifted Gabaldón Sisters* focuses on child captives and on the unmaking of childhood in the course of improving the narrative of respectability undergirding the logic of white supremacy. Yet, unlike *Amigoland* and *Caballero*, *The Gifted Gabaldón Sisters* refutes the scaffold imaginary, insisting on an inclination toward the lingering effects of empty beds and the transformative power of acknowledging the violence that emptied them.

In the years from the end of Mexico's colonial struggle with Spain until the late nineteenth century, captive taking and forced labor as part of warfare gained momentum across North America, becoming a complex and entrenched anchor for the Northern Hemisphere's economy; people were resources and forms of wealth, as Ruiz de Burton posits that Lola functioned for the Norvals: colonial Spain and the Mexican elite also captured people and forced them to labor in mines, on ranches, on farms, and in factories, as did Anglo settlers, who relied on a lack of legal concern for such activities.[4] Settler colonialists exploited the complex practices of the trading networks managed by a broad range of Indigenous nations, including the Apaches, Comanche federations, and Diné, which flourished in northern Mexico and across the US Southwest.[5]

Tacitly tolerated by the US government as unincorporated extensions of the larger effort to take control of the continent, these labor-making networks have mostly evaporated from historical memory, so little studied that their effective burial has produced a kind of plausible deniability about such networks' very occurrence, reducing them to rumors and anecdotes, the legacies left outside of most histories. While scholars have begun vigorously analyzing this history, novelists López and Casares have also turned their attention to this buried history of captive labor. Their novels help to explain why these histories were banished to the archive in the first place, even as they begin to imagine the affective structures that made captivity as a mode of labor management not only possible but logical to some. Their fiction dwells on these histories of captivity and constrained labor, offering contemporary readers a chance to sit among multiple contradictory and contrapuntal voices and forms. These novels encourage one to move past the truth claims upholding authority to unearth the traces of this history, showing not only how these legacies remain active today but also how the active memorializing practices of history argue that such legacies are implausible in the first place. By taking up these traces and legacies, they articulate the ongoing relationship between nineteenth-century forms of captivity, forced labor, and the twentieth-century deportation/labor regime, which, as they illustrate, is a new iteration of captive making and taking. Bringing these practices together underscores how much constraint structures labor and migration, how coercion and migration are intimately connected, thereby belying the idea that captivity was an exceptional practice, one to be spectacularized but not taken seriously as integral to the working of sovereignty, the making of nations, and the brutality of forced movement.

Just as *Who Would Have Thought It?* through its biting burlesque of New England culture offers a doubled captivity tale that forecasts (or prophesies) the entanglements that are laced into US history and that still rupture the structured official narrative of national belonging, *Caballero*, belatedly published in the wake of *Who Would Have Thought It?*, takes up the story of dispossession and elite Spanish and Mexican hostility to Indigenous peoples and similarly tracks the rupturing effects of the US invasion of Mexico.[6] Offering a historical account of the way hidalgo culture held people captive in order to build wealth and standing, *Caballero* also lays out in strikingly clear terms the relationship between these practices and the gendered and racialized norms that were so crucial to the management and maintenance of wealth while providing background for an exploration of the legacies of the Spanish/Mexican/US war against Indigenous peoples that *Amigoland* and *The Gifted Gabaldón Sisters* eloquently and painfully examine.

All four novels center and decenter the hacienda. In *Who Would Have Thought It?* Lola's pregnant mother is removed and traded away from the rural ranch amid a multinational struggle to control the rescaling of North America. *Caballero* returns to the hacienda, taking a more intimate look at it as an active mechanism to scale perspective, hold people captive, and produce intimate emotional attachments to the habit of dispossession, which, as Hagar Kotef puts it, "gives meaning" to people's lives such that violence "conditions one's very being."[7] This chapter reads *Caballero* as a preface to the stories and histories that Casares and López tell about cast-off and captive children in ranchos and haciendas. Both of these more recent novels suggest that a very different kind of captivity tale than that canonized as a prototypical "American" origin story haunts the national imaginary. They follow the traces of captivity by exploring its haunting presence in the contemporary moment with vivid stories of emptied beds. *Amigoland* stages the memory of captivity as an instance of senility and frames the effort to "recover" this memory as an act of hubristic fantasy even as it draws crucial parallels between nineteenth-century captivity and twentieth-century labor regimes. *The Gifted Gabaldón Sisters* suggests that recovering such memories entails, first, returning to the relationship between sexual exploitation and captivity and, second, staring down the legacy of such violence, while unpacking the nostalgia for haciendas in the first place. The two recent novels make it clear that the very form of the captivity tale also engenders a corollary form, the testimonial, which accompanies the spectacularization of captivity. They also illustrate the way the coloniality of gender functions to ensnare people. Yet, unlike *Caballero* and *Amigoland*, *The Gifted Gabaldón Sisters* refuses the ideology that holds to one world at the expense of many and argues awry by rejecting the romantic nostalgia of hybridity that sometimes accompanies Chicanx genealogies. It then models the possibilities reparative witnessing provides, suggesting how such an approach may transform everything through disobjectification. Like González-Torres's billboards, which stand as a witness to the presence of loss and love, this novel, too, suggests how resistance to scale and the scaffold imaginary entails new forms of testimony, of witness, of an inclination toward density.

A Belated Recognition

Part history, part folklore, part feminist critique, *Caballero* offers unflinching portraits of the heteropatriarchal and racist structure of Spanish/Mexican colonialism as it unraveled in South Texas in the late eighteenth through mid-nineteenth century. Ostensibly a portrait of South Texas and an anatomy lesson on the neofeudal hacendado culture as it endured what would be its final crisis of legitimacy, *Caballero* ultimately turns toward an ideology that calls for accommodating or assimilating those aspects of US practices that feature an apparent end to peonage.[8] The plot revolves around the Mendoza family, wealthy ranchers whose rigid patriarch, committed to the culture that thrived on two centuries of violence and fury, slowly dies after repeated strikes at his potency. *Caballero* argues that the family's loss of its ranching empire, and by extension the Mexican elite's loss of wealth and power, results from the family patriarch's refusal to accommodate challenges to his authority or to recognize the inevitability of a new wave of settler colonial activity.

To tell this story, *Caballero* pivots time and again on moments of vulnerability. While the most obvious vulnerability is figured by the arrival of US troops and ideologies of anti-Mexican and Anglo/white supremacy, in the interstices of the plot the novel also illustrates how the wealthy hacendados of northern Mexico/ South Texas had structured their lives against a more complex vulnerability— that is, their vulnerability to the ongoing war for control over the territory, a war waged by multiple parties, including the Comanche peoples, whose sphere of influence encompassed a territory as large as half of Europe and who were uninterested in losing their livelihoods. In other words, the first context for the novel is not the US-Mexico war but rather the ongoing unresolved wars between Spain, and then Mexico, and the Indigenous peoples who had refused to concede any supremacy or sovereignty to either Spain or the Mexican state.

Caballero reveals that the Mendoza clan is not just a family; they are also an assemblage of combatants in a lengthy campaign over resources in which one of their methods of warfare entails holding people in captivity, in peonage.[9] It places this campaign within a historical moment when several competing political economies were wrestling for supremacy, including the plantocracy of the US South, the nascent Mexican liberal republic with its own legacy of casta hierarchies, the US North's expansionist market economy, and the mobile economies of the Apaches and Comanches. Like *Who Would Have Thought It?* the novel portrays the complex process of rescaling the US nation-state, tracking more particularly the machinations of those who wished to avoid being scaled out and those who wished to control the scalar logic as it evolved.

Also like *Who Would Have Thought It?* the novel illustrates the ways in which the process of rescaling the nation and recalibrating the scaffold imaginary entails continual battles over abstract fixities.

Part of what makes *Caballero* complicated is that it draws a connection between the heteronormative and racializing violence of the family patriarch and his treatment of his daughters, his peons, and the "pestiferous small band of Indians."[10] Tejano history, this novel insists, entails an elastic violence. Indigenous peoples are described as "marauding," and the land itself as "infested" with "ornery Indians" and "pagans."[11] This slander of Indigenous people is coupled with an understanding of everyone outside the elite class as peons who are "born to serve." For it is only with a crisis that the hidalgo's daughter, Susana, comes to realize that the man helping her is "more than a *peon* born to serve; he was a man with wife and child, loving life."[12] So while *Caballero* takes great pains to show the don's children pressing against the structures of their received heteropatriarchal gender norms, it offers less effort to force a new conceptualization of racialization.[13] Only as she bursts out of her father's control does Susana recognize the humanity of the man serving her and glimpse their shared vulnerabilities. Yet her realization of his humanity is not an automatic outcome, nor even a fully realized one. She will soon happily marry a Southern slave owner who has offered as evidence of his gentlemanly status his ownership of slaves.

Caballero reveals how that attitude toward "Indians" and "peons" is characterized by condescension, enmity, and vulnerability. They are patronized, infantilized, and characterized as childlike. The text makes it clear that the hidalgos see their servants as nothing more than inferiors like their "Mexican-Indian forebears."[14] This is a structure of ownership that knows no boundaries: the don refuses to order his son to stay away from the head gardener's granddaughter, telling the gardener, "The servant belongs to the master, Gregorio, as does everything he has. God made the one to serve the other and that is the law. You know the saying: 'Tie up your little hen, for my rooster has a world to roam.'"[15] Racialized sexual exploitation instantiates property ownership and produces the figure of the hidalgo and the detribalized Indigenous women as available for rape. The don's address also reveals how his patronizing stance toward Indigenous people ultimately involves treating them as children—children who require *dichos*, sayings, that translate the whims of power for them.

It would be difficult to argue that the diffuse narrator of *Caballero*, moving from the consciousness of one hidalgo to another, articulates anything other than a settler colonial stance toward Indigenous peoples. In other words, the novel's representational economy does not, by and large, undercut the hidalgo's view of them. Indigenous peoples exist only as problems, shadows, and, occasionally, resources. Yet the novel enables readers to understand the ranchers as invaders living on the fringes of a vibrant Comanche territory and an expanding US state. It forces readers to grapple with, even as the hidalgos refuse to articulate, the extent to which Native power shaped hidalgo lives and culture and Indigenous communities provided a refuge for people experiencing the worst excesses of latifundio practices, thereby significantly retarding the ambitions of both the United States and Mexico as the two nations attempted to colonize Native lands and destroy their cultures.[16]

Caballero ends at the beginning of the turmoil that would churn for seventy-five years as the United States wrested control of the region not simply from Mexico, whom it recognized as a nation with similar standing, but ultimately from the many other groups who exercised significant control over the region and held very different sets of visions for it. *Caballero* apparently dismisses the import of the Comanche network or the fact that US troops would subsequently launch a genocidal war against the Apaches and Comanches. The novel instead focuses its narrative energy on a call for Mexican accommodation through marriage to Anglos and adherence to US property laws. The top-line story, then, is of hidalgo-semifeudal vulnerability to Anglo capitalism. The undercurrent story, however, illustrates how these racialized economies were vulnerable to Indigenous efforts to maintain their territories. Read carefully, *Caballero* exemplifies the structures of constraint that hacendado landownership entailed, the extent to which captivity structured relations within families and across the boundaries of racialized economies and territorial warfare.

Caballero proposes a way to come to grips with this underwritten, underacknowledged dynamic; it entails the traversal of a tricky history of violent collisions while entering into a practice of representation that continues the history of imperialist narrative violence. If *Caballero* gestures repeatedly toward conflicts between settler colonial ranchers and the Indigenous peoples who sought to protect their cultures and livelihoods from the vast disruption ranching introduced to the area, it also, of course, mystifies much of the violence of this conflict. If it inadvertently reveals that the people working on the ranches were largely living in conditions akin to captivity and forced labor, it too easily suggests that US capitalism, wage labor, and bureaucracy offered a new, straightforward path to freedom for them. Finally, by stopping short of describing the raiding/captivity economies that underpinned ranching culture and by narrating the arrival of Anglo men and laws as a new beginning and as a break, *Caballero* continues the narrative work of erasing the complex dynamics between Indigenous peoples and settler colonialists so that this work of captivity could be lost to historical memory. In so doing, it helps to produce the conditions in which remembering these dynamics and understanding how much captivity structured labor management would begin to look something like senility, a historical dementia that *Amigoland* ultimately, although perhaps ambivalently, challenges seventy years after *Caballero* was written.

With a Glance in the Rearview Mirror

Amigoland offers a surprising set of linkages between *Who Would Have Thought It?* and *Caballero* and does so while meditating on captivity, history, childhood, embodiment, aging, and family. The novel follows two estranged brothers who struggle to find a connection with each other even as they battle over an oblique family history, over the demands of a masculinism that structures their self-worth, and against their own aging, deteriorating bodies. The novel opens as ninety-one-year-old Fidencio Rosales plots his escape from Amigoland, a nursing home, or "prison" as he calls it. Not only does he find the home belittling, aggravating, and humiliating, but he also nourishes a hope that he can "find some way to escape from this prison where they kept him against his will."[17] As he wrestles with the petty and demeaning rules governing the home and his fury that his daughter has left him there, this sense of entrapment reminds him of other experiences of carcerality and escape, including the moment when, as a young man, he was arrested while picking tomatoes, deported, "crammed into a boxcar," and transported all the way to Veracruz.[18] Penniless, he and the other deportees began the long walk back home, across the river, and back to the migrant labor circuit. In musing on this story of forced walking, he remembers his hunger and the armadillo he and other migrants cornered. Feeling a new empathy for the cornered animal, the aged man recalls the armadillo quivering with fear and then dying of exhaustion before the equally exhausted, famished men can kill it. The armadillo evokes Fidencio's own despair at aging and facing death in a place he loathes—he, too, feels isolated and cornered, as if he is also quivering before death.

Fidencio, whom the narrator affectionately calls Don Fidencio, also remembers the anguish living in Jim Crow Texas could cause, recalling a moment at the close of World War II, when he had left the army and was heading home. The bus stopped for a meal, and "the rest of the passengers were free to enter the restaurant, [but] because of the times he was forced to sit on the back steps of the kitchen and eat a cheeseburger so greasy it stained his uniform."[19] That sense of an uneven relationship to the US polity continues to trouble him as he later remembers struggling to explain to his young daughter why they were prohibited from entering the public swimming pool: "What did the words on the sign say? Why did the man tell us we couldn't go inside, Daddy? Just because. But how come, if they let all the other people? What did the sign say, Daddy? If he was grateful for anything that day, it was that she was still too young to read what it said about the dogs and Mexicans."[20] Each of these memories brings him face to face with varying forms of helplessness, with intransigent systems of exploitation, such that Jim Crow practices, forced deportations as a means of labor management, and rigid segregation dovetail with other forms of carcerality and enclosure, culminating in his own sense of permanent imprisonment and anguished loss of independence. Interlaced with these memories are his recollections of the many erotic affairs he enjoyed while working as a mailman, memories that reveal how much sexual potency structured his sense of well-being over and against these other systems so that the loss of it underscores his intense vulnerability.

Amid these memories, Fidencio and his brother, Celestino, reconnect after a silence of ten years, and Fidencio asks his brother both to break him out of the nursing home (his daughter has forbidden any trips) and to take him to Mexico to visit their grandfather's rancho. Fidencio tells Celestino that he had promised their grandfather on his deathbed that he would visit the "ranchito" from which, Fidencio asserts, their grandfather had been captured by "Indians" and brought to "this side." He lovingly quotes their grandfather's dying wish: "Tocayo, someday when you are older you should go back and see how things are now, what there is of my ranchito. Tell them I always wanted to go back."[21] Throughout the story Fidencio cherishes this request, and as the plot unfolds, he offers increasingly detailed accounts of his grandfather's captivity, the death of his great-grandparents in the battle, and his grandfather's equally sudden release from captivity after the raiders reached the other side of the Rio Bravo. Celestino scoffs at this story, accusing his brother of making it all up, of being senile.

The two men, one weak and infirm, the other struggling with diabetes, continue to wrangle over the veracity of this captivity tale. Fidencio doggedly repeats the story, adding details and embellishing it each time he sees his brother. Over the course of the novel, he recalls his grandfather, after whom he is named, describing a small feria where the rancho had gathered to be entertained by a traveling circus. Then a little boy sitting astride his father's shoulders, Fidencio's grandfather saw men on horses at the horizon and watched in silent wonder as they suddenly swept from the hills and began killing the adults. He and a few other children were gathered up and carried away as soldiers pursued them. While this story is told over the course of the novel and readers must patch it together, Fidencio never discusses his grandfather's experiences after he was abandoned on the US side of the river. How the cast-off little boy survived and found work, a livelihood, or family is left out of the account.

Perhaps because so much is shrouded, Celestino questions the veracity of Fidencio's story of their grandfather's captivity. He expresses even more doubt when his aged brother neither remembers nor cares which Native nation participated in the attack. Such erasure of specificity helps to hide the trace of communities long committed to these territories; it maintains the dominant narrative of a collective construct called "Indian" that is racialized as nonrational and relegated to the status of a perpetual child. It helps to keep the scaffold imaginary in place.

Celestino also questions the story because such captivity tales seem to amount to hearsay. Twice other men remark that they have heard similar accounts of kidnapping during raids. A taxi driver, for example, muses, "They used to tell stories like that when I was a young boy."[22] While he's hospitalized, Celestino's roommate tells him, "One of my uncles used to tell stories like that. . . . But you know how people like to talk, share stories about their families. One never knows whether to believe them, if they're not just stories made up to pass the time."[23] The taxi driver's comments as well as that of the hospitalized roommate suggest that such stories were ubiquitous at one time but that they no longer circulate—as if they have passed out of fashion, into the realm of legend and myth.

Or perhaps Celestino dismisses the story because such stories have been reduced to the "unserious" stuff of film and song. Underscoring this possibility is *Amigoland*'s epigraph, an extract from an 1848 corrido, "Los Inditos":

Ahi vienen los inditos por el carrizal . . .
¡Ay mamita! ¡Ay papito! me quieren matar . . .
The little Indians are coming through the canebrake . . .
Oh mommy! Oh daddy! They want to kill me . . .

While many scholars have argued that corridos are crucial venues for historical narrative, popular culture is nevertheless not always taken seriously.[24] The presence of a corrido account of captivity might, in Celestino's mind, only support dismissal of his brother's story because the account is too vague, too ubiquitous as popular legend, to be believed.

The corrido's role as a herald of the story to follow, as the novel's epigraph, is striking. The use of the diminutive *-ito* along with the hailing of parents as if the song is being sung by a child doubly reinscribes the logic of infantilization at work. Both the singer and the Native peoples are infantilized, thereby subtly stressing that only the non-Indigenous parents can lay claim to Western rationality. Without providing any context for the complex, violent war being waged across the region, the novel reinscribes a settler colonial logic of possession and victimization underpinning both Mexican and US nationalisms. This logic requires the simplification of the story into the structure of the vaguely remembered. Yet in using the corrido epigraph as a herald, *Amigoland* also reinscribes what Christopher Pexa calls the "eradicatory logic intrinsic to settler colonialism" because the epigraph continues the system of draining specificity and complexity from the portrayal of Indigenous peoples.[25]

That Celestino doesn't believe his brother's story may be quite realistic since captivity tales such as the one Fidencio describes are drenched in cinematic legend although such raids were commonplace from the 1830s through the end of the nineteenth century across northern Mexico and what would become the southwestern United States. As Brian DeLay asserts, the wars over territory and resources that engulfed what is now called northern Mexico and South Texas entailed brutal confrontations.[26] María Josefina Saldaña-Portillo, building on DeLay and her own extensive archival research, describes the newly independent Mexican government as conducting a "scalping war" against "equestrian tribes." She notes that Mexico and the United States ultimately hired mercenaries, including escaped slaves from the United States and other Indigenous peoples, to carry out the war against the Native nations that remained independent from Catholic missionaries and the governments of Mexico and the United States. These mercenaries brutally destroyed Indigenous communities and collected as many scalps as they could. "The friendly warriors were paid for the scalps," and they were also then incorporated into Mexican nationhood because, as Saldaña-Portillo puts it, "Apache and Comanche scalps opened the door of advancement for other Indians to step into the nation."[27] In response, Comanche and Apache fighters destroyed as many Mexican settlements as they could in a serious and sustained effort to protect their own lands and kin networks. Even as the US Army killed and forced out Indigenous peoples of the United States, European settler colonists demanded horses and mules for carriages and plows as well as laborers for fields and homes. The trading network supervised by the Nʉmʉnʉʉ, or the Comanche federation, provided these resources, including horses and forced captive laborers, and European settlers did not ask many questions about their origins.[28] With each raid, traders took as taxes horses, cattle, and people, distributing them across the US Midwest, Southwest, and Northeast through elaborate trading networks and markets. Ultimately, it proved a convenient network for the European settlers fanning out across the continent and nursing the myth of white supremacy and manifest destiny. Yet if the practice was convenient, it was also best forgotten.

The legacy of this history of captivity, its trace, has been poorly studied, and *Amigoland* is one of the first contemporary novels to take that legacy seriously and to try to unpack what it might mean for the contemporary inhabitants of a region so jealously guarded and viciously obtained. In a "Reading Group Guide" appended to the Back Bay Books edition of the novel, Casares explains that what he calls "the story within the story" is based on his own family's tale of his great-grandfather's kidnapping in 1850: "This was perhaps the first story I ever heard my Tío Nico, my father's youngest brother, tell me when I was growing up. The only problem was that my father thought the story was all made up." Drawn to the story, Casares wondered if it was "plausible," so he traveled to Monterrey, Mexico, where he met with an archivist: "We met only long enough for him to hand me four books he had written about the Indian raids of the mid-1800s. I stopped my research at this point and started writing."[29] For Casares, the presence of the material in the archives served to verify *the possibility* that his Tío Nico's story could be true. Casares turns this question of plausibility into a thread of the novel—one that the text only vaguely resolves. The tension around plausibility serves as an ongoing comment on historical memory of state violence and the legacies of terrorizing colonization and settlement, prompting the questions, What can be tolerably remembered? What traces can be sustained? Whose empty beds deserve publicity?

The possibility of confirming veracity fades from importance as the story unfolds, but not before Casares introduces a wounded and suffering man who interjects the context of empire and expansion into the story. Fidencio's roommate, struggling with a gaping and torturous bedsore, cries out intermittently, at one point hollering, "Who is Zachary Taylor?" and "Who is Pershing?! Black Jack Pershing!"[30] These, of course, are the names of two US army generals who led invasions into Mexico (Taylor in 1846, Pershing in 1916) and who were critical to the US effort first to subjugate the nascent Mexican nation and then to repress the Mexican Revolution, thereby inhibiting its anti–market economy ideals. That the roommate calls out these names in the form of an interrogative suggests how much US conflicts with Mexico, the nitty-gritty details of national expansion through warfare and exploitation, have disappeared from public memory and seem to reemerge only as the ravings of a wounded man. The seeming randomness of the man's cry, or even its apparent ludicrousness, is so out of context it ruptures the narrative itself. At this point the story has remained focused on Fidencio's deep displeasure with the nursing home and its inhabitants, to whom he gives nicknames (for example, he calls the women patients "Turtles"). The man's cries suggest how structures of authority are attached to honorifics but also how soundly the interrogative undoes such practices by turning titles into ambiguous questions. The narrator doesn't say why the patient asks these questions or what is implied by them, but the reader learns a bit more when the man later cries out, "I DON'T CARE WHO SENT

YOU DOWN HERE—YOU HEAR ME? THIS LAND HAS ALWAYS BELONGED TO MY PEOPLE!"[31] This anguished contention signals an embattled history and, further, what this history cost most Mexicanos in South Texas. As historians have noted, landowning Mexicanos were dispossessed of their lands at gunpoint as Anglos moved into the region and sought to build large-scale ranching economies.[32] His cry signals this new enclosure movement, tying the novel's concerns to those raised in *Caballero* (which looks back on the period just before this enclosure began). Read in the context of the unspooling captivity story, these comments artfully, if in a slippery manner, contextualize the captivity story within the wars waged by Mexico and the United States against the network of nations that included the Apaches, Diné, and Comanches as well as the unfolding history of efforts to rescale ranching, an effort that rescaled agriculture in Texas entirely.

Longing for a little diversion, Celestino's lover, Socorro, urges him to "steal" his brother from the nursing home and travel south to look for their lost family.[33] Celestino does so reluctantly—more to please his lover than to indulge what he thinks of as the whim of his elder brother. At dawn one morning, they sneak Fidencio out the back gate of the nursing home, quickly cross the border, and take a bus traveling into northern Mexico. As they journey, Fidencio recalls more and more details of his grandfather's tale, which Celestino continues to dismiss. Yet as the tale unspools, the captivity conceit and the road-trip conceit cleverly converge, even as the novel plays with the same form of doubled-captivity tale as did Ruiz de Burton.

When the travelers finally find the rancho, they are welcomed by an elderly woman and her granddaughter. She confirms Fidencio's story by remembering that her own grandfather had often told a similar story and that, for the rest of his life, he waited each evening for the young Fidencio to find his way back to the rancho. In a sense, the grandfather's journey as a captive taken away from the Mexican ranchito and into the United States is reversed when his grandson travels away from the "captivity" of the nursing home in the United States to the ranchito in Mexico. Far from feeling triumphant, however, Fidencio is thrown into a new sense of confusion. Told that his grandfather had a cousin who had survived the attack and that the family had awaited his return, he lapses into the story he has been carefully detailing for days. But the elderly woman confuses Fidencio with his grandfather. And so, not wanting to disturb her, he pretends to be his grandfather and to tell a story he both remembers and creates as he speaks it.

This merging of tale and teller gives new ambiguity to the veracity of the tale, but that does not seem to matter precisely. Certainly for Fidencio the thread of the story that has real meaning to him is not the tale of captivity—

which he insists on in part to get his way and get out of the nursing home and which he must excavate from his own memory in short bursts. No, the thread of the story that matters to Fidencio is the promise he had made to his grandfather to find the rancho. The rancho itself offers a promise of connection at a moment when he understands that to stay in the nursing home would leave him profoundly alone and isolated. The effort to keep a promise, then, is an effort to remain connected, not just to his grandfather's memory, but also to a meaningful existence, to something beyond the performance of his own and others' deterioration. His promise becomes both a witness and a trace, a return to the empty bed and a movement away from it as well.

Given this portrait of isolation and age, the novel's conclusion is bittersweet. The elderly woman and her granddaughter invite Fidencio to stay at the rancho and live with them. For Fidencio the road trip ends in a "homecoming" that is also a release from his captivity in the nursing home and a triumphant confirmation of his own memory. The existence of the rancho and their cousin's promise prove that he wasn't senile after all. Fidencio's "return" is, of course, to a home he has never known and to relatives he has never met, but his return is not, as he recognizes, an escape from that overarching sense of being held captive by his aging body. Or, as he muses, having arrived at the rancho, he still had to face "the simple and irrefutable truth that this was where his life was headed now; he had escaped one prison only to discover that there was no escaping his own failing body."[34] Fidencio's painful realization is paralleled throughout the novel as *Amigoland* draws subtle and thoughtful comparisons between multiple forms of captivity.

Not only does the novel mark embodiment as a kind of captivity, as a constraint from which one cannot find release, not only does it gesture to how much Fidencio had been caught in a masculinist ideology that ultimately isolated him, but it also reveals captivity as a form of statecraft.[35] *Amigoland* doubles down on this suggestion in a wry and knowing wink at the present moment. When the taxi driver explains to Celestino how he figured out the location of the rancho they sought, he notes that his aunt had remembered its old name:

"There used to be a ranchito by that name, but with time, more and more people left and then they changed the name to El Rancho De La Paz. For that reason, we couldn't find it."
"And those people who left, did she say the Indians took them?"
"No, those ones, the gringos came and took."
The driver glanced into the rearview mirror.
"You know, to go work on the other side."[36]

This subtle jab at the movement of labor and US systems of exploitation brilliantly links contemporary economic practices to earlier periods in history and in doing so highlights a way to see the captivity practices of the nineteenth century not as warfare alone but also as labor management.[37] Similarly, it reframes contemporary economic policies that seemingly reward migration as actually a new iteration of taking captives. Bringing them together highlights the quality of constraint that structures so much migration, that attenuates so many economic decisions. It also highlights the intimacy between coercion and migration and challenges the notion of captivity as an exceptional practice. *Amigoland* suggests the normality of captivity, subtly upending the exceptionalism of captivity and aligning it with labor control more broadly. This practice of doubling is also signaled by the novel's title. Amigoland is the name of the nursing home from which Fidencio escapes. It is also the name of a once thriving shopping mall in Brownsville, Texas (1974–99).[38] Such an authorial wink at readers further signals the novel's engagement with the relationship between market economies and labor management.

That the brothers haven't spoken in a decade, have each skipped their sister-in-law's funerals, and have not noticed each other's respective trips to the hospital offers an ironic comment on the stereotypical romance of close Mexican families. More important, this portrayal of estrangement suggests how isolation and loneliness come to be forms of captivity, or, more properly, constraint. The brothers' estrangement also surely serves as a metaphor for the manner in which people lose connections with their own history; Don Celestino muses that he "found it hard not to feel as if he were cut off from all that had come before him and, in some ways, all that still remained of his life."[39] The brothers' estrangement also offers a metaphor for the relationship between the United States and Mexico in the sense that the two nation-states share a deeply significant, but inconvenient, history of genocidal warfare about which they cannot or will not speak. Yet the novel explores this history only as a convenient conceit. *Amigoland* does not ultimately undo or undermine the anti-Indian narratives that structure both this history and its forgetting.

For all its engaging meditations on aging, on the temperamental behavior of the elderly, and on the fragility of familial bonds, and despite its portrayal of the violent history of US expansion and Mexican settlement, the novel, perhaps ironically, does not seem to engage with another complex form of estrangement—it does not consider the relatedness of the peoples of El Rancho De La Paz to the Indigenous peoples that found sustenance and established cultures in the area long before the arrival of the Spanish and their descendants. The estrangement of the brothers is metaphoric indeed. But *Amigoland* may not recognize this latter quality in part because, for all its consideration of human frailty, for all its refusal to indulge in the grandiose stereotypes that typify other captivity accounts such as popular westerns, for all its play with the plausibility of the history of raiding and captivity, it seems to be unable to conceptualize the "Indians" with any more depth, with any more recognition of them as people, than that provided by the corrido serving as the novel's herald. Not once does the novel provide even a glimpse of the cultures and peoples who were largely uninterested in Western systems of social and economic organization, who refused to give up their own languages, cultures, and territories, much less consign themselves to the autocratic and violent rule of the US or Mexican armies. This lack of thoughtful representation is both a lost opportunity and a symptom of the problem of plausibility the novel explores. Since *Amigoland* turns on sets of disappearances—disappearing memories, disappearing bodily abilities, disappearing communities—it is extraordinary that Indigenous peoples are also swept into the forgetting of mestizaje as racial management and community formation. Thus, to the extent that *Amigoland*, like *Who Would Have Thought It?*, is also a doubled-captivity tale, it remains caught in the conventions of the Anglo captivity narrative: Indians are spectacularized, their engagements with non-Indigenous communities mere caricatures.

The Other Form of Captivity

If *Amigoland* skips past the slow crime, the deliberate, eviscerating, and chaotic genocidal battle against Indigenous peoples that the Treaty of Guadalupe Hidalgo set in motion in northern Mexico and the US Southwest, it is not alone. Such anti-Indian violence has largely gone unnamed, unseen, and unacknowledged. By contrast, Lorraine López asks her readers to ponder this crime, to consider its happening, to account for the struggle to keep it unacknowledged, buried in silence and in family histories. And in revealing this story of crime, she not only examines it, not only sees it and makes it clear that it is a crime to be faced and acknowledged, but also suggests a beyond to that acknowledgment through a form of witnessing that calls forth the reparative, that refuses the kind of generalizing mandated by scalar narrative formations, or the structures of a scaffold imaginary.

At the heart of *The Gifted Gabaldón Sisters* is a shameful history, the story of a child abducted, forced to labor, repeatedly assaulted, and then denied her identity for the remainder of her long life. The novel acts as a witness to this history, a history that, if here imagined, does not veer far from what the archives suggest happened repeatedly; it compels its readers to witness this history of shame and the rambling effects of so much destruction and violence across three generations. In response to this history, *The Gifted Gabaldón Sisters* offers a theory of reparative witnessing—suggesting through the novel's structure and its themes a way to account for the traces of violence and assault, to acknowledge empty beds. In doing so, the novel articulates a critique of a racialist structure that infiltrates every aspect of interpretive processes. It provides a model for transformative relations that embrace ambivalence and contradictory, demeaning, and empowering histories without languishing in either a sense of diminished plentitude or magical thinking.

The Gifted Gabaldón Sisters sifts through a series of violent encounters and perhaps more violent refusals to acknowledge these encounters. As it does so, it calls on the mechanisms through which belonging and being together are made possible and impossible, but in doing so, it also refuses the ease of narrative command, thereby also refusing to harness a technology of accommodation that, like the law, saturates with a dominant, singularizing voice and account. Instead, it asks readers to engage as witnesses, and it unveils practices of witnessing that form a kind of reparative modality, if a belated one. This belated reparative witnessing practice shows how naming, which in itself is a practice of witnessing, can become a gift, a legacy, and a new form of inhabiting relations that grasp or hold a violent history because it is no longer hidden. The novel illustrates how powerful the movement to name and reveal violence can be in contrast to the tendency to curse, despise, and hide it. To see a crime, to experience profound violence, and then to survive it and find a reparative way forward so that the very recognition of that crime and its legacies becomes a kind of gift, a resource, a way to nurture and confer plentitude, is to open the possibilities of new, sustaining connections. But to achieve this transformation, which is not in and of itself without risk, as López suggests, entails witnessing through multiple forms and across multiple modalities.

This intricately structured novel tells many stories through several voices, utilizing varied formats. It is at once a chronological account of the lives of the four Gabaldón sisters, born and raised in mid- to late twentieth-century Los Angeles, and, at the same time, a biography of Nuvamsa, a Tewa Pueblo woman who lives with the Gabaldón family and whom they call Fermina. The sisters' stories are told through chapters that focus on each sister's point of view and experiences. Interspersed between the chapters are fictionalized Works Progress Administration (WPA) narratives based on interviews with Fermina, conducted in the 1930s, three decades before her death. These narratives tell Fermina's life story, revealing that she had been held captive by the Gabaldóns' great-grandfather and that he had repeatedly raped her, thereby disclosing that Fermina is actually the Gabaldón sisters' great-grandmother.

The sisters, Bette, Loretta, Rita, and Sophia, know none of Fermina's history. As the novel opens, the children have not yet recovered from their mother's death from cancer, and an aged Fermina is mostly confined to her bed. Aching from the loss of their mother, Bette, the eldest, describes herself and her sisters as "cartoon characters who'd had rockets shot through their stomachs, leaving only the landscape showing. . . . We had to walk around for months with that big gap in the middle and the ache of the wind whistling through."[40] Similarly, Loretta, the second-oldest, obsesses over the fact that she didn't get a chance to say goodbye to her mother before she died and so repeatedly asks Fermina, upon her death, to "find her mother in that place she calls Maski and tell her she has to come back, she forgot something—something important."[41] Fermina's place in their home has been ill defined; their father and tía treat Fermina respectfully, yet wave away the older sisters' questions about her. Moreover, Fermina possesses great authority within the household; she scolds, corrects, and orders the children just as she demands kisses, offers blessings, teases, and bosses their father, Juan Carlos, around. She also repeatedly promises the children, "When I am gone, you will get a gift from me."[42]

Fermina dies shortly after the sisters' mother, which locates the sisters in a landscape of loss and silence so that on the night of her funeral, as Bette falls asleep, she muses, "I think about Fermina and the gift thing. Who was she, really? I feel like I should know, like I need to know."[43] This unnamed but promised gift from Fermina ignites Loretta's and Bette's imagination, and their efforts at interpreting this enigmatic promise begin to structure their lives so that they live their interpretation of this promise, in Fermina's absence, as their truth. Indeed, Bette and Loretta eagerly seek meaning and struggle continually with ambiguity, so much so that they cling to interpretative assertions with an assiduity that highlights their stark vulnerability. Bette's question also suggests the problem of the "gift thing," which, as the story unwinds, becomes intertwined with their curiosity about Fermina's relationship to their family.

To some extent the girls fill their losses with Fermina's gifts, or, more accurately, with conjectures about what her gifts might be and how they might identify them. Ultimately, they decide on or discover the gifts, not by reaching consensus, or investigating them, but by swallowing Loretta's declarations whole. It is Loretta who announces each gift, who proclaims them as if she were prophetic. She marshals her slim evidence as she weaves a narrative that the other sisters do not question. With no material objects in hand, no obvious gifts, Loretta declares, and the sisters believe, that Fermina's gifts to them are complex powers: Loretta gains the power to heal animals; Bette to lie convincingly, seemingly without artifice; Rita to curse someone to horrific fates, even death; and Sophia to clown. These "gifts" and the stories they subsequently tell themselves and one another about their gifts begin to govern their lives and relationships as burdens far more than bounties.

If the sisters accept Loretta's declarations as fate and live the stories these gifts seem to tell as truth, they do not, perhaps with the exception of Loretta, embrace them, much less feel gratitude for having received them. Or, as Sophia says of her gift, it feels "like an itchy sweater you can't ever take off."[44] Rita suffers the most from the story of her gift, for it silences her, boxes her into feeling a frightened sense of her own force, because Loretta has told her that her curses are so powerful they can cause rape and death. Eventually, she asks whether Fermina had known magic, whether she had "practice[d] brujería."[45] Her question makes it clear that she senses the gift as a curse itself rather than as a welcome addition to her repertoire for resilience.

Over the next two decades, as the little girls grow up, they wrestle with difficult lives frequently shaped by gendered violence—a violence that began for Bette, Loretta, and Rita when their Tía Nilda's husband repeatedly molested them. The older two protect the youngest, Sophia, and warn Rita, who defies their warnings and so is tormented by the uncle for years. Each sister subsequently struggles, often without the solace of the others, with difficult sexual alliances and loneliness. This dynamic structures their relationships, and eventually the sisters grow apart.

Bringing them together, however, is the story of the gifts and the mystery of Fermina's relationship to them. So desperate are they to discover Fermina's history that long after they have become adults they take a road trip together to New Mexico to see if they can find the WPA narrative that Nilda had once casually mentioned to Loretta. They find no trace of it on this trip, and, flummoxed and saddened, they see and communicate with each other only spasmodically. Eventually Bette and Loretta, while cleaning out their father's storage unit, come across a forgotten maple trunk. There they discover the long-lost WPA narratives and a beautiful letter from Fermina resolving their questions, as the manuscript and letter reveal Fermina's history and transform their understanding of themselves, their family's past, and their futures.

"Unlike Many Ancianos"

Fermina's grim story begins with the massive disruption that US settler colonialists brought to the complex balance of powers within which the Hopi, Pueblo, Diné, and Apache peoples lived. As the United States moved aggressively into the region, whole nations were robbed of their livelihoods, and networks for trading and the means of subsistence were eviscerated.[46] Warfare and raids intensified amid this crisis so that when Fermina was about seven, a group of Navajos stormed her Hopi village, destroying it and carting off the young and healthy to be traded away.[47] The little girl and her mother escaped their captivity, only to be captured again. After being separated from her mother, Fermina was sold to a Hispano ranching couple, the Gabaldóns, where she worked as a domestic laborer and was subjected to nightly rapes by the rancher and frequent beatings by his wife. After all of the Gabaldóns' children died at birth, they robbed the thirteen-year-old Fermina of her newborn son to raise as their own. A priest eventually insisted that they release Fermina because, he explained, slavery was no longer permissible. Fermina, however, tells the WPA interviewer that she decided to remain with the family because she believed her mother was dead, she had no means to reach her Tewa Pueblo extended family, and she wanted to be near her son. The priest forced the family to baptize her, but they refused to give her their family name.[48] In this way they made permanent the secret of Fermina's son's maternity, his heritage, and his connection to the Tewa Pueblos. Fermina's son eventually married a woman who grew fond of and dependent on Fermina, treating her as a central figure in her grandchildren's lives, even though her relationship to them was never acknowledged. Fermina tells the interviewer that this fact saddens her and that she wishes her grandchildren would "see her as she is, in life and death, and not to be afraid."[49]

Fermina's story is at the heart of the novel, and yet it is also scattered across it. Her story is told primarily through the WPA narratives, while each of the sister's narratives returns at some point to the narrative's constant drumbeat—who was Fermina? Her centrality to their lives and the novel is also underscored by the novel's three-part opening, which introduces Fermina in three different ways. This narrative triptych of Fermina offers a complex, fractal framing enabling readers to not simply perceive her from different vantage points but also recognize and even disavow the representation that foregrounds possession and, with possession, a certain kind of objectification. Through such witnessing, the novel practices dis/objectification.

The first introduction is the prologue, "Los Angeles—1966," in which the Gabaldón household is described as comprising a "widowed utility worker, with five children, and an elderly Pueblo woman" whom they call "Fermina, the aged housekeeper." Having named and differentiated Fermina but not the rest of the family, the narrator returns to describing objects, rooms, and the house, which "sighs now with a gust buffeting the curtains and then groans at the joists, like an exhausted woman loosening her girdle in a private moment, as it settles into the foundation." This remarkable comparison, one that plays with the process of adjustment, signals one of the novel's many themes and leads to a maple trunk that "seems to slump, readjusting itself and resetting its contents," which include "a parcel of yellowed pages, printed in fading ink and bound together with twine."[50] The trunk, like the house, seems a bit ill at ease.

Of course, this portrayal of the trunk and the house as sentient could be read as simply another poetic, pathetic fallacy, an enactment of a pluriverse rendered merely cute by the ascendancy of the ideology of one world, by the arrival of representation.[51] The narrative undermines such an interpretation, however, by rejecting the view from the moon, insisting on dis/objectifying the trunk and the house, not by personifying them, but by understanding them in relation, through the constitutive processes of interaction. This attention to interaction as constitutive of things themselves undoes the dualist presumptions of observer and observed. And such an insistence will be further elaborated as the narrative leads readers toward a pluriversal notion of gifts.

A "reproduction" of the first page of this parcel, dated 1938, follows and provides the second introduction to the novel, to Fermina. In a Courier typeface made to resemble that of a typewriter and following the conventions of the WPA interviews, the text describes Fermina as a "petite woman with a corona of braided gray hair . . . born in the 1860s . . . in Walpi, a Hopi village located on the First Mesa." We learn that her father had died while she was young and that her infant brother passed on shortly thereafter. The text then turns to Hopi beliefs. Fermina tells the interviewer, Heidi Marie Schultz, that she remembers "stroking" her infant brother and "whispering her name in his ear, so he would know her when they met in the underworld."[52] The work of naming as a form of witnessing, of producing relation, threads through the novel that follows, although only at the end of the text will readers learn Fermina's given Tewa name. This second introduction signals the novel's play with the historical "real" and its interest in the work of archiving memory. It also forecasts Fermina's desire that her grandchildren "see her as she is," thereby establishing a relay between the reader and the narratives to create a dense practice of testimony.[53]

Following this WPA narrative is the third introduction, the first chapter, "Dog Party—Loretta: 1966." In this third opening, López offers a hilarious account of the second-oldest Gabaldón child's tenth birthday party—a party to which more dogs were invited than children. This was Loretta's first birthday after her mother's death, and she insisted on the canine focus despite her older sister's warning, "Invite all the dogs on earth. Not a single one will bring a gift." It is in this context that Fermina's voice is first heard, recounted by a bitter and strained Loretta as "scrap[ing] through the bungalow like a bad saw on green wood." Fermina's voice scares the one other child attending the party (three dogs will eventually arrive), and Loretta soothes him by saying, "It's just Fermina, her voice. She's a really old Indian." Loretta's friend, Raul, replies with astonishment, "You have an *Indian*? Can I see?"[54]

This moment punctures the chaos and humor of the party and introduces Fermina as an object of possession—a representation that deprives her of dignity and fixes her squarely within an ongoing coloniality. Not only is she some*thing* one has, but her voice "scrapes"—it *sounds* thing-ish—like a razor. This brutal representation is followed by the revelation of a much more complex relationship, one in which Loretta sweetly recounts the hours she spends with Fermina reading and discussing, among other life questions, the merits of various Catholic martyrs. The portrait of Fermina in this opening chapter is the portrait a child might offer. Fermina's status and stature are taken for granted, and Loretta's childish description of the hundred-year-old woman unflinchingly highlights the burnished bumps that age brings. The portrait's tender portrayal of Fermina's and Loretta's intimacy highlights the breadth of loss Loretta feels, the unassuaged grief and sense of abandonment that her mother's death unleashes and that she feels again when, a short while later, Fermina also passes on.

This narrative triptych serves as an introduction to the novel and also to the complex legacy of settler colonialism that the text thoughtfully reveals. Its form and plot set the novel apart from most Latinx literature, which has yet to engage fully with this legacy. By offering different forms of narrative—description, anecdote, and state document—the novel also indicates some of the techniques used to corral captivity narratives into the service of the state's claim to hold a monopoly on movement.

"*Se Acabó*"

Fermina never tells her captivity tale to the sisters; their father and aunt, Fermina's grandchildren, refuse to acknowledge their own heritage or their relationship to her, even after her death. Moreover, as the WPA narratives slowly reveal the story of Fermina's kidnapping, captivity, and rape, the legacy of sexual assault and its impact on the Gabaldón sisters, who have their own struggles with violence and abuse, becomes clearer, as does the smoldering legacy of family silence. The reader thus has the option not only to consider the portrait of Fermina's resilience over and against the portraits of the sisters, whose suffering makes evident the toxic structure of patriarchal categories, but also to wonder if the Gabaldóns' experiences would have been different if their father and aunt, not to mention their grandfather, had been less committed to the kind of silence that protects rapists and molesters and erases the violent exploitation necessary to racial capitalism. The novel dramatizes this silence at several points. Yet it also links this silence to the omnipresence of gendered violence in the Gabaldón sisters' lives.

This dynamic is illustrated at the very moment of Fermina's passing. A young Bette, just twelve, almost casually recounts a story of witnessing a brutal gang rape at a "ditching party," just before she must fight off a boy's efforts to molest her in a choir stall. As Bette recounts her struggles against the unexpected assault, she indicates that she understands the boy's intentions because "he's trying to do me like my uncle used to before I put a stop to it." Bette successfully defends herself, but when the monsignor runs into her after her escape from the choir stall and asks her why she's upset, she thinks, "Sure he's acting all concerned, but if I fink on Jesse, I'll just get myself in trouble; so I go, 'My grandma died.' And I burst into tears." The monsignor ushers her into the principal's office, where her father has just arrived to tell her that Fermina has died. The monsignor responds to the elder Gabaldón, "Why, Bette already knew."[55] This comment will come to feel prophetic as the sisters wrestle with their elders' refusal to answer their questions about how Fermina was related to them.

Later that day, her father asks her why she had told the monsignor that her grandmother had died. Bette dismisses his question with a question, "What's the big deal?" Her father refuses to answer: "Instead, he hauls himself out, leaving me alone in the car, staring at the glove compartment."[56] Bette, of course, doesn't know at this point how very symbolic her long, hard look at the glove compartment might be. Her father's silence is a refusal, and his silence triangulates with the glove compartment itself—the closed space where items are put away, where an acknowledgment of her heritage, her relationship to Fermina, might be legitimated and celebrated; her heritage, the truth about Fermina, has been suggestively locked away, kept from her memory.

The next day, still puzzled by her father's attitude and question, she turns to their Tía Nilda and asks her whether they were related to Fermina:

> "Fermina, rest her soul, was nothing to us." Nilda crosses herself and kisses her gloved thumb. "You know that. She worked for the family. That's all."
> "Yeah, but—"

"She was la criada. And that's all there is to it," Nilda says, her voice rising.

It's pretty weird for a maid to stay in bed all day and have her meals brought in on a tray, the way we did for Fermina toward the end, but I say, "I didn't mean anything."

She points at me. "Don't you start spreading this around, you hear me? And you, too, Rita, you forget about these fairy tales." Nilda dives back under the sink. "Instead of making up stories, you girls ought to mix up some boiling water with Clorox..."[57]

Their father's and tía's responses leave Bette continually wondering, "Who was she? Like, where did she come from?"[58] By this age, Bette knows to be suspicious of any assertion that is followed by the sign of the cross; it's not necessarily for emphasis. She subsequently links this question to the meaning of Fermina's promise of gifts, a promise the sisters never question. They never wonder *if* Fermina had left them gifts—only what the gifts were. Bette also never queries the racism of her tía's response. She catches its evasiveness and doubts it, but she does not question the colonialist structure itself.

The novel, however, clearly critiques the elder Gabaldóns' racism in at least two ways. By locating their evasiveness, it demarcates the shame that such colonial violence and racism conjure and the degree to which secrets must be locked away in compartments or whitewashed with bleach in order to maintain such a violent charade. The text suggests as well how forced these anti-Indian constructions are, how much work they take to maintain, so much so that Nilda must bless herself, making the sign of the cross either to evidence her truth or to make up for the lie she insists must follow Fermina to her grave. Through such portrayals, the novel suggests the demands of an aspirational white supremacy, or one might describe it as the tribute that must be paid to an aspirational normativity that would eschew Nilda acknowledging her own beloved grandmother as *her* grandmother.

Even when the sisters are grown, even after years of wrestling with the contours of their lives, they continually return to questions about Fermina, so much so that their tía accuses them of failing to "see the things your mama left you." An elderly Nilda finally and exasperatedly tells them that she wishes she had "'bought a bunch of Barbies for you girls when Fermina died and told you they were from her. Then that would be that. Se acabó.' She pauses to submerge a skillet. 'Even so, I have told you everything I know about all that business.'"[59] *Business* is both vague and suggestive: Fermina had been sold into captivity, itself a business; *business* also suggests rumors, trouble, and disturbances; to speak of

Fermina truthfully would be to disturb business as usual. As always, Nilda punctuates her movements with domestic labor and underscores her denials with a return to that labor. This relay shuts down conversations and seems to encircle the silence itself, although it is of course complexly symbolic. Fermina was introduced to the family as a captive domestic laborer. It is as if to speak of her is to embody her memory through domestic activities. Nilda is committed to cleansing her family history in order to maintain its claim to racialized respectability.

This commitment to denial and silence is perfectly captured in the recurrent phrase the elder Gabaldóns use in combative encounters with the sisters. Their inverted idiomatic formulation asks and refutes in one deft combination, as Nilda tells a pet-obsessed Loretta, "Qué like, ni like. Animals are filthy, but it's not their fault."[60] Or as their father says in a discussion of a racist boyfriend of Sophie's, "Qué forbid, ni forbid. I don't forbid *nothing*."[61] The *qué/ni* formula roughly translates as "What? Not even!" or "Forbid? I'm not forbidding anything," but its idiomatic meaning suggests a more robust refusal, a ridiculing ("As if?") that dismisses the action identified and denied. López also inverts and expands the more typical, idiomatic *ni/qué* and thereby underscores the parody behind the response. It exemplifies the family code to refuse what is obvious, to underline and then undermine its claims. In other words, the doubling movement plays with exposure and yet ridicules its possibility. Such a rhetorical device encloses the subject of contention—circles it by naming and denying it by dismissing it. This very action signals the continual inaction of the Gabaldón family, in which recognition is simply not tolerated.

It is also in the context of Fermina's death that the narrative veers toward recounting the girls' experience with their uncle, whom Bette calls "the Nasty Thing" and who repeatedly molests three of the four girls. By lacing together the story of the girls' sexual assaults with Fermina's account of the rapes she endured, along with the family habit of harboring secrets, the novel illustrates the relationship between a legacy of sexual assault of Indigenous women and the ongoing violence against young girls of color. Moreover, it shows a family structure mortared together by the effort to hide and deny this violence.

Loretta also recounts the complex way her mother had disciplined her daughters by letting them know that they needed to develop self-control, insisting that they hold their tempers and avoid complaining even as she indulged her son's tantrums and lack of control. Their mother justified this differential treatment by telling her daughters that their female bodies required a firmer hold on their desires and by telling her son, Cary, "Girls aren't supposed to get mad and yell. But you, she said, you're different. You're a boy. You don't have desaguadero like we do, so it's ok for you to have fits."[62] *Desaguadero* ("drain"), a colloquial term for the menstrual cycle, requires a different set of behavior norms, and the four sisters' lives will, in some ways, revolve around the dictates of that desaguadero, around the vulnerabilities and violence of differential treatment based on genitalia. They do not yet know what racialized sexual exploitation their great-grandmother endured and survived during her captivity, nor how their experience links them to her. *The Gifted Gabaldón Sisters* almost trembles with humor. Anecdotes and funny phrases seem to structure each chapter. And yet every chapter and most of the vignettes the sisters tell always return to the desaguadero and to the violence that maintains the coloniality of gender.[63]

Compromised Vision

At the start of the novel, the Gabaldóns' house is described as a "compromise" of styles. This is an interesting word choice because the novel seeks in so many ways to uncover people's dangerous dedication to purity of categories. Compromise, the novel subtly implies, does not fully challenge the work of aesthetics with its reliance on standards and hierarchies, nor is it the failure a fetishization of purity might suggest. Purity fails especially when it is based, as Nilda refuses to acknowledge, on a lie. Keeping distinctions between categories sacrosanct leads to violence. But compromise, especially when it emerges from an effort to avoid a difficult admission, a violent history, cannot be transformative either; it is a settled ambivalence rather than a new vision.

While one could also argue that the novel's own style emerges as a sort of compromise, playing as it does with different narrators and formats, it isn't. Rather, it draws attention to juxtaposition and thereby to the difference between positions, between perspectives, between approaches. Each chapter is focalized through one of the sisters. Loretta's and Bette's chapters are narrated in the first person, while Sophie's is narrated as if she were an outsider to her own life. Her stories are told in the second person, as if she were watching a film of herself and narrating it ("you start the story again"; "you glare at him"). The chapters about Rita are told entirely in the third person. These shifts in narrative persona help establish the distinct personalities of the sisters, but they also repeatedly remind the reader of point of view and of the role of the storyteller. While these shifts seem to isolate the Gabaldóns from each other and the reader, they also force the reader to patch the narrative threads together, drawing the reader into the pleasure of storytelling. The juxtaposition of these various narratives has the interesting effect of keeping readers aware of the importance of perspective, a useful reminder in a novel that wants to tell a different kind of captivity tale, one that proposes a different form of testimony, one that changes the perspective.

This play with narrative personae is striking on its own, but López offers an even more startling move. After each chapter are WPA reports, yet another iteration of the narrative summaries of Heidi Marie Schultz's interviews with Fermina. During the Depression, the WPA employed people to interview "colorful" informants, including the elderly who had been born in slavery as well as cowboys, folk musicians, traditional healers, and so forth. The interviewers would subsequently send their notes to local WPA staff writers to be woven into each state's guide.[64] López cleverly utilizes this historical format to construct the fictional figure of Fermina; the interspersed, fictional WPA narratives obviously differ stylistically from the sisters' chapters, mimicking the reportorial style that the WPA narratives utilized, just as the Grand Central edition of the novel takes care to distinguish the fictional WPA text from the sisters' stories using a courier typeface so that Fermina's story is visually differentiated from theirs as well. Further distinguishing the WPA accounts from the sisters' stories is that each WPA narrative is prefaced by the seemingly official language of a report:

SUBJECT: FERMINA/BURIAL PRACTICES

WPA: 6-13-38-DC: HMS

June 12, 1938

Words: 243[65]

This demarcation inscribes Fermina within the matrix of the WPA effort to collect "folk" knowledge as part of its state-sponsored aesthetic efforts to deepen US nationalism. It also inscribes Fermina as a native informant, suturing her to the structure of an outsider within that views racialized peoples askance the project of state administrative authority. True to the form, the narratives include many details that would count as "folk knowledge" in the WPA's imaginary, all apparently drawn from Tewa Pueblo philosophy and political economy.[66]

Beyond adding to the textual intricacy, the WPA narratives function like photographs: forms of narrative authority that curiously locate the novel in the historical, anchoring the fictional story to a pretend real.[67] This historicizing gesture reminds us that Indigenous people were held as captive laborers by the Anglo and Hispano settler colonialists of New Mexico and that this practice long outlasted the end of chattel slavery.[68] This interweaving of Fermina's story with that of the sisters almost immediately shifts the narrative tension; the narrative is not pulled along by the question, "Who is Fermina?" but by the question, "Will the sisters ever find out?" The answer to the question, "Who was Fermina?" that the sisters repeatedly ask is revealed to readers quickly, thereby positioning the readers apart from the sisters. This dynamic highlights the loss the sisters feel and the damage continually produced in the ongoing wake of historical violence.

Rather than rely on suspense, López cleverly positions Fermina's stories, especially the folk stories, as parables that serve as meditations on or predictors of the sister's story that follows. One tale, for example, describes parents who curse and cast out their child only to see her carried away forever by owls; this tale bears a complex relationship with the plot of the novel, its resonance to Fermina's own experience sounding across the lives of the four sisters, who cannot themselves articulate their own lesser warnings, their sense of abandonment and groundlessness. For example, the first WPA report briefly describes Fermina and focuses on the deaths of her father and infant brother when she was a child. Her loss parallels the sisters' loss of their mother and Fermina.

Similarly, Fermina describes the Hopi clowns who thrilled her when she was a little child, remembering one set of clowns who ridiculed the behavior of a squabbling married couple, to the delight of the audience. Fermina reflectively notes that the clowns were "teachers, showing the Hopi how to behave by ridiculing outsiders and those whose behavior was inconsiderate of others." Fermina further notes that the "clowns were believed to prevent evil by confounding witchery."[69] The next chapter focuses on the youngest Gabaldón, Sophie, who is convinced by her sister Loretta that her gift is clowning. Yet for Sophie such clowning neither seems to confound the menace presented to her by vicious teens nor allows her to escape her own sense of isolation and thereby avoid destructive relationships, particularly one involving a racist, insipid white boyfriend.

Because Fermina's accounts are set apart from each sister's story, the gaps between them force the reader to engage with the complexity and puzzling quality of vantage points. This can enable readers to gain a sense of the work of witnessing and testifying. This gap also underscores the work of silence and secrecy by showing how crucial silence is to the maintenance of hegemonic dominance and to the destruction of the Indigenous peoples whom the state's project of aesthetic, imperial nostalgia seeks to enshrine as once present but now lost. The WPA narratives also continually remind readers that Fermina's story, like the traditional testimonio, is mediated. Her direct voice is largely absent—an absence that serves as witness to settler logics and that helps invoke the loss the sisters feel as their quest to understand her goes unfulfilled.

The WPA interviews describe a period from roughly 1855 to 1938, while the sisters' stories begin in 1966, nearly thirty years after the WPA interviews were conducted. At the same time, the plot proper follows a straightforward and linear logic, moving from 1966 to 1987. Yet the chapters often drop readers into the middle of events and occasionally cast back in time to explain events, offering a sort of temporal hiccup.[70] Thus, readers are asked to work with a multi-contrapuntal voicing within temporal folds that seems to move between the truth claims of testimony and reporting and the imaginative claims of fiction, amid the juxtapositioning of historical documents, albeit ones that are simulacra. Taken together, such traces become witnesses as well.[71]

On the Mother Road

Like in *Amigoland*, the plot of *The Gifted Gabaldón Sisters* turns on a road trip, but unlike in *Amigoland*, the Gabaldóns' road trip neither resolves their quest nor resituates it within the vagaries of a memory troubled by dementia. Having stumbled across a recording she had made as a young teen of an interview she had conducted with Nilda for a school project, Loretta, now a veterinarian, realizes that Fermina had been interviewed by a WPA employee. But by this point Nilda had moved back to New Mexico, and so Loretta packs her grown sisters and two young nieces into their father's old station wagon, and they head across the desert following Route 66, which Loretta, in a nod to John Steinbeck's *The Grapes of Wrath*, calls the "mother road." If Steinbeck also called it the "road of flight" for "refugees from dust and shrinking land," Loretta marks this trip as a kind of pilgrimage that might resolve their decades-old questions.[72]

Along the way, the sisters stop for lunch in Oatman, Arizona, a town named after a more famous captive, Olive Oatman, whose story inspired *Who Would Have Thought It?* among other captivity narratives.[73] With this stop, López underscores the formal connection between captivity and road trips, suggesting, on the one hand, a link within Latinx literature and, on the other, a bridge to the history of captivity as a tool of warfare. If the reference also signals the process of memorialization of history, this novel's gesture also points to the way these experiences of captivity have been variously and unevenly acknowledged. Fermina's captivity narrative has apparently been lost; unlike Oatman's memorial no plaque signals Fermina's experience nor serves the triumphal account of the state. Yet this gesture to the plaque does perform a metaservice since it suggests that the novel itself takes on the task of memorializing lost *historias*, as both histories and stories.[74]

As soon as the Gabaldóns get to New Mexico, they go to the home of Fermina's interviewer, hoping to get the manuscript from her. When Loretta asks the infirm and elderly woman now calling herself Heidi Vigil about a manuscript, Vigil corrects her, explaining that she hadn't written a book; she'd written "retorts."[75] She is too muddled from a recent stroke to say more and can only remember that she had given her notes to Fermina and that Nilda had asked about them. Disappointed, the sisters leave with only a copy of Heidi Marie Schultz's letter of resignation and a photograph of her with a seventy-year-old Fermina.

The letter is tantalizing—it complains that WPA officials have ignored her work with Fermina because of "the information my subject divulges with regard to a leading family in this community." Even more compelling than this hint at controversy is the photo of Fermina and Schultz. Bette sees it and is puzzled by what she thinks is a photo of her Tía Nilda and "some white lady." But all the girls are shocked to hear that it's not a photo of Nilda but of Fermina. As Bette exclaims to her sisters, she "looks *exactly* like Nilda."[76] Upon reflection, she notes to herself, "I'm sure of it. The upright septuagenarian in the picture bears little resemblance to the shrunken, wizened Fermina we knew." They don't confront Nilda with the photograph but ask her about the interview notes—she denies any knowledge, and so they head to the WPA archives at the University of New Mexico. Not surprisingly, they find no records of either Fermina or her interviewer. Puzzled, Rita asks, "But why would she resign from a position she never held?"[77] The logic of the question trumpets the illogic of erasure, and the sisters, defeated, cannot comfort one another.

The WPA narrative that follows this account of the road trip is a rich contrast to their disappointment and has a complex relationship to the novel more broadly. Schultz details the marriage contract negotiations between Fermina's son, Decidero Gabaldón, and Eulalia Torres and their eventual wedding celebration.[78] The narrative spells out in clear terms the business of marriage, its use as a catalyst for wealth management, and women's role as the central medium of exchange. This anecdote also suggests the incredible differences between the gendered violence Eulalia Torres, the Gabaldón sisters, and Fermina each experience. The contrast is further underscored in Bette's narrative that follows, which partly focuses on their brother Cary's wedding and Loretta's simultaneous coming out to her family as lesbian via her introduction of her lover, Chris. Loretta's reticence about her sexuality seems to bother her sisters more, perhaps, than Loretta's identity does, although Rita reacts forcefully: "We're supposed to be sisters. We're supposed to trust each other. I tell *you* things, but you never tell me *any*thing about yourself." Bette responds sarcastically, not to Loretta's news so much as to Rita's drama. In this interaction Bette's refusal to invest in the shame that drives Rita and that has clouded her family becomes clear as she notes matter-of-factly that, despite Rita's fears, her in-laws are "okay people, not the kind to require smelling salts at the sight of lesbian couples, but try telling Rita that, try telling her *anything* when she gets worked up like this."[79] And with this comment Bette drops the subject. But something shifts for Bette at this wedding, and she senses a new "capacious[ness]" and a new willingness to pursue intimacy and love, as if Loretta's refusal to continue to engage in the family shame/secrecy economy has enabled something to open up within her as well.[80]

Perhaps it is fitting, then, that the next WPA account is both the last and the most bittersweet. It focuses on a summary of Fermina's life after her son, Decidero, married Eulalia. It notes that Eulalia tyrannically managed Decidero and bossed around the couple who had held Fermina captive. It also notes that Eulalia adores Fermina and insists that her own children treat Fermina with deference, which they continued to do even after they were grown. The WPA note concludes with this painful reflection: "Though it is impossible, Fermina wishes there was a way for these young men and women to recognize her, as she does them, and one day call her nuestra abuela."[81] The poignancy of this wish is underscored if we remember Loretta's first reference to Fermina as a "really old Indian."

Fermina's wish haunts the novel even as it highlights a colonial legacy that helped to produce gender norms, white supremacy, and the historical disavowal of violent exploitation of Indigenous peoples, in this case Pueblo and Hopi peoples, as part of Spanish/Anglo settler practices. For Fermina this is a wish for recognition, for an acknowledgment that would make filiation a connection, not a disavowal. But the silence that ends the final WPA account hangs over the rest of the text and dislodges the state-making project of the WPA from its power to sediment imperialist nostalgia while also intensifying the silence that ensnares the sisters in a loss they continually struggle against but cannot name.

In the final chapter of the novel, which Loretta fittingly narrates, the two eldest sisters discover Fermina's bird's-eye-maple trunk. They unpack "the photo albums, baby books, year books, and boxes of loose snapshots." They also find "a packet of papers, bound with twine." Loretta responds to this discovery with some ambivalence: "Part of me wanted to take the package from her and read the pages then and there, but another part suspected letdown. How could this stack of yellowed sheets possibly satisfy what I had longed for all these years?"[82] Loretta's fear seems understandable. What would this brittle paper reveal that could accommodate so much desire, explicate so many silences, expunge so much pain and loss?

When Bette hands copies of the manuscript to her other two sisters, she gleefully announces that the bundle of papers, the WPA manuscript notes compiled by Schultz and ultimately given to Fermina, was "our *real* gift from Fermina." For Rita and Sophie, this is especially welcome news. As Sophie says,

"What kind of a crappy gift was I supposed to have gotten—a shitty life, but ha-ha-ha, isn't it hilarious?" And after Rita reads the manuscript, Loretta notices "a fullness in her face I had never seen before."[83]

A letter accompanies the WPA notes. In it, Fermina describes her discovery that she herself had not been abandoned by her mother, as she had feared for most of her young life. At Eulalia and Decidero's wedding, acquaintances tell her that her mother had attempted to rescue her daughter but was once again sold back into captivity. She ultimately died attempting another rescue of her daughter. Fermina muses, "How could I know what she had done without hearing this? It was her last gift to me. Now that I have lost so much, I still have this, and through this, I have my mother with me."[84] Fermina's implicit argument that to know she was not abandoned is itself a gift suggests her understanding of what gifts mean, what gifts can do. Gifts produce connection. They are the golden links sustaining relations that Bette had envisioned during an acid trip on the morning of her first wedding.[85] And, further, this gift that Nuvamsa embraces is the knowledge that she has been neither abandoned nor forgotten. In this manner she underscores a concept of belonging that she then names as her gift to the Gabaldón sisters: "I am your great-grandmother, and this is my story, so you will know how far I have come to be with you."[86] She, too, has stayed near her son, grandson, and great-grandchildren as long as her life held out. She has not abandoned them, even when she could have. She has stayed nearby to nurture and guide despite the knowledge that she had herself been disavowed.

But the story that is revealed here is also a story of Nuvamsa's willingness to embrace her children, grandchildren, and great-grandchildren—to acknowledge them and to give them a chance to acknowledge her. So overwhelmed by her great-grandmother's generosity is Loretta that despite her cynical, hard-bitten determination, she falls into a trance, smelling desert mesquite and seeing "the unbroken and copious wailing of a child borne away from home, from childhood." Loretta's insight that Nuvamsa had been robbed of her childhood captures a central aspect of the production of categories of humanness and belonging. Childhood, within the confines of imperial violence and warfare, is a privilege to be protected and stolen. But Loretta reacts not with the shame that drove Nilda to silence but with an urgency to comfort: "I wrapped my arms about my sides as if to enfold and finally comfort the bereft and shuddering child who was Fermina, and who was also me."[87]

This moment of profound identification shatters the work of settler violence and of the categories of destruction that are the foundation and sustenance of the coloniality of power, of being as the Enlightenment envisioned. Having embraced her great-grandmother, Loretta is subsequently also able to make two more connections: the first to the child from Guatemala that she hopes to adopt (and here she acknowledges the complex politics that such adoption entails), the second to her father, with whom she has had a tempestuous relationship. As if for the first time, she recognizes that he did not abandon his children either despite their many losses; he had held steadfast too, and she is now finally in a position to recognize his love as such.

The irony of what turns out to be Nuvamsa's actual gift, the revelation of their heritage, turns in some measure on the very legacy of coloniality that ensnared Fermina in the first place. When the girls, all really still children, began to look for the gifts, they imagined these gifts by understanding Fermina as magical. They were caught in the Enlightenment's snare—Fermina is an "Indian," and Indians have access to powers that superscribe the presumed real. Such enchantment transforms Fermina into a bruja, a witch, a hybrid human, as Rita feared nearly all of her life. For the little girls grown to women, this category works as a catalyst to snare them and keep them in a psychic holding cell, caught in a belief system that betrays them even as it justifies the violence that menaces their lives from childhood onward. Thus, it's significant that their "discovery" of the real gift comes only after they had emptied out, discarded, and rooted up the layers of things crowding their father's townhome and after they had stopped looking for the manuscript or any interpretive key at all.

If the gifts function psychically for the children as a substitution for their lost mother, they also act as a master narrative, a sort of heuristic against which they strain—like a mother. But to a certain extent the gifts also produce a form of paranoia because their effects—tangible and striking—are not conducive to anything like happiness. Hence, when the sisters realize the misunderstanding that has bedeviled them, they willingly embrace the very gift Nuvamsa granted. But why had Fermina withheld her story from her great-grandchildren? Why wait to reveal her biography until after she has died? The narrative does not dwell on this question but makes it clear that neither the sisters' tía nor their father could embrace their own heritage in the way the girls can. Had Fermina told her story to the children, she would have faced another round of abandonment; her grandchildren might well have denied her claims, and she would once again have experienced being cast out. *Caballero* and *Who Would Have Thought It?* illustrate the imaginary that made Fermina's captivity possible. This imaginary continues to inform Nilda's view as well—and so *Caballero* shows how far Nuvamsa's great-granddaughters had to travel to embrace her as human, as their great-grandmother. The irony of this logical effect is ultimately not lost on the sisters, who welcome their new knowledge not with recriminations but with hope.

Inclining toward Witnessing

Fermina's story as revealed over the course of thirteen WPA documents offers a metaguide for interpreting the sisters' story. But it crucially also gives readers an opportunity to practice what María Lugones and Yomaira Figueroa describe as "faithful witnessing."[88] For philosopher Lugones, witnessing enables collaboration, the chance to produce relations of support and understanding that can undo the entrenched stereotypes and cultural reductionism that undergird white supremacy. While the WPA narratives are mediated testimonies—Fermina's interlocutor retells her story—the structural location of the narratives within the novel disrupts the plot and requires a different set of reading strategies and responses. The WPA narratives thereby put the reader into the position of witness, just as they locate Fermina and her interviewer as witnesses as well.

The captivity genre always requires some form of testimony, some structure that authorizes the captive as witness, to underscore its claims to authenticity. But testimony to what ends? And for whom? In their traditional form, captivity narratives spectacularize Indigenous peoples and make spectacles of captivity as a practice, suggesting its irrationality (shielding the corollary carceral practices of the state). Therefore, traditional captivity narratives' testimonials typically underscore the attendant ideology of white supremacy and the work of captivity to ensure sovereignty's monopoly on violence and movement. To tell a different kind of captivity story, López utilizes the testimonio form but builds a far more nuanced vision of the meaning of witnessing than that typically afforded by the genre.

In López's hands, the WPA narratives function as testimonies to draw readers into a vision of the rarely spoken and even pedestrian structures of violence—this is a history that the habits of domination necessarily keep hidden and silent. As Figueroa puts it, "Faithful witnessing puts the viewer in the path of danger but also enables meaning to be conveyed against the grain of domination."[89] Danger may seem an elaborate term to characterize, in this case, reading, but the opportunity to really hear the voices and see the truths rendered hidden not just in the dominant narrative of US colonial violence but also in the less well-known narratives of collateral violence practiced by communities and peoples often or mostly embattled within the structures of US domination can be risky. These voices and truths demand a refusal to romanticize or to reinscribe a dialectical structure that locates agency and victimization in pure and structural terms alone. The danger can produce an epistemic crisis, or it can produce a "practical attitude that takes seriously the knowledge of those who have historically been silenced, cast as ahistorical subjects, or considered insignificant."[90] To read *The Gifted Gabaldón Sisters* is to become a witness who must acknowledge a caustic violence and the complex, if blundering, attempts to keep that violence repressed but supple, active but unacknowledged.

The Gifted Gabaldón Sisters tells its story through counterpoint, including the contrapuntal sounding of the *qué/ni* formula; the plot is structured through counterpoint—the story is told from multiple vantage points, and the WPA notes produce additional counterpoints—and repeatedly illustrates the role of counterpoint in its deployment of humor. This counterpoint illustrates the novel's deployment of reparative witnessing, because the contrapuntal produces a conversation in which a multiplicity of voices exists in concert with the novel's engagement with the theme of being cast out and erased or abandoned. Fermina's captivity tale is revealed sideways, not as the formal narrative that Oatman's handler produced. Additionally, the sisters are held captive to their "gifts" and to family secrets. Finally, all are held captive by the violence of sexual assault and its resulting traumas. But, crucially, this particular captivity tale engages with the possibility of recuperating, repairing, and incorporating these experiences not through some narrative of escape but through witnessing: by providing testimony, by giving readers the chance to witness these captivities. This seems to happen in Nuvamsa's letter in which she declares her connection and her gift. The text turns to witnessing—Rita witnesses (and stops) a brutal gang rape; Bette witnesses (but cannot stop) a brutal gang rape; no one witnesses Sophia's assault. Yet the sisters do not tell one another about these experiences. They are held captive in their silence, disconnection, and loss. The calamity of their misinterpretation of Fermina's promise holds them apart from each other, just as the revelation of her letter changes the terms of their connections with one another as well as with their history. In this manner the novel suggests how the reparative emerges from the possibility of making connections. If the novel repeatedly shows how starkly the culture that surrounds the sisters is, as Eve Kosofsky Sedgwick says, "indifferent or inimical" to the nurturing the children need, they ultimately find in Nuvamsa's letter the "resources" to help an inchoate sense of being to "assemble and confer plentitude" on their experience.[91]

At the novel's conclusion, all four women realize that they can draw on their own resources to repair, to assemble a new sense of relationality to one another, to their chronicity, to their new history. Thus, for a text that returns regularly to the experience of being cast out, it's more than a little meaningful that its major plotline turns on the effort at recovery—at drawing back into connection. In her discussion of the reparative mode, Sedgwick does not invoke forgiveness; acknowledgment alone enables a pivot to living in ambivalence and contradictions. *The Gifted Gabaldón Sisters* also pivots on acknowledgment and thereby offers a distinct theory of what one way of coming to terms with the inchoate effects of colonial violence and its *longue durée* might look like.

To think without scale, to turn to density, entails a new understanding of gifts. For the young girls, a gift is a possession, something to hold, to have as an object apart. Even when they find an interpretation that mystifies the gifts as powers, the gifts are made real as individuated. They eventually learn, however, that the gifts are not singular possessions; they are revelations, the knowledge of a debt owed, which is to say the revelation of interconnection and of the constitutive force of relations; they gain a new understanding of their dependence on others, that they emerge and are sustained through mutual constitution writ large, a mutuality in which, as Arturo Escobar puts it, "beings of all kinds continuously and reciprocally bring one another into existence."[92] Their consolation, moreover, emerges from such connection and the sense of interbeingness, rather than from distinction, possession, and edified representation. Density, not scale.

The Gifted Gabaldón Sisters tells a difficult story about a family secret. The sisters must confront the fact that their great-grandfather held their great-grandmother captive and abused and raped her; they must confront the history of their own family's participation in a settler colonial project. This story contrasts strikingly with *Amigoland* and *Caballero*, neither of which questions the settler colonial project at all. Neither takes on the complex history out of which a romanticized mestizaje emerged and which continues to be only partially, romantically, acknowledged. If *The Gifted Gabaldón Sisters* focuses on a single family and a single woman, this does not reinforce an individualizing narrative. By introducing the fictional WPA narratives, López reveals the state's investment in celebrating its settler colonial status (by, at the least, reducing complex cultures to the stuff of folktales). By locating Fermina's narrative adjacent to Olive Oatman's captivity narrative (and that of Patty Hearst!), it reminds readers of the service captivity performs for the maintenance of sovereignty, US nationalism, and the coloniality of power.

Tellingly, it offers this story without reference to the Chicano movement (El Movimiento) that swept Los Angeles during the very period the fictional sisters grew up. There are a number of ways to interpret that authorial choice. First, one could read it as "realistic"—not all young Mexican Americans in East Los Angeles were inspired by the movement. Second, all of the sisters, at some point or another, mention their uneven relationship to Spanish. Whether they are asking for translations ("How do you say candle in Spanish?") or struggling to recall words through memory's fog, they often shift their thoughts toward what they don't know. Bette is fluent, but she, too, notes that she runs out of words. This "truth," that young Chicanx have uneven relationships to Spanish and may not have participated in the political movement that flourished around them, might underscore the novel's refusal to engage with a politics of cultural authenticity. But a third interpretation is also worth considering: the sisters' apparent disinterest in participating in a political movement that attempted to build a new cultural imaginary, one sometimes accused of inadvertent romanticism and dangerous inattention to the history of US and Mexican elites' oppressive treatment of Indigenous peoples, might suggest that they were not drawn into that discursive arena because they were caught in the very ambivalence and web of lies and shame that the Chicano movement attempted both to overthrow and avoid. The Chicano movement, however, in its efforts to claim pride in Mexican/Indigenous connections may have given the sisters the conceptual room necessary to understand Fermina as Nuvasma, as their great-grandmother. Such a route entailed moving away from the scalar structures of white supremacy holding their aunt's allegiance and toward a horizontal density, an inclination toward one another that refuses the abstract fixities of a scaffold imaginary.

Conclusion

Like *Who Would Have Thought It?*, the novels *Caballero*, *Amigoland*, and *The Gifted Gabaldón Sisters* all provide portraits of empty beds, of children cast off and cast away, diminished and rendered isolated in their vulnerability, their precarity. Similarly, all three locate their stories, however obliquely, within the precincts of the colonial imperial violence through which the United States repeatedly rescaled itself. As these texts illustrate, this process of rescaling hinged, in part, but at every turn, on anti-Indian ideologies, captivity, and militarized violence. In varying ways, each of these novels serves as a (complicit) witness to this history; each demands that readers acknowledge this history as well.

If *Caballero* inadvertently undermines a romantic narrative of celebratory mestizaje by revealing the structure of a racialist Hispanic imaginary, *The Gifted Gabaldón Sisters* suggests the lengthy chronicity of that imaginary. But as it and *Amigoland* also suggest, the contours of that imaginary and its legacies cannot simply be abandoned. They must be confronted, faced, and witnessed. Such witnessing can result in a new, reparative relation to the past, one that is both faithful and connected. *The Gifted Gabaldón Sisters* refutes the suggestion that these memories may be akin to the memories that suffuse a certain kind of senility. It argues for their importance in the archives, in family storage units, and in forgotten trunks. In doing so, it suggests that coming to terms with this history may be done belatedly, acknowledging that this belatedness will transform into a futurity, one not governed by the prescripts and constraints of respectability. Rather, such belated witnessing might enable a deepened inclination toward one another, toward a new respect for a shared vulnerability, for a growing sense of the collaborative nature of being itself.

| 3 |

SUBMERGED CAPTIVITIES

Moving toward Queer Horizontality

There can be no scale without movement. Even if that movement is necessarily metaphorical, like the conceptual, linguistic transport Juan Maldonado deployed when he sought to scale the world; scale needs some movement, some sort of shift. As the sixteenth-century theologian flew to the moon to imagine the world as a singular object, he sought to rationalize the planet, to utilize the perspective of the moon, a faraway, otherworldly vantage point from which it would be possible to abstract the earth into rationalized homogeneity.[1] Only by stepping outside of density, away from the horizontality of connection, by catapulting past the felt relations of the nearby where one can be jostled by noises and smells and hues, could Maldonado narrate the scalar vision necessary to construct the scaffold that would enshrine an erect, phallic verticality as the grounding imaginary for empire. It's a cool trick, actually, the rendering of the particular, the memorable, the mystical, the scary into the indistinct, the changing same, in order to make a map, to plot a property line, to trace a structure of containment or a line of flight, to calibrate a new imperial poetics, to create the castagories that would delimit new temporalities and new possibilities. Scale needed that move to the moon. And now we seem stuck with it. We can't get the view from the moon off our minds, out of our heads; it's got a lien on our imagination.

If María Amparo Ruiz de Burton's *Who Would Have Thought It?* is not ostensibly about scale, it nevertheless reveals many of the logistics and mechanics underpinning scalar transformations. Its timeline, for example, aligns with three major political and economic shifts that entailed the massing of new capital and resources, the extension of state power, and the reconfiguration of white racialized sensibilities. These were also events, in the grandest sense of the word, that rescaled the United States geographically, economically, and imaginatively. The novel's narrative nod to the US wars against Mexico and Indigenous peoples, which resulted in the physical transformation of the United States and the rush of new resources into the hands of Northeastern financiers; its obsession with the complex racial dynamics in and around the Civil War; and its sardonic look at the political hypocrisy and greed that were entangled in both wars and Reconstruction each signal the multiple vectors attendant to a radical rescaling of capital and states. If its plot tracks this history, its characters also provide an apt illustration of the ideological work, the imaginative quandaries, that scale's scaffold imaginary surely entails. Yet, if it opens up ideological questions about liberal republican claims to moral authority, or exposes the limits necessary for a narrative of freedom by showcasing who cannot move easily within this structure, *Who Would Have Thought It?* does not fully identify the relationship between movement and scale, nor how scalar transformation entails shifts in infrastructure or new forms of enclosure.

More recent texts take up this charge, illustrating the complex ways infrastructure scales choices and opportunities and, more especially, helps narrate socialities. In *Their Dogs Came with Them*, for example, Helena María Viramontes lays out a complex relay among freeway construction, massive policing, Vietnam violence, and new waves of enclosures dispossessing a Chicanx community, all framed as scalar shifts reinforcing the scaffold imaginary. More recent texts also illustrate the way scalar fixes entail forms of containment and captivity, showing that even if the techniques of bracketing change, their importance to scale doesn't.[2] *Their Dogs Came with Them* refuses, however, to offer anodyne, soothing responses to the upsurge of violence that accompanies the scalar ambitions of capital. José Montoya's poem "Gabby Took the 99" offers a painful portrait of what happens when one internalizes the claims of the scaffold imaginary and imagines that instruments enforcing that imaginary also offer a form of escape from it.[3] In *The Faith Healer of Olive Avenue* Manuel Muñoz expands on Viramontes's and Montoya's critiques but also changes direction, offering stories that not only refuse the orientation of scale, what geographers call *phallic verticality*, but also provide a new vision of inclination, of antirectitude, a vision of dense queer horizontality.

A crucial workhorse of the coloniality of power, scale has not strutted across histories without encountering challenges. One could turn, for an example, to various iterations of informal projects, such as piracy or lowriders, to explore resistance to this new globality.[4] Pirates and vatos alike transformed containerization and standardization and shifted the logistical reductions that make containerization possible. Lowriders are not, of course, pirates, but like pirates they have transformed the narrative of movement and labor and the signposts of standardization into something very different, into a little-studied site of theoretical intervention; they have turned cars into mechanisms for creating new relations and new possibilities for imagining being and art and pleasure apart from what a Fordist or even neoliberal imaginary set forth.[5] Lowriders, like pirates, upend the logics of their moment's rescaling movements. Pirates messed up or messed with the scaling of the sea for commerce. Highways, motorways, and freeways rescaled the terrain for commerce, for capital's glee. They made possible the Fordist economic transformation that would fold as container shipping and internet browsing reimagined territoriality entirely. Lowriding, as a multipart practice, challenges the coloniality of scale, the habit of rationalization that eviscerates spatial differentiation and relation. By operating outside of a scalar imaginary, lowriders have fomented, provoked, and procured—through their promotion of car shows, new socialities, and art—an aggressive attention to the mechanisms that are necessary for the ongoing development of a lowrider analytic. That is, while highways were created for capital, for the movement of goods and the efficient transportation of labor (and for ensuring that there is, for some, little to differentiate the two), lowriders argue that the car can also become a device for noncapitalized connections, for habitation, for bodying forth a different relation to the highway and its scalar portents and to capital, waged work, and its (in)human and (un)earthly imaginaries. Lowriders remake the standardized car with gestures that challenge capital's longing for speed and efficiency by building in mechanical jokes and visual delights (cars that hop, swing sideways, and emit loud, long gritos) and by driving home a refusal to succumb to the call for labor's subservience to instrumentality alone; they also relentlessly produce new sites for alterative formations, for people to talk to each other, to think together, to anticipate anew.

It is from this same critical stance that Betsabeé Romero also works. Best known for parking a car in the desert outside of Tijuana, filling it with clothes, and painting it with roses like those that bloom on Guadalupe's image or decorate Talavera pottery, she has also taken the meaning of the car apart: transforming a car into a planter for blossoming nopales or dismantling the car as a whole, engraving tires and side-view mirrors with images drawn from Arab and Aztec visual repertoires and then repurposing the tires further, as stamps to create inked art on dishcloths and ayate fabric. By unmaking the car and lacing into its detached members the aesthetics of many Indigenous cultures, Romero undercuts the apparent instrumentality of the motor aesthetic because the newly recast members are now in dense conversation with one another, a conversation that is not necessarily readily transparent or available.[6] These invocations of other, complex worlds similarly signal the processes by which the instruments of rescaling, and of scale itself, entail standardization, homogenization, and the elision and disappearance of alternative conceptualizations of life and community. Further, this turn to the deconstructed car—like the car repurposed as a lowrider—reminds us that movement is a central part of the work of spatial production and that driving, motoring, in particular, has been pivotal to the production of a Fordist and a neoliberal economy.

Romero repurposes car parts—side-view mirrors, bumpers, doors, tires—as canvases and media to challenge the implicit temporal work of scale as well. Built into the scaffold imaginary is a temporal imaginary that privileges speed, that conflates value with a logic of capitalist development, achievement with wealth. The logic of "low and slow" evoked by lowriders rebukes this temporal normativity, just as Romero's palimpsestic aesthetics delivers a similar message through its juxtaposition of medium and style. By stripping cars, like a crazy chop shop, Romero enables us to see in cars the potential to expand on their meaning and engage with their relationship to people endlessly mobilized, endlessly stuffed into various containers, forced to migrate, barely alive, in the service of capital. Romero's art, like lowriders' artistry, calls attention to the usefulness of the car as a means of producing a scaled world, a world remade not for the driven but for the driver—those who drive mass migration and force new spatial imaginaries, shifting the scales of the possible so that people must struggle to see themselves as something other than shipped, contained, confined.

This dynamic of driving and being driven and its relation to the production of world knowing and the world as limit confer on the powerful a very formidable

FIGURE 3.1. Repurposing cars as palimpsests. From Betsabeé Romero, *Betsabeé Romero: Cars and Traces*, 86.

way to describe and inscribe the earth against itself, and beings apart from each other. Yet many writers and artists are unwilling to sit with this dynamic as if it were settled. They offer both discussions of how scalar restructuring transforms people's lives and a model of thinking without scale, of thinking apart from the scaffold imaginary, of moving from the phallic verticality of the scaffold imaginary to a queer horizontality that insists on the density of connection. Viramontes, Montoya, and Muñoz all challenge the vision provided by a scaled imaginary, even as they mourn scale's costs, especially those people captured in its wake. Their texts each work to imagine a world where scale does not drive relations—where connections and gratitude matter as fully as the acknowledgment of our shared vulnerability, a reciprocity that emerges from a sense of shared indebtedness, or, rather, a shared sense of the obligations that constitute connections and constellate relations.

The Scaffold Imaginary

The hacienda system, whatever its variants (feudal or seigneurial), helped produce the infrastructure necessary to scale Spain's colonial violence. Functioning as spatial containers, haciendas also functioned as systems of constraint. *Who Would Have Thought It?* evokes the hacienda's role as military outpost when it notes that Lola's mother, Theresa Medina, was abducted from the hacienda her family owned, which had kept her in great luxury. That the hacienda system's power had begun to wane by the mid-nineteenth century has been made abundantly clear by *Caballero* and *The Gifted Gabaldón Sisters*, yet, as these texts also show, the impact of haciendas as scalar structures extended far beyond their heyday.[7] One can also read Helena María Viramontes's novel *Their Dogs Came with Them* (2007) as a partial investigation of this hacienda structure. But it flips the perspective illustrated by *Who Would Have Thought It?* As Viramontes suggests, the hacienda spatial matrix provided the brackets that held impoverished Mexicans and detribalized Indigenous peoples hostage. It is from such a confining hacienda that two characters escape, risking their lives to avoid the ongoing violence of the hacienda, although their daughter will face a new iteration of confinement as freeway construction closes in on her Los Angeles neighborhood.

Their Dogs Came with Them is also a disturbingly curious sequel to Ruiz de Burton's second novel, *The Squatter and the Don* (1885), which describes both the decline of the hacienda system and the process by which the southern route for a transcontinental railway was settled and mapped by Callis Huntington and others.[8] Ruiz de Burton, in describing how the incorporation of regions necessitated the decorporation of peoples and cultures, makes it clear that US expansion utilized a refined narrative of race and space. More especially, *The Squatter and the Don* argues that the expansion of the nation, and the creation of a new national scaffold imaginary made possible through the building of railroads, entailed corruption, misinformation, and demagoguery. Ruiz de Burton details the incredible land speculation involved in this process and the economic devastation that rent San Diego when Los Angeles emerged as the railway's terminus. In this sense, her novel sets the stage for understanding Viramontes's own dystopian story of transit gone awry.

After Callis Huntington completed his transcontinental empire, his nephew, Henry Huntington, went to work developing Los Angeles.[9] He purchased vast quantities of land across the Los Angeles basin and built streetcars and a rail system that largely emanated from the central railroad terminus in downtown Los Angeles.[10] In this way he developed new communities such as Long Beach, Santa Monica, and Glendale by creating and extending an interurban housing system that dovetailed with the rail lines, a meshwork of suburban communities that exemplified the small-large imaginary and celebrated the increasing reach of the interconnected region, claiming as its ambit the whole globe, a shrine to phallic verticality set on a horizontal plane.

While his mass transit system lost money, he made millions through real estate speculation, solidifying the philosophy that if you build it, they will come. Yet in a well-told story, his Pacific Electric light-rail system dominated Los Angeles for just a few decades. By midcentury, the city and the nation had committed themselves to an auto-centric organization of space. If the rail system established the pattern for the Los Angeles freeway system, it also helped create and solidify the hypersegregation that bedeviled post–World War II Los Angeles because the success of Huntington's new developments depended on restrictive covenants and redlining practices to keep his new suburbs "white" and to ensnare African American and Latinx communities in the residential areas closest to downtown. In following the route of the Pacific Electric light-rail systems, the new interstate freeway system in Los Angeles further strangled these communities: not only were they cemented into place, but their residents were now utterly dependent on cars and a shaky bus system for mobility across the area. This spatial redesign effectively bracketed and enclosed neighborhoods, thereby creating new forms of containment. Without a car, one experienced new forms of captivity, with mobility limited to a strained, slender bus system.

Los Angeles freeway construction officially began in the mid-1930s with the Arroyo Seco freeway connecting downtown Los Angeles to suburban Pasadena. But before an inch of concrete could be laid down, freeway boosters spent thirty years radically altering the region's scalar imaginary to create a Los Angeles metropolitan area that reduced distinct neighborhoods and towns—from Boyle Heights to Long Beach to Pasadena—to mere nodules on a vertical and greatly expanded scaffold imaginary where the region claimed a larger and overriding significance. Once that rescaled regional imaginary had been established, the freeways could then be celebrated as the logical means to navigate the region. The state, auto, and oil industries, as well as many others, promoted freeways as th best way to give individuals and businesses broad access to the Los Angeles basin—in effect enlarging the scale of movement for individuals and thus "liberating" them from a regional mass transit system that seemingly governed and limited their access: businesses could circulate their products on a grander scale and enhance their profits; individuals could search for work across a broader region, because, as David Brodsly explains, "the area of land within a thirty-five minute drive from the civic center [in downtown Los Angeles] rose from 261 square miles in 1953 to 705 square miles by 1962, an increase of 175 percent."[11]

By the time *Their Dogs Came with Them* opens in 1960, freeway construction was fully underway.[12] Indeed, the region of East Los Angeles and Boyle Heights, where the novel takes place, quickly became home to "the stack"—the euphemism for the major interchange of no less than four freeway systems. Altogether, over half a million vehicles course through East Los Angeles daily along six freeways, making the stack the busiest interchange in the world.[13] Not surprisingly, the language of blight subtended this choice of location for the stack and the freeways: they destroyed and disappeared thriving Black and Latinx neighborhoods; the freeway authorities celebrated their projects' beautifying attributes by claiming to slice through "thoroughly blighted" areas identified by housing authorities as "slums," thereby securing a vision of Los Angeles as the "horizontal city of the future."[14]

In the US spatial imaginary, these supposedly blighted areas disappeared by freeway construction have their roots in the tenements of late nineteenth-century New York. As Priscilla Wald explains, tenements were both "repository and mirror" for anxieties about the spread of disease. The seeming capacity of tenements and slums to breed and grow diseases fostered a crisis narrative demanding that such spaces be sealed off and their diseases spatially contained. As reformers and novels of the period pointed out, however, tenements and slums were anything but "effective spaces of quarantine."[15] Nevertheless, by the beginning of the twentieth century, tenements and contagion were fully intermeshed in the US spatial imaginary. Because tenements, slums, and blighted areas were structured as public health hazards, they became the site of pervasive regulation. "Next to the police and tax assessors," Nayan Shah notes of the early Progressive Era, "municipal public health administrators assumed the most sweeping authority to survey and monitor the city and its inhabitants."[16] The metaphorization of tenements and slums as spatialized loci for disease, as large-scale petri dishes, justified the intensified policing and regulation powers that health administrators assumed.

So if *The Squatter and the Don* ends with Huntington's choice to "settle" Los Angeles and to suture together a new kind of Erie Canal—one in which Los Angeles could be described as the port of Iowa—*Their Dogs Came with Them* begins with Los Angeles's effort to evict the rail system and suture together a new sense of itself as a multiurban metropole whose future seemingly pivoted on freeway construction.[17] But rather than celebrate the effort to elevate Los Angeles, rather than rhapsodize over the rescaled city or signal the "liberation" from the mass transit system's many limitations, *Their Dogs Came with Them* offers a profound critique not simply of the effects of freeway construction but also of the scaffold imaginary whose celebration of a phallic verticality belittles and devastates a Mexican community and also fails to understand the social systems and affiliations that function alongside and apart from that imaginary. In this sense, the novel radically critiques the capitalist/modernist vision that erected the scaffold imaginary in the first place. More especially, *Their Dogs Came with Them* endows its critique with an analysis of the temporal ideology animating the scaffold imaginary and in doing so amplifies that scaffold's weaknesses and viciousness.

The novel opens with an epigraph from Miguel León-Portilla's *The Broken Spears: The Aztec Account of the Conquest of Mexico* that describes the arrival of the Spanish conquistadores: "Their dogs came with them, running ahead of the column. They raised their muzzles high; they lifted their muzzles to the wind. They raced on before with saliva dripping from their jaws." This epigraph ties the freeway not only to the history of colonialism but also to the newly emerging global scaffold imaginary of the sixteenth century and to the technologies that were necessary to demarcate that unfolding scale; it magisterially links the rescaling of Los Angeles to the very coloniality of power that ensnared the Américas in a global capital vision, the view from the moon. The bulldozers are the new dogs: "The earthmovers, Grandmother Zumaya had called them; the bulldozers had started from very far away and slowly arrived on First Street, their muzzles like sharpened metal teeth making way for the freeway."[18] Similarly, the dozers, "their bellies petroleum readied," slowly and methodically chomp whole neighborhoods, creating "condemned, windspooked houses" and "abandoned blocks to get lost in," consuming not just houses but memories and legacies.[19] Through the metaphor of the bulldozers as dogs, the freeway construction is likened to Spain's genocidal habits of dispossession; the freeways and construction vehicles are part and parcel of another wave of community destruction.[20]

Unlike other novels that center on the Los Angeles freeways, such as Thomas Pynchon's *Crying of Lot 49* (1966) and Joan Didion's *Play It as It Lays* (1970), *Their Dogs Came with Them* considers not the effects of driving the freeways, not the sense of "communion" Didion celebrated, but rather those disappeared by the freeways. And, ironically, the novel focuses not on the liberating effects of driving a car on the Los Angeles freeway system, as described by Chester Himes in *If He Hollers Let Him Go* (1945) or as celebrated by Jean Baudrillard in *America* (1989) but rather on their enclosing effects for those who are carless: the pedestrians and bus passengers who must navigate around, under, and alongside the freeways. *Their Dogs Came with Them* follows a set of pedestrians: Ermila, a young teenager, who "trotted the four neighborhood blocks netted together by thick overhead wires, which dipped and lobbed from telephone pole to pole to house to pole in an endless cat's cradle until she arrived on the living side of First Street"; Tranquilina, an impoverished street preacher who, along with her mother, learns the freeway overpasses and narrow alleys while walking East Los Angeles in search of food for their ministry; Turtle, an AWOL member of the McBride Boys who runs from hideout to hideout; Ben, a troubled survivor of a horrific accident; and an unnamed disheveled woman; both Ben and the woman walk up and down the streets of the city, seemingly without connection to much that is near to them.[21] If these pedestrians and bus riders consider the freeways as largely obstacles and destructive forces rather than providers of opportunity and liberation, the novel itself utilizes the freeways in an ingenious way. Much like the four-freeway stack that destroyed Ermila's and Turtle's neighborhood, the characters' lives touch and intersect but never precisely connect—they move around and past each other, seeing each other but not really knowing much about each other's points of origin or crises and trajectories for the present. And in order to assimilate the plot of the novel, a reader must be willing to pay attention to the entire freeway map, as it were, that is, all of the characters' trajectories, as the narrative structure recursively unspools in an intermittent series of revelations, meditations, and mergers.

By refusing to fetishize the freeways as liberating, *Their Dogs Came with Them* underscores the incredible, unaccounted loss that their construction entailed:

> She looked out at her own house and all the other houses on Grandfather's side of First Street; the houses on the saved side were bright and ornamental like the big Easter eggs on display at the Segunda store counter. Some of the houses had cluttered porches with hanging plants or yards with makeshift gardens; others had parked cars on their front lawns. Some built wrought-iron grate fences, while others had drowsy curtains swaying in wide-open windows. In a few weeks, Chavela's side of the neighborhood, the dead side of the street, would disappear forever. The earthmovers had anchored, their tarps whipping like banging sails. . . . In a few weeks the blue house and all the other houses would vanish just like Chavela and all the other neighbors.[22]

Although freeway dispossession had been justified by the discourse of blight, what Ermila sees instead is a thriving neighborhood at the edge of survival. Ermila's sense of being is structured by these disappearances—the vibrancy of half of the street continually utters the lost names of the other half. The young child can only think of Chavela, an elderly woman herself displaced at least once before, by a massive Mexico City earthquake, who had provided a refuge for a then five-year-old Ermila escaping her tense and sorrow-filled house. The construction equipment, like Hernán Cortés's ships, sails into the neighborhood to wipe out and leave for dead any in its way.

For scalar processes to work, space must be rationalized. All spatial differences have to be eradicated (abstracted into homogeneity), and all spaces treated as the same on a theoretical scalar plane. By this method places can be partitioned, mapped, and marked as property, disenchanted and colonized. Such rationalization necessarily refuses to understand places as radically dissimilar or particular and refuses any sense of distinct spaces as sacred or transcendent, or indeed locally meaningful. Ermila's inventory here could be said to refute that logic of spatiality. Within Ermila's view are homes with vibrantly distinct personalities: the yards and homes express different affinities and desires. Not only is this particular place not simply a location on a map, but it is also, the novel suggests, meaningful and creative. Ermila refutes spatial rationalization; *Their Dogs Came with Them* militates against it. In giving us one dense portrait of East Los Angeles after another, Viramontes argues against the inhumanity and reductive aggression of the spatial rationalization inherent to the scaffold imaginary. *Their Dogs Came with Them* indicts spatial rationality as a kind of crime and exposes its dependence on constraint and captivity.

As the novel notes, it is not just people who were displaced by the demands of a rescaled Los Angeles—vast networks of affiliations and place-linked memories got ripped away. The disorientation fueled by the abrupt erection of the freeways underscores this loss for Tranquilina and Mama: "The two women struggled through the rain in a maze of unfamiliar streets. Whole residential blocks had been gutted since their departure and they soon discovered that Kern Street abruptly dead-ended, forcing them to retrace their trail. The streets Mama remembered had once connected to other arteries of the city, rolling up and down hills and in and out of neighborhoods where neighbors of different nationalities intersected with one another . . . But now the freeways amputated the streets into stumped dead ends, and the lives of the neighbors itched like phantom limbs in Mama's memory."[23] The deep texture of a place and its relationship to one's sense of connection and belonging are eviscerated by the anonymous mountains of concrete haphazardly claimed by taggers. The text highlights the argument that the freeways destroyed vitality, and the palpable quality of that long-gone vitality pains with a haunting and forceful memory; Tranquilina's and Mama's spatial relations have been altered, and their memories confounded. The comparison of lost neighbors to phantom limbs highlights the crucial way relationships compose us and structure our sense of selves, providing a kind of embodied connection.

Such discombobulation caused by this new enclosure movement left East Los Angeles residents such as Ermila's grandmother struggling to find some measure of interior stability:

> If she paced up and down the hallway, the repetitious groans from the loose floorboard reminded her she was entrapped. If she looked out the window, the freeway construction bit endless trenches into the earth that resembled a moat, fortifying their safety from all that furious violence outside. No sooner would her sense of consolation override any panic than she realized the construction of the freeway was ridding the neighborhood of everything that was familiar to her. The memory of who lived where, who buried their children's umbilical cords or grew lemons the size of apples, done away. Grandmother thought about how carnivorous life was, how indifferent machinery teeth could be, and all these murky thoughts swirled the dust and tar and heat into a speeding meteor gathering strength.[24]

As Grandmother's survey of loss indicates, the destruction of the neighborhood shatters her relationship to her past as well as to the present. The freeways leave her marooned and ungrounded.[25] She experiences the loss of the neighborhood less like a death than like the disappearance of her own daughter many years before. As the narrator notes, "Death is finite but disappearance is not and so you see her face everywhere."[26] It is this sense of the ever-present quality of the lost neighborhood that *Their Dogs Came with Them* captures—the kind of infinite quality that renders loss an intricately felt aching, outside of a linear temporal structure and thicker than the quotidian. Disappearance is infinite, the narrator tells us; it haunts us, leaving us unsure if we might be surprised or disappointed, continually unsettled in our expectations and confidence.

Their Dogs Came with Them further suggests the tangible quality of disappearance through the story of Renata Valenzuela. The name of the abducted child is repeatedly invoked by parents as a warning to girls who stray. She also functions as a kind of allegory of the lost neighborhoods, as a signal of the fragility of human connections given "how carnivorous life was, how indifferent machinery teeth could be."[27] And she serves as an anchor to a hospitalized and lonely Ben, who feels that her visitations enable him to survive grinding pain. All the children in *Their Dogs Came with Them* struggle to claim some semblance of childhood, yet the story of Renata that laces around and through the narrative reveals how supple the figure of the cast-out child can be, how much it subtends a discourse of blight, renames the coloniality of scale, dissociating it from its abstractive work by individuating loss and dispossession. Yet the story of Renata also hails the disciplinary work of loss and captivity: the parents instrumentalize her disappearance to threaten their children to conform.

While the freeways strangled memories and set them loose like phantom limbs, they have also further impoverished people by shrinking the scale of circulation for laborers and indeed making movement more onerous rather than less. Buses are slower than the rail lines; their routes are not as extensive, nor their travel as frequent. Ermila, who must take buses to get anywhere she cannot walk to, meditates daily on the centrality of the bus to her working neighbors' lives:

> Four freeways crossing and interchanging, looping and stacking in the Eastside, but if you didn't own a car, you were fucked. Many were, and this is something Ermila always said in her head: You're fucked. Though this morning she said, We're fucked, as the men passed her window to gather on the corner for the Rapid Transit 26 bus where the women already waited, all ready. Each morning Ermila saw them from her window: several women in several sizes and ages who carried with them the weight of a family or two or three, their backs slumped over as they sat on the bus bench, their sweaters draped over their shoulders for protection against the morning chill. They toted their history of muted desires packed tightly in the bags under their eyes, and carried with that the poker face of their responsibility, a grimace left over from their splash of cold water on their cheeks each morning.... They sat on the bus bench, canvas bags beside them, filled with the day's essentials: fearlessness scrambled with huevos con chorizo and wrapped in a tortilla as thin as the documents they carried to prove legality.... Why bother looking at the bounce of purposeful step, their bus timetables tucked inside wallets, these men and women who hastened to their destinations feeling a sense of commitment, compelled to believe they held the world together with the glue of their endless sweat? They carried everything needed to assist them in holding up the operations of commerce, and carried it all onto the bus except laziness.[28]

In this exquisite praise song for laboring Mexicans, Ermila emphasizes the costs the freeways impose on the carless. Ermila asks us to admire the steady determination of her neighbors to take care of one another, to incline themselves toward their felt relations despite the infrastructure built to undermine their futures. It is as if the freeway stack itself rubs their class position in and forces those who ride inefficient, packed buses to greet their labors with ever more determination. Without cars, people must rely on an unfriendly, thin public transit system. *Their Dogs Came with Them* illustrates how the lack of a car produces a new form of captivity; it draws attention to the limits of car culture and the way mobility became necessary to access the means for living an unexploited life.

In this vein, the novel should be read as a Fordist captivity tale, as the freeways literally enclose neighborhoods, closing off connections and the means to move from one place to another, limiting mobility and all that mobility can enable. The novel also reveals the constraints that the lack of a private car produces. But while the novel lays out this new form of enclosure and carefully illustrates an economy that doles out bracketed possibilities—which is to say it illustrates the costs of the scaffold imaginary, the price affective survival entails—it also, in meditations such as this one, refocuses attention on horizontal connections. This thick portrait of people leading obligated lives threaded together by their sense of commitment to their ancestors, their futures, their loved ones, refutes the dominant narratives that structure them as figures of blight, as left behind by the ferocity of development and progress. By braiding together this dense set of connections, the novel honors and celebrates relationships "already, all ready."

In dwelling on the residents' "sense of commitment" and their "muted desires," Viramontes also takes up another aspect of the scalar masquerade of spatial rationalization. On the one hand, for Los Angeles to rescale itself, it had to embrace the logic of spatial rationalization by treating space as the same. On the other hand, oddly enough, it could not fully achieve that desired scalar leap without justifying or rationalizing the choice of freeway routes through the discourse of blight. One kind of rationalization entailed another kind of rationale. Such inherent contradiction meant Los Angeles could suggest that for the purposes of achieving new market efficiencies, all space was the same. But precisely in order to make that claim, it had to argue that some spaces were less deserving (i.e., more blighted) than others. Viramontes pushes back against that spatial rendering with a reverent portrait of the barrios' inhabitants as they wait for buses to take them to work. She insists that we understand East Los Angeles not as blighted but as home to brave and determined people caring for other people who find ways to navigate around their bracketed options, around the impossible conditions that capital, through intensive rescaling, imposes.

The alienating effects of the freeways are further underscored by an exceptional series of observations Ben makes as he imagines a woman struggling across a pedestrian bridge spanning the Hollywood Freeway. Ben muses in his journal about how little the drivers zooming beneath this woman on the freeway overpass might care about her disheveled state or think of her fragility. Terrifically scarred and fragile himself, Ben projects onto the woman his own sense of how others might perceive him as he seeks to understand the workings of empathy: "One would have to be close enough to look into her eyes, jump into the trunk of her heart, lift the stage curtains to see behind her props. It was one thing to assume, another to conjure, and yet another *to feel for her. One would need metaphor to love her.*"[29] In a novel that steadily considers harsh and violent situations, this quiet metacomment on the significance of imaginative labor disrupts the text's almost-cantankerous attention to the coloniality of power.[30] Ben senses the bridging function of metaphors, their capacity to transport or carry concepts, and so grasps how metaphor enables the work of love, particularly within and amid the omnipresence of violence. How often are metaphors used to move affectively? As conceptual and emotional means of transport, where do metaphors take people? If metaphors can enable generous relations, they can similarly stir hate, as the novel suggests; its examination of the power of the metaphor of blight offers a prime example.

Just as *Their Dogs Came with Them* uses the freeway stack as a model for narrative structure, it also uses the image of a woman alone on a pedestrian overpass above thousands of disinterested, moving cars as an image of the freeway system's isolating and alienating effects—and yet it envelops that sense of alienation within the folds of vividly sculptural language, suggesting a detour around that very alienation. Ben's insights also argue that the scalar processes that are so much a part of the working of coloniality can indeed be circumvented through literature and the imagination. The strategies behind the scaffold imaginary can be made clear and less potent. Metaphor does the work of love; the hard streets of a poststack East Los Angeles also require that translational act of labor that the novel attempts to provide. For if Ermila offers a praise song about her neighbors in their "fucked" situation, the novel as a whole offers a praise song for the people and communities who navigate their new enclosures, a spatial transformation that entails ongoing dispossession (of time, of mobility, of money, of memories, of each other).

If the freeway construction grounds the novel historically, that historical modality is twice signaled for readers before the novel even opens. The first indication is the epigraph from Miguel León-Portilla, which both explains the novel's title and signals its ongoing engagement with coloniality; the subsequent page offers the boldfaced "1960–1970," which seems to suggest the facticity of the novel itself.[31] Overlaid onto the story of the freeways' arrival is a postsurrealist account of the Quarantine Authority (QA), whose mission, we are told, is to rid the barrio of rabid dogs. The QA is the counterhistorical aspect of the novel; it's a story of the enforcement of deranged power.³² And it works brilliantly as a seemingly real story of police force, framed by the very real and very smoggy freeways structuring the plot.

If the bulldozers are the new dogs in 1960 when the novel opens, the helicopters are the new bulldozers by 1970. The QA establishes a set of checkpoints and a curfew and demands that residents prove their right to enter the QA zone—a zone patrolled by police and guns where documents structure mobility. At night, squadrons of QA helicopters fly over the quarantined area shooting stray dogs as they roam the streets. Characterizing the arrival of the QA as a subsequent invasion within a history of invasion and conquest, the novel insists on this framework:

> Ten years later the child becomes a young woman who will recognize the invading engines of the Quarantine Authority helicopters because their whir of blades above the roof of her home, their earth-rattling explosive motors, will surpass in volume the combustion of engines driving the bulldozer tractors, slowly, methodically unspooling the six freeways. She will be a young woman peering from between the palm tree drapes of her grandparents' living room, a woman watching the QA helicopters burst out of the midnight sky to shoot dogs not chained up by curfew. Qué locura, she thinks. The world is going crazy. The chopper blades raise the roof shingles of the neighborhood houses and topple TV antennas in swirls of suction on the living side of First Street.³³

It may be difficult to imagine even the Los Angeles Police Department claiming it could eliminate a rabies epidemic by shooting dogs from helicopters. The surreal quality of the plotline is hard to swallow unless one considers Ben's ode to metaphor. The QA plotline doesn't just tie the novel to the Vietnam War or to the long history of imperial conquest; it also underscores the effects of scalar processes. To reduce East Los Angeles to a blighted area entailed a further reduction and dehumanization of its inhabitants. The QA reinforces that work. The freeway construction that the novel memorializes worked to perform a scalar fix that enabled a new round of capital accumulation by rescaling capital relations from a series of small-scale relations to a larger, regional scale while simultaneously rescaling the barrio itself. This process reduced East Los Angeles's importance in terms of capital flow and also enhanced its policability by enclosing it.

The QA helicopters cast a spotlight on the effort to make East Los Angeles a carceral, captive space because the helicopters construct the hedges that limit mobility—their guns and spotlights demarcate the area, enclosing residents and removing them from the pleasures that mobility enables. The characters whose stories *Their Dogs Came with Them* tells must navigate these scalar forces, finding the interstices between carceral structures and captive encounters, even as the novel asks readers to engage with their stories as forms of testimony. Put differently, the QA illustrates how the economies of free movement also entail a process of instantiation, of rendering captive, so that "freedom" is more aptly understood as a masquerade for violence.

In giving us the ludicrous story of the QA, Viramontes pulls from the shadows the operative legacy of coloniality. She asks us to think about the ways different scales frame realities differently, and in juxtaposing the real scalar fix of the freeways with the surreal scalar fix of the QA, she shows us how particular scalar fixes are only, in Neil Smith's words, "temporary spatializations of certain social assumptions."[34] The story of the QA makes those social assumptions visible. Viramontes hones our attention and hones our capacity to pay attention to those segments of spatial processes where the narrative about a place (as blighted, for example) instantiates the practices that indeed incapacitate it. In other words, the discourse of contagion produces the supposedly contaminated space.

The QA reinforces the scalar structure of the entire region by further strangling East Los Angeles. If the freeways create one set of enclosures and rescale the barrio within a rescaled Los Angeles, the QA further solidifies these enclosures and indeed reduces the scale of movement for the residents even further, explicating how the threat of violence produces a different kind of "gated community." As the narrator dispassionately recounts:

> The girlfriends lived within the shaded boundaries of the map printed in English only and distributed by the city. From First Street to Boyle to Whittier and back to Pacific Boulevard, the roadblocks enforced a quarantine to contain a potential outbreak of rabies. . . . *Let's work together to keep our families and our city safe*, the end of the message urged.
>
> Yea, Mousie added. You know some culero will be, like, "You got your ID or INS or SS card wit you?"
>
> For sure, like, "Hey, let me see your IUD?" Lollie joked, opening her knees wide and then saying, "Yea, wanna check it out?" . . .
>
> Except for troublemakers, the neighborhood people bit into the quarantine without question. Ermila's own grandparents were convinced that the curfew and the shooting and the QA all *contained the rabies epidemic*.[35]

Here Viramontes draws together two racializing forms; the narrative notes the official discourse of scale, the map with its boundaries demarcating the barrio's place in the broader bounded region of the city; placed into a flattened relationship here is the cutting phrase "printed in English only." The narrator's reversal of the more colloquial "printed only in English" signals the anti-immigrant (English-only) movement and rhetoric that have served as a neoliberal version of Jim Crow segregation across the country and clearly indicates how the QA functions as a racializing mechanism. The girls' jokes challenge the policing mechanisms that support the scaling processes that would contain them and turn those mechanisms into a means to signal their own desires to resist that containment by taking control of their bodies and their reproductive capacities. The narrator then continues the joking by noting that the barrio "bit" into the quarantine. Viramontes here puns further on "contained" as if to suggest that the actions of the QA both have stopped the rabies epidemic and actually possess it, that is, have spread rabies (in a writerly deconstructive move—the quarantine produces what it claims to prevent). This pun also reinforces the narrator's suggestion that the rabies epidemic is not real at all. Finally, the use of "contained" challenges us to consider what and who are contained by the curfew, signaling the state's desire to contain and to penalize, to create penal end points for denigrated residents. The narrator's implicit critique of the barrio's passive acquiescence, however, is framed by examples of the girls' own critique. As Ermila later complains, "She wondered if she was the only person to doubt this peculiar situation or had found it as confusing and crazy as she."[36]

The surreal quality of the QA is further reinforced by Ermila's strange encounter with a dog. One evening, lying between sleep and wakefulness, Ermila vaguely hears "the freeway bumble" as well as "the sporadic spray of bullets" and the "drone of engines," and then she sleepily spots "a small curled-up dog" who is "ludicrous on its sausage legs." Ermila is at first convinced that her grandmother had placed the dog in her room to guard and restrict her movements, and then she is terrified when the dog suddenly "gnashe[s] its fangs" and bites her.[37] The next morning, with a throbbing wound, Ermila asks her grandparents about the dog, but despite her bandaged hand, no one evinces any belief that such a dog might exist or even be allowed in the house in the first place.[38] Is the dog an apparition? Only Ermila's bleeding body can tell her that it is not. But how, then, could the dog suddenly appear, and appear only to her, and yet still bite her? The dog is both phantom and figural motif, a signal of the ongoing violence of imperial structures, whether they be rigged ships, freeway stacks, or rabies quarantines. The dog continually threatens Ermila over the course of two days and opens another aspect of Viramontes's critique of the scaffold imaginary.

One problem with the phallic verticality that structures the scaffold imaginary and scale production more generally is that in fixing capital by narrating and rationalizing space, scale also fixes time, locks it down into a linear structure. Woven into the scaffold imaginary is the Enlightenment's temporal narrative of history as a record of linear progress. The corollary to this account is the assumption that the further along one moves on the spatial scale, from village to metropole, the further along one moves temporally from the past into contemporaneity via the track of modern future movement. DeWitt Clinton grasped this structure when he argued so persuasively that building the Erie Canal was not simply a means to transform the scale of US industrial production but also a way to construct the future. The regional, the local, and the parochial are not merely spatial or figural structures; they are temporal coordinates. In the scaffold imaginary, they are inevitably left behind, left back, not just left outside the "horizontal city of the future" but also relegated to the past to serve as contemporary ancestors.

And that exchange, that slipping of a certain temporal logic into scale production, partly accounts for the power of scales and scale jumping in the first place. In the scaffold imaginary, one scale is always left behind, set back in time in a linear, temporal logic of progression and development. That is what Viramontes points to in *Their Dogs Came with Them* as Ermila contends with the dog that materializes seemingly out of nowhere and bites her viciously. The dog's haunting materialization is of course a reference to coloniality, an allegory of sorts, but it's a rupture that also asks us to think about the way haunting troubles linear time and thereby bites into the phallic verticality of scalar thinking.

Haunting refutes linear temporality; it mocks it. If linear temporality suggests "there is no going back," haunting suggests the effervescence of a denser now that is endowed with a more complex temporal structure of flows, swirls, and connections. The dog bites Ermila for realizing the "locura" that surrounds her, for not biting into the phallic verticality that renders East Los Angeles captive, obsolete, primordial, and heavily policed. But the novel rebukes linear temporality not just in its deployment of the haunting dog but also through its narrative structure. Because it weaves through and around the plot's basic events (which take about forty-eight hours) by moving in and out of the decade of the 1960s and back and forth within the decade so that the reader is constantly unsettled by such temporal shifts, it uncovers a conventional desire for linear temporality and highlights the extent to which readers have been trained to think through it. In this manner, it further rebuffs the scaffold imaginary along with Newtonian logics of time and space deployed through scalar politics.

The massive outlay of public money to fund the Los Angeles freeway construction and to keep it operating despite its environmentally devastating effects requires a great love of phallic verticality and a naturalized faith in the abstraction of space. *Their Dogs Came with Them* refutes this loyalty and argues that phallic verticality—the love of the large with its entrenched faith in a scaffold imaginary in which the transnational, the hemispheric, and the global are seen as more vital than the local, the barrio—depends on a bankrupt philosophy of temporal linearity and spatial rationality. It suggests that like the snarling and gnashing dog, this philosophy bites us, but no one knows who did it or how it happened; we simply find ourselves bleeding. *Their Dogs Came with Them* reveals the scaffold imaginary's willingness to wound and draw blood in order to keep its spatial/temporal cover.

María Amparo Ruiz de Burton represents Lola as cast out, stuck, a perpetual but resilient child. In *Who Would Have Thought It?* Lola, from the moment she appears as a silent and remote ten-year-old child, must endure one structure of captivity after another. Her occasional brief appearances in the novel are marked by her refusal to define herself in the terms her captors apply. Treated by the Norvals as a perpetual (monster) child, as unable to develop, she seems to confine herself to these limits until she finally undermines the strictures that would hold her permanently captive. To a certain extent, her captivity not only reveals the economic basis of such practices by showing the extent to which capturing the resources of Indigenous peoples enabled the United States to develop the means to rescale its geography and economy so that it could begin to imagine itself as a global power but also reveals the scaffold imaginary, which sees the local as stuck and limited. Further reinforcing that imaginary, Ruiz de Burton repeatedly makes fun of the provincial Jemima Norval, who cannot handle the sophisticated New York social heights. She is still stuck.

Their Dogs Came with Them also tells a captivity tale about castaway and cast-out children. Turtle and Ermila in particular are figured as caught and stuck, developmentally frozen within a catastrophic local, without access to the vibrancy of the global and the cosmopolitan. But Viramontes does not dally with the scaffold imaginary. Even as the novel closes with the violent actions of the state attacking East Los Angeles, Turtle and Ermila, Tranquilina and Ben, each without apparent options, are represented as stuck or frozen in time, developmentally askew, even as each eschews a normative narrative of development. At nearly every turn, rather than understanding themselves as stuck, the characters refuse that label; instead, they incline toward one another, toward care and compassion, even as that inclination costs them their lives. If the scaffold imaginary provides only the possibility of a formal captivity for those hedged out by capital, *Their Dogs Came with Them* illustrates that that the conditions of captivity do not necessarily mean one is indeed stuck or captive, however much one must struggle with bracketed possibilities; such containment can be worked, undone, bent, and shifted. People move and contend with possibilities and with the inclination to resist the rectitude of the scaffold imaginary for the opportunity to love.[39]

The 99

North and east of the Los Angeles stack is the legendary Highway 99, which runs up and down the spine of California following a Spanish colonial route, which followed a Miwok and Yokut route along the edge of the Sierras up the San Joaquin Valley, often called the "world's richest agricultural valley" and the stuff of legendary literary works such as Frank Norris's *The Octopus* and John Steinbeck's *The Grapes of Wrath*. Anglos began farming the region after Confederate sympathizers arrived in Visalia in the mid-nineteenth century, transforming the region into one dependent on subsidized water and draconian labor policies.[40] Agribusiness spread, developing a multifaceted crop base that initially depended on the railroads for distribution and still partly does; by 1909 the bustling Highway 99 stretched 274 miles, linking together a huge swath of California. As agribusiness intensified, the highway was enlarged so that it functioned as a carceral artery depositing prisoners and farm laborers, crops and fuel. Its work, like the freeway stack in East Los Angeles, was designed to enlarge the scale of distribution and to transform regional agriculture into world agribusiness. Its success, as José Montoya suggests in "Gabby Took the 99," has been achieved, like all scalar work, through entrapment and blood.[41] Here Montoya considers a highway made robust by the valley's irrigation canals, which poet Wendy Rose evokes as "churn[ing] poison between claws and fins."[42]

Montoya describes the crucial role the highway plays in laborers' lives because workers must grab "el troque" to work down and up the highway, "por el todo el 99." But the irony the poem points out is that the highway does not provide a route away from labor, only back to it again and again. If the highway is "hot slippery / bloody," it is also "foggy / sleek / powerful." Yet "who ever leaves"? Montoya answers this question by pointing out that the highway circles lives like a prison fence—an idea made painfully clear as the poem describes a youthful Gabby's rueful dream to achieve "the riches that passed" on the highway. But Gabby's dream turns sour, not in the grape fields, but in those other California industries: war and narcotics. Gabby's "escape" leads only to a death ritualized by the poem's rhythmic mimicking of the army's staccato taps.[43]

Montoya's poem invokes the memorial crosses planted along rural highways after violent accidental deaths. The poem's sense of the memorial, however, is tinged with a grief made furious by the desperation of labor conditions, the structures of enclosure that force Gabby and others to watch "the riches that passed" and to feel the waste of an economic system that seems to laugh at those struggling to escape it: "Y el 99 laughs." Like lowriders or Betasbeé Romero's tires, "Gabby Took the 99" plays with the relationships among motion, scalar rationalism, and a dense engagement with the interanimating and immanent connections among many forms of beings in motion. Both the poem and *Their Dogs Came with Them* propose that knowledge and understanding shift in motion; they suggest how much driving shapes a modality of seeing and cognizing relations. Yes, movement also underlies precarious working conditions, the force of needing to move, always moving. As these texts suggest, movement also shapes relations; it cements, in every sense of the word and world, a scalar scaffold imaginary, as *Their Dogs Came with Them* and "Gabby Took the 99" explore. Phallic verticality, so damaging if one remains within it and near its nether regions, also contains the sloppy marks of its own dismemberment: generosity, forgiveness, empathy, engagement. These undo the scalar sensibility because they refuse a demonic scaffold, the view from the moon, by engaging connections and moving within the irreducibility and immutability of being and being together, of looking for the horizontality of inclination and connection.

Seeking a Queer Horizontality

Highway 99 connects the freeway stack of East Los Angeles to the fields and farms south of California's capital city, Sacramento; to the small towns of Visalia and Danuba; and to the locus of Manuel Muñoz's collection of short stories, *The Faith Healer of Olive Avenue*. Building on the critique of scale and the scaffold imaginary proffered by Viramontes and Montoya, this collection suggests that the point is not to rue scale, to dwell in its losses and damage, but to refuse it its meaning or reach and to seek out instead connections that defy the logic of phallic verticality by embracing a queer horizontality. Scalar logic suggests that only at the level of the world, the global, do actions matter; only within a schema with global reach can real change occur or agency acquire value. *The Faith Healer of Olive Avenue* highlights the emotional cost of scalar thinking and suggests a different conceptual possibility, one without scale as an organizing force. Rich, suggestive, delicate, and searing, these stories together offer an eloquent portrait of a place where "deep green water rushed icy from the tops of the Sierra Nevada," with "roads so skinny they don't need painted lines" and with "orange groves nestled on the brink of the foothills" where meth labs lie hidden among "the deep green leaves."[44] This is a place where a "treacherous" highway will take you past "empty cotton fields," where "a dust devil swirled lazily, meandering" over to "a miraculous horizon—the sheer blue line of the ocean meeting its own impossible expanse."[45] Each of the stories in *The Faith Healer of Olive Avenue* offers portraits of a place that phallic verticality insists has been left behind, where nothing ever happens. Phallic verticality teaches one to think that what is nearby is "a mess of lack," that thriving always entails departure, abandonment, disconnection in order to move outward, upward.[46] As the narrator in "Tell Him about Brother John" explains, everyone asks him about Allá (over there)—that vague and distant big city that promises a better life. The narrator feeds that fantasy: "I say that Over There is tall buildings. Over There is restaurants and the people who eat in them.... Living Over There is cars and taxis, vans and too many horns, a bus to get you from one side of the city to the other whenever you needed."[47] Beyond the implication that "Over There" you don't need a car to work, what the narrator notes is that the fantasy of escape is belied by his own experience: "My life is this: I'm broke, cramped in my apartment, on edge in the late night."[48] Folded into the density of refuting phallic verticality is the unwillingness to remain within categories and their organizing principles; it is to think against the logic of containers; it is to hold a general antagonism toward subjectivity as transcendent and apart from complex reciprocities. Phallic verticality insists on the rectitude of individualist rationalism rather than acknowledging the more bountiful movement toward inclination and care with a sense of indebted responsibility and out of the knowledge that beings find themselves indebted to one another.

To step outside of scale, away from phallic verticality, is to challenge one's training in categories, to shift from looking for models, for transpositions, for transcendences. It is to shift into the instance and out of the generalizing, with all of its laws and norms. This shift means understanding beings not as authors or agents per se but as part of the "dense materialities that compose sites" connected and formed by shifting aggregates of (im)material bodies of many forms. To step outside of scale is to connect as various forms (called ghosts and people and things and trees) inhabit one another collectively and aggressively and dynamically.[49] Thinking by looking around, thinking through a hug, an abrazo, by attesting to the outstretched set of relations characterized by horizontality, entails refusing the easy logic of categories, suggesting instead that interactions among various forms of beings, from people to plants to oceans, highways, houses, and streets, are richly interactive rather than rigidly distinct. The focus in thinking as embracing rather than delineating is not on locating the agency to move up the ladder as dictated by the "rigidities of hierarchical thought" but rather on participating in all the connections and blockages that help constitute situations, peoples, linkages.

For this reason, when the narrator of "Tell Him about Brother John" explains, "I imagine Gold Street as a living being, an entity with arms waiting," he is not offering one more instance of a pathetic fallacy (a theoretical concept derived from a rationalist categorical epistemology if ever there were one) but rather naming a way of being that recognizes a denser, more animate set of relations and connections, that understands the material, the real, as vibrant and engages with a sense of immanence rather than transcendence.[50] *The Faith Healer of Olive Avenue* offers one instance after another of narrators who look around, not nostalgically or romantically, but generously. Even as they look at scourging loss and profound blockages, they nevertheless look around thinking densely and calling readers to ride along with them.

Put another way, Muñoz's narrators take readers along as they drive, suggesting as they go the densities of spaces, their vibrancy, the overlapping mesh of relationships, the convergences of relations stretched out, stretched open. Some stories highlight driving dangers—crippling, death-dealing accidents—and every story entails moments of driving, most frequently to work. Like in *Their Dogs Came with Them*, where the stack serves as a model for both human sociality and the novel's form, *The Faith Healer of Olive Avenue* utilizes Highway 99 with its various tentacles immersed in a quotidian, unexceptional moment where understanding and the beat of daily living and slow forgiveness, slower empathy, can happen. For the narrators, driving is the moment for musing and observing the interconnected roads stringing together memories, change, and development, just as the stories slowly lace together characters so that the collection illustrates and engages readers in a mesh of relations. In some moments, the highway and driving function as metaphors for temporality: "I never thought about what can happen down the road."[51] And while it is clear that *The Faith Healer of Olive Avenue* suggests how crucially highways can shape how people perceive a relationship to time, to experience, Muñoz uses these moments, pat as they are, within and against careful observation so that the tired, trite connections recede as markers of loss just as "Fresno receded into a shimmering line in her rearview mirror."[52] The roads are scalar forces, as the collection repeatedly suggests, but Muñoz's stories also show them as knit into relationships that exceed their service to capital even as the global scale intensifies people's dependence on cars, a point Muñoz's stories also underscore.

Not surprisingly, the highways signal multiple structures of longing for escape and connection, but they also work as a carceral form, as the walls of enclosures that circle around financial debt and low-wage jobs. As the stories suggest, the highways seem to offer escape, "the open road to pursue whatever he craved."[53] Ultimately, they don't actually provide it. Or consider how Christian puts it in "Señor X": "We headed east up into the Tehachapi Mountains on Highway 58 and the darkness, leaving the Valley behind, and even in the night I knew my life had changed without my wanting it to. The fruit trees were gone, the vineyards. In the dark was the dry rustle of the mountains at the burst of fire season. In the dark was the edge of the desert and its frightening jaws." At the edge of the highway, promise gives way to threatening consumption. The promise of the highways is repeatedly revealed as a betrayal: "He felt his loneliness stretching before him like a road, the mirage of water at the end of it wavering, beckoning him."[54]

If the narratives frequently focalize from behind the wheel or, more vulnerably, from the passenger seat, the rhythm of the text itself reinforces a drive-by quality. Throughout the collection the narrative pauses to enumerate what a car passes or to suggest movement and the accumulation of changes, of memories. Such lists draw the characters, who look into an engagement with what they see, creating not a series of objects but a set of relationships: "There now is the fog gathering faintly. There is the barge, so far away, its destination still imperceptible. There is the sun beginning its embrace of the horizon, its dark time coming, its rest."[55] The narrators also ask readers to think about the logistics of driving, pointing out "treacherous" roads that "twist, climb, and dip"; clogged interchanges; and avenues that "slithered," all suggesting how much driving encloses and shapes their lives just as capital's flight does: "The deterioration of Olive Avenue, in the older part of Fresno, spoke everything about where the money was headed nowadays. Here were the cars with dangling mufflers and work trucks with bad paint jobs, the meat markets with their hand-painted signs in Spanish, the long-closed beauty salons with their broken neon signs, and everywhere people walking because they had no choice. On and on they went..."[56] Throughout the collection Muñoz illustrates the importance of looking through embracing rather than through a scalar analytic with its focus on the difference between alli and allá and the "riches that passed"; he provides not an ocularcentric vision (where vision structures through hierarchy) but instance after instance of felt engagement in particularity.

The stories in *The Faith Healer of Olive Avenue* trace, albeit with various permutations, the experience of feeling like an outsider, an estrangement that comes from the deeply felt and unarticulated sense of being a stranger to those supposed to be closest: one's families, one's neighbors. Gaps, bridges, silences, and slashes fill these stories of queer desires refuted and acknowledged, silently shamed and resisted. Satiating the portrayal of queer desires are the complex receptions these desires' articulation receives. In dwelling in woundedness, in the "fists of daily living," *The Faith Healer of Olive Avenue* refutes the truth claims of a performative masculinity produced through New York and Hollywood characterizations of Latinx masculinism with its fetishized bravado and strutting figurations of heteromasculinity.[57] In contrast, *The Faith Healer of Olive Avenue* walks or drives readers in and around gay desires and the struggles to articulate these desires amid all the protocols attempting to maintain heterosexual masculinity at all costs. It brilliantly links these queer longings to another aspect of desire: the stories largely twine around the gashed yet sinuous bonds between sons (often queer) and their parents.

The text begs a reading that focuses on the controlling power of the closet. And the closet might well be understood as a captive space, as a form of containment and bracketing. Story after story might be described as illustrating life in the closet: the belated experience of homoerotic desire, the discovery after tragedy of a son's gay affair, a character's sorrow over the toll his refusal of gender norms exacted, another character's smoldering alienation after confusing erotic encounters. The melancholy tone of so many of the stories might easily be attributed to the myriad ways queer desire is not simply not articulated but rather disarticulated, closeted. Eve Kosofsky Sedgwick's own proclamation that "the closet is the defining structure of gay oppression this century" seems to simmer through the collection.[58] This understanding of the closet's role in *The Faith Healer of Olive Avenue* seems perfectly reasonable.

Yet such an easy conclusion would then lend itself to conflating the closet with the rural, thereby reducing the stories to gnarled portraits of the intersections of Mexican and queer identities as closeted in California; this reading misses the collection's dramatic rejection of a phallic verticality. In other words, within the representational economy of phallic verticality, *The Faith Healer of Olive Avenue* offers portraits of closeted, stuck lives left behind. Not only does Muñoz resist such an economy, but he counters it with a queer horizontality, a queer density, that reveals a far more vibrant and dramatic set of networks and connections. This queer density can be found not through stories of heteronormativity but through the stories of youth who find themselves cast out and cast away, alienated precisely because they are not normative. So while the closet is not the crucial signifier, the process of dispossession is. Cast-out youth, dispossessed of a comforting set of affective ties, attempt to rebuke a set of imaginary, but real, structural hierarchies that would reduce them to failures. In the portrait of their thick connections, Muñoz offers a vision of inclination.

The Faith Healer of Olive Avenue doesn't overtly pay attention to categories such as gay or straight. It doesn't offer a set of narratives that we might expect—bold coming-of-age accounts that report a liberated proclamation of gay identity; such triumphant coming-out stories are not offered here, nor are the narrative energies focused on a nostalgic fondness for "small-town America" or an iconic and neighborly (Mexican) Main Street. These representations seem unimportant to a writer who, in rejecting the scaffold imaginary, knows that such coming-out stories frequently include the drumbeat to rise above and get out—a theme that leaves the closet and the rural in the dustbin of power.[59] Instead, the collection urges us to think more densely, more intricately, about the network of relations that knit people together.

The Faith Healer of Olive Avenue begins this effort of thinking densely with a warning: "People knew that road, that intersection, how often it happens."[60] This opening sentence of the first story in the collection, "Lindo y Querido," refers to a highway intersection where accidents frequently occur. But it is also an apt sentence to open a story and a collection deeply engaged with the contours of public knowledge, open secrets, things known (particularly intersections of various kinds) but not said. Similarly, it is a touching way to annotate the frequency with which boundaries are broken, while also emphasizing a kind of communal vulnerability. The open secret is, of course, a desire that refuses the constraints of heteronormativity. But as the story unfolds, we learn that the *other* open secret entails a woman's tenuous relationship to her legal status in the United States. Continually sounding this connection (this set of shared vulnerabilities between immigration status and sexuality), the collection repeatedly traces circuits of prohibition and constraint.

This intersection is a dangerous one; the story follows the death of a young man, Isidro, killed in a motorcycle accident at that intersection. As his mother empties his room, she comes across love letters to her son, written in a language she doesn't know; she easily recognizes, however, that they are love letters and that they have been signed by Carlos, the other young man killed in the accident. At this intersection of loss and revelation, Isidro's mother, Connie, tries to collate her new knowledge of her son with her old knowledge of her estranged husband. Muñoz gives us a portrait here of isolation and loneliness—not a nostalgic and stereotypical image of a supportive and mutually engaged community but rather an image of one that knows things but doesn't speak them. The narrative won't let us forget that intersection; it repeats the formulation two more times over the course of the story, the second time as Connie remembers a sexual encounter with Isidro's father: "Everyone knows that road, that intersection." The story folds this memory into the fierce evocation of Connie's sense of pride, which, the narrator dryly notes, in telling us of Connie's delicately forged immigration papers, "can be an enormous crushing weight."[61]

Connie destroys the love letters: "She rips the letters angrily, just as she did her husband's magazines all those years ago. . . . She would not be alone in this house as she is, with the pile of letter scraps on the mattress, scraps she will wet in the sink and squish tightly into the garbage."[62] Just as she had destroyed her husband's porn after he had abandoned Connie and their young son, Isidro, she makes the letters go away because they are documents that attest to some knowledge she does not want to assimilate. The letters are signs of an illicit desire and a signal of a son's unspoken experiences. They also painfully remind her of her own letters sent to parents "who shipped her off to a husband when she was very young," which go unanswered. This mesh of paper—from forged citizenship documents purchased for $1,500, to returned letters, to porn, to love notes from one young boy to another boy—serves as a screen for her memories and for her navigation of an increasingly isolated existence. Working recursively, the narrative suggests that Isidro's father may well have been gay, but, more important, we ultimately see Connie now grieving the loss of her son, the loss of his love letters, the loss of a connection to Carlos's mother.[63] She is swamped by grief, and her son's accident haunts her as it fills her dreams: "She will dream of her son hugging Carlos as the motorcycle speeds faster. This was love. At each of the intersections, she is there watching as Isidro hugs Carlos, feeling with her son as Carlos takes in a deep breath, the boys waiting for clearance, Carlos's back widening."[64] In her loss, she begins to love her son as who she now understands him to have been. At the close of "Lindo y Querido," the killing intersection signals not danger but interconnection. And it is this interconnection that *The Faith Healer of Olive Avenue* repeatedly asks us to consider. The stories mold events not in terms of individual actors but within the sites of their coming together—a coming together that is not just of bodies and (heroic) actions but of disparate memories, shifting economies, and representational struggles in local places, the shared knowledge of which reinstantiates connections.

To step outside of the scaffold imaginary means, at the very least, to look closely at these interconnections and their sites of coming together (and thus to step away from reductive comparisons). *The Faith Healer of Olive Avenue* amplifies the ways sites stretch to include multiple temporalities and breathing, shifting materialities. The stories locate events and experiences but do so with a sense that these locales are constitutive of the events. Such an understanding of place eschews panoramic visions, or as one character says, "Sometimes I imagine Gold Street as a living being, an entity with arms waiting."[65] In this sense, the stories suggest that not only are lives braided with other lives, but they are woven in and through a particular place. It further suggests that one must look really, really closely at a place, its peoples, at the events that are their coming together. Just as crucial to the stories' coherence are the accounts of the valley, which entail understanding it in terms of its "liveness," its interactivity; "[when] night came, the temperature would plummet, the open Valley sky snatching away all the heat."[66] "The Valley" is not iterable, duplicable, abstractable, or rationalizable. Similarly, to give place texture is also to show that the characters invent themselves and their experiences through spatial transformation. So their comments on the areas around them are not mere asides but rather engagements with the place as a way to understand themselves, as a way to see themselves densely emplaced.

The text allows us to understand that to follow a character's story, it is also important that readers learn, for instance, about a town's "expanding, eating up the farmland, the field lizards still confused as they scampered around in the dust."[67] Changing economies swirl through the stories as they trace the transformations of development, often cynically:

> On this side of town there has not been much construction in a long time. Over on the north side, the town is stretching its way toward Fresno, swallowing up farmland sold by farmers who claimed that the soil was too acidic. But that's a lie. The peaches, the nectarines, were growing just fine. Then one foggy day in January, I drove past the Northern fringe of town and saw acres and acres of fruit trees pulled up, the trunks and branches gathered in piles. January: there were no leaves, no buds, just the bare dead trees, and as soon as the sun came to stay and the county waived air quality restrictions for a few days, the farmers were allowed to burn their tree piles. That's greed for you: now there are beautiful, beautiful houses up there.[68]

The movement of capital is registered here as a changing relationship to the nearby. This kind of engagement with the valley bespeaks a sense of relationship with a place, an acknowledgment of place as enmeshed in sociality and not simply a notch on a vertical hierarchy where real living happens elsewhere. Individuals, the stories teach, are not outside of places; they are not apart from the "dense materialities that compose sites," nor are they the "transcendental author of those sites."[69]

This sense of people and place as interanimating does not give much room to a social imaginary that isolates individual actors with heroic coming-out accounts. Instead, *The Faith Healer of Olive Avenue* highlights a set of intermeshed relations far more in sync with Mary Gray's argument in *Out in the Country*. There Gray persuasively shows how the politics of visibility that has emerged as a product of the contemporary gay rights movement depends for its political utility on urban living. Visibility and the closet therefore are inadequate metaphors for approaching an understanding of nonurban queer cultures. As she argues, "At the moment, queer desires and embodiments are popularly and politically tethered to prescriptions of exacting kinds of LBGT visibility. These politics and practices, however, fail to recognize the price rural LGBT-identifying youth pay for this 'claustrophilia.'"[70] Understanding queer cultures beyond urban locales entails refusing the normalizing mechanisms of queer visibility and assembling such a sensibility via other mechanisms and technologies. Gray suggests that rural queer youth "constantly reworked boundaries" without queer visibility as the normative or utopian end marker.[71] In rejecting the universality of visibility politics, Gray shifts the focus "away from the private world of individual negotiations of the closet" so that we learn how queer identities can be understood as "collective labor" and as "work shared among many rather than the play of any one individual."[72] That many includes place and the complex of relationships among beings (including orange trees and lizards).

Three stories in *The Faith Healer of Olive Avenue* in particular illustrate Gray's concept of collaborative labor by suggesting that what characters move toward is not a named identity but rather a sense of living and working together, collaboratively pursuing fulfillment or survival. The stories show that such mutuality entails a carefully wrought series of negotiations in which many characters labor together to find room for each other's approaches to living, carefully acknowledging, in keeping with the collection's interest in empathy, how bodies in motion and materialities have an impact on each other. Put differently, to understand queer identity as a collective labor is also to understand how dense relations emerge from indebtedness, from a knowledge of responsibility and shared vulnerability. To see identity as collaborative is to undo the individuating logic of market capitalism. The scaffold imaginary doesn't have any leeway for collaboration.

In "Bring, Brang, Brung," the narrative follows Martín after he has reluctantly returned to his hometown in "the Valley." A single father whose lover has recently died of a stroke, Martín must wrestle with his grief, which comes "like a ghost at the foot of the bed, just as he was sleeping."[73] He must also wrestle with the financial demands of raising his young son, Adán, on his own, in the town he despises: "the Valley was a mess of lack, of descending into dust, of utter failure, and he had learned that long, long ago."[74] But what Martín finds in the valley is not isolation or rejection because of his queer desires but a complex network of care. The very people whom he had once rejected now find room and ways to make him and his son welcome, finally convincing him to display a photo of himself and his lost lover, Adrian. What Martín finds, ironically, is not lack, although people are poor, but engagement and the realization that he is part of a mesh of connected people who collectively build a collaborative sense of themselves, in part by admitting their debt, their connection to one another.

In "Tell Him about Brother John," the narrator accedes to his father's request to visit a downcast neighbor called Brother John. What unfolds in the conversation is a blisteringly sad story of queer love gone awry. The unnamed queer narrator hears Brother John's story with grudging ambivalence but refuses to give him any empathetic recognition at all. Nevertheless, the narrator finds, to his surprise, that his own father wishes to acknowledge his son's queer life, not by naming it, but by encouraging his friendship with Brother John. The father wants to build a collaborative sort of solidarity.

And, finally, in "Ida y Vuelta," Roberto recounts how his ex-lover's parents slowly accepted his relationship with their son. Their acceptance moves between the parents' own troubled marital relationship and Roberto's generous willingness to help them with business matters. It's a kind of bargain that Roberto does not regret because he inhabits a network of relations that acknowledges shared vulnerabilities, in which responsibility is a way to also acknowledge an indebtedness that marks connection.

In each of these stories, *The Faith Healer of Olive Avenue* helps us to see this complex mesh of relations, particularly as it tracks its subjects coming to terms with this interrelatedness and with their own movement within a relational mesh. The form of the collection also highlights the collaborative labor of building identity and writing densely. Rather than highlight the agency of individual actors, the collection repeatedly weaves the lives of various characters into and out of the stories. The same place-names appear across the different stories. Minor characters in one story become the narrators of other stories. Lives and events and places overlap and fold together. This interbraiding also further undercuts the possibility of abstracting the valley into the scale of the rural. It emphasizes instead a specificity that in its unfolding challenges the way scalar structures empty out difference and political possibilities. Even if the closet and the rural are perceived as captive, stuck spaces, *The Faith Healer of Olive Avenue* suggests that people are nevertheless on the move, that a lot happens, and that the normative, scalar scaffold imaginary misses all the action.

Temporal Girders

To fully understand the collaborative work of identity, it is useful to disentangle identity from linear time. Just as *The Faith Healer of Olive Avenue* rejects the scaffold imaginary, it similarly rejects that imaginary's dependence on linear time. The problem is that linear time is, like the rural, an abstraction. We live in jagged, cut temporalities overlaid and decollaged upon each other. And yet the momentous explanatory power of linearity swamps the language of time. Linear time works in concert with a scaffold imaginary, delimiting worlds into the past and the present, giving the global and the abstract the swoosh of movement, power, action—and draining what is not global of its vibrancy.

To resist the power geometry of such a temporal/scaffold imaginary entails refusing its claims to aggregated accuracy. It refuses the seeming efficiencies of abstractions that crush temporalities into one seamless line.

The Faith Healer of Olive Avenue suggests that we don't live and breathe in a straightforward temporal clime. Instead, it argues that every experience depends not just on memories but on the intrusiveness of other people's memories and on the vibrancy of what seems past but isn't. For that reason, no one person is immune to the temporalities of another. Instead, as the stories suggest, empathy, understanding, and a sense of being in place depend on concatenated memories, on sudden linkages and burst obstructions.

Repeatedly, the stories hold a character in sharp light, focusing intently on the way a long-held memory inflects the present and, on occasion, enables one to begin understanding another person. For example, at the end of "Bring, Brang, Brung," Martín, having reluctantly cared for his ailing son all day, finds himself flooded with a memory: "He thought, for the first time in years, of his father, and in the quiet of the apartment, Martín let himself inch toward understanding him."[75] A ruptured present allows Martín to shift toward, if not compassion, then a recognition of the emotions that might have pushed his own father to abandon a young Martín. Similarly, a bullying father suffused with pain after his son's suicide in "When You Come into Your Kingdom" moves between temporal planes over and over again until he begins to "see how his son saw, and he knows what it is to be him and prove incapable of resisting his own body, how his hands and feet could move forward as if on their own."[76] As in so many moments in the collection, the verb tenses shift from phrase to phrase and within phrases (from present to past: *see/saw*; from present to future subjunctive: *knows/could move*), illustrating the instability of time. Jagged time, cracks in a linear movement from past to present, enables the possibility of empathizing and of understanding our indebtedness to one another.

One of the ways linear time structures the scaffold imaginary is by holding temporal movement to a single direction, forming nostalgia. Nostalgia finds the rural quaint, discarded, left apart, and crushed. Characters in *The Faith Healer of Olive Avenue* often rail against nostalgia, seeing it as damaging, as an intrusive attitude that freezes memories, tweaks time so that one feels "fooled and hypnotized by" it.[77] Nostalgia, in other words, prevents temporal movements that enable empathy and resilient connections, because it is "the will of memory to rectify everything" and nostalgia serves as an obstruction, gathering power if one allows it.[78]

Memories shape the present so that the present tense is never quite a linear marker from past to future but is always embedded in becomings and endings and enfoldings of the experiences of not just one person but of everyone coming in contact with each other. No time is its own; the present is a product of collective memories, of everyone else's times; this moment doesn't exist in isolation. It is in thinking backward and around and through time that the characters in Muñoz's stories reconstruct family ties both present and dissolved, but they do not think backward as if to trace direct connections. Rather, they find themselves inhabiting seemingly prior moments fluctuating within a present temporal bouquet.

The larger form of the stories themselves also reflects this interbraiding of temporalities. The stories never trace a linear series of actions or events. The narratives dwell on minor moments, microscopic observations. Although one must read sequentially along the page, the stories disrupt a linear or straightforward plot by repeatedly spinning in different directions so that a reader's understanding is enlarged not just by the explanation of a prior event but also by the combustion of memories and realizations within a particular interaction. Thus, a character begins to describe a series of actions, but before the actions can be fully explained, the character offers an associative memory that leads to another memory, which then pulses forward again or sideways into the realm of could have/should have. This formal density creates a kind of discombobulated time for the reader and, most important, shows that people live in a mesh of temporal relations and collaborations.

The Faith Healer of Olive Avenue offers an abrazo, an approach to knowing and engaging with the meshes of relations, events, temporalities, and sites in which people find themselves located. Its motion is not up, up, and away but toward and with and through generosity and a sense of indebtedness and a willingness to find a route to empathy and connection. The collection offers, then, a crucial contribution to considering shared vulnerability against the scale of the world and its globe and with the peculiarities of the earth and its being. In other words, to think about living queer is not to create an algorithm that fits every place queer people find themselves. Rather than seek out ways to buttress and add density to formulaic descriptions, *The Faith Healer of Olive Avenue* calls for a radical shift away from the scaffold imaginary and linear time, away from iterative and abstracting naming practices or categorical solutions. It dismisses a liberal call for queer visibility as an end in itself and asks instead that people listen to and walk with each other in a place that matters. Perhaps one reason the collection attends so fiercely to highways and roadways is that these forms shape the scaffold imaginary that would represent the local, rural, and queer as stuck and contained. If it offers a series of portraits of children, cast away and captive, struggling across bracketed lives, it also shows that in seeing them through a queerly horizontal lens, rather than through the phallic verticality that prizes an urban gay cosmopolitan vibrancy, we see a rich and deep set of connections. And in casting readers' eyes toward highways, toward the stretches and turns of the intimately familiar roads people travel, *The Faith Healer of Olive Avenue* emphasizes how highways work as conjoiners and threats. Yet rather than presume the scalar force of highways, *The Faith Healer of Olive Avenue* strips them of their power to frame and instead weaves them into storied lives. The cast-off children and the beloved children that people *The Faith Healer of Olive Avenue* also find these highways crucial for articulating their sense of relationality, for articulating their own textured mesh of connections.

Conclusion

If the road-trip novel celebrates the open road, then *Their Dogs Came with Them*, *The Faith Healer of Olive Avenue*, and "Gabby Took the 99" meditate on the costs the road itself exacts. Helena María Viramontes suggests that freeway construction worked to force a new kind of enclosure, while José Montoya slices through the rhetoric that promises highways as an escape, and Manuel Muñoz shows that the liberatory rhetoric highways symbolize intensifies the sense of isolation and entrapment people come to feel, especially as they struggle with their responsibilities toward each other, their indebtedness to one another. All three writers illustrate the damage scalar forces wreak as devices that striate and differentiate, whether it's the railroad, the highway, or the freeway stack, the clock or the castagory. All three invoke their readers as witnesses who must find a way, via metaphor, to question how and whether their destinies are bound up with people very much like those portrayed by the writers. Viramontes and Muñoz further suggest a vibrant way of pursuing relations, irrespective of scale, a way of stepping away from its work of confinement to pursue connection amid precarity. In many ways Viramontes and Muñoz tell Fordist captivity tales, but in other ways they eschew that form's vision of capitalist individuation by insisting on the emotional tangles that emerge from recognizing our indebtedness to one another—to beings of every form, despite the "fists of daily living," by offering instead praise for the abrazo in all its manifestations. Put differently, Viramontes and Muñoz highlight the kinds of collectivities and movements that disappear in a scaffold imaginary, the ways that bracketed, snared lives can be overturned when the scalar, when coloniality, does not govern the processes of articulation and interpretation, when a phallic verticality is rejected to embrace queer horizontality instead.

4

N + 1

Sex and the Hypervisible (Invisible) Migrant

> When did immigration assume a place next to abortion and traditional marriage as a "family" issue for the religious right?
> —ALEXANDER ZAITCHIK, "Who Would Jesus Deport?"

Enmity lies at the heart of the liberal moral imaginary, as María Amparo Ruiz de Burton's *Who Would Have Thought It?* (1872) vehemently insists: social relations in a liberal market economy depend on enmity. Enmity, not the consent of the governed, pumps through the ideological heart of liberal democracies. And such enmity inspires erotic fantasies. Certainly, in the novel's portrayal of the allure surrounding a young child, Lola, readers see that the perception of enmity engenders desire as much as wealth inspires desire. Written in a moment when the United States was restructuring political citizenship to include (theoretically) African American men, the novel nevertheless defiantly argues that such restructuring would not undermine this fundamental premise of liberal democracy, nor would it undo the dynamic that eroticizes enmity. That enmity has such an erotic component might well explain why nearly every effort to articulate, revise, or implement US immigration laws has been saturated not just with enmity but also with sex.

Obviously, Ruiz de Burton's novel does not provide a clear answer to Alexander Zaitchik's question, posed in an essay for a publication sent to the donors of an antiracist organization, the Southern Poverty Law Center. Yet it certainly maps some of the implicit assumptions that continue to trouble US governance and nearly every effort to envision a different structure of belonging than that defined since the passage of the Thirteenth and Fourteenth Amendments to the US Constitution. Zaitchik posed his question about twenty years after the Cold War had ended, during a period when the United States more generally was seeking a new portfolio of enemies that could be used to maintain its defensive posture and its mantle of supremacy. Zaitchik of course posed his question with an eye toward not the Cold War but rather legislation and ballot propositions aimed at restricting access to normative citizenship via homophobia and villifying migrants while narrowing their access to humanitarian care, including hospitalization and schooling. Thus, the narrator of *Who Would Have Thought It?* would certainly have told Zaitchik, in answer to his question, that immigration had always had a place next to "traditional family values" on the conservative agenda.[1]

A little over a century after Ruiz de Burton sent her novel off to a Philadelphia publisher and it and she fell into obscurity, the question of immigration would emerge with a new force, yet the rhetoric framing immigration remained substantially stuck in the discourse Ruiz de Burton radically critiqued. It is this history lesson that would help Zaitchik analyze what he perceives here as surprising and peculiar bedfellows. It is not just, as Karma Chávez so effectively illustrates, that "even as it may seem that LGBTQ politics and migration politics are opposed, queers and migrants have been attacked through shared logics of scapegoating, threat, and deviance."[2] The strategies demonizing both migrants and LGBTQ populations are clearly the same. But this point provides only one necessary connection for Zaitchik. Another, Eithne Luibhéid insists, is that sexuality "structures every aspect of immigrant experiences."[3] Yet despite this structuring, Chávez notes, "immigration scholarship virtually ignores connections among immigration, sexuality, and heteronormativity."[4] The refusal to see these relationships leads to a repetition of Zaitchik's question in multiple arenas, not just in immigration scholarship, but in queer studies as well as civil rights studies of citizenship more generally, and even in more general Latinx studies. Immigration policy seeks to establish boundaries for normativity, and in this it relies on the social norms defining sexuality. For most of the twentieth century, the norms structuring sexuality were articulated with recourse to the "threat of homosexuality," but immigration policy debates at crucial moments in the 1960s, 1970s, and 1980s were largely free to maintain a cone of silence around these relationships.[5] This capacity to conceal the connections among concepts of sexuality, concepts of citizenship, and concepts of movement (as immigration can be understood) began to change only in the late 1980s, when queer activists started to successfully challenge normative assumptions.

And to look at this moment is to understand at least partially how it is that in the third decade of the twenty-first century the problem of enmity and the challenge to belonging that Ruiz de Burton articulated in 1872 continue to structure lives and reproduce conditions of violence and exclusion. Seemingly discrete events and the scholarship on these events, scholarship that maintains the discreteness or that dismisses relationships among the events as incidental, help to feed this problematic, to maintain the structures of knowledge that prevent a movement outward from narratives of inclusion that depend on exclusion.

To tangle with exclusion, with its stickiness, its tacky and spongy qualities, without reinforcing the right of exclusion, is a difficult task. Contemporary writers such as Eduardo Corral, Bettina Restrepo, and Reyna Grande, for example, complicate the system of discrete, objectifying, and decontextualizing analysis, as do the filmmaker Laura Angelica Simón and the visual artist John Sonsini. All insist on a prolonged view of exclusion, of the methods and values of it. All offer portraits of the costs of new rounds of global scaling, the costs of our dependence on a scaffold imaginary and our inattention to its evolving dependence on captivity. Ruiz de Burton identified a dynamic between captivity and scale that remains germane even as processes of rescaling shift: contemporary writers must contend with new forms of rescaling economies and with the attending differences in structures of containment that such scalar projects require. Like Ruiz de Burton, Restrepo, Simón, and Grande offer complicated portraits of cast-off children forced to negotiate a post-NAFTA political economy, children who must navigate what could easily be understood as a new form of bracketing, of captivity: life in the United States without papers.

The work discussed here emerges not just in concert with *Who Would Have Thought It?* and not just in opposition to it but in the aftermath of a spectacular rupture, a rupture in which the implicit work of immigration law—to police and maintain white supremacist heterosexuality and to cordon off queer life from the protections of citizen rights—began to be unsettled. This rupture has multiple parts, and its implications are still unfolding. The power of this rupture can be seen in contemporary electoral politics as well as in the continually befuddled efforts to understand them. And this rupture occurred in the midst of yet another round of economic rescaling, signaled by NAFTA, signed by Operation

Gatekeeper, enforced by the collapse of the Immigration and Naturalization Service and the Border Patrol into Homeland Security.

The writers and artists I analyze here work in the wake of this rupture. They write in a contemporary moment of crisis for people living "deportable lives." Ruiz de Burton may have predicted this crisis, may have seen its antecedents in liberal governance and market capitalism, but it's doubtful she would have predicted the particular series of events and actions that led to this rupture. Yet they are worth recounting because their ramifications are so significant and because they have been so understudied. Furthermore, they highlight, as do the cultural texts studied here, the complex role sexuality plays in the battle over the scale of the nation, the scale of belonging, which is to say over immigration. Moreover, each text offers a decolonial shift away from the view from the moon that helped map imperialism in the first place.

The fiction, poetry, and film echo an earlier moment, one presaged by Ruiz de Burton, a moment when surging economic anxiety and industrial descaling collided with an intensified effort to narrate white supremacy as in crisis, justifying new bracketing practices and more cast-off children. Created in the wake of California's voter-approved anti-immigrant ballot initiative, Proposition 187, Laura Angelica Simón's 1997 film *Fear and Learning at Hoover Elementary* features a child, Mayra, who meditates on the abyss before her, on the possibility that electoral politics and sovereignty's war to ensure its perpetuity will cast her out.[6] Noting that her mother could be deported and reeling from the recent death of her father, Mayra quietly comments that if her mom leaves, she will have to leave with her: "Who will I stay with? I don't got nobody." This sense of lack exemplifies the shredding of sustaining relations that accompanies scalar crises. Acutely aware of her own vulnerability, Mayra already feels cast off and bracketed.

This articulation of potent loss, this request that viewers peer over the abyss with her, is also reinforced by the framing: Mayra is consistently alone—alone on the playground, alone in the apartment describing her life. This solitude is underscored by the numerous establishing shots that feature cheerful children walking to school with adults who caress and bless them as they say goodbye. Such framing deliberately reveals her thin base of support—only a photo of her deceased father is offered to viewers. Instead, Mayra is surrounded by spent bullet casings, threatening building tags, used condoms on raggedy roofs, and the fears that Proposition 187 fomented and furthered. If she is portrayed as solitary, the film also emphasizes her affability and the pleasure she takes in playing for the camera and the filmmakers.[7]

Fear and Learning illustrates how the proposition's affective register delineated scarcity by evoking the discursive register of the home and its apparently exploited hospitality, but it also illustrates not only the immediate impact the proposition's passage had on children but also their understanding that they were meant to be threatened. The voter-approved proposition explicitly attacked children as the illegitimate recipients of publicly funded education, once again reinforcing the jarring distinction between the experiences of racialized children and the guarantees collated under the umbrella of childhood. Or, as the narrator (who is also the filmmaker and a teacher at the featured school) notes with acerbity, "I knew it was aimed at my kids." Mayra similarly articulates the sense of being targeted: "Only cause we're Latinos, they don't like us"; after this perceptive formulation, the film cuts to a shot of a policeman beating a Latinx protester at an anti–Proposition 187 march.

By portraying the school as at the intersection of embattled informal economies (narcotics, green cards, sex work) and more general labor exploitation, the film insists that the abandonment of the crucial infrastructure that supports social well-being aligns with the opening of a new regime of captive taking and captive making. The school responds to this blatant disregard for social well-being by reinvesting in the already failing and inadequate strategy of promoting rectitude. As the news about who publicly supported Proposition 187 sweeps through the school, staff meet to argue over why students don't come to school. This conversation predictably leads a Proposition 187 supporter to invoke the discourses of development and respectability, the normative logics of schooling as producing not just disciplined labor but better assimilated subjects. Other teachers counter with arguments that highlight family needs. The debate goes unresolved as the narrator, confronted with the news that Mayra and her mother have left for El Salvador, despondently wonders about the effectiveness of education as a liberatory practice: "Will I have to apologize for what we took away from her?" With this note of dispossession, the film closes on images of Mayra playfully dancing alone, a bittersweet contrast from the film's opening images of surveillance helicopters moving across a smog-encased landscape.

Fear and Learning effectively captures some of the shock that the passage of Proposition 187 engendered. It does not ultimately nod toward the complex political landscape that made its passage possible, nor could it have predicted the legacy, the thousands of deaths, the millions of deportations, that would soon follow. What it does make clear, however, is the centrality of social reproduction to immigration policy as well as the instrumentalization of children in furthering it. To understand why Proposition 187 would come to influence politics for more than a decade and would so thoroughly destroy affective structures and material economies for millions while also enabling the broader

United States to so casually slough off the lives of so many children, it's helpful to study a little-known antecedent.

An Archaeology of the Future

In 1991 the California State Legislature passed AB101, a bill prohibiting employment discrimination on the basis of sexuality.[8] Exempting churches and small businesses, this seemingly humble step complemented existing administrative practices already in place. By linking the rights of citizens to multiple sexual identities, AB101 sexualized citizenship or, better said, uncoupled it from presumptive heteronormativity, thereby articulating the rights and guarantees, the succor and expectations, proffered by a citizenship made less deceptively heteronormative. Extending the mantle of "rights," AB101 undermined the supposition that citizenship is a neutral and transparent category, revealing it to be fully imbricated in the creation and support of heterosexuality. For this reason, AB101 inspired a cultural storm out of which conservative activists and Christian fundamentalists inaugurated a great rights awakening, ultimately yoking issues once considered distinct and thereby harnessing additional political power with surprising reach and exceptional impact.

Understanding this 1991 storm helps to answer Zaitchik's question, "When did immigration assume a place next to abortion and traditional marriage as a 'family' issue for the religious right?," because this now-obscure political event inspired a new family-values campaign, one that was subsequently appropriated by the successful campaign for an anti-immigration initiative, California Proposition 187, thereby bringing together battles over social reproduction and border control. Indeed, Zaitchik might not have posed his question if he had realized this extraordinary but forgotten link among a 1991 legislative effort to create a more equal citizenry, the national disruption to immigration norms provoked by Proposition 187, and the subsequent *longue durée* of anti-immigrant fervor and violence that has engulfed and even commandeered US political culture as well as stolen the lives of thousands of people since then.

This is not to say that Zaitchik's question is naive. There is a reason the obscure 1991 legislative effort was forgotten; the practice of forgetting, as well as Zaitchik's question, emerges from the interstices created by two analytic frameworks. Studied separately and conceptualized differently, the frameworks for analyzing immigration and family values engage with two distinct sets of questions: (1) What forms the limits of the nation? and (2) What structures the relations within this nation, once formed? As Linda Bosniak argues, the two resulting frameworks fail to acknowledge their interdependence, and the accompanying academic disciplines shore up that failure in similarly facile ways, leading to Zaitchik's surprise and enabling conservative organizations to exploit general anxiety about social and political change.[9] Thus, it's crucial that we understand the profound interconnection between the discourses of social reproduction and migration control. The storm inaugurated by AB101 reveals the extent to which migration control functions through social reproduction, and so attending to it provides a better understanding of the violence and durability of contemporary anti-immigration sentiment, sentiment that has meant that life without papers in the twenty-first-century United States might be akin to a form of captivity, to a kind of enclosure that constrains, delimits, and obscures hopes, dreams, and relationships through a migration system determined to ruthlessly shred the affective networks that enable social lives to exist and flourish.

Yet while this brief social and political history is helpful in understanding how dependent border control is on discourses of social reproduction, including the normalization of heterosexuality and the instantiation of homoerotics and homophobia, contemporary Latinx fiction and poetry unpacks these interanimating structures in revealing ways as well. The poetry of Eduardo Corral and the novels of Bettina Restrepo and Reyna Grande each counter the structures deployed to intensify anti-immigrant affective relations through careful consideration of the relays between anti-queer hysteria and anti-immigrant fervor. Approaching their subjects in radically different ways, they nevertheless all expose the complexity of social reproduction, which controls relations within the nation by policing the limits of the nation. They articulate the questions, costs, and fictions that are built into the system of managing belonging, managing citizenship, even as the system belies this complexity. They do so in part through a focus on the cast-out child: the figure of a social reproductive system gone awry.

Their texts also answer Zaitchik's question, albeit indirectly and with no specific reference to public policies, state legislative maneuvers, or national treaties. Poetry, fiction, and artwork reveal a much more complicated relationship between sexualities and migration than that portrayed in the media or presumed and perpetuated by politicians. The novels, poems, and paintings discussed in this chapter all pursue the relationship between migration and freedom and all work in the shadow of the religious right, each wrestling with the way migrants have become captive to the whims of activists fighting against the transformation of equality, and each reworking sanctioned forms of belonging by ungluing citizenship from heteronormativity. In other words, each insists, however variously, that sexuality must be at the center of analyses of both civil rights battles (or social values campaigns) and immigration debates.

This chapter maps these two approaches, the literary and the historical, in order to shine as bright a light as possible on the myriad ways immigration control depends on social reproduction, and social reproduction depends on immigration control. It takes up both sets of frameworks by first looking at historical moments when a bold new era of violent border control was enacted and then looking at the contemporary literary interpretations of border control's violent and far-reaching impact.

Spectacularizing Heterosexual Anxiety

The story of AB101 does not stop with the assembly's passage of legislation outlawing discrimination on the basis of sexuality. Newly elected California governor Pete Wilson, a Republican, initially suggested he would support the legislation. But as soon as the California legislature voted, opponents to the new law inundated Wilson's office with postcards, phone calls, and letters. Their campaign continued for months, tying up Wilson's phone lines every day during the summer and fall.[10] Not surprisingly, Wilson buckled to conservative pressure and vetoed AB101.[11]

Before the ink was dry on his veto, outraged queers across the state took to the streets, snarling rush-hour traffic in Los Angeles for the next fourteen nights. One evening, protestors rushed a runway at Los Angeles International Airport, bringing air travel to a halt for several hours.[12] As geographer Moira Kenney writes, "For the first time in recent Los Angeles history, and for the first time in gay and lesbian movement history, the streets of Los Angeles were the sites of sustained, often-anarchic protests, overwhelming neighborhoods from the Westside into downtown."[13] The protests subsequently spread across the state and included flag burnings at the state capitol building. Overwhelming numbers of protestors also took to the streets in San Francisco for several nights, culminating in an uprising that brought the city center to a halt for several hours.[14]

The veto and the ensuing protests rounded out a terrible first year for the governor. Elected by a very thin margin, Wilson pushed through a large tax increase to bolster the state budget during a blistering recession and vocally supported social welfare measures, including Head Start.[15] His veto of AB101 and his steadfast refusal to engage with queer protestors did little to improve his popularity with social conservatives, whose money-raising prowess had already pushed President George H. W. Bush much further to the right. Wilson spent the subsequent months and most of 1992 trying to outflank his opposition within the Republican Party.[16] Nevertheless, the emboldened hard-right wing of his party added antiabortion proposals to their annual state convention platform in defiance of Wilson, as well as several other invidious resolutions, including one against same-sex marriage, one promoting new restrictions on the privacy of people testing positive for HIV, and a third demanding mandatory HIV testing for food-service workers.[17] Wilson responded to the right-wing platform by boycotting his party's state convention and urging his supporters to do so as well. Not surprisingly, speakers at the convention boldly and publicly denounced their own party's governor. The very next week, a clearly annoyed Wilson defied the right wing and signed the revised, though nearly identical, version of AB101 (called AB2601), to the surprise of most observers.[18] Like its previous incarnation, AB2601 made it illegal to fire employees on the basis of their sexuality.[19] The new law was a triumph for activists who had worked through the haze of AIDS-related deaths and paranoid homophobia, including the vitriolic campaigns led by Jimmy Swaggart and Anita Bryant. But if Wilson hoped to outmaneuver his opponents within his own party and style himself as a Reaganesque fiscal conservative and social moderate, he failed. Six weeks later, not only was his own budget proposition defeated in the general election, but so were virtually all of the candidates he had supported.[20] His clout diminished, and his popularity continued to sink.

Already engaged in an all-out party war, conservative groups put new pressure on Wilson by recruiting a radical conservative to challenge him in the next primary. Only six months after he signed AB2601 into law, political hecklers began predicting the demise of Wilson's career. Wilson watched his statewide approval rating sink to a desolate 15 percent as he withstood repeated attacks from jubilant Democrats as well as furious conservative forces.[21] Conservative groups subsequently put even more pressure on Wilson when they released films highly critical of his actions.

The most well-known of these films, *Gay Rights, Special Rights* (1993), included a then-surprising innovation. It utilized iconic images of African American civil rights struggles to argue that gay activists were trying to cut in on hard-won Black claims to civil rights. Beginning with a clip from Martin Luther King's March on Washington speech, the film argued that African American claims to protection from discrimination were threatened because decadent white elites would steal the rights earned by iconic, respectable, apparently heterosexual African American activists. As Ioannis Mookas puts it, *Gay Rights, Special Rights* "cynically seeks to cash in on the moral capital accumulated by the civil rights establishment by having African American fundamentalists, who are presented as the ultimate arbiters of 'legitimate' and 'illegitimate' minorities, inveigh against the lesbian and gay movement—and by extension, lesbians and gay men as a whole—as a fraudulent trespasser upon the hallowed ground of the civil rights struggle."[22] Without explicitly saying so, citizenship rights, the film tells us, function within a zero-sum economy. In other words, the claims to protection that gay activists sought somehow diminished the claims to protection from discrimination that an earlier generation of civil rights activists had struggled for and won. Or, put differently, the film, in Jacqui Alexander's words, "spectacularizes yet again heterosexual anxiety in a manner that puts homosexuality on display."[23]

The homophobic response to AB2601 occurred within the context of California's deep recession—then considered the worst since the Great Depression. The end of the Cold War had forced California's vast defense business to scale down while few other industries were expanding. The state coffers were shallow, forcing Wilson to issue IOUs to vendors. Wilson deflected this problem by claiming that the state suffered because federal policies, especially immigration policies, placed undue burdens on California's schools, hospitals, and businesses. Such rhetorical deflection did little, however, to help California climb out of its economic malaise, nor did it do much for the governor's popularity.[24]

Ultimately, Wilson's strategy to placate his base and regain political prominence entailed a brilliant change of subject: he shifted the locale for his constituents' anxiety rather than challenging the validity of their fears about gay rights. A few months after signing the controversial gay rights legislation, Wilson kicked his anti-immigrant marketing machinery into much higher gear and began amplifying a pitch that had already proven very useful.[25] He gained national attention by publishing editorials, giving speeches, and filing lawsuits calling for the federal government to revise its immigration strategies and direct new aid to border states. He scheduled multiple press conferences in a single week, even appearing at a freeway checkpoint where a new border fence was being built. He also purchased full-page advertisements in the *New York Times*, *USA Today*, and the *Washington Times*.[26] The advertisements complained not about immigrants themselves but about the way the federal government's immigration policies off-loaded costs onto states. His claims cleverly linked immigrants to crime and dereliction by focusing on rising prison, health, and welfare costs. In other words, Wilson made immigration control an issue of social reproduction rather than a project of economic management or labor relations.

These advertisements, editorials, and speeches were a pretense for what his efforts really entailed: a clear scapegoating of immigrants in order to deflect attention from an economic and cultural transformation entirely out of his control. The problem, his new public relations campaign implicitly suggested, was not queers dancing in the streets, not the broad economic changes that were bedeviling a cultural system organized around the behests of a now-defunct large-scale manufacturing economy, but immigrants, and specifically immigrants who had entered the United States without papers. For the next two years, Wilson made immigration policy and the supposed costs of immigrants the centerpiece of every move and every speech. Effectively reframing the debate by simply sliding away from his unpopular signature on antidiscrimination legislation, Wilson took command of another platform. Since he couldn't openly defeat the social conservatives gaining control of his party, he simultaneously joined them and co-opted their tactics with a new message more to their liking.

As a capstone to this broad publicity campaign, Wilson eventually supported, popularized, and campaigned for Proposition 187, an anti-immigration ballot referendum in California that refuted a century of US thinking about citizenship and immigration and took as its charge the statewide regulation of immigration.[27] Known as the Save Our State initiative, Proposition 187 prohibited immigrants lacking formal recognition by the state from using any social services, including health care and public education.[28] It effectively turned nurses and schoolteachers into immigration officials by charging them with surveillance responsibility, denied basic emergency care and benefits to anyone whose immigration status was questionable, and rescaled state authority by extending it into the quotidian practices of social life.[29]

Perhaps the first emblem of the neoliberal structural adjustment programs that came home to roost in the United States in the mid-1990s (like so-called welfare reform), Proposition 187 conveniently shifted the focus from gyrating gym boys protesting public policy and the corporate malfeasance that had led to economic debacle to the abjected bodies of the poor immigrant mothers and children who were supposedly sucking welfare money and hospital care from a recession-weary state, as well as, and more particularly, the migrant men who embodied some vague threat to the nation as they waited for work on a street corner.[30] As Michael Peter Smith and Bernadette Tarallo note of Wilson's maneuvering, "It was a remarkable narrowing of the complex political and economic conditions besieging California, but a politically astute move. Wilson thereby obfuscated the causes of California's economic and fiscal problems and redirected them to the immigration issue, arguing that federally mandated services provide a magnet which attracted immigrants to California's 'generous' social services, imposing an impossible burden that was bankrupting the state's economy."[31] Wilson's campaign completed a "remarkable, if politically opportunistic, turnaround." And this turnaround led not just to his reelection but also to the cementing of anti-immigration fever as a potent political tool for the foreseeable future. The change of "subject" galvanized conservative support for Wilson, who went on to win reelection in 1994 on Proposition 187's coattails, just as the proposition gained nearly 60 percent of the ballots cast.[32]

Wilson's eventual shift from AB101 to Proposition 187 was not merely or only a clever politician's ruse. Rather, the homophobia generated around AB101 (and the notion of gay rights it solidified) helped sustain and nurture the anti-immigrant fervor that propelled Proposition 187 from a crackpot, unconstitutional idea into a widely copied national anti-immigrant campaign that would lead to the deaths of many thousands of people. Tying Proposition 187 and AB101 together is the underlying assumption that both the "gay agenda" and the "immigrant agenda" take aim at the patriarchal white family. The move between AB101 and Proposition 187 was not simply a shift from a battle over the regulation and production of sexual citizenship to the sharpening of economic nationalism in nativist guise but also the ignition of the vibrant relay that derives from, even as it enhances, a nationalist, racialized, sexualized discourse of citizenship built through the framework of respectability.

California's AB101 and Proposition 187 emerged after a sea change in the US economy. The demise of a national economy organized around the Cold War and manufacturing necessitated the reorganization of the nation's political economy when the locus of capital accumulation in the United States transferred from manufacturing to the global management of money. This phase of economic transformation began in the late 1960s as US-based manufacturing plants closed and reopened in so-called developing nations, where they could employ young women for substandard wages. At the same time, large corporations began developing new flexible labor strategies that undermined organized labor and shifted the burden of pensions and risks to their employees. Ronald Reagan's "revolution" shut down some social programs and limited others so that public education, housing, and welfare assistance declined significantly. Corporate tax rates were reduced as well, justified as a response to a profit squeeze that US companies faced as the international economy expanded; these tax reductions freed corporations from the expectations that they had any responsibility to their locales.[33]

The particular vein of nativism that proponents of Proposition 187 mined was linked to this transforming national economy and was heretofore unique in the annals of nativist responses to economic crises and rising immigration in the United States. Proponents reimagined migrants as "tax burdens." As Kitty Calavita notes, if "immigrants serve as scapegoats for social crises, it stands to reason that the specific content of anti-immigrant nativism will shift to encompass the prevailing malaise."[34] Not surprisingly, then, at various moments over the course of the past century, the demonized immigrant in the US imaginary has served as strikebreaker, socialist and anarchist, depressor of wages, and, most recently, tax burden.[35] And as scapegoats, immigrants joined the other already identified scapegoats of the era, including multiculturalism, affirmative action, crack babies, teen mothers, and queer folks.

Of course, the central motif of Proposition 187—the immigrant as a leech on social services—emerged only *after* the social safety net had largely been dismantled by Reagan, and in a period of intense economic insecurity.[36] In other words, as the welfare state was dismantled, the resulting economic and cultural chaos was blamed on immigrants, said to have stretched the "system beyond capacity."[37] So Wilson could turn the tables on his conservative opponents and gain the upper hand in a political sphere that had been determined to dismantle his ambitions in part because he pulled on another set of strings undergirding cultural security. If the advent of campaigns against discrimination on the basis of sexuality signaled a shift in the social organization of capital relations, increased migration signaled that shift as well.

By the time propaganda like *Gay Rights, Special Rights* first began circulating, the storied nuclear family that it claimed needed protection could no longer function easily with only one wage earner. In short, when apparently childless, partially clothed gay men and women were dancing in the streets and demanding protection from discrimination and therefore seemingly threatening the viability of white heteropatriarchal families, the much-vaunted two-parent, single-breadwinner family structure was already under profound economic duress—a duress made fiercer by a series of recessions in the 1980s that caused most wage earners to feel their vulnerability to global economic change. It was in this political-economic climate that the battles over enlarging the concept of citizens' rights and guarding access to social services developed. Emerging from this context, traditional-values campaigns hooked together queers and migrants as threats to the heterosexual white family. Queers and migrants became easy villains or targets to blame for an already nearly completed transition to neoliberalism that had shredded the economic support structure undergirding a racialized (white supremacist) heteronormativity.

In their response to Wilson's signature on a gay rights bill, Lou Sheldon and others suggested that broadening the state's protective mechanisms to include protection against discrimination on the basis of sexuality threatened the heteronormative family structure and came at the expense of families. In a similar manner, Wilson turned the spotlight on working migrant laborers, arguing that the very presence of people without documents threatened the heteronormative family structure and came at the expense of families, further removing from blame or attention the increasingly globalized finance capital system wreaking havoc on every working and poor person on the planet.

By and large, the relationship I am outlining here between the homophobia surrounding AB101 and AB2601 and the subsequent anti-immigration fervor that Proposition 187 created and stoked has been ignored by historians and social scientists. Proposition 187's moniker, Save Our State, even echoed Anita Bryant's famous anti-gay campaign, Save Our Children, thereby reinforcing the link between the policing of sexuality as a means to reinscribe normative (white) heterosexuality and broader immigration control.[38] Yet none of the scholarship on AB101 and subsequent protests and none of the scholarship on the initiative Proposition 187 and its aftermath references the other bodies of scholarship.[39] Scholars studying Proposition 187 have tended to focus on the very significant economic problems in California at the moment when anti-immigration fever reached a new pitch and have ignored the protests over gay rights that engulfed Wilson's first two years in office.[40] While the declining economy enabled nativism to flourish, in skipping past Wilson's tussle first with party moderates in vetoing AB101 and then with party conservatives in subsequently signing AB2016 and thereby bringing a cascade of conservative criticism down upon his administration, immigration scholars miss a significant relay.[41] This relay illustrates that long-standing assumptions about the meaning of citizenship were already in play before Proposition 187 became more than a crackpot scheme. More important, the tangled, if subterranean, relationship between AB101 and Proposition 187 helped fuel mass anxiety over the status and stability of white heterosexual norms, often signaled by a melodramatic threat to the white child as stand-in for property and capital, and thereby encouraged the resurgence of nativism, in particular a nativism that focused on social reproduction.[42]

Too much is at stake here to simply ignore this lack of scholarly attention. This scant attention mirrors a problem Karma Chávez identifies as endemic to immigration studies more generally. As she points out, despite the centrality of sexuality to immigration policies and experience, "immigration scholarship virtually ignores connections among immigration, sexuality, and heteronormativity."[43] Part of the reason for this gap lies in how citizenship has been conceptualized and studied. Legal theorist Bosniak argues that citizenship studied as aspirational or endogenous perspective explores the "nature and quality of relations among presumed members of an already established society."[44] Or scholars may take up the "ways in which that community—usually a nation-state—is constituted and maintained *as* a community."[45] Citizenship is here understood as "rationed and the limitations on its availability mark the limitations on belonging."⁴⁶ Scholars studying what is sometimes called *sexual citizenship* or *gay rights* begin from the first perspective—from a discussion about what constitutes the relationship between presumed members of a society; immigration scholars, in contrast, usually begin from the second point of view—asking how a nation constitutes itself by the creation of an outside. Only a limited degree of interchange takes place between inward-looking and sometimes nationalist civil rights scholarship and boundary-conscious immigration scholarship. This lack of interchange between approaches means that in the effort to understand citizenship as a "commitment against subordination," many of the proponents of civil rights have not also considered how "citizenship can also represent an axis of subordination."⁴⁷ Scholarship on gay rights has not, then, fully contended with the boundedness of citizenship or with the extent to which, as Bosniak puts it, "noncitizen immigrants have entered the spatial domain of universal citizenship, but they remain outsiders in a significant sense: the border effectively follows them inside."⁴⁸

Not only does the border follow people around, but in the post–Proposition 187 world, citizenship has increasingly become a zero-sum game. Many gay rights advocates, as well as many scholars and activists intent on expanding the meaning of citizenship, often fail to acknowledge the fantasy of enmity, the set of exclusions on which citizenship depends and which constitute and vivify it.⁴⁹ But when they are forced to admit its constitutive exclusions, they understand them as relevant "out there" at the community's edges, on the other side of its walls. As Bosniak puts it, "It is in the very nature of alienage to bring those boundaries to bear in the territorial inside; alienage entails the introjection of borders."⁵⁰ Borders follow you everywhere, constituting conditions of possibility or obliterating them.

All Immigrants Are Queer, but Not All the Queers Are Immigrants

What, then, are the chains of equivalence connecting queers and their allies snarling rush-hour traffic a quarter century ago over a flailing politician's veto and the anti-immigration ballot proposition whose reverberations continue to structure US politics?⁵¹ If the causal or casual relationships between AB101 and Proposition 187 have been disregarded, immigration and gay rights are nevertheless now broadly linked in the US political imagination, thus giving Frank Rich, writing for the *New York Times*, the opportunity to joke that "Hispanics" are the new gays.⁵² Such a joke works because in many states anti-immigrant proposals have played tag with anti-gay-marriage or anti-gay-adoption proposals. Like bellowing twins, the ballot measures and legislation have shown up together, or in repeated iterations year after year, their sponsors angrily chasing fearful voters and successfully dividing people over differently perceived values. These ballot and legislative proposals have been successful wedge issues; they have worked together to produce a siege mentality and a nostalgia for what is imagined as a virtually extinct white and classically patriarchal middle-class family structure well serviced by the national economy and public policy.

Yet if nativism and homophobia are yoked, we should continue to do more to understand precisely how they assist each other. Two decades of scholarship on the subject has shown just how much ideas about sexuality have emerged through the management of the immigration process in the United States. For example, as Margot Canaday reveals in *The Straight State* (2009), welfare and immigration bureaucracies bloomed into existence and flourished in the United States by policing citizenship through exclusions based on homosexual practices or status.[53] Similarly, Eithne Luibhéid shows that sexual discourse around immigration, particularly antihomosexual discourse, has been used both to sustain and undermine existing social policies. In other words, "sexuality has long been a concern to the framers of US immigration law and policy, and it has consistently comprised an important axis for the regulation of newcomers."[54]

The US Border Patrol itself has also helped to develop these relays between sexuality and nation through border management. Not only did the nascent Border Patrol experiment with various concepts of manhood in a region that Alexandra Minna Stern argues has "long served as the stage for the articulation of hyper masculinity," but in framing its own mission as an effort to protect the national body and "the American family from unwanted intrusion," the Border Patrol snared the concepts of family, borders, and nation together in the service of militarism.[55] This not-uncommon move on the part of police agents of a state inscribes all of the actors in a sexual drama overwritten with patriotic and patriarchal rhetoric.[56] These processes of migration and immigration, sexual pleasure, sexuality, policing violence, and their various image repertoires invoke each other while repressing that invocation so that the one appears to have nothing to do with the others. Yet if current statistics are to be believed and the price of admission to the United States includes not just cash but rape, then the machinery to manage sexuality through migration continues to churn unabated.[57] Another way to say this is to say bluntly that in envisioning the Border Patrol as a protector of the American family, the Border Patrol's own mission statement enthralls its organization in narratives of sexual management and containment. Attacks on that mission necessarily engage sexuality as well as revenue collection.

The interstices between the study of civil rights and that of immigration enable the ongoing fortification of heterosexuality and heteronormativity through racialization, perhaps especially because it helps to hide the way US labor practices have historically isolated people of color from heteronormativity, queering them despite whatever claim to normativity and respectability they may seek. Indeed, such practices have their origin not just in chattel slavery but also in Spanish colonial organizational structures. Put differently, the constitution of the concept of Latinidad in the hemispheric racial imaginary has been laced with references to sexuality, beginning with the casta paintings and continuing through to contemporary representations. As feminist-of-color scholars have repeatedly taught, racialization entails sexualization; each instantiates or enacts the other: to see race is to know sex.[58] If the casta paintings were one of the earlier instances in which sex, reproduction, and race were linked as constitutive of this rubric called Latinx, three centuries later, and especially during the nineteenth century, the language of manifest destiny and the conceptualization of Latinidad in white popular culture were contoured through sex so that the invention of Latinx—the castagory's conjuring in the US imaginary as outsiders and as threats—entailed an invocation of excessive sexuality. This representation has further been stunted by cultural stereotypes of migrants. When Latinas are represented, they are typically visualized as mothers, toting, protecting, or feeding children, or they are represented as "hot" erotic objects, lascivious and hypersexual. Leo Chávez argues that Latinx have generally been characterized in the US media as a threat, as a group whose "loyalty to the nation, danger to the nation, and legitimate claims to membership in the nation" characterize them as a coercive and threatening invading force.[59] Part and parcel of this myth, Chávez argues, is the characterization of Latinas as hyperfertile and hypersexual; such accounts of fertility help justify the conspiracy theory that Latinx aim to reconquer the Southwest. Viewed as hypersexual, Latinas threaten to entrap men. Such a representation appears repeatedly in the national media; Latinas, Mary Romero notes, are frequently associated with animals that breed excessively and are even more dehumanized by virtue of their participation in a supposed culture of immorality and deceit.[60]

This sexualization continues to subtend images of migrant border crossing, whether these images are homoerotic or homosocial, whether they invite rape fantasies or empathetic pathos or seem to combine some set of fantasies and threats. Thus, while migrant Latinx are rarely represented as explicitly gay, their sociality is depicted as extra-ordinary, a depiction that *New York Times* columnist David Brooks has no problem underscoring. In a column advocating restrictive new immigration measures, Brooks conjures this portrait of a befuddled white Texan: "He's no racist. Many of his favorite neighbors are kind, neat and hard-working Latinos. But his neighborhood now has homes with five cars rotting in the front yard and 12 single men living in one house. . . . He read in the local paper last week that Anglos are now a minority in Texas and [he] wonders if anybody is in charge of this social experiment. . . . What we can do is re-establish law and order, so immigrants can bring their energy to this country without destroying the social fabric while they're here."[61] Put aside the point that Brooks undoubtedly doesn't know whether these men are single or not. Put aside as well the disavowal of racism that initiates a racist rant. Focus instead on the relay Brooks conjures between "12 single men living in one house" alongside "five rotting cars." The rotting cars are meant to signal a slovenly poverty, dead-enders functioning without the domesticating value of women, inhabitants of a home who do not properly value property. Further, the demographic shift is called a "social experiment," and the implication is that immigrants destroy the existing social fabric (i.e., twelve single men living together in one house) and that their presence undoes "law and order" (signaled by the abandoned cars). The singleness of the men works in relay with the unstated implication that the men are living in the United States without formal documents. Their sociality is queer or nonnormative by implication; their ontological status is illegal by implication. The relays between these statuses—the ideological traffic between immigration status and sexuality—do not have to be explicit to function visciously.

Brooks's complaint that male migrant workers live in clusters without the domesticating presence of women ignores the historical effort in the United States to disentangle racialized labor power from heterosexual social relations and then to blame the resulting homosocial structures on the laborers as if they are somehow deviant. Consider, for example, (1) chattel slavery's prohibition of heterosexual family sociality among enslaved groups; (2) the 1882 Exclusion Act, which essentially prohibited Chinese women from immigrating to the United States and so created what came to be called "bachelor" societies of Chinese male laborers; and (3) the Bracero program's disaggregating of Mexican male laborers from their broader sociality.[62] Such state-engineered socialities subsequently get narrated in various ways, of course, but men in these constructs have consistently been labeled nonnormative, rendered either unmasculine or hypersexual. Sutured into US labor practices is a habit, so to speak, of isolating nonwhite men from heteronormativity, of, in a sideways manner, queering men of color, particularly men on the move.

Two other aspects of Brooks's screed bear attention. His complaint about the single men relies on not only homophobia to intensify his audience's distaste, to underscore his image of the nonnormativity of the living arrangements (after all, if he had wished to render the men "normal," he might have called their home a fraternity), but also the long-debunked stereotype of gay men as hypersexual predators. He doesn't need to articulate that stereotype to invoke it—its cultural prevalence maintains its power and familiarity. The second point has been made repeatedly by political economists but should be underscored as well. That is, the US preference for male laborers unaccompanied by kin reflects the ongoing practice of shuffling the costs of social reproduction onto another country. As one scholar notes, this shuffle allows "the costs of reproducing the migrant labor force to be totally hidden with the economic, social and psychic costs transferred to a different location and state."[63]

A crucial part of the problem is that a well-cultivated but hidden homophobia underpins anti-immigrant sentiment—not simply because immigration has been managed through the regulation of sexuality, thereby cementing the link, but also because the anti-immigrant narrative builds on homophobia even when it does not articulate such homophobia explicitly. Thus, artwork and literature that bring into focus the interanimating relationship between sexuality and citizenship, and between homophobia and nativism, are particularly relevant and valuable to study.

Visualizing Immigration Askew

Despite state policy and the mass media treatment of immigrants, artists and writers over the past two decades have readily and provocatively explored immigration. In doing so, they have engaged with the representation of migrants in the mainstream media by tangling with that representation. These creative efforts are unsettling because they reveal crucial aspects of the way sexuality, implicated as social reproduction, structures migration, refusing to adhere to the conventional ways in which migration and civil rights are studied and discussed. They see not an interstice between frameworks but a relay between interanimating structures. This enables them to highlight immigration control's dependence on sex.[64]

John Sonsini has been particularly interested in this relay between sex and migration, between civil rights and border control.[65] Since the late 1990s,

Sonsini has exhibited a series of portraits of day laborers whom his lover, Gabriel Barajas, originally a schoolteacher from Michoacán, hires from a corner near their local Home Depot. Sonsini typically pays his subjects standard daylaborer wages.[66] At his first Manhattan show in 2005, these paintings, most of them six by seven feet, sold for $20,000 to $70,000. His work is now in major US collections, including those of the Solomon R. Guggenheim Museum and the Whitney Museum of American Art.

Day laborers might at first glance appear to be an unusual choice of subject. They have been reviled in the press, by politicians, and by hate groups and have been the subject of intense zoning campaigns across the United States. Day laborers spend hours on street corners, waiting for odd jobs and work in construction—hauling debris, painting, or cleaning. Some wait all day without luck, only to show up again the next morning hoping to secure a job for the day.[67] As researchers suggest,

> Day laborers are among the most vulnerable of the immigrant working populations in the United States. Day labor is a highly precarious employment arrangement.... Employment agreements are unwritten and difficult to enforce, and redressing violations of labor standards is difficult to achieve. In the United States, as in many other countries, day labor serves as a point of entry into the labor market for migrant workers. However, the exploitive nature of the day labor economy makes subsistence within, as well as mobility out of, this labor market and into more formalized sectors extremely difficult to achieve and it hinders the economic incorporation of day laborers.[68]

So Sonsini's choice to paint los esquineros, day laborers, is a complex one. One could argue that these day laborers are the vanguard of the gig economy; they are the epitome of what corporations glibly describe as flexible labor practices. Rarely earning a living wage, these laborers are precarious in every sense of the word; their employers pay no attention to employment law, and the laborers themselves do not have easy recourse for redress when they experience dangerous conditions or wage theft. As the highly visible sign of migration from Mexico and Central America, they also stand in as the image of a neoliberal economy writ across the hemisphere. And just as their status as flexible makes day laborers enticing to employers—employers make no commitment to long-term employment, no commitment to getting to know their employees, to registering a relation of affiliation with the employees and their larger networks, as the laborers exist for the day's job alone—Sonsini's choice to focus on day laborers enacts a similar dubious, flexible practice. His paintings render the subjects as without context, as aestheti-

FIGURE 4.1. Day laborers by John Sonsini. From John Sonsini, *John Sonsini Exhibition Catalog*.

cally flexible. Sonsini uses the same model repeatedly. The same man may sit for several individual portraits as well as stand in several group portraits. This repetition has the effect of abstracting individual subjects, and their abstraction subtly emphasizes their iterability, their status as $N + 1$.[69] The effect is of serial laborers, iterations of one another, flattened images outside of all sociality.

Los esquineros appear in Sonsini's paintings alone and in groups. Lushly painted, the portraits are fraught with homoerotic possibilities and tensions, a homoerotics signaled by the *New York Times* when it primly notes the artist's

"Whitmanesque affection" for his subjects.[70] Sonsini offers these figures on a strange crosscut plane. They wear giant shoes, way out of proportion to their physical frames. In some portraits it is the hands that are outsized—their magnificence resting against seemingly shrunken frames. This makes the viewer perceive the figures at a kind of distancing slant; their heads are comparably tiny in contrast to the dominant capaciousness of the shoes or hands, and their nearly generic forms against the white, unpainted canvas shrink the men. This shrinking sets up a contradiction between their status as laborers, signaled by their strong, muscular poses with tightly dressed shoulders, and their shrunken frames. Their heads are also rendered tinier by virtue of their muscular necks. To some extent, this odd hyperexaggeration intensifies the apparent pathos implied by the somber faces. None of the men smile; it is difficult to know what they are thinking and feeling.

In classical portraiture the objects accompanying the figure indicate the subject's status, wealth, or interests; these objects are intricately necessary for individuation. In other words, they provide a kind of authorization of the figure portrayed; they provide documentation, authorization. Bereft of any of the typical tools of portraiture used to provide biography (no hunting dogs, kids, mansions in the background) or other clues to their individuality, Sonsini's subjects are apparently impenetrable. They don't hold tools. They stand without context. As in nineteenth-century photographs of American Indians, Sonsini's figures are without individuating signs. The only objects to appear regularly in his paintings are suitcases and backpacks. The laborers' clothes are unmemorable. Thus, the figures are, as it were, undocumented. We know they are day laborers only because the exhibition material, catalog, and press reports tell us so. In a gallery filled with these paintings, the effect is not of portraits of individuals but of blended subjects visually abstracted into the category of laborer by the accompanying narrative. The washed, unfinished, and disappearing backdrops behind them reinforce this tenuous and ephemeral quality of the figures themselves.

The catalog for the first New York show offers biographical details that identify some sitters' home countries and their language proficiencies. For example, the catalog tells us that Manuel speaks a "a rather ancient Mayan dialect which is native to his region [of Guatemala] but he does speak a bit of conventional Spanish as well."[71] The catalog constitutes Manuel as a relic, a contemporary ancestor, yet this detail describes a Manuel that is nowhere to be found in the catalog itself; he is not identified as present in any of the paintings reproduced in the catalog.

Claiming a lack of interest in politics but a stake in a humanist account of his subjects as beings worthy of art, Sonsini sees himself as challenging the history of portraiture and its focus on the wealthy elite even as he wishes to see his "artistry" as the important contribution. The exquisite quality of the paintings emerges in part through their metaquality. The paintings call attention to themselves as paintings; the brushstrokes and the colors are built up on the body of the laborers as if the men work to call attention not to themselves as subjects but to the painting of them, to the paintings as art. Further belying Sonsini's claim that he has no stake in politics is his obvious participation in the discursive processes that endow his paintings with meaning. Why else indeed would he go to so much trouble to underscore his sitters' relationship to citizenship as he does in the catalog discussion? In this sense, Sonsini draws attention to the modes of representation that frame los esquineros, offering an implicit challenge to those modes by drawing attention to them; he nevertheless participates in an ongoing coloniality in which sociality is continuously subsumed into the next level of global scaling: $N + 1$.[72]

By disappearing context and floating his subjects, Sonsini remands his viewers to the moon. By evacuating specificity from his subjects, Sonsini ultimately underscores the logic that keeps day laborers vulnerable. The figures can replace each other; they stand for a concept; they are mere iterations of each other. The supposed intimacy of the portraits works because of the extent to which the mechanics of migration depend on scale, on a process of rationalizing people with ideas, dreams, kinship networks, and commitments into the content-free category of migrant. The sparseness of Sonsini's visual grammar and vocabulary emphasizes this iterability further. What he achieves, then, perhaps contra his stated intentions, is to draw attention to the lack of background or context allowed migrants. Their anonymity underscores their vulnerability.

Further differentiating Sonsini's representation of immigrants and migrants is the absence not only of the typical mother-child pietà but of children entirely. No photograph of a small child peeks out from a bag, no suggestion of a gift, a toy, tenderly collected for a loved one. This representation of adult men who appear childless further abstracts them from socialities, delinks them from the mesh of connectivity that forms so much of the substance of living. Were they soldiers, then the absence of enfolding care networks—small children or the signs of their presence—would be less expected. To some extent, then, this portrayal not only isolates the figures but de-adults them; it strips them of the signals that implicitly name responsibilities, possessions, affections. Childless but childlike, they are remanded to the position of subservience, cut off from the discourses of development and rectitude that underpin eligibility for citizenship. These men, too, are cast-off children.

But what of that Whitmanesque affection? These portraits emerge for us through subtle clues as homoerotic objects; the figures' butch postures, their well-dressed shoulders reminiscent of gay porn, seem to push back against the enclosing vulnerability rendered through painterly manipulations. The subtle erotic tensions within the paintings are magnetized not simply by the manner in which the men's poses allude to the muscle men of gay erotica but also, more important, by the subjects' relationship to US entry regulations. The figures' immigration status, their vulnerability, is used to eroticize them. The effect of the portraits, their status as art, depends on understanding the figures as lacking formal documents in the first place.[73] Without naming the migrants as queer, Sonsini returns us to this long history of US labor management in which workers are unwillingly extracted into a state-constructed homosociality only to be pathologized as nonnormative, as twelve single men in a house. However problematically he gets us there, Sonsini's art asks us to revise Frank Rich's quip that "Hispanics are the new gays." Practically speaking, in terms of US labor practices, "Hispanics" have always been queer.

Scale Can Seduce

It may be a bit surprising to find Sonsini's approach somewhat validated in the work of poet Eduardo Corral, a winner of prestigious prizes, who similarly takes up the figure of "the jornalero," or day laborer. Corral's collection *Slow Lightning*, published in 2012 as part of the Yale Series of Younger Poets, is breathtaking. In these poems AIDS, ICE, love, and desire move around and with each other; the poetic portraits of estrangement nurture joy in surprising ways, offering playful engagements with present poetry's pasts. The center of the collection is a long rewriting of José Montoya's "El Louie," entitled "Variation on a Theme by José Montoya"; elsewhere, Corral names and invokes poets such as Lorna Dee Cervantes and visual artist Esthér Hernandez.[74]

Like Sonsini, Corral also muses on the erotic possibilities of a male figure on the move. And to some extent he, too, empties the space surrounding the figure. Just as Sonsini's figures float vaguely, their identities and connections stripped from the visual grammar of portraiture, just as viewers are given no web of connections with which to understand the men sitting and standing before Sonsini's brush, so, too, in "To a Jornalero Cleaning Out My Neighbor's Garage" Corral seems to offer a stripped portrait of a figure whose experiences, relationships, and aspirations cannot be known. Corral dedicates his poem to this unnamed jornalero, offering an immediate structure of (dis)identification as the poem begins:

> You are nothing like my father.
>   And like my father
> you are nothing.
>   Zambo. Castizo.
> Without draft animals
>   the Mexica used the wheel
>   only as a toy.[75]

If the jornalero's position reminds the speaker of his own father's experiences as a migrant laborer, he nonetheless refuses to conflate the two men. Here the unnamed, undescribed jornalero is not quite Sonsini's figure. The poet insists on recognizing the jornalero, if only through the admission of another relationship. But the second nothingness that Corral asserts here is harder to decipher. Perhaps it can be read as "no-thing." This would suggest the poem critiques the treatment of the hardworking man as a thing—as an object. With this meditative observation, the poet takes two surprising turns, shifting focus to coloniality and to the casta system that Spain introduced in order to collate people, property, and rights. Does "Zambo" here describe either the jornalero or Corral's father? Does it refer obliquely to the treatment and rights of people of mixed African and Native descent? A status named as if to enclose. At the very least, this invocation of a caste system reminds readers of the way sexuality subtends coloniality as well as contemporary labor policy. The subsequent shift is even more evocative. Is this an implicit comparison between the jornalero or the poet's father and a draft animal? In naming an immensely prosperous culture, the Mexica, does he here suggest a counter to Spanish and US colonial practices? Certainly, the move links Spanish castagories to present-day US labor practices and implies that the poet's gaze is mediated by ongoing coloniality—a coloniality indicated by the authoritative warning about borders and limits: "Please keep off the lawn."[76]

This practice—not of disidentification but of dis/objectification—continues as the speaker recalls a moment in graduate school when a prospective landlord sees him, not as a graduate student at a prestigious writers' workshop, but as a farm laborer working the strawberry harvest. The chain of resonances between the unnamed jornalero and the poet's own experiences renders the laborer knowable and familiar, at the very least recognizable as a human living within a web of relationships. This memory of the racist assumption then folds into an erotic reverie in which the poet imagines caressing the jornalero's fingers only to have the erotic object (figured as a pomegranate) transform into a weapon of destruction (a grenade). The grenade leads to a second round of musing on racism as the poet quotes a misbegotten slur molded into a child's word game and then humorously quotes Américo Paredes's authoritative work on corridos, *With His Pistol in His Hand,* to dismiss the slur as beneath the dignity of an expert crafter of words.

Sonsini may wish to humanize his subjects, to bestow on them the grandeur of portraiture, a grandeur typically the province of the wealthy. Yet in molding his subjects through a form of iterability, refusing to grant them the distinction of individuality (which is not singularity), he removes them back into the category of in-distinction, of mass and object or category. Corral, by contrast, suggests that we pursue a clearer relationship. The poet suggests that desire and estrangement compose each other, that to see the jornalero is not to see a laborer merely but to see the web of processes and relationships that compose each person. It is with this argument that the poem closes:

> You walk out with a French horn in your arms
>   And you're a butcher
> in El Dorado holding
>   the golden entrails of cattle.[77]

The unnamed laborer pulls a French horn out of the garage, and the poet transfigures him into a mystical figure floating in a jumble of myths while simultaneously invoking the work of the US meatpacking industry, which has become wholly dependent on immigrant labor.

"To a Jornalero" samples Chicana feminist poet Angela de Hoyos; poet, novelist, and scholar Américo Paredes; and British Renaissance poet Michael Drayton. These multiple, interspersed voices seem to come out of the garage along with the French horn—turning the poem into a sort of storage shed but also placing the speaker and the jornalero within a shared mesh of relations, thereby refuting the jornalero's status as "alien," "inhuman," or, indeed, "castizo," even as the poem conflates the stuff in the garage with the repertoire of literary texts the poem samples.[78] Here Corral invokes the discourse of the United States as the land of riches—ironically recalling the mystical El Dorado that had lured explorers for three centuries and that now lures hardworking people to risk their lives, only to find themselves performing even riskier tasks (working, for example, as a butcher or meatpacker in El Dorado, California, or El Dorado, Arkansas). Through this web of connection, the poet suggests a complicated sensibility: the jornalero's destiny is bound up with the speaker's and with the poem's readers'. Corral invokes a witnessing that does not tend toward empathy, with all of the traps of condescension such empathy can enable (even as empathy is necessary for complex collaboration); rather, the poem suggests a witnessing that connects suffering to the longer history of coloniality and to the most recent search for El Dorado, a metaphorical name for the current round of global recapitalization at Latin America's expense.

Like Sonsini's paintings, Corral's poems speak to one another as well. His father's story, referenced obliquely in "To a Jornalero," is given a more explicit account in "Want." And, again, in "Want" Corral insists on linking the courage that migration entails to the courage that desire, sexual and otherwise, requires. The poem describes the speaker's father crossing the rabid heat of the Sonoran Desert, cut by the sharp spines of cholla cacti and, in desperation, finding a lizard to eat:

> he tore it
> apart, shoved guts & bones
> into his mouth the first
> time I knelt for a man, my
> lips pressed to his zipper,
> I suffered   such hunger[79]

"Want" asks readers to imagine the edges of vibrancy, the strains of survival that threaten to stop their whispers, to consider a moment in which breathing is a task to be achieved, not called to mind, and in which the father's experience of bare finitude blooms before the speaker as the relay between his lunge into pleasure and the conditions that structure it. Formally, the poems suggest the bridging work analogies seek to do. The gaps between words suggest not just line breaks, or breaks in ideas, but gaps that must be anticipated, crossed, bridged. They suggest unaccommodating, empty, and maybe treacherous desert spaces.

Corral's portrait of his father's desperate act could be said to respatialize the migrants that Sonsini and the US media strip of context. In other words, what Sonsini offers, in portraying migrant men as nearly floating in space, as without background, as iterative substitutes for each other, is a depersonalized vision of migration. Not only are the men taken out of context—no cities, no ranchos, no communities to link them to a larger history—but, like the men in the Bracero program in the mid-twentieth century or Chinese laborers in the nineteenth century, they are also identified and classed through a kind of homosocial practice that strips them of a larger relativity. In some sense, Sonsini's figures comprise the very vision offered by David Brooks's "12 single men living in one house."

By contrast, Corral asserts relationality, connection: "my father." He searches for ways to identify with his father's experience, to understand migration and its attendant dangers in analogous terms. This movement enables him to ground his experiences together with those of migrant men. Desire plays an interesting role here. For Sonsini, the portraits offer the opportunity for empathy. In attempting to humanize and dignify migrant men, he relies on a strand of the politics of respectability bedeviling liberality. Corral, by contrast, does not consider the question of respectability, nor does he appear, at least in these poems, interested in empathy precisely. It's as if he is saying, "not that migrants are *like* us"—a position that could implicitly maintain their status as other—but rather that we *are* them. He unshackles empathy and respectability from analogy; his poems suggest not that one person can care about another person, but that both people recognize that their futures and their presents are inherently interlinked and interdependent, bound together. They are indebted to one another.

And yet, like Sonsini, Corral engages his portrait of migrants through a reference to erotic desire. This move implicitly acknowledges the extent to which immigration has been managed in terms of sexuality. It acknowledges that, to some extent, immigrants are always queered, rendered nonnormative. It further signals the history of discursive construction of Latinidad *through* sexuality and perhaps subtly explains the emphasis in so much Latino writing portraying the hyperheterosexuality of Latinos in general.[80] It may well also explain the reticence of many scholars to spell out, to seriously investigate, this ongoing relationship between the construction of Latinidad and sexuality, particularly a sexuality that the US nation-state has a stake in rendering nonnormative. At the very least, the contrasts among Sonsini, Corral, and even Brooks and the work of two Latina novelists are worth examining because they attend to this question of social reproduction and take the relay between sex and transnational movement very seriously.

Remember the Women

When visual artists such as Sonsini or poets like Corral step into the process of representing migrant experiences, they, like media and migration scholarship more generally, focus on the experiences of men. And while Sonsini and Corral shift away from one dominant portrayal of migrants—as animals who threaten—Sonsini and, to a lesser extent, Corral maintain the perception that migrants are mostly men. This image persists despite the fact that women comprise an increasingly larger percentage of migrants worldwide and despite the vociferous arguments from feminist scholars of migration that the experiences of women and migration as a gendered phenomenon have been woefully understudied. Obviously, the lack of attention not only reinforces the concept that most migrants are men but also reinscribes the homosocial account of migration, the notion that migrants move without reference to broader relations of intimacy.

That migration studies are inflected by gender—that is, that men and women experience migration differently—should not be a surprise. Women are more commonly portrayed in migration scholarship, according to Caroline Archambault, as "left behind."[81] Migration scholarship, she and other scholars point out, depends for its models on an image of the young, male migrant, searching for wage labor. Women in this model are viewed as beside the point, merely passive bystanders to male decisions. As she notes, this image of women reinscribes a patriarchal narrative of women as passive agents in a system of movement in which they are prohibited from participating because of the high costs of social reproduction. The "left behind" narrative also tends to be subtended by the urban/rural narrative, in which the rural is understood to be outside of the modern. This narrative also ignores the many reasons women may choose not to migrate, just as it ignores how male migrant networks tend to limit how much information about the physics of migration is shared thereby keeping the technology of migrating gendered as well. Put differently, migration scholars argue that women face very different hurdles when migrating, and a vastly different set of narratives accompanies those hurdles. That does not mean, however, that women don't migrate.

Certainly within US popular culture, the portrayal of Latina migrants has been extremely limited, even though the experience of migration has been a central subject of Latinx literature. Influential texts such as Ernesto Galarza's *Barrio Boy* (1971), Julia Alvarez's *How the García Girls Lost Their Accent* (1991), Angie Cruz's *Let It Rain Coffee* (2005), and Cristina García's *Dreaming in Cuban* (2004) focus on migration. They also evoke that experience from the perspective of a child and the experience of a childhood shaped by the repetitive erection of many types of boundaries.

Yet only recently have writers begun to focus on the experiences of young girls migrating to the United States alone and without state consent. This strand of writing expands the cultural understanding of a significant and shaping experience. Reyna Grande's *Across a Hundred Mountains* (2006) and Bettina Restrepo's *Illegal* (2011) provide moving portraits of young women who must cross the US-Mexico border without formal papers, young women who are not mothers but would not be called adults either; they draw together a set of complex issues encompassing the costs of migration, the social transformations mass migration has wrought, and the problematics of sexuality within the migration-for-profit industry. In these novels Restrepo and Grande offer another side to the anti-immigrant dehumanization campaign initiated by Pete Wilson and Bill Clinton and resist the iterative characterization that scales young women out of the frameworks of the human, the citizen, or the migrant. And while the two novels provide a crucial corrective to the "left behind" narrative, they offer much more than that. They map a portion of the complex economy of migration and explore how intricately gender and sexuality figure into migration, into the mechanics of migration. They do so while also tapping the layers of affective relations that media coverage about migration has yet to unearth. If they challenge the left-behind myth, both novels also demand that we pay attention to another form of leaving: the deaths that go unacknowledged, untraced, because no one knows the dead migrant, no one either finds or identifies the body. In this manner, both novels outline the shaping force of death that contours and scales migration and the narrative traffic built into it.

Curiously, both novels, although not as dramatically as Sonsini's paintings or Corral's poems, also omit a kind of background to their tales. While they provide compelling accounts of family stories, *Illegal* and *Across a Hundred Mountains* do not outline, much less hint at, the context of their stories: the devastating consequences of border militarization and the neoliberalization of the US and Mexican economies. Instead, they offer dramatic illustrations of how such economic and political changes are experienced and interpreted. Yet their stories, like Sonsini's paintings and Corral's poems, exist in tension with the very same dynamics that structure anti-immigration fervor and family-values campaigns funded by conservative organizations. That is, these two novels necessarily grapple with the great new right's awakening that followed AB101 and resulted in Proposition 187's violent reimagining of the borders of the nation, the borders of belonging, and, ultimately, the borders of being within the nation-state.

When the Border Became a Mass Grave

If the new right targeted Pete Wilson, they also repeatedly linked the newly elected Bill Clinton to partying and parading queer activists. Already under attack by conservatives for his apparent support for broader sexual freedom, concerned that Proposition 187 demonstrated wide crossover appeal for voters, and cognizant of his need to hold onto California's electoral votes, Clinton appropriated the anxiety about immigration, all the while decrying what he characterized as the antihumanitarian aspects of Proposition 187 (even though his own evacuation of welfare would mimic its prescriptions two years later). In the very heat of the Proposition 187 campaign, Clinton sent attorney general

Janet Reno to visit California, where she announced the new federal program Operation Gatekeeper.[82]

Operation Gatekeeper emerged as a new form of border policing. The Border Patrol began massing agents at popular crossing points on the US-Mexico border, effectively funneling people into the treacherous terrain of the Sonoran Desert, where they had to cross large stretches of desert on foot.[83] Operation Gatekeeper became a centerpiece of Clinton's reelection campaign; it was then welcomed and augmented by George Bush as part of the post-9/11 security apparatus and has now become the condition of impossibility for many thousands of people. Since its inception, on average, one person has died every single day trying to cross the US-Mexico border. Occasionally these deaths gain national attention, as when eleven skeletons were found in a railroad car in the Midwest months after the car had entered the United States, or as when a Border Patrol agent transported a body like a hood ornament across the desert. But most often these deaths go unnoted in the mainstream media. They occur in an underdeveloped region of the country; they occur regularly, most frequently from spring through early fall, during what one human rights activist calls "the dying season."[84]

Operation Gatekeeper prepared the terrain for the consequences NAFTA would set rolling. Because the end of the Cold War coincided with the ongoing crisis in Fordist manufacturing, employers sought to alleviate their collapsing business models by seeking new supplies of cheaper, more precarious labor. Forcing more women into the wage-labor market provided one new source of relatively inexpensive labor. Unions especially worried that NAFTA would create a significantly larger pool of labor, fearing that corporations supported the trade deal because it would provide both new markets for their products and new sources of less protected labor. For this reason, trade unions and foes of immigration alike welcomed Operation Gatekeeper and the coercive new immigration laws that followed two years later. The program helped reassure nervous constituents by ensuring the free movement of finance and commodities but constraining the mobility of labor.

The trade deal demanded Mexico make dramatic constitutional changes, and farmers felt the first wave of that transformation. Before NAFTA, Mexico had relied on its network of small farm collectives, ejidos, to provide the basic grains and proteins for the country; in turn, its farmers relied on a stable price system to sustain their farms. The trade deal undid this system and forced Mexico to allow large-scale grain imports while also removing price supports on basic commodities such as beans and corn. The immediate result was that people in Mexico grew hungrier as food became more expensive and farmers fled to cities in search of work and new sources of livelihoods. Individual farmers had to sell their shares in their ejidos, and large US agribusinesses quickly nabbed the land to create farms on an industrial scale. Thus, NAFTA forced rural farmers from their homes and to the new factories in northern border states; when these were shuttered as the factories moved to China, workers fled to the United States to search again for a new source of income. The United States gained a new market for its corn and wheat and a new set of laborers desperate to work and willing to do so at substandard wages, thereby creating new pools of profitability to fund the massive US expansion into technology and global finance. Put bitterly, Operation Gatekeeper gifted unions with new gains: it resulted in the massive expansion of unions for border policing, detention-center policing, and prison policing, while the global finance industry also welcomed a profoundly enhanced new revenue stream: remittances.

Across a Hundred Mountains and *Illegal* explore how both NAFTA and Operation Gatekeeper transformed the lives of ordinary Mexicanos. Grande's sprawling and formally interesting novel follows the experiences of a young cast-out child, Juana, born in a small town in the southern Mexican state of Guerrero. As the story opens, Juana's infant sister perishes in a flood; amid the family's grief, her father departs for the United States, where he hopes to find work to pay off the greedy mortician who prepared his daughter for burial. The child's burial costs only intensify a poverty his work as a farm laborer cannot relieve. Spiraling from abject poverty to even more intensive misery, Juana and her mother barely survive for months, hearing not a word of their father/husband. Eventually the mortician demands that Juana's mother repay the debt with sex and then steals Juana's newly born brother as a "final" payment. Grief-stricken and furious, Juana's mother murders the mortician. Juana then leaves for the border and Los Angeles, hoping to find her father and rescue her mother from madness. Prevented by youth and poverty from paying a coyote enough to take her across, she takes up sex work in order to sustain herself while she questions various coyotes about her long-absent father. Only after more than nineteen years of searching, only after entering the United States by ingenious means, only after she has pursued an education and taken up work as a social worker for a domestic violence center, does she find her father. He had been bitten by a snake and died trying to enter the United States. When the coyote who buried her father shows her his remains, she recognizes a small rosary buried with her father. The novel closes as she takes her father's ashes back to her dying mother and claims a new relationship with her younger brother.

Across a Hundred Mountains hints at the devastation that Mexican farmers faced in the wake of NAFTA when it recounts how Juana's father, Miguel, revealed to her that he would be leaving for the United States. The young girl accompanies her parents to a spot where her father would frequently "point to the crops in the distance and tell them how much he'd harvested that day." But on this particular trip, Miguel shifts her attention to houses with electricity and notes that "when it rains, the houses never get flooded, and the roofs don't leak, and the people stay warm."[85] Of course, such a home would be appealing to a family that had just been devastated by a flood and whose home is one of many "little shacks made out of bamboo sticks and cardboard, some leaning against one another like little old ladies tired after a long walk."[86] Juana is too young to understand her father's logic and is perplexed: "Those houses made of brick and concrete had never existed for them before. Only the stalks of corn swaying in the breeze, only the orange, red, and purple hues of the setting sun, only the river snaking its way around the mountains, had mattered."[87] Miguel insists that his daughter see the material commodities they lack, acknowledge their precarity, as a way to justify the expense, the cost of his departure from her. Her father subsequently describes the enormous amount of corn he had harvested that day, but this does not undermine his larger point. It does not matter how much corn he had harvested that day; it would not be enough to provide basic shelter. Despite their sense of commitment to their lands, NAFTA had impoverished them to the point of starvation.

To further convince his daughter that migration provides their best option, Miguel shows her a letter: "Apá's friend wrote about riches unheard of, streets that never end, and buildings that nearly reach the sky. He wrote that there's so much money to be made, and so much food to eat, people there don't know what hunger is."[88] In spelling out the complex equation people must make between survival and the immense risk of crossing the border, a risk that Operation Gatekeeper seeks to make insurmountable but has succeeded only in making more expensive and more dangerous, the novel shows the alluring function of border-crossing propaganda. Yet a young Juana does not embrace this logic and begs her father to stay. In response, he compresses the risk and the distance: "El Otro Lado is over there, on the other side of those mountains.... I won't be that far from you. When you feel that you need to talk to your Apá, just look toward the mountains, and the wind will carry your words to me."[89] This compression of distance reinforces the fantasy her father has already spun. Shortly thereafter, he leaves, and Juana never hears from him again.

Much of the novel follows the struggles Juana and her mother subsequently face. Having lost Miguel's income and not receiving any remittances, the two struggle to survive as their neighbors ruthlessly tease them that Miguel has found another woman and has abandoned them. *Across a Hundred Mountains* insists on an unsympathetic portrayal of rural Mexico within the structure of the migrant system—just as the two women, mother and daughter, feel abandoned, the village must contend with the forced migration of its population. The village experiences many losses, many shifts in relationships, and a strained dependence on a system of promises through exploitation. The novel offers a portrait of a town drained of its inhabitants, where children taunt other children about their missing family members, where rather than acknowledging their vulnerability to a vicious system, children "make a mockery out of [each other's] pain."[90] But if the novel portrays Juana initially as "left behind," it neither drains her of agency nor leaves her simply abandoned. Instead, it shows Juana's resilient efforts to survive, to take care of her devastated mother, and to build a network of care that would sustain them. It subsequently shows her systematically preparing for her own departure, after her mother is sent to prison.

Through an interesting formal innovation, *Across a Hundred Mountains* portrays two young women, Juana and Adelina, in alternating chapters. At crucial points their stories begin to converge even as they are formally juxtaposed with half-page chapters opposing each other across the book's centerfold. Suggesting the relationship between the two evolving stories of Juana and Adelina is a kind man who tells a homeless Adelina where she can find shelter in Los Angeles. He points out that the moon has two faces: "She only shows one face to the world. Even though it changes shape constantly, it's always the same face we see. But her second face, her second face remains hidden in darkness. That's the face no one can see. People call it the dark side of the moon. Two identities. Two sides of a coin."[91] This description of the moon gestures toward the main conceit of the novel; only toward the end do readers learn that the two girls, Juana and Adelina, are actually the same person. Juana has assumed her friend Adelina's identification by taking her birth certificate after her murder. While the text is plotted as if it is pursuing the course of two distinct lives, it ultimately shows that one life has been doubled and turned like the moon. This conceit also reflects Adelina's struggle to integrate her labor in the sex industry with her desire to pursue a relationship with a caring Chicano doctor. But this image of doubleness also suggests the interanimating relationship between the United States and Mexico, just as it exemplifies the extent to which people have been rendered objects that speak, commodities: "two sides of a coin." The phrase also underscores the indebtedness to contemporary conditions of servitude that the formal economies of both nations obscure through recourse to legality, rendering invisible the "face no one can see," the people who are compelled to move without protection and who labor for others' benefit.

If Grande shows the force of desperation that stokes so many decisions to migrate as well as the costs to families and towns that must accommodate a brutal labor system, she also takes up another image, that of the thief, to challenge the representation of migrants. Living in the equivalent of a cardboard shack, Juana and her parents must navigate an unreliable river that, the narrator notes, sometimes "swelled so much the water would overflow, creeping into the shacks like un ladrón."[92] The river steals Juana's little sister from her sleeping arms. Later, another migrant father uses the image to describe to his young daughter how they will enter the United States: "We must go like thieves."[93] Just as Juana later appropriates a newly deceased Adelina's papers, assumes Adelina's legality, and crosses without difficulty into the United States to continue her search for her father, the language of law, the sinews of force and constraint indicated by various forms of thievery, of compliance and refusal, continually asks readers to wrestle with the violence of a hemispheric economy that may best be described as a form of cannibalism, a consumption of people through servitude. Who, the novel prompts, is actually the thief?

By representing the effects of migration on women, *Across a Hundred Mountains* does not flinch in showing how it affects and strains kinship ties. Yet it goes much further than so much migration scholarship by portraying a young girl's experience of migrating, of traveling alone, without any support. This portion of the novel illustrates how much strength of will is necessary for a cast-out child to migrate alone—Juana can count on no help, must make do with little food and less money, must hope for the friendly assistance of strangers. When she reluctantly begins work in the sex industry, she does so with none of her father's romanticism. She sees this as labor that provides her with the necessary flexibility to search for her father as well as with the access needed to question the coyotes she hopes will lead her to him. Her choice, if realistic, may replicate stereotypes of Latinas as hypersexual, but in linking Juana's hypervulnerability to her decision to earn a living via sex work Grande refutes the sentimentality that helps lock women into a patriarchal structure in the first place. Further, she underscores that Juana makes her own constrained decision, refuting the anti-sex work hysteria that accompanies so many normative narratives about human trafficking.[94] Her decision, described largely as a practical one, contrasts entirely with her mother's complex reaction to sex work—Juana sees her decision as one she can independently make, while her mother was forced by her creditor to acquiesce to undesirable sex in an effort to survive, in effect to not call his actions rape. Yet in portraying sex work as integral to the migration process, *Across a Hundred Mountains* reinforces the relationship between social reproduction and immigration control. By linking them—as Zaitchik noticed that conservative activists had also done—Grande's novel refuses the interstices created by a scholarly refusal to study civil rights, sexuality, and immigration together.

The rescaling of the US and Mexican economies at the turn of the century created new conditions of bracketing and captivity as well as new captors and new technologies of retention. As the novel shows, living a deportable life comes to be a form of captivity, and, ultimately, the threat of deportation serves as a psychological ankle bracelet reinforcing the sense of impingement and impossibility. Juana represents the many cast-off children forced into a system that cleaves them from their childhood, hurling them into the latest iteration of constraint demanded by a newly rescaled economy. Yet Juana also suggests an opening. Grande portrays a child who refuses the terms of captivity offered to her, including the terms of normativity that would constrain her either in her home village or in the United States. The cleavage becomes a rip and an opening into the possibility of dis/objectification.

Before. Antes.

Published five years after *Across a Hundred Mountains*, Restrepo's *Illegal* covers some of the same ground. Here, too, a little girl must gather the inner strength to leave her rural village and poverty-encased life to travel to the United States. She, too, chases after a father who no longer communicates or sends remittances.[95] He, too, had left not long after the death of a beloved sibling. And he, too, has died, in this case from a construction accident. This young protagonist, Nora, must also search for him and migrate on her own terms, although she has a healthy, if anxious, mother to assist her. The novel traces their family's economic decline, the challenges they face crossing the border, and the hurdles they encounter establishing a new life without formal authorization. *Illegal* concludes as Nora begins school in the United States while also working alongside her grandmother and mother in a small Houston restaurant. Without actually naming NAFTA, the novel identifies it as the partial source of its protagonist's poverty: NAFTA renegotiated water rights for the Rio Bravo/Rio Grande, causing significant hardship to Mexican farmers who depended on it for irrigation. *Illegal* links this shift to the decline of the small town of Cedula and suggests that the drought had drained the region of people as well as water.

To convey this change, the novel uses an interesting maneuver that functions both temporally and narratively. In a moment when Nora is recalling life with her father, she remembers an earlier sensation: "I had felt like this only once before. A large crop of grapefruits had come in from the trees and every hand was needed in the orchard. We couldn't stop picking and boxing and selling. That was before the water ran out in Cedula. That was before Papa talked about America. It was before the school closed. Before. *Antes.*"[96] On the one hand, Nora is remembering the feeling of exhaustion after immense and continuous labor. On the other hand, the text is suggesting a significant temporality. The shift between English and Spanish is both a technique of emphasis and a division of time, movements of loss and exchange and stasis. This moment describes conditions of labor and the condition of drought just as it signals the time before her father's departure and the unspoken after; the doubled "Before. *Antes*" is a crossing and a braiding in temporal, linguistic terms that suggest stasis rather than movement, and gaps that cannot be accommodated.

That structure of stasis is also formally conveyed quite slyly. The novel is narrated by Nora, who we are told has had very few opportunities to enjoy formal education. She also tells the story in English about a self that cannot understand the English language. While this is not in and of itself formally innovative, the novel does not hesitate to draw attention to this problematic. Nora, the narrator, signals her lack of ability to follow conversations that are taking place and that she herself is reporting even while she is also reporting that she cannot understand the conversations. Consider, for example, a scene shortly after Nora begins to work for a food-truck owner. He directs her to sell drinks at the neighborhood pool and tells her that she can do so if she gives the lifeguard a free drink each day:

> "Lifeguard." Jorge told me. I tried to get the words to slow down, but I was only catching pieces. *Tacos. Swim. Free.*
> I tugged at Jorge's shirt. *"Jorge. No entiendo."*
> "Don't worry about Lauren," he said. "I have a deal with her that you can sell poolside as long as she gets free drinks." . . .
> Lauren raised her voice. "I don't speak Spanish. I don't know why they assign me to this pool."[97]

How can Nora report this comment when she has just reported that she cannot understand a conversation between Jorge (her boss) and the lifeguard? This disjuncture underscores a recursive movement inherent to a text that wishes to convey an experience felt in one language but reported in another, as if the language difference matters but must be muddled. This curious authorial choice ensures that readers can only partially track the efforts at translating that migration entails, the way moments of translation inundate and adumbrate every quotidian encounter. To draw attention to translation and yet to inhabit it without portraying it creates a kind of friction for the reader that may well serve to produce a sense of viscerality, an embodied experience. It also curiously suggests that gap, the moment between translations and before comprehension; like "Before. *Antes*," this passage requires the reader to pay attention to the complex crossings soldered into the structure of experience and the novel itself.

This scene also underscores the racialization of childhood. Nora is no older than most of the children enjoying the pool, to whom she sells snacks and drinks. But she has been denied her childhood; the rescaling of water rights under NAFTA has made her future in Mexico barren. It has forced her into the position of racialized subservience. That her work takes her to the obscenity of a swimming pool (when it was a lack of access to water to maintain their orchards that led to the debacle of her father's migration and death) is not underscored by the novel. It's left to the reader to see the irony of water rights and the lack thereof, as well as the long life of a racializing project that would repeatedly deprive Nora of access to the supposed humanity of rectitude signaled by racialized adulthood.

Less formally complex than *Across a Hundred Mountains*, *Illegal* also focuses on a child who must negotiate her way past the expectations that she will use her body as an ATM machine, use it to obtain the cash necessary to cross. As the mother and daughter prepare to cross, their coyote demands more money. They refuse to pay, and he replies, licking his lips, "Then go back to your village, unless you want to pay with your virginity."[98] This sort of endangerment continues after Nora has successfully established a life in Houston. There she must negotiate and beat back a bullying young man, tattooed with the mark of a local gang. But in this case, *Illegal* counters this part of the crossing with multiple portraits of kindness, of a web of strangers who make an effort to help people they recognize as their other selves. The novel offers the possibility of beating back vulnerability, of making a life more substantive, less fleeting, through interconnection.

The interwoven relations that *Illegal* emphasizes contrast slightly with *Across a Hundred Mountains*. In the case of the latter, Adelina both builds networks as a social worker and keeps her own complex history enclosed, encased in silence. Only after she reveals to a young woman, devastated by the accidental death of her son, that her own infant sister had died as well does a new network of relations open. After that revelation, Adelina finds the remains of her father and reconnects with her brother. The suggestion, of course, is that the secrecy that illegality and loss force on people also makes many sorts of connections difficult. In both novels it is the blossoming of relationships that counters the corrosive effects of the violent structure made possible by linking legality to humanness, by criminalizing movement, by leavening desperation with an accusation of crime.

Both novels also illustrate the central role remittances play in migration, again highlighting the relationship between social reproduction and border control. In both cases, the absence of remittances triggers crises. Migrants send billions to Mexico each year to support relatives and businesses. A recent report noted that remittances make up a larger share of Mexico's gross domestic product than does the sale of its crude oil.[99] In both stories, remittances have stopped because the fathers have been killed—one by a snake bite while crossing the border, the other in a construction accident. Obviously, the violence and danger attendant on crossing the border and working without state authorization have been extensively studied. Less attention has been paid to the efforts of families to cope with the disappearance of their kin. Yet what both texts offer here is a crucial meditation on how hard it is to search for lost migrants. Both young women face the daunting prospect of searching for men no one else seems to know, all the while staring down the possibility that they have been abandoned by their fathers. As Marta Caminero-Santangelo insightfully notes, novels such as *Illegal* form a new genre of testimonio fiction dedicated to the "border-disappeared" that "construct[s] migrant disappearances as a new form of cultural trauma that violently separates families and introduces profound instability into notions of individual and group identity."[100] In connecting the end of remittances to death, the novels force a return to the vacuum between civil rights and migration. The men's deaths fall into the interstices, and the sign of this loss becomes the absent money.

Both novels ask their readers to think through the peculiarities and particularities of gendered precarity. Both refute a romantic nostalgia for a stereotypically supportive and nurturing mother. Grande offers a portrait of a mother's grief intensified into incapacity. Restrepo portrays a mother driven by fear and paralyzed by a sense of inadequacy. In both cases, the young children must draw on their own fierce will and the generosity of others and learn how to move through the world without parental support. In their portraits of missing fathers, the novelists suggest not simply how intensely migration stresses bonds but also how lives become almost ephemeral within a system of illegality, within the constraints of a new form of captivity that has emerged with the rescaling of the hemisphere engineered by NAFTA. In other words, both missing men lack a system of connection that would notify their families after their deaths. And if both deaths reflect tragically common occurrences, their aftermath does as well. The silence of the failure to arrive, to continue to remit, haunts this hemisphere. And that silence is made louder, the novels suggest, through the activity of other villagers, who build and buy and survive on the strength of the remittances that continue apace.

Both novels borrow from the long tradition of melodrama to emphasize the suffering of the vulnerable children portrayed. In this sense, they could be said to add to a tradition that Ana Elena Puga has astutely named "migrant melodrama." Puga argues that this suffering, particularly gratuitous displays of "virtuous suffering," have been transfigured as the "price of inclusion in the nation-state"[101] and that this "reconfigures suffering as a necessary step in the progress toward inclusion and belonging."[102] As such, migrant melodrama requires a suffering child, a failed mother, a stigmatized nation, all of which are necessary to produce an end result in which the child may or may not "deserve" inclusion in the US polity. Crucial to her argument is the claim that melodrama "reformulates collective conflict as personal and individual experience" in order to mediate who does and does not deserve entrée.[103] Yet if melodrama provides a familiar track for stories about migration, these two novels veer from its well-established path. By connecting children's experiences to the broader political economy, to the transformations wrought by NAFTA and the intensified policing of the US-Mexico border, to the exploitative system of labor relations, and, indeed, to the intricate relations between sexuality and immigration, Restrepo and Grande undo melodrama's dependence on individuation as an ideological workhorse for racial capitalism.

Both novels also think about temporality through meditations on faith. The two young women experience the cost of migrant time—the time waiting to hear (from the fathers, from the coyotes), waiting to receive, waiting to see; this migrant time folds into mourning time as the silence stretches to weeks and months and then years. They also must endure another kind of migrant time, the time waiting to get the money to cross, waiting to cross, to recross, to make do and redo. In such moments both novels peruse the offerings of faith—the silence of gods and saints and the promises made by nuns and grandmothers on God's behalf. Less interested in exploring the nuances of faith, the two novels suggest how clumsily hope must be held aloft and how useful, if sometimes disingenuous, a rhetoric of faith might be.

But the signature of faith also sutures together the possibility of recognition that the two novels consider. In both novels a religious object—a cross or a rosary—is the sign of the lost father, the material memento that each man carried with him and that confirms his body for his daughter. These signatures stand in for the tenuousness of a faith that both young women struggle to embrace at the same time that they link that faith to the irredeemable loss of beloved parents. Loss, hope, and a memory signaled by a rosary or a cross connect the young women's past to their present and to their struggle with what might be called a phenomenology of unauthority, of being as an unauthorized presence.

It should be noted that the two novels focus on children, young girls who make the journey to the United States under profound duress. This representation dovetails with DREAMer narratives in that it focuses on children who must migrate. The dominant DREAMer narrative frames migrant children as being unable to choose to migrate, because they were minors when "brought" to the United States and thus were under the control of their guardians; they were brought to the United States before they had the option to consent or had reached the age of reason, and, therefore, they have not committed a crime. These two novels resist that framing. Indeed, they dismiss and disavow the language of racialized legality or the liberal rhetoric of consent. They provide portraits of young girls who drive their own migration, who organize their own movement, and who manage their own journey's multiple dangers and transitions. In this they refute the liberal imaginary construction of a child and go further, to undo the racist narrative of people of color more generally as perpetual children. This refutation undermines what Ana Mae Duane, following historian Holly Brewer, notes as "the emerging emphasis on consent" that has "progressively denied children even the small power they had previously been able to access via birthright and bloodline. The child effectively came to represent all that should exclude and subject from citizenship."[104] The novels refute this largely sentimental version of children, depicting the young girls as adept, capable, and resourceful. At the same time, it could be said that the two novels reinforce the liberal sensibility that all children of color, including immigrant children of color, lack access to childhood.

Illegal and *Across a Hundred Mountains* operate outside of and against this liberal rhetoric of citizenship with its built-in dependence on borders, rectitude, and legal violence. The liberal imaginary fueling the management of citizenship and the nation-state still demands this concept of the racialized child, because it reinforces the nearly hallowed link among reason, consent, and citizenship. Yet if the novels operate without reference to this structure of citizenship, they do not do so outside of the structures of normativity entirely. While both novels reject a sentimentality that underpins the long legacy of Anglo-US novels focused on women and girls, and while both suggest the extent to which the childhood envisioned through consumer culture is a privilege rather than a universal experience, both texts also portray young women who long for permanent and stable kin relations. That is, neither text proposes a completely antinormative model of living outside of the normative force of legality. They do, however, insist on a different vision, one not scaled by liberal notions of agency, consent, or sentiment.

Whose Streets? Our Fucking Streets!

Protestors opposing AB101 chanted, "Whose streets? Our fucking streets!" repeatedly as they challenged the police and sheriff patrols to leave them alone while they staged their outrage. The mobilization of their fury was productive of new possibilities. Their demand to occupy public space as outraged people contributed to the transformation of employment discrimination law. It also helped to create a new platform for gay activism that shifted attitudes toward public policy and heteronormativity and created a new sphere of homonormativity that laid siege to the liberal hetero-family narrative of property and kinship.

This turning of rhetoric upon itself has an interesting history if we look at another convergence between homophobia and nativism. Recall that when gay activists were first championing civil protection against employment discrimination in the early 1990s, sodomy was still illegal in many parts of the United States. Only five years before the AB101 protests, the US Supreme Court in *Bowers v. Hardwick* reaffirmed the right of states to criminalize gay sex acts. Coming out as gay in the 1980s and early 1990s still held the risk of attracting the violent attention of the government, of criminalization, even as it held the promise of new political affiliations. Nevertheless, as more and more people came out of the closet, joined gay rights movements, and demanded greater relief from discriminatory practices, state statutes defining sodomy as criminal began to be repealed or declared unconstitutional. This movement toward decriminalization culminated in 2003 when the Supreme Court reversed the *Bowers* decision. Coming-out actions by gay activists challenged the dehumanizing structures of legality, laying claim to normativity, although perhaps with some ambivalence.

For migrants, a kind of reverse history has been underway. When gay rights protestors swarmed the streets in the early 1990s, overstaying a visa or entering the United States without papers, even repeatedly, was a violation of immigration procedures but had not yet been ensconced in the discourse of crime. That shift was one of Bill Clinton's central dis-achievements. Clinton's 1996 immigration bill depended on the rhetoric of "legality," of "breaking our laws." That rhetorical flourish, repeated by Clinton throughout his reelection campaign and as he pressured Congress to overhaul immigration, had the effect of reinforcing a concept of "our"—of reinvigorating nationalism—and remaking migrants as lawbreakers, while reimagining US citizens as law abiding. Thus, over the very period in which queer sex acts were decriminalized and civil rights expanded, albeit unevenly, for same-sex kinships, culminating in the 2013 decision overturning the Defense of Marriage Act and California's Proposition 8 and the 2015 decision declaring the constitutionality of same-gender marriage, a haunting, daunting, violent policing system of migration and detention grew and intensified, brutalizing millions of people.[105]

In their efforts to challenge AB101, conservative family-values activists successfully siphoned the energy generated by homophobia and used it to narrow the margins of legality for migrants. Many immigrant rights activists have responded to the nativism campaign by asserting their own ownership of family values and embedding in the political discourse the language of "Hispanics" as committed to traditional conservative family values. That effort can claim few successes in stemming border violence or anti-immigrant fervor.

Another set of efforts by Latinx activists has had far more visible results. Rather than battle nativism on its own grounds, DREAM activists decommissioned nativism's overt use of homophobia by delegitimizing its claim to a monopoly on citizenship.[106] They did this by taking a page from gay organizing: using the technologies of coming out, drawing attention to the pathologizing of their humanity, and defying it by unclosing it, unsecret-ing it. These practices of disclosure intensified the pressure on Congress to reform immigration procedures and were instrumental in leading to Barack Obama's deferred deportation policy known as DACA (Deferred Action for Childhood Arrivals). They were later fundamental to slowing the subsequent presidential effort to revoke DACA. By "coming out" as DREAMers, activists seized the rhetoric of US nationalism and the techniques of a contemporary civil resistance movement. Their coming-out strategies disentangled one of nativism's support structures, homophobia, and effectively mobilized the shameless practices of queer activism to unshame a migrant status vis-à-vis a fortress United States.

Both the gay rights movement and DREAMers have seen success through an engagement with heteronormativity, with capitalist claims to property and achievement. The new right emphasized the nonnormativity of sex acts attributed to a "homosexual lifestyle." In response, the mainstream gay rights movement pivoted toward marriage, toward overturning "don't ask, don't tell," toward gaining recognition of civil partnerships by working with corporations to obtain access to health care and retirement benefits. That is, they sought to show themselves as consonant with normativity. This decades-long effort helped lead to the 2013 Supreme Court decision (*Windsor v. United States*) and the subsequent transformation of legal interpretations of civil rights. The coming-out-of-the-shadows actions by DREAMers have similarly pivoted toward normativity, alluding to their aspirations to attend college, to settle into a normative (and largely heterosexual) life of civic quietness.

In the long, twisted corridor leading from AB101 protestors burning flags at the California state capitol through deserts strewn with unmarked bodies, past a neglectful media and political culture that could well be accused of a genocidal malfeasance about a slow-motion massacre, to the present moment of anti-immigrant violence, forced sterilizations, shredding of kin ties, and open hostility, the journey to improve structures of belonging and affiliation, and to make respect and integrity watchwords of the hemisphere, has only been bumpy. We must embrace the insights of the "undocumented and unafraid" artists who refuse to allow citizenship to serve as an arbiter for humanness and who, ultimately, eschew the violence that these categories of the human and citizen produce, as antithetical to liberation itself. Similarly, we must listen to the writers and artists who refute the gap between border control and civil rights, who call for an end to borders and citizenship, who insist that political economy cannot be conceptualized apart from sexuality, that consent as a fundamental formation within legal structures must be bypassed.

| 5 |

MISPLACED

Peopling a Deportation Imaginary

> I desire to know wherefore I am banished.
> Say no more, the court knows wherefore and is satisfied.
> —"The Examination of Mrs. Ann Hutchinson at the Court at Newtown"

> The western archive is premised on the crystallization of the idea of the border.
> —ACHILLE MBEMBE, "The Idea of a Borderless World"

What desire does deportation enact? What impulse lies behind the legal violence of forced removal? What leads to deporting people often, repeatedly, and relentlessly, even to their death?[1] Forced removal is a tactic of war and, by extension, of nation building. Integral to the constitution of sovereignty, deportation also contours citizenship. As such, strategic deportation produces hierarchies, stabilizes existing hierarchies, requires a commitment across all levels to the habit of capturing, caging, and repelling people for profit. It scales the nation-state.

Since the mid-1990s "terror" has handily catalyzed an ever-expanding border abjection machine.[2] As it has been deployed rhetorically by politicians and materially by the violence-hungry agents of the state wielding bluster, guns, and indifference to suffering, deportation terror operates as a torrential storm of destruction—one that seems to continually expand and that consumes and threatens communities across the hemisphere. Terror takes the form of traffic stops and roadblocks; terror takes the form of detention centers without proper plumbing where children are beaten, drugged, and exploited; terror takes the form of men with guns demanding papers at dawn in homes and fields and hospitals; terror takes advantage of the suffering caused by thirst, sun, rattlesnakes, coyotes, and bajadores.[3]

Deportation produces a new form of subjectivity—people find themselves situated but without state attachments, returned to the nation of their birth, perhaps, but certainly not returned home. The complications for people expelled from the United States are significant. Birth countries may not recognize their education, their labor history, their skills. They may find themselves penniless, homeless, without family or connections, bereft of the linguistic skills necessary to navigate a largely new sociality, and too frequently the ready-made victims of kidnappers, thieves, and cartels; they may be shamed and shunned, dispossessed in every way. Moreover, those remaining in the United States may find themselves impoverished, homeless, cut off from sustainable support systems and the possibility of material well-being. Forced removal spreads its largesse around.

Contemporary scholarship on deportation terror has tended to focus on the roundup, on the experience of carceral zones and the tropologies necessary for snaring people, as well as the experiences of waiting, of detention, and of the mechanics of expulsion; scholars have focused to a lesser extent on how such mass disappearances disrupt lives and violently shred socialities. In other words, while scholars have tracked the transformations in immigration policies that enabled the legal violence that is mass deportation, have carefully traced the effects and experiences of living deportable lives, and have shed light on the broad effects of these policies for people across the United States, they have written substantially less about what it feels like once one has been deported; once one finds oneself the target of the state, caught by an arsenal of tactics that eviscerate a sense of belonging; once one is, to use a terrifyingly bland, mundane word, *removed*.[4]

Indeed, on the rare occasions when popular media attend to life after removal, journalists tend to repeat two or three stories; they have favorite types. For example, they often feature a single person, usually a parent with children who are US citizens and a partner who may or may not fear deportation. The person deported is portrayed as lonely, ill at ease, and isolated, despite having some family member, often an aunt, with whom they can live. The deportation story depicts deportees as spending most of their time alone, looking forward to phone calls with their children and, crucially, not interacting with those around them. Described as unmoored, they are represented as disconnected from a local culture or disengaged from any effort to find meaningful new relations. Or the media might describe youths who are on the hustle or are joining/avoiding gangs. Or they might offer a glimpse of the narco/gang violence a deportee attempts to avoid. These stories are short and offer little real information; in their stereotyping and repetition, they further serve to make the deportee invisible. Mexico is described as an end point—not a place for a new beginning. These stories may wish to evoke pity at seeing a person so bereft, but they are so narrow that they accomplish little more than to cloak deportation in silence. Such silence about this form of exile is a significant and powerful tool of the deportation regime itself; it sustains the claims of sovereignty that the state has a right to deport.[5] The silence helps reinforce the terror and shame that the system induces, perpetuates, and thrives on. Ultimately, the silence helps to further disappear the millions of people deported since the twenty-first century began.

While the work of scholars who study the "real" methods and the "real" effects of deportation counters this silence, the work of the imagination provides another significant part of the analysis of deportation. It allows people who have not been deported to imagine the experience. The purpose is not to gain empathy, inasmuch as empathy has become a mechanism of the liberal racial imaginary, one that fails to shift the actual structures producing legal violence. Fictive portrayals, however, can bring about the more potent loss of indifference and hence the possibility for new enactments of solidarity. Surprisingly perhaps, María Amparo Ruiz de Burton's 1872 novel, *Who Would Have Thought It?*, characterizes the experience of deportation (its protagonist, Lola Medina, voluntarily deports herself to Mexico) in a way that anticipates contemporary news stories.[6] At the end of the novel, an isolated and bereft Lola misses her loved ones and seems to sink into a dangerous depression. Lola's suspended, static, even fugue-like state as she sits dejected and isolated in her father's mansion eerily predicts the complex experience forced removal imposes. It is, of course, a stretch to characterize *Who Would Have Thought It?* as a novel about deportation, but it does presciently critique the legal and moral groundwork justifying deportation today. Roughly tracking the period when the juridical justification for a national deportation policy was firmly established, the novel lays out the logic of respectability that supposedly encases the structure of rightful belonging and reveals that logic to be suspect at best, hypocritical and demeaning, dependent on a nefarious process of racialization and hedged by unfreedom. As it does so, it also lays out the crucial relationships among a racialized childhood, captivity, and witnessing, while illustrating the dynamic processes by which racialized children are hailed as suspended in infancy, their potential for maturation foreclosed, their futurity denied and devalued. Ultimately, this quirky, disturbing nineteenth-century novel, obsessed with proving elite Mexican claims to whiteness rather than the fallacy of white supremacy, nevertheless keeps company with a set of novels far more critical of such racializing practices. These texts begin where *Who Would Have Thought It?* stops, with the story of life after forced removal. And if *Who Would Have Thought It?* shows a deported Lola at the hinge between two scalar shifts, contemporary novels also underscore ongoing deportation as a result of the post-NAFTA scalar changes that global financial restructuring produced. More important, perhaps, they also show how, along with the newly scaled financial landscape (globalization), a new form of mass captivity arose: forced removal, instantiating this century's newest iteration of captivity.

In this chapter I turn to three novels and a remarkable installation project, all of which try to imagine life after removal and comment on the surreal emptying out and "repopulating" of Mexico that the migration/deportation machine enacts. Alejandro Santiago's massive sculptural project *2501 Migrantes* offers a visually compelling account of the processes by which forced migration empties towns, even as it challenges audiences to consider the processes by which the concept of the human is structured through exclusions. Malín Alegría's 2007 young adult novel, *Sofi Mendoza's Guide to Getting Lost in Mexico*, depicts the shock of finding out your citizenship status is different than you'd been led to believe and thus considers how it feels to be refused reentry to the United States. In *The Deportation of Wopper Barraza* (2014), Maceo Montoya examines the impact of deportation at the hands of the court system and tracks the ripple effects on its titular character, Wopper, and his family. The third novel is the least utopian of the three; Daniel Peña's *Bang* (2018) forces readers to look at the ruthless sociality that awaits deportees, a sociality that the United States has helped to produce and that it exploits as part of its strategy of maintaining thickened borders, of off-loading immigrant deterrence.

All three of these novels, along with Santiago's sculptural installation, recalibrate the story of deportation. Taken together, they provide an intimate portrait of removal and expulsion, a portrait of the density of feelings that expulsion promulgates; they also offer an opening counterweight to the silence that deportation seems to create. Finally, as if answering Ruiz de Burton's own critique of the hallowed relationship between respectability and the right to give consent, and hence to belong, all of these creative projects refute that key tenet sustaining the work of violent citizenship and the practice of sovereignty, even as they follow characters who refuse to accede to the new form of captivity that forced removal imposes, even as they struggle against the temporal suspension and the shredding of affective relations that deportation produces.

The novels and artwork discussed here refuse to participate in the production of unpersonhood, insisting on the trauma that deportation causes and illustrating how creative literary and visual forms refute the loss of personhood that deportation enacts. Opening up questions about form and containment, captivity, restraint, and witnessing while ultimately revealing sovereignty's dependence on containment and capture, these projects show why it is so necessary for sovereignty to mute captivity's witness. By refusing to forget, by illustrating the way in which creative engagement, the use of the imaginary, produces a resilience against the legal violence of the state, these creative works counter the national imaginary that seeks to disappear those it has expelled from the national space. Rather, they insist that "the removed" live in a dense field of sociality by acknowledging their presence, their continued coming together with others, their resilient making of worlds and relations. These texts also deny forced removal its ideological cover as a supposedly inevitable and natural arm of sovereign power.

Creative works such as these write against and alongside five hundred years of common sense, which is to say, against the logic of sovereignty, which is also the logic of deportability. England's forced removal of children and its slave policies coincided with the emergence of theories of the liberal state and new concepts of freedom. The unimpeded movement of capital, goods, and services signaled freedom. Theorists such as Thomas Hobbes foresaw this movement as a manifestation of freedom, but when he and other philosophers folded people into this understanding of freedom, a problem emerged. For Hobbes, the unimpeded movement of all people constitutes a threat, especially a threat to order, which is to say sovereign power.[7] Movement, then, is both a signal of freedom and a form of danger, one that must be contained to ensure the power of the state. In imagining freedom, theorists understood that pure freedom could not coincide with the management of a territory, so if they envisioned freedom of movement for capital and goods, they simultaneously understood such freedom as contradictory. Borders instantiate the state's claim to both enable freedom of movement and view it as a threat to its own order, its own power over territory and people. Central to the workings of territory-based power, then, is the need to control movement into, out of, and within the territory.

According to this logic, without a removal policy, there is no state.[8] Thus, as Hagar Kotef argues, the carceral and disciplinary structures of the state are arrayed against the free movement of everyone, not just those directly targeted.[9] So while the state may celebrate itself as a guarantor of freedom, it simultaneously depends, for its logic, on the vision that it need only protect the freedoms of those it deems capable of self-restraint, those who embrace self-regulation according to the state's terms. And, of course, this logic of who is and isn't capable of self-restraint (of rectitude) is embedded within the logics of gendered racialization and crystallized in the idea of the border. The philosophical emphasis on self-restraint and rectitude, on a claim to govern by the rational alone, as Adriana Cavarero makes clear, is an avowedly misogynistic project.[10] It is also clearly racist. To take on the taken-for-granted status of forced removal, as these novels do, is to counter the logic of sovereignty freighted with racism and misogyny and to advance new possibilities of connection, possibilities that hinge on queer horizontality, on living such connection in a web of acknowledged debt.

A Brief History of Deportation

The current deportation regime is obviously a new iteration of captivity, a new instantiation of the seemingly insatiable need in the United States to produce inequality in order to sustain capital and a facade of freedom. The practice of bordering, of enacting borders through deportation, has been from the first instance a racializing practice. And while such a violent practice was crucial to building the infrastructure of the current regime, scholars of forced removal see far longer roots, arguing that the concept and practice of deportation stretch back to the emergence of the idea of the liberal republic and reach into the very sinews of the United States as a settler colonial state.[11]

The stark history of British imperialism began from a habit of dispossession that became a practice of deportation. In *The Many-Headed Hydra*, Peter Linebaugh and Marcus Rediker argue that expropriation entailed not just the hedging of the commons, the felling of forests, or the draining of swamps but also the impressment, expulsion, kidnapping, capture, and deportation of hundreds of thousands of poor people from England, Ireland, and eventually Africa. "The many expropriations of the day—of the commons by enclosure and conquest, of time by the puritanical abolition of holidays, of the body by child stealing and the burning of women, and of knowledge by the destruction of guilds and assaults on paganism gave rise to new kinds of workers and a new kind of slavery, enforced directly by terror."[12] Enclosures undermined subsistence economies, forcing people to seek out new means to survive. Refugees from the lost commons and forests had no homes or means of subsistence. They were first hedged out and then hedged in by one draconian law after another: "Under Henry VIII vagabonds were whipped, had their ears cut off, or were hanged (one chronicler of the age put their number at seventy-five thousand). Under Edward VI they had their chests branded with the letter V and were enslaved for two years; under Elizabeth I they were whipped and banished to galley service or the house of corrections."[13] The production of the category of the beggar or vagabond entailed the emergence of the condition of being "affectable" and thus of "feeling like a problem."[14] Such naming inscribed within punishing held as its charm the magic of removal.

Forced removal and transport to the nascent colonies began under Elizabeth. Writers as various as John Donne, Richard Hakluyt, and Francis Bacon celebrated removal, impressment, and transport. Donne crowed that the policy of forced removal "shall sweep your streets, and wash your dores, from idle persons, and the children of idle persons, and imploy them: and truly if the whole Country were such a Bridewell, to force idle persons to work, it had a good use."[15] The Virginia Company even claimed deportation provided a form of public service.[16] Richard Hakluyt argued that "irregular youths of no religion" should accompany people condemned to deportation because they could not pay their rent and suffered such "extream poverty" that they "cannot lie at home." He put it this way: "[A] swarme of unnecessary inmates, [are] a continual cause of death and famine, and the very original cause of all the plagues that happen in this kingdom."[17] Targets for deportation were associated with jails and with dirt. By associating the poor with filth, Donne and others coagulated an onto-epistemological assemblage (the poor are filth; you know they are poor through their filth) that produced the distinction between the proper and the common and thereby assembled a network theory, an algorithm of belonging mediated by respectability. Put differently, people who were deported were represented as outside the strictures of respectability, spectacularized so that they were available for removal.

Such conceptual work helped lawmen like Francis Bacon justify the shipping of young children spirited away to their deaths in the colonies. Of the many thousands of children who were shipped to the colonies, only 7 percent were alive six years after being taken from their beds, stolen from their parents, or snared on the streets and in the forests of England and Ireland. Even as the slave trade intensified between Latin America and Africa and the Caribbean, the English continued to impress children and the poor from their own territory. Records show that as late as 1660 "ordinary parents pitifully followed ships carrying their children to the West Indies down river to Gravesend, crying and moaning for Redemption from their slavery."[18]

Daniel Kanstroom suggests that the concept of removal and its corollary, "the right to remain," that is, to not be deported, are modern modalities.[19] He notes that English subjects had limited and controlled mobility, governed by laws stretching back to the fourteenth century and to feudal practices before that. The right to remain did not emerge until after the forced mass removal of poor people engendered a backlash. Before that backlash, Queen Elizabeth developed "brutal" expulsion practices in Ireland and England. James I demanded that "rogues, vagabonds, and sturdy beggars" be removed to the colonies. A 1662 law insisted that a man entering an area who could not prove that he would not become a burden (i.e., was not poor) had to be "summarily removed, in custody together with his wife and children."[20] Kanstroom concludes that, "in effect, the poor were always subject to removal."[21] English removal laws facilitated colonization efforts. Sir Walter Raleigh, along with many others such as John Donne, demanded the deportation of the poor. "England," Raleigh wrote, must "disburden" itself and "lay the load upon others."[22] The Crown sent tens of thousands of its poor to forced labor in colonies in the Americas, hurtling them to an almost certain death. Forced removal and deportation are at the heart of US history, as much as chattel slavery, voluntary immigration, and the genocidal destruction of Indigenous peoples.

US deportation law was modeled after these practices and, Kanstroom argues, has repeatedly been used as a "system of social control against people of color."[23] Almost immediately after independence, for example, Massachusetts enacted laws deporting "strolling poor people," aimed at African and Native Americans, and so the practice of removal continued.[24] Other states followed suit, signaling that deportation would largely serve white supremacist efforts. Yet the right of the state to remove people from within its boundaries was not universally assumed. Thomas Jefferson, for example, argued that laws enabling the removal of "friendless aliens" created the proverbial slippery slope: rules attacking noncitizens could easily be transformed into rules attacking citizens.[25] Mindful of the potential for such slippage, nineteenth-century practices emphasized the foreignness—the noncivilized, non-Protestant attributes—of those who should be removed. Deportation functioned as a tool to contour white supremacy and thus to undermine belonging for people of color.

Given this history, it may not be surprising that there are striking similarities between nineteenth-century congressional efforts to seize American Indian territory and contemporary administrative deportation practices.[26] Crucial to the justifications for violence against American Indians was the idea that Native peoples were deemed foreign noncitizen subjects within US territory, or foreign in a domestic sense. This concept would be used again and again: to apply to Asian immigrants, to justify the colonial occupation of Puerto Rico, and, ultimately, to form the logical foundation of the current deportation regime. Throughout the nineteenth century, courts justified this refusal to give people the protection of the Constitution (that is, this maintenance of plenary power as administrative power) by declaring Native and Asian peoples a "menace to our civilization."[27] This allowed unchecked executive power over American Indians and immigrants, particularly those from Asia, with "no constitutional limitations and no judicial oversight at all."[28] Supreme Court decision after decision reinforced this view, insisting that "the right of a nation to expel or deport foreigners . . . rests upon the same grounds and is as absolute and unqualified as the right to prohibit and prevent their entrance into the country."[29] With this, deportation gained a taken-for-granted status as a legitimate act of sovereignty.

Deportation continued throughout the twentieth century, initially focusing on union organizers and anticapitalists such as the Wobblies. In the 1930s the federal government began to use trains and then buses and airplanes to shuttle people from one state to another as they awaited deportation, thereby producing a form of "carceral mobility" across state lines.[30] Other administrative logistics were slowly collated in order to refine the labor market for capital, as the Border Patrol attempted to do after World War II through Operation Wetback.[31] But logistics could only form part of the foundation for the current mass deportation effort. A more intensive ideological groundwork was also necessary, and that began to emerge when the administration of Richard Nixon deployed immigration control and deportation as a weapon in its newly decreed war on drugs.[32] The ramping up of funding for increased policing and a new "security" industry entailed creating stronger relays between the discourses of crime and immigration. By the end of the 1970s, the US government had cemented a discursive relationship between Latinx immigration and criminality but had failed to build a widespread anti-immigrant machine.

The subsequent step of transforming immigrants from laborers to de facto criminals emerged after Ronald Reagan steered legislation known as the Immigration Reform and Control Act (IRCA) through Congress and widened the scope of immigrant policing still further, making people conscious of such a status and rendering it quotidian. This step, the creation of the I-9 form with which people must certify their status when they begin a new job or apply for aid, was advertised as a means to prevent employers from hiring people and exploiting them because of their immigration status, yet it also made the practice of requiring citizenship authorization not only quotidian but so familiar as to erase the memory of an era in which such surveillance did not exist. As Keramet Reiter and Susan Bibler Coutin explain, "IRCA's employer sanctions provisions were a key step in diffusing the enforcement of US immigration law throughout society; key gatekeepers—for example, employers, welfare officers, school admissions officials, airlines, banks—now indirectly enforce immigration law, by denying services to individuals who lack appropriate identity documents."[33] By transforming immigration status into a matter of quotidian reporting by any business, IRCA also normalized the link between status and legality, creating another layer of exclusion, an exclusion policed by secretaries, administrative assistants, and others charged with clerical routines.

In the decade after IRCA, anti-immigrant fervor intensified, enabling politicians to merge aspects of criminal law into immigration law (which is largely understood as administrative and therefore outside the scope of juridical or congressional responsibility). During his reelection campaign, for example, Bill Clinton moved the debate from what laborers "deserved"—that is, a debate over rights to health care, education, and protection from exploitation—to a rhetoric centered on migrants' *status* as "legal" or "illegal." This shift produced a new grid of intelligibility with legality as the central hermeneutic. The emphasis, Clinton repeatedly claimed, should not be on *all* immigrants but rather on those who enter the country informally or overstay their visa. By emphasizing such "illegality," he shifted the focus in the US imaginary to immigrants' so-called criminality, to their supposedly bad behavior, and away from issues such as disappearing jobs, wages, and poverty. Clinton also promoted legislation that created a new class of crimes, increasing the arsenal of weapons the state could deploy to forcibly remove people from the territories claimed by the United States. Leisy Abrego and colleagues argue that these new laws transubstantiated once-informal practices that skirted the law into "offenses that qualified as an 'aggravated felony,'" encompassing "a range of misdemeanors and minor offenses, crimes which are neither aggravated nor felonious—such as prostitution, undocumented entry after removal, drug addiction, shoplifting, failure to appear in court, filing a false tax return, and generally any crime warranting a sentence of one year or more." Abrego and colleagues warn that this logic creates a "noun-centric logic of 'criminal alienhood' at the core of immigrant criminalization, thereby reinforcing the links between criminality and immigration."[34] By creating a new grid of immigrant intelligibility, Clinton and Congress established a new subjectivity, one that constricted the space between two nouns—*criminal* and *immigrant*—while rejuvenating their intricacies as castagories. In other words, new laws focused on beings rather than doings.

Crucial to the new policing of immigrants was the insistence that people without citizenship status are dangerous, which rhetorically conflated status with danger.[35] As Patrisia Macías-Rojas explains, Clinton's legislation (the Illegal Immigration Reform and Immigrant Responsibility Act) expanded criminalization practices to the interior of the United States because it "linked unauthorized migration with criminality, and fundamentally restructured immigration enforcement and infused it with the resources necessary to track, detain, and deport broad categories of immigrants, not just those with convictions."[36] Looking back on this law, Abrego and her collaborators note, "The policies of 1996 used the term 'criminal alien' as a strategic sleight of hand. These laws established the concept of 'criminal alienhood' that has slowly but purposefully redefined what it means to be unauthorized in the United States such that criminality and unauthorized status are too often considered synonymous."[37] This conflation invigorated a new practice of captivity—one that brackets and constrains those forced to live through the threat of forced removal.

The Clinton administration ultimately created a doubled structure of containment. Through Operation Gatekeeper it essentially trapped people in the United States by making it much more difficult for people to come and go informally, restricting them from regularly visiting families and friends. Not surprisingly, they subsequently sought to bring their families to the United States, where they were met with a new mesh of laws and an intensified punishment regime that ultimately further contained their mobility and their efforts to build habitable lives.

After the United States declared a war on terror, a new process of "securitization of migration" began linking migration not just to criminal law and the prison-industrial complex but to national security as well, further augmenting the enormous sums now spent on policing and making the effort to enter the United States informally more and more dangerous while also spreading additional funds across the country to encourage local police and sheriff departments to intensify their surveillance of Latinx communities.[38] Under Barack Obama, Homeland Security accelerated the mass deportation of people, focusing its energies largely on people with family ties to Latin America, the location to which more than 90 percent of people were removed in 2008-16. His administration also launched Predator drones to surveil larger and larger swaths of the border, hired tens of thousands more agents to staff ICE and the Border Patrol, amassed financial resources for detention camps and tracking systems, and ultimately spent more on immigrant policing than on other policing agencies such as the Secret Service and the Bureau of Alcohol, Tobacco, and Firearms.[39] The number of people expelled from the territorial United States rose from fewer than 20,000 per annum before 9/11 to an average of 400,000 per year afterward. By the end of his term, Obama could count the forced removal of more than three million people. The number of informal removals can only be imagined.[40]

Taken together, the resulting immigrant detention and removal processes, along with a border enforcement regime that is effectively a war on migrants and refugees, have resulted in thousands of deaths—between 350 and 450 people die every year crossing the border and crossing a policy put in place in 1994 when the government declared that people in the United States informally were now effectively contained. They might leave; they couldn't easily return. The thousands of deaths over the past twenty-five years at the border with Mexico and in detention centers around the country have been machined through the mill of legality to become nearly the proper punishment for violating an unquestioned law. The emphasis on legality removes the deaths from the context of a policing system that forces people to enter the US political territory (they are always already in US economic territory) in extremely dangerous ways. It contextualizes these deaths as a kind of passive capital punishment for a desperate migrant's willingness to skirt entry regulations. Put differently, any sentiment that might be mobilized by so many horrific deaths remains out of bounds owing to the narrative tangle that puts illegality out of empathy's reach.

By naming people as criminals, by marking them as beyond the margins of legality, by spectacularizing them so that they seem supposedly unworthy of empathy, the US government effectively reinforced its own role as the keeper of propriety and the agent of social well-being. In particular, by treating people with an informal immigration status in the same manner it treats convicted felons (shackles, incarceration, armed arrests), the state powerfully delimits their claims to the respectability so fundamental to the discursive rubric of citizenship status. In other words, the logic of legality functions to dehumanize people—not simply to shame them but also to render them beyond the norms of the social.

A Geography of Our Indifference

The policies Bill Clinton initiated beginning with Operation Gatekeeper turned Mexico's border with the United States into a graveyard, an abjection machine, and a gallery spectacularizing all those caught in its snares, thereby creating an icon of loss in the name of deterrence. Those who survive but are deported find themselves bereft of many of the intimacies and material signs of their existence, of their connections to life. Additionally, the towns they return to have been emptied out, their residences boarded and shuttered, establishing, according to the noted writer Cristina Rivera Garza, "un rosario de pueblos fantasma."[41] Can the "returned" repopulate such a rosary of ghost towns? Does the US government's active effort to render people nonhuman taint them once they find themselves in the ostensible locale of their birth?

FIGURE 5.1. Grouped migrantes by Alejandro Santiago. From Alejandro Santiago, *Alejandro Santiago: 2501 Migrantes*, 38.

These are some of the questions evoked by Alejandro Santiago's massive, intriguing sculptural project *2501 Migrantes*.

In 2001 Santiago, a highly regarded abstract artist, returned to his birthplace of San Pedro Teococuilco, in the state of Oaxaca, Mexico, after several years of living in Paris. He learned that more than half of his hometown had been forced to migrate to Mexico City and the United States. Shocked to hear that so many people had left, the artist decided to cross into the United States without papers himself. He wanted to know what the experience felt like. Quickly caught and returned to Tijuana, Santiago noticed an exhibit of crosses on the border wall placed by activists to signal the number killed attempting to enter the United States. Inspired by these protests, the artist decided to begin repopulating his home village of Teococuilco, Oaxaca, and conceived the project *2501 Migrantes,* a massive grouping of individually sculpted clay figures in human proportions.

Santiago originally envisioned his project as an effort to repopulate his village, to mark each absent member with a new presence. The sculptures consist of the young and the old, grouped as kin and alone, displayed walking, walking, walking, or lying in coffins. Each figure represents one of those forced to leave his village, and each is meant to suggest their return.⁴² The migrantes are only vaguely figural; their bodies and faces fade in and out of abstraction, yet they convey a theatricality that indicates a vitality against the seeming transience of migrants' valuation. The sculptures are beautiful, each with individual features—simultaneously referencing Pablo Picasso, Alberto Giacometti, and, just as important, the late preclassical figures displayed in cases at El Museo de Arte Prehispánico de Mexico in Oaxaca City. While many of the migrantes, even the majority, have their arms crossed in repose, supplication, or death, they have precise facial features, hair, and other distinguishing details. Santiago sculpts each migrante as a distinct individual, resisting any effort to suggest that they are simply iterations of each other.

2501 Migrantes plays with mass and scale. The migrantes function individually as solid sculptures; their outsized feet and thick, trunk-like legs hold them upright. In its many public displays, *2501 Migrantes* has depended on a kind of mass: the migrantes never stand alone, either in death or in movement. Instead, they have been exhibited in large groups—crossing plazas and hills. Such massing calls to mind the range of people forced to journey for sustenance—young and old and elderly, uprooted by their loss of the right to stay at home and farm and work and thrive on the land where, in the case of the Zapotecs, their communities have lived for a millennium or more.

Massed together, the sculpted migrantes highlight alienation, a practice inherent to statecraft and necessary for the state's claim to hold a monopoly on movement. Santiago makes that logic visible, forcing spectators to come to terms with the visual repertoire from which migration regulations draw. Further, in abstracting the figural and shifting out of a realist register, Santiago suggests that forced and massed migration dis-humanizes people, tears apart complex ties to places, as well as cultural practices embedded in specific locales and attendant to precise or regular climate patterns. Migration, Santiago's sculptures suggest, at the very least undoes what people have worked to create and sustain—languages, arts, relations, connections to place. The abstraction of migrants also underscores the indifference with which global austerity (or economic liberalization achieved via NAFTA and other modalities) treats people; the migrantes have been treated indifferently, inhumanely; state policies do not respond to their lived and embodied violent effects.

Santiago's grouped sculptures inevitably draw comparisons to zombies. This analogy is complex and ambivalent. Zombies have circulated as a film genre for nearly a century, but in popular culture they are often invoked as at war with the living and as vaguely organized only around their hunger for human (non-undead) flesh. By insisting on the density of the project (all 2,501 migrantes must remain on display together), Santiago also mines the zombie repertoire, invoking the way the zombie, as Camilla Fojas argues, "elucidates the social life of capitalism in ruins, where existence is reduced to a mere struggle for survival."[43] So while zombies signal a voracious consumerism, they also signal the labor necessary to produce things to be consumed. By invoking the zombie, Santiago's project offers a sidelong critique of iteration, of the unspoken assumption that the iterability of migrants is inherent to the definition of migration—the guarantee that there are always more, that they are replicas of one another.

The scaffold imaginary requires the homogenization of iteration, the scaling of people into abstractions, into iterations of one another. To refute that process is to see without a scalar perspective, to see across the horizon densely, queerly, as Santiago insists when he stretches his sculptures across and around public space. The migrantes tear open the visual norm, cut through the everyday expectations of "the normal" to comment almost dispassionately on the treatment of migrants. Migrants, the project suggests, have been shorn of the visible markers of their social relations, rendered undead but also unloving as figures, laborers without humanness. Santiago challenges this representation by creating connections between pedestrians and the sculpted migrantes; they are always installed so that people can walk around them and past them, sit with them. In the migrantes' very sociality, that is, in the multiple generations and life stages and configurations displayed (from babies, to toddlers, to youth, to adults, to bodies in coffins), *2501 Migrantes* ultimately works against the antisociality entailed in the US state's habit of deeming migrant laborers as outside of and apart from multiple social relations (including familial ones). That is, Santiago gives viewers a chance to imagine or recognize themselves among the migrantes, as migrants, in part because these very nonrealist sculptures move in very real configurations (the dead together like a moving campo santo: the young with the old, in the real space of the city and the desert). He thereby creates a larger aperture for recognizing oneself as a zombie, as a migrante under the duress and pressure of capital's might. Alternately, the interpretive occasion that Santiago makes possible may well be traced back to the display culture of the nineteenth century, to the practices of othering and parading, producing an estranged normativity and even an equality and superiority among the nonothered. Yet, in seizing that stance, Santiago wrests away the terms defining migrants as everywhere yet invisible, anomalous before the law, friendly behind the counter and with a leaf blower and at the car wash. *2501 Migrantes* offers an homage, a critique, and a rebuttal to the systems that legitimate the processes of violence and discrimination against people forced to migrate in order to eat and breathe.

Feeling Forced Out

2501 Migrantes illustrates the haunting and dense structure of departure and return, of the stretched-out social relations texturing geographies from Mixtec villages to Bakersfield suburbs. Yet these stretched relations, frayed and rutted, are far more chaotic than Santiago implies. As Deborah Boehm argues, mass deportation creates an enormous amount of chaos across communities and kin networks since people lose track of each other; intimate relations are disrupted or demolished, and assets are lost or seized. Additionally, people are often cast into a form of legal limbo when their cases are tossed about between bureaucracies and administrative courts, thereby creating new levels of uncertainty for those named deportable and for their loved ones and dependents. Because people may also seek informal routes back to the United States or may be forced to wait for cousins, partners, children, or parents to join them after they've been deported, they find themselves blockaded by uncertainties. So, in addition to losing jobs, homes, cars, clothes, money, and photos (i.e., all the material forms that people need to take care of themselves) as well as love, affection, connection, and a sense of belonging (i.e., all the affective forms that people need to take care of themselves), they are dispossessed of their *time*. They find themselves uncertain about what future they will have, unclear about what they can plan for, expect, or even dream about. The future, Boehm argues, becomes "unimaginable" for many deportees. As she notes, people are dispossessed of real time and relocated to the dream time of "what could have been."[44]

For mixed-status families, deportation entails a broad set of effects. Deported parents may take their US-citizen children with them, rendering those children even more vulnerable since they may subsequently reside in Mexico without formal status. Or, if the children are left in the United States, their care may devolve to their older siblings or other members of a kin network, or to foster care, making every aspect of children's sociality murkier, so that they, too, are dispossessed of a clear future. Added to all of this is the trauma that such disruption begets and the lack of formal structures with which to heal. Deportation produces vast social suffering; the legal violence of the deportation regime causes unexamined damage translocally, chaotically dislocating lives, memories, and futures.

In addition to all of this disorientation, deportees face the vulnerability of transit. Frequently, ICE drops people off far from cities, shelters, or other people so that they are especially vulnerable to criminal networks. Not only is the transportation of people into the United States an industry, but deportees with US relatives have also become a profit center for organized crime. They are kidnapped and held for ransom until the kidnappers receive payment from US relatives. If payment does not come or too little arrives, people are forced to work for the kidnappers or are killed.[45]

The process of treating migrants as criminals produces a cloud of shame that follows people around. Returnees can find themselves shunned, presumed to be criminals, or failures at the migration game, and thus are left even more vulnerable. Such shame often represses any energy toward political activism or collective organizing to improve the treatment they receive in their new locale.[46] And this is significant because while Mexico, for example, has benefited from the immense flow of remittances into its economy, state agencies have often refused to acknowledge the education and training people receive in the United States.[47] Mexican state agencies unevenly certify or recognize US diplomas for high school, college, or technical training. This means that people can be effectively deskilled since, without Mexican state licensing, they often can't work at the job for which they have prepared and at which they may have a wealth of experience.

What Boehm calls a "fog of vulnerability" almost always entails disappearances that take many forms, from actual disappearances in which no one knows whether the missing person is alive or dead to the variegated disappearance of those one loves, whom one can no longer see, touch, or even talk to regularly. This freezes people in place, rendering them immobile, unable to travel to see their loved ones, and produces a whole new structure of mourning, a mourning that lacks the rituals and public acknowledgment or sense of finality that death brings, because one is mourning the loss of the living present, a shared sociality.

In Deportation's Wake

In *The Deportation of Wopper Barraza*, Maceo Montoya offers an account of deportation that is at once painful and humorous. It is also a strangely stilted bildungsroman with a central character who rarely speaks, who offers little self-reflection, and who is largely portrayed through recourse to other people's memories. Giving a glimpse of deportation's wake, showing the grief, chaos, mourning, and melancholia that attend a sudden, unplanned removal, *The Deportation of Wopper Barraza* conjures a particularly attuned (and attuning) portrait of the way forced removal dissipates time and also of the sense of lost futures, thereby creating a new experience of temporal immateriality. It achieves all this through a set of complex formal moves, slyly bringing together the "novel of development" with a covert critique of the discourse of development, ultimately rebuking the logic that sustains both by implicating them in the structures of captivity and removal enabling sovereignty and the deportation regime.

Montoya's novel is a surprising blend of genres: part parody, part satire, part roman à clef, laced with noir-ish tropes, it is sardonic, bitter, and oddly distant. The central plot revolves around an unemployed, seemingly directionless youth whose green card is revoked after his fourth DWI; he is then ordered to be deported. Shocked and insulted, he tells the judge, "But that doesn't make any sense, sir. I don't know anybody there. I came here when I was three years old! I'm American. You can't send me to Mexico—what the hell am I going to do there?"[48] The novel then follows just what Wopper does in a Mexico where he really doesn't know anyone; he has no affective relationship with Mexico, nor any memories of it. Fortunately, his father had purchased some land in his hometown, and so Wopper has a place to go, although he leaves behind his furious and pregnant girlfriend. When he arrives in Mexico, he finds an elderly man squatting on his father's property, happily cultivating his fields. Wopper, rather than evict the squatter, goes to work for him; becomes involved with his daughter, Mija; and, at her urging, enters local politics. Mija teaches him the political ropes, and together they set about improving the condition of their rancho, getting roads paved, building soccer fields, and laying the groundwork for a new development of upscale vacation homes marketed to people living in the United States. Their real estate scheme draws the unfortunate attention of a local kingpin, who throws a wrench in their plans, ruins the couple's relationship, and scares Wopper enough that he flees Mexico and returns to his home in rural northern California. Now without papers, Wopper finds a steady job, quits drinking, and begins to take care of his toddler son.

While the plot revolves around Wopper, the novel also examines the deportation regime's ripple effects on kin networks and reveals an intimate sense of subjunctive mourning, that is, mourning for the loss of what could have been. Partly a story of family estrangement, *The Deportation of Wopper Barraza* is also a story of the grief deportation causes by shredding kinship ties, undoing intimacies of every form, and ultimately ensnaring many people beyond those deported. His father misses him terribly and muses on his own reasons for migrating to the United States; his mother remains angry at him even as she longs to reconnect with her son. Most distressed is his ex-girlfriend, Lara. Pregnant and feeling abandoned, she cannot articulate or explain the loss, so, like Wopper's parents, friends, and acquaintances, she dwells not on Wopper's disappearance but on memories of her life with him before his removal. If these seem like obvious people to feel affected by Wopper's removal, the novel also details the responses of a bar owner, a childhood friend, a former racquetball partner, and a college counselor. By attending to these various experiences, the novel refutes the assumption that removal affects individuals alone; instead, forced removals transform the life of whole networks of people, splitting and fraying and stretching these networks.

The form of the novel also brilliantly underscores deportation's wake. Wopper's story is told largely through the recollections of other people, as if it were a scripted documentary, as if the characters were sitting before cameras, documentary style, chattily remembering Wopper, describing their reactions to events, pondering Wopper's motives, and repeatedly expressing surprise at his transformation. These various voices are interwoven across the novel, forwarding the plot as people remember and sometimes marvel at Wopper, making the novel a collation of testimonies by witnesses to Wopper's removal, by those affected by it.

By beginning with a prologue by Julio Caesar Tamayo, owner of the bar that Wopper frequented before being deported, the novel establishes this documentary format and the colloquial quality of the text: "I have a sign up in my bar, directly behind the tap and right next to the flat screen television, so you can't miss it. In neon pink and yellow marker it says: 'If you're drunk, 1. Call a cab. 2. Walk. 3. Call your Mom! Now you have no excuse.' . . . Every now and then we'll add a few more entries just to fuck around. A while ago we wrote, 'Remember Wopper Barraza!'"[49] In addition to suggesting that Wopper had reached the status of an icon in Woodland, California, the prologue goes on to offer a capsule version of Wopper's story. The warning also initiates the novel's meditation on deportation by revealing how forced removal structures social relations and economies of pleasure. With its curious anti-Mexican echoes of "Remember the Alamo," Tamayo's warning also draws a long line between one century's anti-Mexican militarism and another's. These undercurrents belie the seeming informality and joking tone of the narrative and establish the tension between the novel as serious critique and as easygoing romp.

The prologue is followed by a brief interlude in the close third person and then by the narrative of Raúl Leon, a childhood friend and drinking buddy; followed by Lara González, Wopper's ex-girlfriend; followed by Jorge Barraza, his father; and so on. This multivoiced form is significant for several reasons beyond underscoring the testimonial or documentary quality of the novel. Not only does this format lend a kind of realist effect, but it also makes Wopper a bit mysterious, turning him into an icon as well as an omen.

Such a documentary-like form doesn't suggest a conventional bildungsroman. It even seems to go to a great deal of trouble to belie the bildungsroman by deploying a complex if perhaps meaningless chapter notation system that reads more like a muddled outline for a research paper, complete with "parts" and "chapters" subdivided into sections numbered with roman numerals—none of which follow a pattern or even conform to the rules for the outline of a research paper taught in old-fashioned middle-school curricula. For example, the prologue is followed by "Part I. Chapter One. I." This vaguely officious structure contrasts with the jokey tone and kaleidoscopic quality of the novel, making it less evocative of a bildungsroman than of a poorly organized policy brief or a loose ethnography, one that relies on structuring forms for narrative authority in an effort to impose order.

These links to the documentary form also gesture toward the ethnographic form and thereby double us back to the captivity narrative (one of ethnography's ancestors), emphasizing *The Deportation of Wopper Barraza* as a kind of community testimonio and reinforcing the importance of testimony, of witnessing as formally inherent to narratives of capture, containment, and removal. By evoking the captivity narrative, the novel underscores a critical component of the contemporary deportation regime: it spreads containment and captivity far and wide. People are not simply removed; their movements are also circumscribed and defined. The removal of deportees constrains the movements of others, who live in enhanced fear and increased economic precarity every time someone is removed. Finally, Wopper's exile to Mexico ultimately entails a form of captivity, just as his secretive return to California further envelops him in a web of constraint.

Subjunctive Mourning

When the novel reveals the ripple effects of deportation, it also illustrates how forced removal messes with time, skewing and fragmenting temporalities and leaving people bereft. Part of the suffering that deportation causes has to do with the way futurities seem to evaporate. Boehm highlights this aspect of deportation, arguing that as relationships are shredded, strained, and stretched out, those affected by deportation find themselves stuck in time. Without a clear sense of how to move forward with their lives that are so interrupted and often locked in limbo, people cannot plan, cannot imagine new futures. They may not know whether loved ones will join them in exile; they may not know whether they will be able to navigate a country's labyrinthine bureaucracies to obtain jobs for which they are qualified; they may not know whether they will be able to assemble the money to return to the United States; they may not know whether their legal status will change as their case winds through the courts. So, in addition to mourning their lost connections, mourning those who have been disappeared from their life even if they can be reached by phone, people mourn subjunctively; they mourn "the loss of what could have been" because "deportation renders lives frozen in the moment" and "frames the future as unimaginable."[50] Forced removal kidnaps time.

The Deportation of Wopper Barraza illustrates this temporal sensation formally and within the narrative. First, it emphasizes the shredded relationship to time by refusing to provide regular temporal markers. Readers must piece together the time of the novel, assembling a sense of the temporal duration of events via clues such as the birth of Lara and Wopper's son or a stray comment about how long Wopper had been gone. This temporal disorientation gives readers a glimpse of what it would be like to lose ordinary markers such as the past, present, and future.

As the narrative unspools, the novel also examines this experience of temporal loss through the story. One of Wopper's friends describes that newfound relationship to time with an ironic envy. Raul explains, "We envied Wopper because he had no idea what tomorrow would be like. And we all knew exactly what it would be like. Like yesterday and the day before."[51] Such a sentiment belies the situation Wopper finds himself in, but it also speaks to the complexity of possession. Raul possesses a sense of the past and future, even if he finds them dull and uninspired. Yet, as he points out, Wopper has lost the sense of the future. And if Raul sees it as an adventure, Wopper assuredly does not. Instead, Wopper grieves what he has lost:

> His misery was such that all he could think about was his own misery. How he missed home, how he missed his parents and Lara, how he would do anything to be back in Woodland, to have his life as it once was.... Day after day he spent pacing the light blue tile floor of his one-bedroom shack as if it were a jail cell, a cell of crumbling plaster walls, nothing hanging, not even a wooden cross or an old calendar.... It felt as if he spent his days crying or trying to cry, or, even more pitiful, thinking about how he felt like crying.[52]

If Wopper struggles with an unfamiliar new reality, finding himself longing for what is lost, he also finds himself immobilized, unable to imagine or plan—which is to say unable to look for work or do more than act as a witness to his own grief. What the narrator elliptically suggests is that the passage of time does not interest Wopper because he no longer has a sense of its materiality.

Wopper ultimately finds his way out of his grief, and here the novel offers a remarkable argument about how time can be restored after it has been kidnapped and how the grief over its loss can be lessened—by the crucial work of witnessing (which underscores what the novel's form has already emphasized). Shortly after he arrives, Mija begins bringing him an evening meal. He waits for her to leave it and then "hungrily devour[s] whatever she left for him." This routine continues until "one evening she set the tray of food down and stayed. She didn't even talk to him; she just placed her back against the wall and in one motion slid down so that she sat with her legs crossed." Mija then sat mutely each evening for several days, until she finally asked him, "Do you like my cooking?"[53] In her mute silence she witnesses Wopper's presence, perhaps his grief, and gives him the gift of her time as well as her labor. Her question, importantly, demands reciprocity, thereby serving to underline the work of witnessing. If she cannot replace what forced removal has taken from him, she can provide the possibility for new connections and, in doing so, create the possibility of a new futurity. This moment between Mija and Wopper also comments on the work of the novel itself, especially on the way the novel centers witnessing as a crucial part of the response to captivity, a response that is also a rebuke to the long history of spectacularizing the captive.

Shrug Theory

Further establishing Wopper's status as an icon in Woodland is that he rarely speaks for himself. Communicating mostly by shrugging, Wopper shrugs his answer to virtually every question. Sometimes Wopper's shrugs are funny and provide him with paths out of trouble since they leave people to draw their own conclusions, conclusions that turn out favorably for him. His ambiguous shrugs leave his interlocutors wondering, meditating on the reasons they interpreted the shrug as they did, and leaving Wopper even more opaque. What the novel reveals, and part of its joke, is that by simply shrugging, Wopper enables others to transform him into a screen onto which they project their own desires.

The shrugs are also tragic because they appear to be the effect of a corrosive sense of shame. In Woodland only his father and a childhood friend don't disparage Wopper. Everyone else characterizes him as a loser, from his mother, who complains that he "drank too much, worked too little, and let life make his decisions for him," to an apparently corrupt businessman, Don Elpidio, who mockingly calls him "Don Nobody" and derides him: "You exist to be used by others. Back home, no one had any use for you, so you did nothing."[54] Wopper even articulates a sense of himself as a loser when he tells Lara that he doesn't want a son because "he would be ashamed of me just like everyone else."[55] He subsequently insists to Mija that she overestimates him, arguing, "I'm not capable of shit! Just ask anyone who's ever known me. My favorite thing to do back home was play racquetball, and I'm not even good at it."[56]

So when people in Woodland hear that this hapless youth, an out-of-work shrugger, a loser who loses his green card, has taken a leading role in district politics in Mexico and is actively reshaping his family's rancho, La Morada (which translates simply as "residence"), by getting roads paved, attracting a soccer team, and collecting funds for a new upscale housing development, they are shocked. Or, as his ex-girlfriend, Lara, notes with astonishment, people in Mexico "trusted him, respected him, whatever. They thought Wopper was a man on the rise, and they wanted to rise with him."[57] Such sentiments are repeated by nearly every character in the novel except Wopper, who shrugs.

If Wopper's silence, his recourse to the language of shrugs, underscores his sense of shame, it also highlights the work of interpretation and, especially, the testimonial quality of the novel itself. The novel keeps Wopper at a remove from readers, a technique that echoes the defamiliarizing mechanisms states use to manage and scale their populations, rendering people as "aliens" who are "illegal" and "deportable." Montoya exploits this strategy to suggest how easily people adopt such defamiliarizing techniques to characterize their own sons and lovers. While it's an aggressive authorial choice to refuse to represent Wopper's interiority beyond a few snippets, it suggests an unwillingness to satisfy a bourgeois curiosity about a figure marked by his refusal to concede to aspirational market ideals. Through the shrug, the novel offers its extraordinary critique of the discourse of development, of the very concept of liberal subjectivity, of rectitude as the mark of superiority. It may also be a sly critique of not simply the educational system in the United States but also the early rhetoric of those who advocated for DREAM legislation by arguing for a kind of capitalist assimilation, to the disadvantage of those who don't fit such a model.

Dropout or Licenciado?

That Wopper is so successful in rural Michoacán comprises the novel's farce. His and Mija's "success" depends on a series of misrepresentations that portray Wopper as a respected, influential university graduate, a "licenciado," while deploying an intricate set of maneuvers in which they pit rival businessmen against each other, dupe his ex-girlfriend's family into giving them a substantial sum to keep the scam from falling to pieces, draw in former La Morada residents now living in California to invest in their development scheme, and ultimately inspire a retired California real estate tycoon to help them build a housing development in an area prone to floods. The scheme unravels only when Wopper realizes that Mija may have been a bit duplicitous, and he a bit naive.

But to get at how this farce is also a complicated critique of liberal discourses of development and assimilation, it's helpful to look at *The Deportation of Wopper Barraza*'s most self-reflective voice, Arnulfo Beas, a college counselor and Lara's cousin, who had known Wopper as a diffident student in Woodland. He cannot understand what he sees as Wopper's transformation and tells him, "It's throwing me for a friggin' loop. I can't make sense of it. Here you did nothing back home, and all of a sudden I show up and you're playing me for some pawn in your intricate scheme. What happened to you? I want to know. I seriously want to know."[58] Wopper of course shrugs a response, and Beas begins to doubt the educational methodologies that have guided his graduate research and work as a college counselor.

Throughout the text, Beas brings Wopper's story into the context of a liberal discourse of education and management. Beas is burned out; his ambitions to solve the "Latino educational crisis" have dissipated with promotions, a mortgage, the search for a girlfriend. In his haplessness he seeks to understand Wopper's transformation by linking it to the failure he sees in the educational system and then to Wopper's encounter with the US judicial system: "I considered Wopper's deportation as the greatest thing to happen to him if only because it woke him from a senselessly inane existence."[59] So committed is Beas to uplift and respectability—that is, to the assimilationist demands placed on racialized peoples—that he actually imagines forced removal as a good thing. Beas's approach is that of the well-meaning mediator of social control and its sustaining logic of respectability. Wopper is unvalued and unrecognizable outside of the narrow aperture of aspiration and striving productivity. Beas can't imagine that Wopper, far from being without ambition, is unpersuaded by capital's promise and has refused the system of respectability, the grind of labor without end; he even walks away from the real estate scheme just as the lure of flowing money seems most promising, telling Mija, "I don't care, I never cared!"[60]

For Beas, Wopper's deportation is a break from an educational system that diminishes people, grinding their ambition and sense of possibility to nothing: "Seeing students with so much potential, students who wanted to be astronauts and presidents and soccer stars, become slowly anesthetized, numbed to a point that they couldn't move forward, so that by the time they were fifteen, sixteen, seventeen, they could no longer even understand the concept of envisioning a future for themselves. They couldn't see past Woodland. They couldn't see past tomorrow."[61] Beas's critique of the education system depends, in a sense, on his faith in the possibilities of uplift through respectability. He sees a system that, for students like Wopper, anesthetizes ambition, or what another character, the retired real estate developer who joins Wopper and Mija's scheme, calls, less grandly, "momentum." Wopper's refusal both reinforces his iconic status and stymies those like Beas and the real estate developer who are committed to the aspirational romance that structures capital's allure.

When Wopper returns to Woodland, somber and silent about his exile to La Morada, unwilling to discuss the scheme he has abandoned, Beas is so puzzled that he admits to a kind of defeat: "I couldn't enter Wopper's thoughts. I couldn't know what was going on inside his head. And I realized that I would never know. That was when I pushed myself away from the computer and placed my forehead on the edge of the desk, and I said to myself, *Damn it, Arnie, you don't know anything at all.*"[62] For Beas, perhaps for the very form of bildung, only an aspirational approach to consumer culture, to normative white respectability, is legible as valued and appreciated. Thus, in its insistent effort to draw readers into a position where Wopper is appreciated rather than dismissed as a reckless drunk with four DWIs and countless hours of counseling and community service behind him, as a loser who loses his green card, *The Deportation of Wopper Barraza* reveals a slender, very interesting critique. Beas has functioned as the novel's mouthpiece for bourgeois subjectivity, the warden of respectability, and the signpost for assimilation to a liberal (white) individualism. For Beas, Wopper is ultimately unintelligible. He can't understand such a refusal or the affective relations that enable it.

Perhaps that push away from the computer signals the failure of the standard rags-to-riches narrative. The novel suggests, in fact, that Beas is actually the teller of the tale, the producer who assembled the many voices across the documentary text, the narrator who imagines Wopper's consciousness. It's a clever turn, and Beas's despair before his computer screen can be read as despair at the genre of the bildungsroman, which is to say at the discourse of development as it applies to both subjects and locales, which he now suspects as having done a disservice not only to him but to Wopper and everyone else. It's a really interesting move on Montoya's part because if the formal quality of the novel draws from multiple narrative traditions, the plot itself looks like a standard-issue bildungsroman up until the very moment Wopper walks away from his and Mija's scheme.

Perhaps the form could be characterized as a bildungsroman lite. Wopper is not transformed but chastened; the quivering final chapters do not offer satisfactory closure: Beas tries to convince Wopper to return to school; Mija dreams that he will return to La Morada. Apparently offering a tale that weaves forced removal, deportation, into the arc of the bildungsroman as a "crisis" that enables maturity and liberation, *The Deportation of Wopper Barraza* ultimately refutes what it seems to have promised. Such a refutation of the premise of liberal subjectivity can be most clearly understood if the novel is seen as offering a bildungsroman plot focused not just on Wopper but also on La Morada.

At first, both rancho and man appear listless, underdeveloped, abandoned. When Wopper leaves for La Morada, his parents pack a suitcase full of gifts and a "makeshift map" identifying cousins and compadres who would welcome Wopper and help him adjust. But Wopper encounters a very different rancho than his father's map of memories had predicted. The town is still small, with unpaved roads and brick structures "plastered and painted bright colors—yellows, pinks, and greens, seemingly the brighter the better." These homes, however, do not have occupants: "The largest ones were empty, boarded up, some Northerner's dream home rarely visited." Wopper sees almost no one on the streets and discovers that everyone his father "had instructed him to visit was gone or, like Don Martín, dead."[63] Or as Don Cirilo, the squatter, notes, "Everyone his age or every age except for my age and older has left."[64] Wopper's father ultimately finds out about this depopulated town not from Wopper, who never calls or writes, but from a compadre who tells him that everyone had moved either to a larger city or to the United States: "'Don't you remember, compadre,' he said, 'La Morada is disappearing.'"[65] So Wopper is sent to a devastated town, bereft of its long-term inhabitants, in which he must find some way to survive and respond to the question the few remaining children ask, "How come [you] don't go north like their parents?"[66] In this sense, Wopper's first encounters with La Morada seem not very different from Alejandro Santiago's description of his return to his hometown in Oaxaca. And if Santiago set about "repopulating" his rancho, Wopper finds himself rebranding his.

While the parallels between La Morada and Wopper may be obvious, Montoya plays with these parallels by revealing that the people in Woodland who hear about the changes to La Morada and celebrate its development also see them as a sign of Wopper's transformation. When Wopper's father hears that Wopper has begun having La Morada's streets paved, he joyfully crows to Raquel, Wopper's mother, "That's not just any rancho . . . that's my hometown, your hometown, too, if you weren't so ashamed! And everybody knows that paved streets are necessary for anything and everything to progress."[67]

Paved streets signal a kind of arrival for Jorge, especially in a town where no one seems to show up and where few people seem to have vehicles in any case. If the paved streets signal potential market integration, they are only a part of Mija's scheme, catalyzing a broader plan to develop the local reservoir into a vacation resort, appealing first to former La Morada residents now living in the United States and, ultimately, according to the practiced eye of a California real estate developer, to a much larger market. Here, in people's wonderment at the change in Wopper and La Morada, the novel reveals its critique of the politics of respectability that undergirds the deportation regime, the novel of development, the educational system, and the racial work of a liberal imaginary which imagines education can soothe the ravages that capitalism enacts.

Far more than easing the integration of La Morada into the market economy, Wopper and Mija's scheme would completely transform the town itself, shifting it from subsistence farming—from the cultivation of corn and agave with profit margins so miniscule that Don Elpidio sneeringly tells Wopper he would make more money working at a car wash than farming—to another tourist zone dependent on the movement of people and capital rather than the maintenance of a sustainable culture and way of life. Furthermore, the larger infrastructure scheme depends on fraud: by constructing the homes in a flood zone, Mija expects to trigger government money for flood abatement, benefiting the concrete companies lured into doing much of the paving and rebuilding for free. This plan will further degrade the arability of the region, further disappear farming from the local economy. Ironically, paved roads may ultimately make it harder to get crops to market since there will be fewer crops to travel the roads. Wopper abandons the project, and the novel closes with La Morada paved but empty, the shell of the house planned by Mija and Wopper sitting atop the reservoir, virtually abandoned. The real estate developer continues to plan, but the scheme is stunted by Wopper's departure.

Part of what conflates La Morada and Wopper is that transformation for both seems to hinge on migration. Wopper's efforts to change the rancho rely on the influx of cash from former La Morada residents now living in California. He hitches this scheme to their dreams of return, to a vision of La Morada as a "sanctuary," as Jorge calls it, and even to an effort to transform their affective relationship to their hometown. Just as Raquel is ashamed of Wopper, Jorge sees her as ashamed of their rancho. The promise of transformation, of the development of man and town, is a promise of a new affective sensibility toward origin and future.

Neither Raquel nor Jorge, much less Wopper or Beas, ultimately acknowledges that the scheme to "improve" La Morada relies on neocolonial logics that undo land-based community in favor of the movement of global capital and the consumption of leisure. It is of course this same movement of global capital that enchanted Jorge away from La Morada in the first place and that Wopper ultimately resists, to the disappointment and mystification of everyone. Yet, perhaps unlike others, Wopper realizes that if paved roads are the beginning of the adventure, they do not signal freedom for him since his deported status limits the roads he can travel openly, at ease.

The novel leaves so much undone and unmade in the rancho and in Wopper and thereby offers space for a set of questions about deportation. How complicit, the novel seems to ask, is the assimilationist politics of education and achievement not just with global capital but with the ideologies subtending the deportation regime itself? What sorts of achievements and integration (market or otherwise) appear to justify the casting out of some, in the loud clamor to make room for others? What values does the discourse of development underscore? In formal and narrative terms, *The Deportation of Wopper Barraza* not only offers a picture of deportation's wake, the ripples of loss and devastation, the kidnapping of time and of the sustaining sense of what could have been, but also provides a devastating critique of the structures of liberal subject making, the scaffolding of growth and achievement that subtly justifies persistent legal violence.

Sola; Sola

If Maceo Montoya, like María Amparo Ruiz de Burton, provides a complex portrait of the politics of respectability underpinning the logic of citizenship and the deportation regime, he does so at the expense of offering nuanced representations of either women or Mexico. By contrast, an earlier novel, one set just as mass deportation was beginning, portrays women, Mexico, and forced removal in a way that is ultimately more complex, far less sardonic, and more earnest— even as it is aimed at a less "respectable" audience (after all, *The Deportation of Wopper Barraza* was published by a venerable university press). Malín Alegría's 2007 novel, *Sofi Mendoza's Guide to Getting Lost in Mexico*, is targeted at the chica lit market.[68] As such, the novel utilizes familiar tropes of romance and thwarted teen crushes, female competition for the star athlete, and drunken antics. It weaves into this familiar plot, however, a very unfamiliar story of border politics, border crossing, and the long legacy of US imperial ambition, an ambition that has required Mexican labor even as it refuses Mexicano cultures. If the novel reinscribes heteropatriarchal romance as an antidote to much that ails youth, it nevertheless strategically leverages this platform to portray the anguish deportation can cause and the duplicity of US immigration practices.

The novel opens with a portrait of a preening teen, Sofi, the daughter of parents who came from Mexico to the United States as young adults, as she instant-messages her friends about sneaking away from their homes for a weekend bash in Baja California. Sofi feels anxious about lying to her parents but gains new resolve when, over a Taco Bell meal, her parents tell her that she will not be allowed to attend the University of California, Los Angeles, the next year because they want her to live at home. So furious is she with this manifestation of parental protectiveness that she joins her fellow high school mat maids and defiantly heads across the line.

The first third of the novel follows the girls on a typical binge-drinking, house-party hookup escapade. Sofi is not especially likable, nor is she comfortable in Mexico. She has not been there since she was three, knows very little Spanish, and indulges in as many anti-Mexican stereotypes as her white friends, even going so far as to call a woman working at a café a "wettie" while criticizing her parents' failure to fully assimilate:

> Sofi looked at her mother with feelings of shame and pity. She couldn't help it. Her parents were fixated on the American dream and talked constantly about how America was the best country in the world. It was the only place where hard work and persistence actually paid off. It was nothing like Mexico, where politicians were crooks, cops abused their power, and if you were poor, there was no way to get ahead. They were so proud to live in America, yet when they interacted with Americans, they grew quiet and nervous. After fourteen years, her parents were still uncomfortable with their accents and lack of formal education. They tiptoed around their white employers, white neighbors and anyone in an expensive suit as if they were God Almighty. It made Sofi's skin crawl. Sofi refused to be like them. She was just as American as her friends, and once she went to college, she could stuff her parents' issues in a closet.[69]

What Sofi does not yet know is that she and her parents do not have formal authorization to live in the United States, which partially explains their apparent anxiety. But this portrait also reveals a Sofi whose US education and cultural assimilation have not provided a nuanced understanding of class practices or of a labor economy that depends on systems of exploitation. Her judgments both utilize her parents' gross generalization about Mexico, conflating "America" with whiteness (all of her friends, she later notes, are Anglo) and class mobility, and also draw on the structure of entitlement provided by her education; her parents' ambitious decision to rent a condominium in a well-funded public school district gave their daughter the opportunity to obtain an education that would enable her to apply to and be accepted by an elite public institution. Characterizing her parents as "caged behind their fears of the unknown," Sofi patronizingly assumes her own superiority.[70] Her affective stance, shame and pity, mirrors her sense of both identification and disidentification—a form of splitting that will only grow more intense as the plot unfolds.

When the teens head home at the end of the weekend, Sofi is pulled aside at the border and told that her green card is a fake. After a panicked phone call to her parents, a confused and miserable Sofi makes her way to her tía's home, where she meets her cousins and uncle for the first time. Presuming that there is just some mistake with her paperwork, she haughtily enters her aunt's home, exhibiting the self-assurance of an overprivileged snob. Per the setup, Sofi, an only child, is unprepared for less luxurious living conditions. Outraged at finding herself cast out, she is also horrified by ranch life: the rooster attacks; she witnesses her first pig slaughter; the chinche bugs bite her when she tries to sleep; she has to share a bedroom with her three cousins; everyone makes fun of her Spanish; no one has a phone; and her internet access is confined to a nearby café. At seventeen, Sofi is forced to acknowledge that she may not be able to return to the United States legally. To Sofi's immediate horror, her tía has no sympathy for her and puts her to work doing the laundry by hand, babysitting her rambunctious twin cousins, cooking for everyone, and cleaning. Sofi, furious and pouty, behaves intolerably.

While Sofi slowly recognizes the structures of legality that hold her, her parents, and many others captive, she does not actually question the terrorizing governance that she has encountered. Instead, Alegría forces readers to see Mexico through the eyes of this unlikely teenager, and it's an uncomfortable experience for sure. She also enables readers to see that in coming to terms with her legal status vis-à-vis the immigration machine, Sofi must understand the work of borders that she had never envisioned as applicable to her. Like Wopper Barraza, Sofi initially moves from outrage to grief. When the immigration agent confronts her, she thinks, "She had lived in San Inocente most of her life. She was a Mat Maid, for God's sake. She couldn't be illegal."[71] Her own sense of the impossibility of her situation underscores just what her parents had been closeting but also her own ignorance of the structural system of immigration underpinning the neoliberal economy. Like Wopper Barraza, she mourns her kidnapped future, her now-inaccessible past. Described as "lugging her heavy heart" around the rancho, she ultimately isolates herself in her grief: "'Leave me alone.' Tears streamed down her cheeks. Sofi muffled her sobs into her pillow. Yesenia turned off the lights and closed the door, leaving Sofi alone in the blackness."[72] This blackness suggests Sofi's incapacity to see things differently. Yet the novel argues rather sweetly that for Sofi to accommodate herself to her new situation, she needs precisely the opposite of isolation; she has to give up the scaffold imaginary, stop demanding that she be left sola, and begin to understand the possibilities of queer horizontalities. This change starts when she meets María Rita, who gives Sofi a necklace commemorating Santo Juan Soldado, the patron saint of the US-Mexico border, whose miraculous appearance had saved María Rita from an attempted rape while she tried to cross into the United States in a remote region.[73] She also tells Sofi about the caravan of loss, the accumulation of deaths of people attempting to cross the border informally. Her cousin Yesenia subsequently takes her to a curandera, where Sofi sees a candle with a picture of Juan Soldado and reads a prayer asking for his intervention so that people may safely cross the border. After giving Sofi a limpia, the curandera outfits her with a miniature statue of Juan Soldado. These meetings introduce her to a new meshwork of relations. Sofi is forced to see herself not in isolation, not as the sole figure to suffer in an inhuman system of degradation and control, but as someone who might well be part of a collective she hadn't known existed. Additionally, Liliana's and María Rita's stories illustrate a broader history of struggle and force, thereby prodding Sofi to slowly relocate herself into a history of struggle and thus into a set of relationships she had previously eschewed.

Sofi's journey from San Inocente, Alta California, to Rancho Escondido, Baja California, is also a journey from her privileged life to a new consciousness about her broader sociality. The text winks at this journey, since she travels from innocence (San Inocente) to consciousness and compassion through a hidden detour unknown to most of the inhabitants of San Inocente: that is, Rancho Escondido. Rancho Escondido is the zone where Sofi learns to confront her own ignorance, stereotypes, and self-centered behavior. In tracing this journey, the novel offers its compelling critique of the cultural processes and imperial machinations that produced Sofi's ignorance and nasty behavior in the first place.

True to the generic conventions of a popular teen romance, Sofi meets a handsome young man named Andres, who takes her on a tour of the ejido system, explaining Mexico's revolutionary history, as well as the political economy of tourism and self-fashioning. According to Andres, Rancho Escondido had originally been a large ejido, which, he explains, "are communal lands that people can farm at no cost." Sofi responds with some astonishment, "That's strange. I never heard of people sharing land."[74] Such a vision of collectivity or interdependence is fully incompatible with the commodity-fueled dreams that Sofi had lugged to Mexico along with teen lovesickness or "curdled pain."[75] But as she begins to recognize the possibility of land held outside of capital, she also begins to see the beauty of the countryside around her: "She smiled at the little black-headed brown birds chirping melodiously in the evergreens. The turquoise blue sky contrasted with the dark green plants and brown hills. It was a soothing sight."[76]

Her appreciation of her location as a meaningful place, as a place worth attending to, is further intensified when her tía makes her join a church group handing out clothes and other supplies at a nearby migrant camp. At first Sofi is shocked by the "makeshift box houses; they looked like they'd been constructed overnight with the resources found around them: portions of cardboard, loose bricks, old wood, anything flat to keep the sun and rain away." She learns that many of the camp's inhabitants have traveled thousands of miles from Oaxaca and Chiapas, do not speak the settler colonizer's language of Spanish, and have few resources. Not surprisingly, as she hands out clothes and greets people, she at first sees only difference: "Sofi realized that this was another world, one she never knew existed."[77] Yet as she continues to meet people, her sense of disconnection shifts:

> She recognized her mother's strong nose. Behind her stood a man who looked just like her uncle. Everywhere she turned she saw familiar-looking faces. Sofi felt their eyes in different ways, too: from some she felt warmth, acceptance, and appreciation of an honest attempt to make someone's life better. From others she felt the cold stare of judgment or maybe resentment for being an uninvited guest and rubbing their noses in their neediness. But Sofi dismissed those negative thoughts. A new feeling was spilling into her heart. It was a crystal-clear awareness that she was related to all these people. *They are Mexican like me*, she thought.[78]

If Sofi initially saw her parents through the doubled frame of "shame and pity," she now rejects the tendency to produce such frames and focuses on a sense of relationship that entails acknowledging a fundamental connection to the Mexican, Mayan, and Zapotec refugees before her. This is a dramatic shift for a teen who had, before her exile, remained aloof from other Latinas while befriending only white girls.

As Sofi accommodates herself to her new life and as her consciousness shifts, she becomes increasingly likable: kinder to her younger cousins, friendlier with her neighbors, less hostile to the differences she does not understand. She does favors for Yesenia, teaches her uncle yoga to help relieve his pain from a debilitating back injury and to lift his depression, learns to wrestle and play with her wily twin cousins, and seeks to establish a relationship with a grandmother she hadn't even known was alive before her exile. It helps that her tour guide, Andres, is handsome and that she develops a crush on him.

Her budding romance will exceed the boundaries of the plot and carry across the border line, but it does not emerge until she recognizes that she can have a meaningful relationship with Mexico, her new home, and her generous family. Although she never really acknowledges that they didn't have to shelter her, she does begin to appreciate them. More especially, she starts to see that if her US status renders her "illegal" over there, it resembles a different sensibility in Rancho Escondido, and a "new feeling" spills into her heart as she begins to feel a part of Mexico, connected to her family and the culture she is meeting for the first time. Her sense of superiority, a sense intrinsic to her assimilation to the dominant norms of whiteness, an assimilation that also entails her internalization of the norms of respectability, begins to dissipate.

One of the novel's surprising moves—because one might not expect this turn in a teen romance—is its insistence that Sofi's transformation entails a new political consciousness, not simply more empathy. Beyond learning that she can understand herself within a broader sociality, she also begins to learn something about the structures of capital that rely on criminalized labor to increase profits and produce docile consumer citizens. The narrative turns on these revelations. For example, having just been publicly humiliated by her mischievous cousins, who convince her to use the wrong (and inappropriate) Spanish words at a public market, she meets a man who explains the use of black ribbons to signify the death of a relative crossing the border. He describes the border violence and then notes the intensive anti-Mexican militia that had formed along the border: "'What those fools don't understand is that it is we Mexicans who make it possible for them to have big cars, big houses, and even bigger guns. It's these hands,' Lalo said, lifting up his wide, callused palms, 'working in the fields, washing dishes, and cleaning their houses. You can't have a superpower nation without stepping on someone's back to get there.'"[79] Lalo's comment is not simply a quotidian critique of hemispheric labor management, or discipline through violence; it is also a specific critique of the erasure of interdependence. He argues here that the US economy requires exploitation to flourish. This critique is underscored later when Andres notes how policing has intensified: "You know, the INS pulls over trains and buses at random to check people's paperwork. It's ridiculous. The United States is so scared of dishwashers and cleaning ladies taking over that it's becoming a police state."[80] In both of these moments, the text produces a pause; it cuts the structure of the narrative so that an analysis of power dynamics can disrupt the romance novel's tendency toward integration through accommodation to structures of power. The text further underscores how grasping these dynamics forces a broader transformation by illustrating more than one moment when Sofi begins to confront the ugly prejudices of Anglo tourists as well as her own faulty assumptions.

To some extent, this critique might appear pedantic, even patronizing; yet in weaving the critique into the process by which Sofi learns of her own immigration status and then is forced to understand the larger social structure that produces the concept of status in the first place, Alegría transforms a teen romance/coming-of-age narrative into a contemporary captivity narrative, one in which Sofi is forced to witness a set of cultural practices that differ from what she is used to—and more important—to grow to appreciate those practices outside of US capitalist, racialized norms. By suggesting that a critique of US power is a part of daily conversations in Mexico, Alegría also articulates a crucial point—that Mexico is as much a zone of theorization as the more typically sanctioned US academic institutions (which would largely ignore her novel in the first place).

Locating a meaningful critique of US hemispheric practices within the quotidian experience of Mexican life is one way *Sofi Mendoza's Guide to Getting Lost in Mexico* differs radically from *The Deportation of Wopper Barraza*. Yet another way in which Alegría's novel proffers a more complex portrait of Mexico is in its mapping of rich social practices—from illustrations of daily forms of generosity from portraits of quinceañeras and tardeadas to the informal economies that produce more viable lives. In this novel Mexico is a substantial place, not a flat backdrop for loss, corruption, or disappointment. By illustrating how Sofi changes and comes to recognize Mexico as the name for rich socialities and complex histories, the novel suggests that the US imaginary is itself rather stunted, that it has failed to grow and develop into the capacity to recognize and appreciate different structures of being, different worlds.

Perhaps the richest critique of the US deportation regime lies within the novel's most romantic gesture. Early in her sojourn Sofi is shocked to learn that her grandmother also lives in Rancho Escondido. She had never heard her mentioned and is disturbed to hear her characterized as mean and crazy. As she adjusts to her new life in Mexico and comes to embrace the people who have welcomed her, Sofi decides to meet her grandmother. After rejecting Sofi's initial efforts, her grandmother ultimately invites her into her house to talk. Describing her life, Sofi's abuela notes that she and her family had also been deported:

> "I was born in 1940 in a small town called Lemoore." *That's a strange name for a Mexican town,* Sofi thought. "My daddy, your great-grandfather, worked as a farmworker. In those days the *gringos* wanted our money. He

paid three cents to cross the border in El Paso." The old woman smiled softly. "I don't remember much of that time. But there was this huge raid. INS officers swarmed into our barrio and took everybody. They called it Operation Wetback. We were brought here, to the border. My father refused to ever go back. He was so disgusted with the United States, he made me swear never to go back there again."[81]

This moment, in addition to providing the clue that enables Sofi to return to the United States and allows her family to claim citizenship status, offers some important insights. First, Sofi's grandmother, Abuela Benita, reveals a longer history of deportations, one that depends on a set of contradictory practices creating disjunctures and erasing refusals. Second, the citation of Operation Wetback historicizes Benita's experience, but it also creates a reverberating irony given that the text opens with the teen girls' plan to help Sofi hook up with her dream date, Nick—a plan they jokingly dub "Operation *Papi Chulo.*" Finally, the moment suggests an alternative affective relationship with the United States, one in which it is not designated as desirable, as the place where people can get ahead, but instead is a site to be eschewed, a place held in contempt.

The larger argument that Sofi has something to gain by pursuing a closer relationship to her grandmother, especially since the grandmother has been described by Sofi's tía as the woman who abandoned her and her brother, is obviously reinforced when Benita locates the paper that proves she was born in the United States. But the romance of this plot move should not be dismissed as simply that. Sofi has pursued someone who has been despised and rejected and in this finds a way through her captivity, even as it reveals a doubled form of capture. More important, Alegría provides a portrait of transformation that depends on recognition of relationality. In this, the novel provides for a more complex portrait of transformation than does the farce Maceo Montoya offers. Not only does *Sofi Mendoza's Guide to Getting Lost in Mexico* challenge *The Deportation of Wopper Barraza*'s stereotypical portraits of women alongside a flattened, even stereotypical Mexico, but it also offers a denser analysis of the psychic effects of deportation, even if the map it offers for adjustment to such an experience is more than a bit unrealistic.

Sofi's desire to meet her abuela, whom the family has shunned, finally leads to the romantic ending to the story. As it turns out, her grandmother is a US citizen, a bit of data her father and aunt lacked. So, miraculously, this deus ex machina of a birth certificate liberates Sofi from the deportation machine and enables her parents to adjust their residency status as well. But as the novel argues, the real transformation is not Sofi's status but her new sense of self as proudly Mexicana, eager to make a life for herself in her new home in Rancho Escondido. Of course, the novel could have ended with the more realistic portrayal of Sofi finding a way to reenter informally, thereby veering sharply from the dictates of the romance genre.[82] And in this allegiance to the genre perhaps Alegría offers a second kind of pause—a pause that asks readers to think about the fantasy of legitimacy and the way "authorization" enables a kind of closure that "informally authorized" methods of movement cannot, or cannot yet.

Mourning the Misplaced

Wopper and Sofi contend with the liberal state's instantiation of sovereignty in the "liberal" manner through its habit of controlling people by controlling territory. Their deportations are enacted by agents of the state (a judge, a guard) who reenact the border and illustrate how the border walls people in and out, producing the state through its capacity for refusal and ejection. A more recent novel, Daniel Peña's *Bang*, illustrates how another model of power entraps people not through the spatial structures of grids producing scaled states but through informal meshworks of people and places, attending to how flows of people and products can interact with other forms of movement and other forms of being. This form of power is less static, less structured around places, less defined by spatial grids, because its strength comes from attention to movements and flows, diversions, conversions, interactions. And as a response *Bang* focuses far more on its characters' movements, their resilience to shifts in situations; it also attends to both the mechanics and lyricism of movement itself.

In the years between the publication of Alegría's novel and Peña's novel, the war on drugs engulfed Mexico, shattering many lives and regions; these are also the years in which the deportation regime accelerated to the vicious pace that marks it today. So starkly has the narco-deportation regime's violence remade northern Mexico that to read these two novels side by side is to wonder if the settings, both nominally Mexico, are comparable at all. Peña's *Bang* offers a portrait of the tangled relations between forced deportation and the narcospaces of a frontera embattled in a complex drug war. With vivid language it shows the constraints placed on people with an informal immigration status, illustrating a terrifying landscape of forced labor and brutality. By offering a portrait of a northern Mexico in which routinized violence is a form of advertising and in which death, kidnapping, and assaults impinge on people expelled from the United States, corroding their options to such an extent that the narcoterrorism practiced by cartels aids and abets the deportation regime, *Bang* shifts the story of forced removal from the nearly benevolent experiences imagined in *Sofi Mendoza's Guide to Getting Lost in Mexico* and *The Deportation of Wopper Barraza* to a representation marked by a far more visceral cynicism and violence visited on the vulnerable.

Bang opens as a woman awaits the return of her husband, who had recently been deported: "Misplaced is the word Araceli would use. Like her husband was a lost set of keys or a good pair of scissors she doesn't want to return to the neighbors yet. *Misplaced*. First in the spring when he was deported, when the earth was full of holes and the air was spiced with baby citrus trees starving to be grounded. Then in the summer when the rattlesnakes multiplied at the end of the great drought, when the rains brought the crops back from the dead and still her husband hadn't arrived."[83] Araceli refuses the language of permanence, of death or abandonment. It's not clear whether she has heard from her husband, but in thinking of him as "misplaced," she invokes the spatial relations of border management. Her husband is not in the place one would expect. Like necessary or admired objects, he holds significance and affection; he just can't be located. Araceli's refusal of finality is underscored by the narrator's recourse to the subtle signs of seasonal change, the passage of months in the Southwest, signs marked by sweetness, danger, despair, and even a resurrection; yet all are spoiled by the husband's continued displacement, his status as missing and misplaced. These opening sentences also announce the plot; almost immediately, Araceli and her two sons will also find themselves misplaced, misplaced from their home in the United States and misplaced from each other. Their involuntary removals are a draconian result of their father's forced removal and disappearance.

Bang follows Araceli and her two sons, the high school student Uli and older brother Cuauhtémoc. After a stupid accident separates the two boys and strands them in Mexico, leaving Uli badly wounded, they each find themselves in binds, unable to return home easily because they do not have formal status. Neither does their mother, who also suffers from severe complications from diabetes; she nevertheless sets out in search of her sons, presuming that they will have returned to the town in Mexico in which they were born and partially raised. All three must try to survive the tricky terrain dominated by ruthless cartels, corrupt police and military, and a shattered sociality. While only the father has been formally deported, the rest of the family suffer from his disappearance and find themselves de facto deportees, their mobility limited by their status and their lack of a social net within Mexico that might sustain them. Uli, despite his serious injuries, makes his way to their hometown. Cuauhtémoc is lured and trapped into working for a ruthless drug dealer, flying beat-up old planes loaded with cash and cocaine. Araceli searches for them while growing sicker and more desperate, finding herself tracked by narco entrepreneurs and left to die from gangrenous injuries alongside other prisoners held for ransom by a cartel.

If quirky, funny, and surprisingly lyrical, *Bang* refuses to offer anything like a romantic or nostalgic portrait of life for deportees. Each of the three characters must navigate a series of traps by constantly negotiating their way out of one dangerous situation after another, utilizing their skills, initiative, and resilience at every turn to survive a site bathed in violence, dependent on the narcotics trade, and under siege by cartels and the military. In offering this portrait, Peña refuses to provide any kind of refuge for the reader; he offers neither a happy ending nor romantic turns of luck that enable people to survive. Only one character, the hapless older son who survives the brutalities of a kidnapping by a cartel only because he can fly a plane, seems to be alive at the end of the novel—but there, too, the text offers only a weak reason for hope.

Like *The Deportation of Wopper Barraza* and *2501 Migrantes*, *Bang* also portrays Uli's birthplace as nearly abandoned: "On Calle Ocotepec, the houses are all close to each other. They all look the same. Block after block of beige single-story boxes with square concrete facades and haloed arches above the doors like miniature Spanish missions. Adobe, cement, plaster and wrought iron. There's splayed rebar where the concrete's been knocked away from a shifty foundation. Everything is overgrown with weeds and unruly magnolia trees never meant to have grown that large. Everyone is missing. The roads are full of sand and concrete barricades and boulders that look like they were dug up from the guts of the earth."[84] Peña also deploys the language of loss. People have not left; they are "missing." And the town that has misplaced its inhabitants is structured further by earlier misplacements, as it were. Uli looks at a street whose very name, Ocotopec, signals a Mixtec presence but whose architecture and faulty building designs reflect the ongoing imperialist nostalgia for Spanish coloniality.[85] Even the landscape implies the disintegration of a social network structured now more by absence than presence: an earth disemboweled to ward off even further violence. Uli quickly discovers that people have left not only because they have been forced to migrate but also because "immediately after the cartel arrived, everyone else left. Everything was abandoned."[86] The scene of abandonment instantiates the characters' own sense of disintegrated connection; what they find in San Miguel, if they don't meet up with kidnappers and army troops, are crowds "mostly comprised of women and children. Uli assumes that, like his father had, all of the men have gone north. To Texas, Arizona, California."[87] Taken together, Montoya, Santiago, and Peña all depict a Mexico with gaping absences—absences discovered by unbidden returns.

Repeatedly flying into the United States to drop product until he finally crashes a plane full of cocaine, only Cuauhtémoc survives the cartel. As the novel closes, he has found his way to a truck stop and traded his $400 in pesos for a ten-minute shower: "Cuauhtémoc pulls himself up, turns both diamond-cut acrylic knobs at the same time so that the water pours hot and clean onto the crown of his dry head and then over his clothes and then over his aching body. He watches the water swirl pink down the drain, and he cries. He cries and cries under a shower that's so hot it puts a chill in his nerves."[88] Such is his "survival"; his escape from one war entails only a tenuous possibility of further escape. And though he has "returned" to the United States, it is a return more abject and isolated than any he might have imagined. The family has disintegrated. Cuauhtémoc has escaped captivity only to find new forms of constraint. *Bang* leaves readers unsettled, without the comfort that all will be okay for anyone caught in the deportation/narco morass.

Conclusion

The Deportation of Wopper Barraza, *Sofi Mendoza's Guide to Getting Lost in Mexico*, and *Bang* all conclude with a protagonist's return to the United States. Like Wopper, Cuauhtémoc will attempt to live in the United States informally, negotiating his daily life with the skills gleaned from years living as a "de facto citizen."[89] Unlike the other two novels, *Bang* does not offer much hope for Cuauhtémoc—its bleak outlook is underscored by the movement of the novel, which closes, not with his escape, as he contemplates the reach of a furious cartel, but with a detailed description of his brother Uli's murder after a bomb explodes. The narrative notes that as he dies, Uli remembers his mother: "She's forever shouting like that, her voice fading into oblivion. Words that have no meaning."[90] In the moments before the bomb exploded, Uli had been listing both what he would eat when he returned to Texas and what gifts he would bring his mother, but the bomb underscores the precarity that seems to emphasize that words can "have no meaning." In this sense, *Bang* seems to dismiss the possibility that the novel form can counter the US national imaginary, striated as it currently seems to be with a kind of hatred, a commitment to the pursuit of inequality in order to maintain a racialized order of capitalism. It offers a dystopian picture of the deportation regime, underscoring how crucial the work of narcoindustries has become to the maintenance of this regime. It illustrates how the kidnappers, bajadores, and cartels have become the unincorporated, unacknowledged arms of the deportation regime and how unrealistic it might well be to envision a happy ending with words that can "have no meaning" against the spreading intensification of containment.

Each of these novels ultimately illustrates how the threat of deportation and the experience of deportation, of captivity, produces a form of suspended animation for youth contained and denied childhood, stretching the experience of growing across dimensions that do not easily fold into the logic of heteronormative (and white and papered) development. These novels focus on youth whose lives have been bracketed by the practices of structured mobility and by the efforts of the state to repeatedly reinstantiate itself as sovereign through the logic and ferocity of removal. Two of the three novels seek a sort of emotional release (and relief) for the presumably papered, English-speaking reader: their romances and narratives of maturation offer a kind of sigh, even a return to the individuating logic of the liberal republic. So while they serve as witness to the violence of sovereignty and offer robust critiques of education, of the logics and politics of respectability, they nevertheless sidestep the possibility that the story of freedom the United States continues to tell remains a story predicated on the captivity not only of people constrained within its own territories but also of people now constrained across the hemisphere.

Although both *The Deportation of Wopper Barraza* and *Sofi Mendoza's Guide to Getting Lost in Mexico* were published within a dozen years of *Bang*, the intensifying narco war in Mexico and the escalation of white supremacist legal violence in the United States provide little cover for a utopian romance. To move between these three texts is to see the flattening of the reservoir of optimism. Such a narrowing is not totally surprising given how violently Mexico and Central America have suffered because of the continued transnational movement of narcotics into the United States and the ongoing displacement of the dangers of narcotics production and distribution to these zones. Nor is it surprising given the narcogenre's commitment to spectacular narratives of violence and death. But it is surprising to see the arc that the three texts collectively offer, which move from a sustained hope, an affirmation of solidarity, especially in *Sofi Mendoza's Guide to Getting Lost in Mexico*, to the breathless despair that closes *Bang*. Or is it? If we consider Alejandro Santiago's *2501 Migrantes*, then the violence that closes *Bang* in 2018 may not be very different from the vision Santiago first offered in 2006 when he began displaying coffins in the regal rooms of Oaxaca's contemporary art museum at the very same moment the streets of the United States were filled with people protesting its draconian immigration schemes.

What *2501 Migrantes* and these three novels make clear is that the logics of captivity, scale, and sovereignty reinforce each other. Borders seek to produce constraints; scale abstracts to produce borders. Sovereignty needs both. The deportation machine continues to churn just as other legal-violence systems before it have: by shredding social relations and affective connections that sustain belonging and thereby isolating labor from life, by imposing a phallic verticality that weights some lives and depletes possibilities for others. Unimpeded freedom for all people will be possible only if we abolish borders and the scaffold imaginary that produces citizenship. To do so we need to abandon the logic of scale, the perspective from the moon, and recognize that there are many worlds. We need to draw from different archives to do the conceptual work necessary to think without borders, without scale, and without sovereignty. These texts offer a beginning, a rough guide.

CONCLUSION

Density's Resistance to Scale

If we linger with Édouard Glissant's injunction to "bring an end to the very notion of a scale" and simultaneously ponder Fred Moten's observation that "every local place is a gathering place," then we can feel density's resistance to scale, the queer proximities of the felt-nearby dissolving, as Linda Hogan puts it, "in the give and take that is where grace comes from."[1] Such resistance endures despite scale's lien on the Western academic imaginary, a lien entrenched by our gratitude. For scale, like it or not, is beloved by scholars, beloved for its promise of mastery, its premise that we live in only one world, not many, and that such a world can be wholly known, contained, bracketed, held captive. Yet as the expressive practices studied here suggest, within the folds and pockets of relations lie very different notions of connection and worlding than those enabled by the scaffold imaginary.

Moreover, if scale holds a lien on our imagination, so, too, does its literary minion, the novel of development. The bildungsroman—the story of an orphan, of a cast-out child's progress through trials and suffering to achieve social integration and assimilation—is profoundly familiar, which is to say resonant with the coercive tactics that produce racializing capitalism, including the castagories that limn rectitude: heterosexuality, white propriety, and civility. This story is both quotidian (or endemic within the Western imaginary) and a key girder in the narrative of the white family, so familiar it sustains the family. It illustrates the triumph of rectitude and rationality over any inclination toward sensuality, pleasure, embodied connection, gratitude, debt; it objectifies and models an autonomous individual child who, as if by alchemy, learns to consume and prioritize competition and success over and against collective well-being, thereby rebuking the claims of reciprocity and precarity while reinforcing a liberal ensemble of governance. The path this iconic white child charts includes not simply the temporal, reproductive, and linear markers of progress but also the technologies of comparison, which require benchmarks, signposts for normativity and neurotypicality that pit children against one another. The pedagogy behind these novels is clear: to be a child with access to a childhood is to have the capacity to unfold through normative time into a properly upright adult, citizen, or citizen-mother. To inhabit childhood is to accede to the notion that when one is not presumed a perpetual child, one can escape separability.

The slow reveal of orphan Lola's undyed, unspotted white skin suggests that with *Who Would Have Thought It?* María Amparo Ruiz de Burton intended to localize and spectacularize this well-worn narrative convention. But while *Who Would Have Thought It?* assembles the accoutrements of a bildungsroman, it swerves toward burlesquing liberal logic instead of celebrating it. Ruiz de Burton's protagonist does not weather trials and tribulations to achieve successful integration as a master of the material world. At the novel's close, an elaborate farce hinging on silly impersonations saves Lola from a fortune hunter and hurtles her into the arms of her birth family, her "real" family. Shrouded at her introduction to the Norvals, she flees at the end of the plot proper, shrouded from their machinations, disguised as the nonother. Such stasis in representation underscores the stasis of Lola's character at the novel's end: the orphaned Lola, upon discovering that she is not really orphaned, does not celebrate her newfound status as the daughter of a wealthy Australian/Mexican family nor revel in a relationship with a father she had never met. Ensconced in luxury, she pines away in solitude, consumed by her inclination to be near her lover. Her grand tour from rural Arizona, to New England, to New York City, to

Mexico City has not educated or redeemed her; it has flattened her, just as her fortune, diverted to fund the Civil War, is now in the hands of yet more grifters. At the novel's close, Lola refuses the geometry of modernity. Rectitude will not sustain her sense of isolation and loss.

By opening with a complex(ion) masquerade, a masquerade that is not revealed as such until midway through the convoluted plot of *Who Would Have Thought It?*, Ruiz de Burton breaks apart the realism that sentimental fiction and the bildungsroman deploy and that burlesque ridicules. In a world conceived of as real and distinct, Lola's dyed skin enables her to impersonate a Mojave child—a manipulation of the authentic self and a challenge to the established order of representation. Impersonation was, of course, a trademark of burlesque theater, an effort to make fun of proprieties and dislodge tired perceptions by capitalizing on an audience's discomfort with the realization that an authentic self could be undone, that selfy-ness was a performance, and realism a charade. It is worth recalling, however, that the ruse to keep Lola safe from marauding Anglo troops signals a different conceptual structure, one that deploys masquerade against possessive individuation. If Lola's masquerade as a Mojave child helps maintain the safety of the whole people and if her revelation as non-Mojave provides the promise of access to white supremacy, they also showcase another masquerade well underway. For Lola's entry into the heart of northern values sets off another slow reveal: the Norvals collectively hide the source of their wealth (the dispossession of Indigenous and Mexican resources funneled through Lola) by masquerading as successful prospectors and entrepreneurs. But this masquerade is not the novel's last. Its more important reveal spotlights the extent to which the claims of individuation, of the rational individual who consents to be governed, are also farces, charades to mask the claimants' posing, first as simple yeoman farmers; then as successful, lucky prospectors; and, finally, as real estate barons, all in the effort to make time via someone else's deeds (deeds also obtained by theft). These masquerades capitalize on yet another scandal: the proclamation of equality via the consent of the governed masks vast inequities and coercive normativities, performing what Ruiz de Burton, writing to a friend, grumpily called a "Manifest Yankie trick."[2]

The burlesque and the reveal work for Ruiz de Burton as they will operate for others; they are effective tools to manage up and against power structures. Contemporary writers also similarly turn to ruse as a means to make manifest yet more iterations of the "Manifest Yankie trick."[3] They, too, highlight how modes of capture and apprehension are crucial to efforts to rescale power, to naturalize the scaffold imaginary, even as these modes of bracketing and enclosure shift as economies and modes of control are repeatedly rescaled. Not surprisingly, then, masquerading imposters tramp across the pages of many if not all of the texts discussed in *Scales of Captivity*. In *Amigoland*, for example, the grumpy old man, Don Fidencio, resorts to pretending he is his own grandfather, returned to the rancho after a long absence. In *The Gifted Gabaldón Sisters*, Nuvamsa is forced to masquerade as the servant Fermina, hiding her identity as both great-grandmother and a captive. In *Their Dogs Came with Them*, Turtle's sense of belonging is encased in a discourse that doesn't make room for a non-binary child growing up in 1960s Los Angeles, just as the narrative itself struggles to find ways to accommodate Turtle's complex relation to structures of belonging that resist giving voice to sexual desire or really any form of desire beyond base survival; at the close of the novel, after Turtle's death, the narrative once again links Turtle's gender presentation to the tradition of masquerade, or rather to the shaken faith in transparency that gender challenges can initiate. Character after character in *The Faith Healer of Olive Avenue* will slip and slide into convenient masquerades produced by others' assumptions and presumptions about them, thereby inhabiting the figure others imagine them to be. In *Across a Hundred Mountains*, after her friend Adelina is murdered, Juana assumes her persona in order to cross easily into the United States to search for her missing father, gain an education, and survive into adulthood. Finally, *The Deportation of Wopper Barraza* features its protagonist masquerading as a licenciado sucked into an elaborate development scheme that is itself also a kind of masquerade.

Impersonation is productive because it not only showcases the constructed quality of personhood but also undermines a logic of transcendent authenticity. In doing so, it makes room for a broader critique of rectitude and the assumptions that scale helps to naturalize. Impersonation makes clear that rectitude, with its parading of claims to rationality and independence, masks a determined reliance on bracketed others, on an exploited but deauthorized support system. It disrupts the demarcations inherent to castagories and reminds us that abstract fixities are ongoing theatricals. It opens the door to a new conceptualization of relationality, one that dis/objectifies nature as distinct and separate from human agency, so called. And in the splitting that impersonation offers, the cut it knifes, it produces a new and reparative opportunity for witnessing constellations of connections without denigration, inclinations without bracketing, politics without scale.

Of course, there are crucial points of divergence between how *Who Would Have Thought It?* deploys impersonations and how the more contemporary novels studied here utilize them. Burlesque, like Ruiz de Burton, relies not just on trickery but also on stereotypes and gross generalizations. Ultimately, both that novel and its theatrical mentor reinforce the claims of representation, evoking abstract fixities and castagories even as they burlesque them. However, most of the other texts discussed here swerve from Ruiz de Burton's approach, and burlesque itself is not their touchstone. Their closer generic model is, of course, the bildungsroman. Yet none of these texts, including *Who Would Have Thought It?*, ultimately embraces the tenets of the novel of development. Instead, impersonation allows all of these novels to unfurl an analysis of the tenacious scaffolding sustaining a narrative of racialized, cast-out children cleaved from childhood, produced as perpetual children without access to a childhood, denied the experience of protection or its promise of privilege.

These texts' attention to the cast-out child who does not get to assimilate and integrate as a citizen, and their focus on the way practices of rescaling economic and geographic power entail new iterations of captivity, ultimately also suggests that scale itself is a masquerade. Scale creates the facade of coherence by showcasing nested hierarchies as inevitable and ideal, locking up people and locking down castagories through containment and comparison. Impersonation immobilizes scalar claims, not to deceive and con, but to burst the perception of singularity, to suggest the mutually constitutive processes that constellate relations rather than stratify them. Masquerades enact what the texts studied in *Scales of Captivity* all repeatedly insist: living is a reciprocal, not a scaled, process, and relations are constitutive of being itself. Beings of every form continually "and reciprocally bring one another into existence," as Arturo Escobar puts it.[4] Because beings do not preexist their constitutive relations, their natality is not in their naming or their hailing but in their myriad connections, their generative debts.

This understanding of relationality and indebtedness is not meaningful if it does not also entail a different concept of spatiality. Beyond rejecting the view from the moon, taking relationality seriously means more than refuting the colonist's claim that the world is one and not many. This imperial perception of materiality as the passive and singular ground enabling what Kemi Adeyemi, drawing on Cavarero, perceptively describes as "90° living" requires a thin materiality, one that is nonimmanent, lacking agency and imagination.[5] A world that is one and not many conjures a transparent space, an objectivity available for property, meant for deeds, circumscribed into markets. A concept of earth as a passive plane solidifies a larger understanding of the world itself as distinct, composed of individuals and other already existing objects placed upon that world. Such objects may be manipulated and perceived as abstractions, but they, like the upright individual, merely occupy space while the individual, living in this preexisting world, a world that contains everyone, also possesses a discrete mind. The vision of the rational, upright individual is bound together with a concept of a distinct, impassive, and singular world. This is the globe with its objects and agents, scaled and desperately alone.

The Gifted Gabaldón Sisters, *Sofi Mendoza's Guide to Getting Lost in Mexico*, *Their Dogs Came with Them*, *Bang*, *The Deportation of Wopper Barraza*, and *The Faith Healer of Olive Avenue* critique coloniality's elaborate scaffold imaginary with its abstract fixities, castagories, and phallic verticalities, just as they illustrate the price of rectitude, restricted movement, captivity, and the cleavage between child and childhood that creates perpetual children and unachievable adulthood. The critique they mobilize extends beyond their attention to the instrumentalization of the racialized child and the scaled globe. Put differently, the series of impersonations in these novels can be understood not as mischievous rebukes to authority and rectitude's proprieties but as openings to a broader repertoire of challenges to the coloniality of power. What emerges across these stunning texts is a broad vision of approaches to life without a globe, to living in situations instead of on the earth.

Manuel Muñoz, Helena María Viramontes, Reyna Grande, Malín Alegría, and Lorraine López offer density, queer horizontalities that attend to the felt nearby and dis/objectify relations as techniques and methods to resist scale, to live without it or its minions. They attend to proximities, to connections and reactions, rather than privileging narratives of transformative resistance and triumphant arrivals. They suggest that a dense mesh of congealments, folds, and relays constituted through changing and immanent relations compose our "throwntogetherness," as Doreen Massey would put it, rather than a distinct reality materialized in preexisting space and time.[6] This shifts the emphasis from occupying space to dwelling together amid a variegated, thick aliveness.

Density names the multiplicities of interactions, materialities, memories, and articulations that fold together with smells, inclinations, graces, breezes, organisms, ideas, idiosyncrasies, jokes, as well as solar, seismic, lunar, and gravitational movements to enact together unfolding relations. Taken together, the texts taken up by *Scales of Captivity* highlight the mesh of obligations and interactions cocreating each other, signaling the constitutive quality of relations. Moreover, nearly all of these texts underscore the violent loss caused by the upright geometry of the rational, scaled human by illustrating the conjunctures acknowledging debt can bring into being. The interexistence, the interbeingness, the throwntogetherness of situatedness can be conceptualized best via dis/objectification, which is to say an insistence on interaction against stratification via isolation and separability. Dis/objectification enables us to understand all beings and all the stuff we have been taught to think of as things as mutually constitutive of one another; it disaggregates materialities and energies from the narratives comprising them as mere objects and ordered movements to acknowledge the complexity of interactions, that is, of relations as a making do, making with, as constitutive, a practice Gloria Anzaldúa astutely named "haciendo caras."[7]

As the literature discussed in *Scales of Captivity* suggests, density does not easily fold together with romances that reinscribe market primacies. The movements along queer horizontalities do not produce orientation for mastery but rather offer an articulation of shared vulnerabilities; such horizontalities open onto the interdependence of all things and beings and further reveal the textures of indebtedness that rectitude eschews and euclidean geometries occlude. Writers as different as Eduardo Corral, Reyna Grande, Malín Alegría, and Manuel Muñoz continually weave together texts that connect people and places—connections that refuse the distinctions and binaries between them—that emphasize the blockages and openings people and beings create for one another. In this sense, indebtedness dis/objectifies: it offers an acknowledgment of interconnection, a refutation of individualism and singular rationality.

By *debt* I do not mean only the forms of extraction, accumulation, and expropriation that we associate with finance, colonialism, and slavery capitalism. To acknowledge debt is also to acknowledge the legacies of exploitation, the extent to which life has been destroyed to better and maintain other lives. If chattel slavery no longer serves as an overt structure of the US economy, its offspring—the starkly visible bracketing practices that compose what Achille Mbembe calls the "carceral landscape" (prisons, jails, detention centers) and those bracketing practices that are less visible: the informal practices of containment, apprehension, and bracketing sutured into US empire making, such as ongoing segregation, uneven access to health care, food insecurity, and the threat of deportability that serves, in effect, as a psychological ankle bracelet for millions—all produce the structures that enable rational European white people to stand erect, maintaining vast inequities and keeping exploitation both vibrant and unacknowledged.[8] The form of debt articulated by the writers studied here, furthermore, understands the connections, the responsibilities, one has to those who came before and those who will come after, to the lands and places and creatures that nurture people, each other. Rectitude can't stand this form of indebtedness because it must deny the way in which debt is, as Mbembe notes, "constitutive of the very basis of relation."[9] Such debt, Fred Moten and Stefano Harney argue, is a "debt that cannot be repaid, the debt at a distance, the debt without creditor" that calls other debtors together into a "refuge, this place of bad debt," where density refuses scale.[10]

Scalar logic, and one could say the logic perpetrated and perpetuated by the social sciences, the academic disciplines most likely to continually enforce scale, can accept change only if it can be classified as structural, fundamental, systemic. Such change requires coherence, adherence to a narrative framework that synthesizes all the aspects of a transformation, reflecting consistent values and beliefs. Such an approach emerges only with the scalar masquerade that is spatial rationalization and the casting of abstract fixities.[11] If you want to believe the world is one and not many, you need to collate whole domains of the netting of life around you into cubicles called *animate* and *inanimate*. You need to see yourself walking on earth, not dwelling within the netting of life. You need to refuse to acknowledge a sentient, all-encompassing (maybe we call it a universal) blanket of being, the multiple reals and the dramas that interactions set in motion. You must be willing to ignore the violence our investments in scale make possible.

Density, queer horizontality, and dis/objectification do not easily resolve the scalar violence perpetrated by state and informal actors; they do not prettify cages and brackets, but as part of a repertoire of resistance, they do reveal the possibilities reparative witnessing to this violence can generate. As Lorraine López, Oscar Casares, Helena María Viramontes, Malín Alegría, Bettina Restrepo, Eduardo Corral, Manuel Muñoz, Reyna Grande, Maceo Montoya, and Daniel Peña each suggest, such reparative witnessing, instead of separability, distinctions, and comparisons, enables ruptures and refusals that go unmarked as resistance precisely because scalar logic insists on a simplistic idea of transformation. What matters differently, these writers teach us and *Scales of Captivity* argues, is the unfolding materialities that cannot be easily reconciled as abstract fixities but are rather sentient places and beings in dynamic aggregates of one another. Density and dis/objectification offer unmeasurable resistances, instances undermining the reduction of agency to simply a collation of mass, scale, and force.[12] Density and dis/objectification open up the possibility of different capacities and narratives: occlusions and shrugs and boulders and nods that cannot be accumulated into a synthesizing narrative create discontinuities that are far more generative than scalar logic realizes.

The 2020 whistleblower's report that a contract doctor was secretly sterilizing refugee women in ICE detention centers signals that agents of the state seek to rejuvenate the violence that enabled the US state's creation with its roots in a refusal to allow stable, reliable affective ties among people of color.[13] That forced sterilization remains possible indicates the depth of allegiance to the maintenance of a racial capitalism striated by impossible childhoods, demarcated by denied adulthoods. But, indeed, so does the ongoing practice of child separation and the increasing violence of the camps that have sprung up across the border, where hundreds if not thousands of people have been kidnapped, raped, or assaulted. Children continue to be cast away: put on planes to places where there is no one to greet them, sent to foster care facilities, disappeared into labor camps on factory farms. Trump officials even instrumentalized SARS-CoV-2 to force further separations of children from their guardians. These are all practices of war and terror that produce separability, that depend on and enforce the castagories that scale describes and the scaffold imaginary naturalizes. That such a war has emerged again as a terrorized planet intensifies its inhospitability to exploitative violence may suggest that a fraying socioeconomic structure that sustained racial capitalism requires old-form violence as well as new-form logics for its survival.

In the expressive practices studied here, the cast-out child serves as a figure for the shared vulnerability that Western notions of individualist rationality and rectitude deny. The lie of the self, the upright geometry of the liberal human, masks the vulnerabilities castaway children must confront, and as such these texts reveal that the self is only a temporary nexus in a continuously unfolding and dense field of relations. These texts compel a sense of density without scaffolding by dis/objectifying relations; this density resists scale and the scalar lien on our imagination. In their density the expressive practices studied here repeatedly demonstrate how indebted people may be to one another and to the thick materialities and beings encountered across the horizon of situations. In our dwelling together, we know nothing exists by itself alone in our many worlds that are not one, as the cast-out child quietly witnesses for us.

Notes

INTRODUCTION

1. See US Commission on Civil Rights, *Trauma at the Border;* Miriam Jordan, "Family Separation May Have Hit Thousands More Migrant Children Than Reported," *New York Times*, January 17, 2019; and Molly O'Toole, "Family Separation Returns under Cover of the Coronavirus," *Los Angeles Times*, May 27, 2020. Note also that while the Biden administration has tempered some of the worst aspects of Trump's border policies, it has not eliminated the understanding of "family." Miriam Jordan, "Migrants Separated from Their Children Will Be Allowed into US," *New York Times*, May 3, 2021.
2. For decades the United States has attempted to devise various mechanisms to "deter" people's efforts to enter the United States by forcing people to cross in desolate, dangerous desert areas. I was first alerted to such efforts when, in 1997, I visited the Border Patrol Museum in El Paso, Texas, and a retired border guard, a volunteer docent, explained that they sought measures "to drive people" into the rural desert where the Border Patrol could isolate them and discourage attempts to migrate. For a detailed history of instrumentalizing the ferocity of the desert and border management as deterrence more generally, see De León, *Land of Open Graves*.
3. Linebaugh and Rediker, *Many-Headed Hydra*; and Jordan and Walsh, *White Cargo*.
4. Ngai, *Impossible Subjects*; and Ling, *"Reading."*
5. Haley, *No Mercy Here*; and Martinez, *Injustice Never Leaves You*.
6. Rifkin, *When Did Indians Become Straight?*
7. Alvord, Menjívar, and Gómez Cervantes, "Legal Violence."
8. Reséndez, *Other Slavery*; and J. Brooks, *Captives and Cousins*.
9. See Wheatley, *Writings*; Douglass, *Narrative*; Du Bois, *Souls*; and Equiano, *Interesting Narrative*.
10. For discussions of the racialization of children, the construction of childhood, and the particular role of literature, see Thomas, *Dark Fantastic*; L. Jones, "'Most Unprotected'"; Haywood, "Constructing Childhood"; Stephens, *Children*; Bishop,

Free within Ourselves; Martin, *Brown Gold*; Kelen and Sundmark, *Nation in Children's Literature*; Monaghan, *Learning to Read*; MacCann, *White Supremacy*; Murray, *American Children's Literature*. See also Gill-Peterson, *Histories*; Wilson and Gabriel, *Asian Children's Literature*; Jiménez García, "En(countering) YA"; and Cox, *Shapeshifters*. For discussions of how Latinx children are racialized, particularly around language use, see Orellana, *Translating Childhoods*; for helpful discussions of Latinx literature for children, see Jiménez García, "Lens of Latinx Literature"; Jiménez García, "Pura Belpre"; Jiménez García, "Side-by-Side"; and Aldama, *Latino/a Children's and Young Adult Writers*.

11 Stephens, *Children*, 8–24.
12 Levander, *Cradle of Liberty*, 25.
13 Levander, *Cradle of Liberty*, 79.
14 For a full discussion of this relationship, see Sánchez-Eppler, *Dependent States*.
15 Quoted in Brewer, *By Birth or Consent*, 43.
16 Quoted in Brewer, *By Birth or Consent*, 43.
17 Alryyes, *Original Subjects*; and Nixon, *Orphan in Eighteenth-Century Law*.
18 Levander, *Cradle of Liberty*, 3.
19 Bernstein, *Racial Innocence*, 4.
20 Levander, *Cradle of Liberty*, 4.
21 Levander, *Cradle of Liberty*, 19.
22 Bernstein, *Racial Innocence*, 33–36.
23 Brewer, *By Birth or Consent*, 365.
24 Bernstein, *Racial Innocence*, 8. It is no surprise, then, that in the period in which cartes de visite of children displaying a range of skin colors became popular as part of an abolitionist effort to brand whiteness as endangered (as potentially infiltratable), the regulation of immigration also picked up steam, culminating in Abraham Lincoln's signature on the first immigration reform measure. For more on the role of cartes de visite in revising racial imaginaries, see M. Mitchell, *Raising Freedom's Child*.
25 Lipsitz, "Possessive Investment in Whiteness"; and Harris, "Whiteness as Property."
26 For a rich discussion, see Stockton, *Queer Child*.
27 As Ruth MacDonald notes, one crucial aspect of this effort to wrest control from the propertied elite was assisted by the Puritan commitment to reading. Settler colonists adhering to Puritanism encouraged literacy because they believed a direct relationship with God could only be obtained by reading the Judeo-Christian Bible. MacDonald, *Literature for Children*, 7.
28 Laura Briggs argues that the foster care system was used to punish African American civil rights activists by separating them from their families. Briggs, *Taking Children*, 32–45.
29 See Rooks, *Cutting School*.
30 Paredes, *George Washington Gómez*; T. Rivera, . . . *Y no se lo tragó la tierra*; P. Thomas, *Down These Mean Streets*; and Mohr, *Nilda*.
31 Terminology here proves very difficult. *Latina/o* (and, eventually, *Latinx*) emerged as a scalar attempt to draw together different constituencies; it names a desire for

a new collectivity that signals multiple and overlapping diasporas, one that scales up people who may be hailed by their own or their great-great-grandparents' nation of origin or their settler/colonial status or even their status as what Jodi Byrd in *Transit of Empire* calls arrivants. Jane Juffer in *Intimacy across Borders* offers a rich engagement with this emergent collectivity, with the complexity of writing about overlapping diasporas. An alternative approach unpacks the concept of "greater Mexico"; this approach offers the advantage of attention to spatial relations without attendant assumptions about racial authenticity. For an extraordinary unpacking of this concept in relation to art see Amy Sara Carroll, *Remex*. A different kind of collectivity, that is the market/brand called *Latino*, was also called into being by advertising executives, according to Arlene Dávila in *Latinos Inc*. That *Latina/o/x* leaves something to be desired is eloquently articulated by Virginia Grise, who notes, "Pan-Latino(ism) is killing me, as Latino is not a politic nor an ideology and does nothing to prepare us to defend ourselves against what is actually killing us (Grise, *Healing*, 57). For in this very naming of Latina/o/x, the haunting presence of anti-Black, anti-Indigenous articulations remains nearby. After all, Latin America was a name meant to associate the hemisphere with France and all things European by invoking the Roman Empire's language of Latin and thereby disentangling the former Spanish colonies from their reputation as the scene of multiracial intimacies (see Arturo Ardao's *Génesis de la idea y el nombre de América Latina*). *Chicana/o* and *Nuyorican* were attempts to unbundle naming from empire and thus to disrupt the scalar work of castagories. Not surprisingly, the critique of the term *Chicana/o* emerged out of a scalar ambition. The label *Chicana/o* was seen as too fully linked to a messy activist nationalism that was misogynist and homophobic, a failed collectivity that embarrassed a certain kind of assimilative academic scholarship. More significantly, a critique of Spain's and postindependence Mexico's genocidal practices has rendered distasteful the romanticism of some Chicana/o writing about Indigenous histories. Scholars inspired by queer studies have distanced themselves from this debate by turning to the concept of "brown" developed by José Esteban Muñoz (see his *The Sense of Brown*). Others, such as Marissa López, have sought to undo the assimilative narrative rebuking Chicanx scholarship and activism and to reinvigorate its critique and disruption of scalar ambition (see *Racial Immanence*). Other scholars, such as Patricia Ybarra, Ricardo Ortiz, Ralph Rodriguez, and Frederick Aldama, have sought to understand what is at stake in the naming of cultural practices as Latina/o/x (Ybarra, *Latinx Theater in the Times of Neoliberalism*; Ortiz, *Latinx Literature Now*; Ralph Rodriguz, *Latinx Literature Unbound*; Aldama, *Routledge Concise History*). Richard T. Rodríguez in "What Lies Beneath" has offered a significant and stellar meditation on the friction between such practices. For the purposes of *Scales of Captivity*, when I seek to name a broad constituency that can be signaled by its relationship to Spanish coloniality and US imperialism, I will use *Latinx*; if a writer or argument is especially associated with Chicanx politics historically, I link the two as such. To the extent possible, I do not invoke scalar narratives in order to avoid using abstract fixities to homogenize dense materialities.

32 For an alternate and very compelling use of witnessing, see Figueroa, "Faithful Witnessing as Practice."

33 The Trump administration's innovation in May 2018 was to declare all minors as trafficked. This allowed the administration to then charge accompanying adults with more serious felony trafficking charges, thereby justifying the separation of children from caregivers and blocking asylum options.
34 Atiya, *Rise and Fall*.
35 Kotef, *Movement*, 4.
36 Kotef, *Movement*, 5.
37 Kotef, *Movement*, 9.
38 See Torpey, *Invention*; and Weber, *Politics as a Vocation*.
39 Kotef, *Movement*, 15.
40 Linebaugh and Rediker, *Many-Headed Hydra*, 59.
41 The captivity narrative has figured in canonical US literary studies for nearly a hundred years. See Slotkin, *Regeneration through Violence*.
42 Rowlandson's narrative takes pride of place as a genre-defining text, but of course it was not the first captivity narrative. These accounts were abundant—largely following the work of empire building and resource theft. See Carroll, "Captivity Literature."
43 See Castiglia, *Bound and Determined*; Namias, *White Captives*; and Tinnemyer, *Identity Politics*.
44 L. Brooks, *Our Beloved Kin*.
45 Wynter, "Unsettling the Coloniality of Being," 299.
46 L. Brooks, *Our Beloved Kin*, 255.
47 Higginson, "*Caught Up*," iii.
48 Kotef, *Movement*, 29.
49 C. Smith, *Prison*, 23.
50 López de Gómara, *Historia general de las Indias*, 7.
51 Ferreira da Silva, "On Difference without Separability."
52 Carrillo Castillo, "'The World Is Only One,'" 142.
53 Carrillo Castillo, "'The World Is Only One,'" 142.
54 Marston, Jones, and Woodward, "Human Geography without Scale," 422.
55 Marston, Jones, and Woodward, "Human Geography without Scale," 422.
56 In earlier work I examined the border as fungible, as an abjection machine, and as the mediator of homoerotic desires expressed though a repertoire of homophobic attacks. See Brady, *Extinct Lands, Temporal Geographies*; "Fungibility of Borders"; and "Homoerotics of Immigration Control."
57 For the most innovative critiques of scale, see Marston, Jones, and Woodward, "Human Geography without Scale"; J. Jones et al., "Neil Smith's Scale"; Woodward, Jones, and Marston, "Of Eagles and Flies"; and Marston, Jones, and Woodward, "Flattening Ontologies of Globalization."
58 See Escobar, *Designs for the Pluriverse*.
59 Katzew, *Casta Painting*, 39–63.
60 Carrera, *Imagining Identity*, 2. For a helpful discussion of the way some African descent peoples negotiatiated the casta system see Williams, "My Conscience."
61 For a thorough history of the emergence of capitalism and its racializing technologies see Robinson, *Black Marxism*.

62 See Ferreira da Silva, "On Difference without Separability."
63 Earle, "Pleasures of Taxonomy," 428.
64 Ferreira da Silva, "Notes for a Critique," 140.
65 Ferreira da Silva, "Notes for a Critique," 139.
66 Ferreira da Silva, "Notes for a Critique," 140.
67 Escobar, *Designs for the Pluriverse*, 86.
68 Clinton, "Opening Speech," 966–67.
69 For a wonderful discussion of peoplehood, see J.-M. Rivera, *Emergence of Mexican America*.
70 Marston, Jones, and Woodward, "Human Geography without Scale," 421.
71 Marston, Jones, and Woodward, "Human Geography without Scale," 422.
72 Marston, Jones, and Woodward, "Human Geography without Scale," 427.
73 Marston, Jones, and Woodward, "Human Geography without Scale," 425.
74 Marston, Jones, and Woodward, "Human Geography without Scale," 428.
75 As Alicia Schmidt Camacho brilliantly outlines in "Hailing the Twelve Million," the rhetoric of scale enables a set of political practices that have no actual relationship to the lived conditions of people in the United States.
76 For this reason, perhaps, much of the revelatory theoretical work of Indigenous scholars goes unconsulted because Indigenous studies tends to challenge cavalier scalar claims, articulating a set of values and insights that take *place* (as opposed to the scalable fiction of abstract space) seriously as real, vibrant, fecund, and constitutive of culture and meaning, which is to say avowedly not scalable. This does not mean, however, that scholars working from within Indigenous studies do not see connections across cultures and languages, nor do they refuse networks of meanings and histories. Chadwick Allen, for example, in *Trans-Indigenous* argues for attention to just such a mesh of relations. Yet Allen's work also keeps time with the attention scholars such as Daniel Heath Justice (*Why Indigenous Literatures Matter*) and Christopher Pexa (*Translated Nation*) give to the importance of attending to heuristics focused on nation and tribe. Making connections, locating shared histories and epistemologies, does not reduce such relations to easily scalable forms that can be inserted into an already existing nested, scalar hierarchy; it does not mean that cultural, tribal, linguistic, and cosmological differences can be swished away into a homogenized narrative of an empty category of indigeneity that can be accommodated by universalizing narratives (one/not many) or simple dualisms. This critique of sovereignty is linked to its emergence as part of the scalar imaginary. Indigenous Studies offers a very different model of sovereignty than that explored here.
77 Jones, Woodward, and Marston, "Situating Flatness," 274.
78 For an elegant argument that places this critique in an earlier moment, see Ross, "Trans-Atlantic Parochialism." For a thoughtful engagement with the use of scale in contemporary cultural theory, see N. Mitchell, "View from Nowhere." For an extraordinary discussion of place as a dense ensemble of practices thereby illustrating orientation without scale, see Alexandra Vazquez, *The Florida Room*.
79 Ilene Grabel makes this case eloquently when she notes that change can be found in the "disparate, the seemingly trivial, or the experimental . . . because they are not scalable." Grabel, *When Things Don't Fall Apart*, 23.

80 Agard-Jones, "Bodies in the System," 184.
81 Agard-Jones, "Bodies in the System," 192.
82 This argument has been developed in a sophisticated, engrossing manner by Indigenous studies scholars. See especially Justice, *Why Indigenous Literatures Matter*.
83 Marston, Jones, and Woodward, "Human Geography without Scale," 424. For a helpful critique of worlding see Woodward, Jones, and Marston, "The Politics of Autonomous Spaces."
84 Saldívar, *Trans-Americanity*, xvii.
85 Moten, *Black and Blur*, 198.
86 Moten, *Black and Blur*, 199.
87 Ferreira da Silva, "Notes for a Critique," 142.
88 Byrd, "Souths as Prologues," 26.
89 See J. Muñoz, "Feeling Brown, Feeling Down"; "Feeling Brown: Ethnicity and Affect"; "Theorizing Queer Inhumanisms"; and "'Chico,'" as well as his recorded lecture "The Brown Commons." Special thanks to Joseph Miranda for thinking through this work with me.
90 J. Muñoz, "The Brown Commons."
91 Cavarero, *Inclinations*, 11.
92 As Hamer explains, "And until I am free, you are not free either." Hamer, "'Until I Am Free, You Are Not Free Either,'" 125.
93 See Bosniak, *Citizen and the Alien*, for an elegant discussion of this problem.
94 Castiglia, *Bound and Determined*, 1–15.
95 Kotef, *Movement*, 24–26.
96 For a foundational essay, see Alemán, "'Thank God.'"
97 See Blackwell, Lopez, and Urrieta, "Critical Latinx Indigeneities."
98 J. Montoya, *In Formation*, 52.
99 Nyers, "Abject Cosmopolitanism," 420–25.
100 For extended discussions, see Macías-Rojas, *From Deportation to Prison*; Kanstroom and Lykes, *New Deportations Delirium*; and Menjívar and Kanstroom, *Constructing Immigrant "Illegality."*
101 For further discussion, see Boehm, *Returned*.

CHAPTER ONE. CAPTIVATING TIES

1 See J. J. Rodríguez, *Literatures*. See also Lazo, *Letters from Filadelfia*, for a magnificent analysis of early transnational theories of liberal formation and democracy. For an important contextualization of the novel, see Lazo and Alemán, *Latino Nineteenth Century*. Lucas Dietrich draws on archival material to argue that Ruiz de Burton paid for the novel's publication. See Dietrich, "On Commission."
2 For a splendid discussion of Ruiz de Burton's meditation on suffrage and her analysis of the economy of the "alien," see Arrizón-Palomera, "Trope of the Papers." For a helpful history of the emerging vision of citizenship in concert with Reconstruction, see Hyde, *Civic Longing*.
3 From its first reintroduction to the reading public, scholars have correctly noted the novel's racism and especially its racist portrayal of African Americans as well as

its celebration of a white supremacy calibrated to include those of Spanish descent. See, for example, the first wave of criticism in R. Sánchez and Pita, introduction; McCullough, *Regions of Identity*; and Saldívar, *Border Matters*. José Aranda's "Contradictory Impulses" and Jesse Alemán's "'Thank God, Lolita Is Away from Those Horrid Savages'" argue persuasively that the novel is hopelessly mired in the logic of white supremacy. Pablo Ramírez in "Conquest's Child" situates the novel in terms of the logic of contractual relations, as does John-Michael Rivera in *The Emergence of Mexican America*. Bernadine Hernández argues for the importance of spatiality to the novel's project in "Rewriting Space in Ruiz de Burton's *Who Would Have Thought It?*," and Brook Thomas places the novel as working from and against Reconstruction in *The Literature of Reconstruction*.

4   See Bogdan, *Freak Show*; and Qureshi, *Peoples on Parade*.
5   Retman, *Reel Folks*, 5.
6   Retman, *Reel Folks*, 5.
7   Ruiz de Burton, *Who*, 9.
8   Ruiz de Burton, *Who*, 10.
9   See Lowell, *The Biglow Papers*.
10 See Cotera, *Native Speakers*.
11 Szeghi, "Vanishing Mexicana/o," 100.
12 For a discussion of Clinton's vision see Sheriff, *The Artificial River*.
13 Menjívar and Abrego, "Legal Violence," 1381.
14 Pateman, *Disorder of Women*, 135.
15 See Pateman, *Disorder of Women*; Saccamano, "'Le plus fort lien'"; and Mills, *Racial Contract*.
16 Ruiz de Burton, *Who*, 14.
17 Ruiz de Burton, *Who*, 13–16.
18 The *Oxford English Dictionary Online* notes that *deed* can also be used as the past participle of *damn*. Oxford English Dictionary Online, s.v. "deed," accessed July 31, 2019, https://www-oed-com.proxy.library.cornell.edu/view/Entry/25830#eid10948520.
19 Vazquez, *Listening in Detail*, 57.
20 Ruiz de Burton, *Who*, 16.
21 Ruiz de Burton, *Who*, 17.
22 Ruiz de Burton, *Who*, 17.
23 Ruiz de Burton, *Who*, 20, 79.
24 See Frost, *Never One Nation*; Blanchard et al., *Human Zoos*; and Bogdan, *Freak Show*.
25 Aguirre, *Informal Empire*, 103–30.
26 Aguirre, *Informal Empire*, 121.
27 Qureshi, *Peoples on Parade*, 128.
28 Quoted in Durbach, *Spectacle of Deformity*, 117.
29 Quoted in Bogden, *Freak Show*, 129.
30 Durbach, *Spectacle of Deformity*, 125.
31 R. Sánchez and Pita, introduction, xxxv.
32 Quoted in M. Mitchell, *Raising Freedom's Child*, 83.
33 Quoted in M. Mitchell, *Raising Freedom's Child*, 84.
34 M. Mitchell, *Raising Freedom's Child*, 86.

35 For a fuller discussion of *Ida May*, see M. Mitchell, *Raising Freedom's Child*, 71–74.
36 M. Mitchell, *Raising Freedom's Child*, 74.
37 Quoted in M. Mitchell, *Raising Freedom's Child*, 74.
38 Ruiz de Burton, *Who*, 25.
39 See Harris, "Whiteness as Property"; and Lipsitz, "Possessive Investment."
40 More than once the narrator takes readers into the mind of a canary.
41 See Pateman, *Disorder*; Brown, *Consent*; and O'Neill, Shanley, and Young, *Illusion of Consent*.
42 Mills, *Racial Contract*, 73.
43 Miller, *Prose and Cons*, 62–77.
44 For a careful survey, see Fahs, *Imagined Civil War*.
45 See Sánchez-Eppler, *Dependent States*; Bernstein, *Racial Innocence*; and Levander, *Cradle of Liberty*.
46 Sánchez-Eppler, *Dependent States*.
47 Bernstein, *Racial Innocence*, 2.
48 Stockton in *The Queer Child* suggests that children who are not welcomed into the developmentalist narrative of (white) rationality grow sideways.
49 Bernstein, *Racial Innocence*, 23.
50 Certainly more should be said about the novel's prophetic and astute effort to show how the infrastructural work that chattel slavery performed to enable the growth of racial capitalism shifted after 1848 toward speculative finance. Jemima's biography illustrates the imaginative cultural work that had to accompany this change in financial infrastructure as she morphs from an ardent racist, abolitionist, working *farmer* to an ardent racist, abolitionist *consumer*. Moreover, the novel repeatedly shows how capitalists mystify the source of their wealth in order to further hide the way captive taking and bracketing of life inhere in such scalar jumps.
51 See Barr, *Peace Came*; J. Brooks, *Captives and Cousins*; Hämäläinen, *Comanche Empire*; and DeLay, *War of a Thousand Deserts*.
52 Scholars have argued that the Comanche helped make further US incursions against Mexico impossible. But see Ned Blackhawk's critique of this argument more generally in *Violence over the Land*.
53 On captivity as a justification for imperial expansion, see Castiglia, *Bound and Determined*.
54 The crucial link between Oatman's case and Ruiz de Burton's novel is that Ruiz de Burton locates Dr. Norval's encounter with Lola's adoptive family at the same point where the US soldiers encountered Oatman and her adopted kin.
55 See Barr, *Peace Came*; J. Brooks, *Captives and Cousins*; Hämäläinen, *Comanche Empire*; and DeLay, *War of a Thousand Deserts*.
56 See Blackhawk, *Violence over the Land*; Reséndez, *Other Slavery*; J. Brooks, *Captives and Cousins*; Barr, *Peace Came*; Hämäläinen, *Comanche Empire*; and DeLay, *War of a Thousand Deserts*.
57 See Reséndez, *Other Slavery*.
58 See Barr, *Peace Came*; J. Brooks, *Captives and Cousins*; Hämäläinen, *Comanche Empire*; and DeLay, *War of a Thousand Deserts*.

59 Mifflin, *Blue Tattoo*, 2. Mifflin sees *Who Would Have Thought It?* as one of the first of many fictionalizations of Oatman's experiences (one among many burlesque parodies, plays, and children's books). See Mifflin, *Blue Tattoo*, 199.
60 Mifflin, *Blue Tattoo*, 183.
61 For discussions of feminism in the novel see Soares, "From Canary Birds to Suffrage'"; and Arrizón-Palomera, "Trope of the Papers."
62 Castiglia, *Bound and Determined*, 114.
63 Castiglia, *Bound and Determined*, 123.
64 Castiglia argues that the captivity narrative "played a central yet largely unrecognized role in literary history." Castiglia, *Bound and Determined*, 111.
65 Castiglia, *Bound and Determined*, 89.
66 Castiglia, *Bound and Determined*, 103. The end of the seduction plot is worth considering here. In one sense, traditional captivity narratives promote the concept of a new "us." In their critique of nationalist domesticity, the captivity narratives give voice to an outernational "us," according to Castiglia. Such may be the case with the end of *Who Would Have Thought It?* Four ships weave in and out, somewhat like the main strands of the plot: one, a steamer, departs with Lola and her father, bound for Cuba; a second, from Europe, arrives with James Norval; the third contains the masquerading figures of Julian, Mattie, and Isaac; and the fourth contains Hackwell and his henchmen. In a certain way Lola never figures into the "us" created on the third ship, but this "us" defines a new relationship to the domestic maelstrom established by Jemima and so trenchantly critiqued by the narrator.
67 Fahs, *Imagined Civil War*, 6.
68 Fahs, *Imagined Civil War*, 12.
69 Fahs, *Imagined Civil War*, 94.
70 Fahs, *Imagined Civil War*, 118.
71 Fahs, *Imagined Civil War*, 286.
72 Fahs, *Imagined Civil War*, 300.
73 Fahs, *Imagined Civil War*, 316.
74 It is clear that Ruiz de Burton paid attention to other genres, including sentimental fiction and theatrical melodrama. Yet neither of these forms affords the recourse to sarcasm, outrage, and humor that *Who Would Have Thought It?* deploys.
75 Compare, for instance, the narrative intrusions in Trollope's novels such as *Can You Forgive Her?* or Mark Twain's use of an interruptive narrator in *The Prince and the Pauper*.
76 In "Precarious Performances," Beth Fisher demonstrates that theater indexes the transformation of Anglo middle-class culture by showing Jemima's shifting attitudes toward theater. Patricia Ybarra, in private conversation with this author, suggested that another model for Ruiz de Burton may well have been the Mexican variety shows popular in nineteenth-century California (April 25, 2019).
77 D. Brooks, *Bodies in Dissent*, 8.
78 Burlesque fiction thrived while Ruiz de Burton lived on the East Coast. But it tends to rely on a strict relationship to a prior work of fiction. *Who Would Have Thought It?* is more engaged with the structures of burlesque theater. See Shepperson, *Novel in Motley*.
79 R. Allen, *Horrible Prettiness*, 104.

80 R. Allen, *Horrible Prettiness*, 12.
81 R. Allen, *Horrible Prettiness*, 147.
82 R. Allen, *Horrible Prettiness*, 147.
83 Quoted in R. Allen, *Horrible Prettiness*, 25.
84 The most notorious example of burlesque in the period was probably Lydia Thompson's *Ixion*, which featured female actors as cavorting male gods.
85 R. Allen, *Horrible Prettiness*, 148, 156.
86 R. Allen, *Horrible Prettiness*, 81, 129.
87 Quoted in R. Allen, *Horrible Prettiness*, 18.
88 How else to explain that even though Lola lived with the Norvals for years before Jemima's brother, Isaac, was captured at the First Battle of Bull Run, Isaac fails to connect the dead letter manuscript with the young woman in his sister's home, the source of his family's prosperity? How else to explain that at her first appearance, as a child newly "rescued" from a decade of life with the Mojave, Lola is fluent in English? Ruiz de Burton insists finally on Lola's opacity to the US reader.
89 J. J. Rodríguez, *Literatures*, 118–30.
90 J. J. Rodríguez, *Literatures*, 118–208.
91 J. J. Rodríguez, *Literatures*, 121.
92 J. J. Rodríguez, *Literatures*, 117.
93 Ruiz de Burton, *Who*, 11.
94 According to the *Oxford English Dictionary Online*, cackle can be traced to the Middle English *cakelen*. *Oxford English Dictionary Online*, s.v. "cackle" (v.), accessed May 20, 2019, https://www-oed-com.proxy.library.cornell.edu/view/Entry/25830#eid10948520.
95 Ruiz de Burton, *Who*, 11.
96 Ruiz de Burton, *Who*, 11.
97 Ruiz de Burton, *Who*, 62.
98 Ruiz de Burton, *Who*, 136.
99 Ruiz de Burton, *Who*, 136.
100 Ruiz de Burton, *Who*, 231.
101 Ruiz de Burton, *Who*, 231.
102 D. Brooks, *Bodies in Dissent*, 14.
103 Ruiz de Burton, *Who*, 179, 180.
104 Peter Linebaugh and Marcus Rediker highlight the logic by which landowners developed a critique of the "common" as an aspect of their own structure of eligibility for the category of citizen (which would exclude the "peasantry"). The language of the common easily translated in the United States into the concept of respectability. See Linebaugh and Rediker, *Many-Headed Hydra*, 108.
105 Ruiz de Burton, *Who*, 180.
106 Ruiz de Burton, *Who*, 153.
107 Ruiz de Burton, *Who*, 100, 241. For a discussion of the history of the concept of "Sambos" see Wynter, "Sambos and Minstrels," 149.
108 Ruiz de Burton, *Who*, 100.
109 See Brody, *Impossible Purities*.
110 Poovey, "Trollope's Barsetshire Series," 32.

111 Ruiz de Burton, *Who*, 136.
112 Ruiz de Burton, *Who*, 75, 155.
113 Ruiz de Burton, *Who*, 188.
114 Ruiz de Burton, *Who*, 103.
115 Ruiz de Burton, *Who*, 194.
116 Ruiz de Burton, *Who*, 263.
117 Allen, *Horrible Prettiness*, 81.
118 Brewer, *By Birth or Consent*, 351.
119 See Barack Obama, "Remarks by the President on Immigration," White House, June 15, 2012, https://www.whitehouse.gov/the-press-office/2012/06/15/remarks-president-immigration.
120 Clyde Haberman, "For Private Prisons, Detaining Immigrants Is Big Business," *New York Times*, October 1, 2018. My thanks to Larissa Brewer-García for directing me to this subject.
121 My thanks to Esmeralda Arrizón-Palomera for showing me the Bieber memes and discussing the weirdness of the novel with me. Thanks also to Ella Diaz for helpful comments on this chapter.
122 Du Bois, *Souls of Black Folk*, 3; Chandler, *Toward an African Future*, 62.

CHAPTER TWO. PLAUSIBLE DENIABILITY

1 hooks, "Subversive Beauty," 46.
2 See Castiglia, *Bound and Determined*, for a discussion of the importance of these narratives.
3 Kotef, *Movement*, 71.
4 For a full account of the practices of captivity in New Spain, see Reséndez, *Other Slavery*.
5 See J. Brooks, *Captives and Cousins*; and Pexa, *Translated Nation*.
6 The novel was written during the 1930s and 1940s but languished among González's papers until the early 1990s. See Kreneck's foreword to *Caballero*, ix.
7 Kotef, "Violent Attachments," 6, 21. See also McMahon, *Domestic Negotiations*; and Garza-Falcón, *Gente Decente*, for related arguments.
8 *Caballero* has been the focus of some of the most impressive criticism in the field of Chicanx literary studies. My interest here is simply in the novel's engagement with the historic intersections of a set of competing political economies (the semifeudal latifundio system of northern Mexico, the chattel slave system of the United States, the liberal republican system of market capitalism and financial speculation that Ruiz de Burton lampoons, and, to my mind the least carefully studied, the Comanche and Apache Indigenous networks). All these systems are overlaid with two other systems: the gendered and racialized economies that the novel unpacks with surprising care, if not always admirable results. For an important critique of the novel's deployment of Indianness, see Olguín, "Caballeros and Indians." For a splendid discussion of transnational Indigenous communities, see Portillo, *Sovereign Stories*. For arguments about the novel's polyangular engagements, see P. S. Ybarra, *Writing the Goodlife*; Cotera, *Native Speakers*; M.

López, *Chicano Nations*; Cutler, *Ends of Assimilation*; Roybal, *Archives of Dispossession*; John González, "Terms of Engagement"; Pérez, "Remembering the Hacienda"; Guidotti-Hernández, *Unspeakable Violence*; P. Ramírez, "Resignifying Preservation"; and Vizcaíno-Alemán, "Rethinking Jovita González's Work."

9   See Alonzo, *Tejano Legacy*.
10 Jovita González and Raleigh, *Caballero*, 23.
11 Jovita González and Raleigh, *Caballero*, 22, 20, 282, 71, 224.
12 Jovita González and Raleigh, *Caballero*, 263.
13 See Cuevas, *Post-Borderlandia*; and Bebout, "First Generation," for exemplary queer readings of the novel.
14 Jovita González and Raleigh, *Caballero*, 224.
15 Jovita González and Raleigh, *Caballero*, 297.
16 For a full discussion, see Hämäläinen, *Comanche Empire*.
17 Casares, *Amigoland*, 10.
18 Casares, *Amigoland*, 15. This is a gesture toward Operation Wetback.
19 Casares, *Amigoland*, 86.
20 Casares, *Amigoland*, 168.
21 Casares, *Amigoland*, 147–48.
22 Casares, *Amigoland*, 296.
23 Casares, *Amigoland*, 64.
24 See Herrera-Sobek, *Mexican Corrido*, for an important discussion of the corrido form and popular culture.
25 Pexa, "Futurity Foreclosed," 3.
26 DeLay, *War of a Thousand Deserts*, xiv.
27 Saldaña-Portillo, *Indian Given*, 132.
28 For more details of the reach of such forced labor into the European expansion across the US Midwest, see Proyect, "Political Economy of Comanche Violence."
29 Casares, "Reading Guide" in *Amigoland*, 9.
30 Casares, *Amigoland*, 85.
31 Casares, *Amigoland*, 125.
32 For a full discussion, see Martinez, *Injustice Never Leaves You*.
33 Casares, *Amigoland*, 206.
34 Casares, *Amigoland*, 285.
35 The novel offers a painstaking critique of the anti-Indigenous ideology structuring heteromasculinity. One can see the evocation of the corrido in the novel's epigraph as a nod toward that violent history.
36 Casares, *Amigoland*, 308.
37 Of course labor practices are also forms of warfare. But see Johnson, *Fear of French Negroes*.
38 According to "The Louisiana and Texas Retail Blogspot" Amigoland was once a thriving mall located near the USMexico border. The mall is now a technology training center for a local community college. "Amigoland Mall Brownsville Texas March 2020," *Louisiana and Texas Retail Blogspot*, Mary 21, 2020, https://southernretail.blogspot.com/2020/05/amigoland-mall-brownsville-texas-march.html.
39 Casares, *Amigoland*, 68.

40   L. López, *Gifted Gabaldón Sisters*, 38.
41   L. López, *Gifted Gabaldón Sisters*, 8.
42   L. López, *Gifted Gabaldón Sisters*, 8.
43   L. López, *Gifted Gabaldón Sisters*, 63.
44   L. López, *Gifted Gabaldón Sisters*, 80.
45   L. López, *Gifted Gabaldón Sisters*, 248.
46   See J. Brooks, *Captives and Cousins*; and DeLay, *War of a Thousand Deserts*.
47   See Hatch, "'Lords of New Mexico.'"
48   As David Weber explains, Spanish and Mexican colonists used baptism as a significant distinction. A baptized person could not be forced into slavery nor sold or traded. For the Spanish, baptism symbolized conversion not just to Catholicism but to the sovereignty of the Spanish Crown. See Weber, *Barbaros*.
49   L. López, *Gifted Gabaldón Sisters*, 26.
50   L. López, *Gifted Gabaldón Sisters*, 1, 2.
51   Escobar, *Designs for the Pluriverse*, 80.
52   L. López, *Gifted Gabaldón Sisters*, 3.
53   L. López, *Gifted Gabaldón Sisters*, 26.
54   L. López, *Gifted Gabaldón Sisters*, 9, 6.
55   L. López, *Gifted Gabaldón Sisters*, 30, 31.
56   L. López, *Gifted Gabaldón Sisters*, 33.
57   L. López, *Gifted Gabaldón Sisters*, 40–41.
58   L. López, *Gifted Gabaldón Sisters*, 46.
59   L. López, *Gifted Gabaldón Sisters*, 254.
60   L. López, *Gifted Gabaldón Sisters*, 98.
61   L. López, *Gifted Gabaldón Sisters*, 181.
62   L. López, *Gifted Gabaldón Sisters*, 24.
63   The legacy of this violence wounds Rita deeply; she tells her dying uncle that she hopes he will die but that she forgives him: "I have to, because if I don't, you'll always be there, like a splinter in my heart." L. López, *Gifted Gabaldón Sisters*, 161.
64   For a terrific discussion of New Mexico's guide, see Marez, *Drug Wars*.
65   L. López, *Gifted Gabaldón Sisters*, 26.
66   Many of Fermina's stories have corollaries in Albert Yava's *Big Falling Snow*.
67   López's WPA narrative gambit runs the risk of reinforcing a romanticized view of Native peoples as possessors of an elaborate past that is indeed past and gone.
68   See Reséndez, *Other Slavery*; and Trujillo, *Land Uprising*.
69   L. López, *Gifted Gabaldón Sisters*, 78.
70   My discussion of temporality here and across the book has been immensely influenced by Patricia Ybarra's *Latinx Theater in the Times of Neoliberalism* and Kate McCullough's brilliant work on queer temporality in "'The Complexity of Loss Itself.'"
71   Fermina's letter to the sisters adds another layer of temporal complexity. It is also the only significant example of Fermina's unmediated voice.
72   Steinbeck, *Grapes of Wrath*, 123.
73   For a further discussion, see Mifflin, *Blue Tattoo*.
74   The reference to Oatman is preceded by a discussion of Nilda's obsession with another white captive, Patty Hearst, whose own celebrated experience and similarly

best-selling memoir and story of identification with her captors also functioned in part as a mechanism for producing a continually consolidated white supremacy. The sisters don't take Nilda's obsession very seriously, and yet it's quite interesting because it accompanies her as she sits by her dying husband's bed. Nilda objects to the sentiment that Hearst should be punished and imprisoned and in this context tells Rita that her husband, José, had also had a period of captivity: "Did you know his mother was a prostitute? She worked in one of those houses in Tijuana, raised him there. Made him like a slave in that house. She hired him out, too, when he was just a kid, sent him to work on a rancho" (159). This story does not move Rita to greater sympathy with the man who molested her. But the anecdote does suggest to readers Nilda's contradictory position: her sympathy for captives does not seem to translate to Fermina.

75 L. López, *Gifted Gabaldón Sisters*, 248.
76 L. López, *Gifted Gabaldón Sisters*, 251.
77 L. López, *Gifted Gabaldón Sisters*, 248, 250, 251, 252, 256.
78 Note that one translation for *Decidero* is "declarable."
79 L. López, *Gifted Gabaldón Sisters*, 280.
80 L. López, *Gifted Gabaldón Sisters*, 284.
81 L. López, *Gifted Gabaldón Sisters*, 286.
82 L. López, *Gifted Gabaldón Sisters*, 311–12.
83 L. López, *Gifted Gabaldón Sisters*, 313–14.
84 L. López, *Gifted Gabaldón Sisters*, 315.
85 L. López, *Gifted Gabaldón Sisters*, 127.
86 L. López, *Gifted Gabaldón Sisters*, 315.
87 L. López, *Gifted Gabaldón Sisters*, 316.
88 See Lugones, *Peregrinajes/pilgrimages*; and Figueroa, "Faithful Witnessing as Practice."
89 Figueroa, "Faithful Witnessing as Practice," 643.
90 Figueroa, "Faithful Witnessing as Practice," 644.
91 Sedgwick, *Touching Feeling*, 138, 149.
92 Escobar, *Designs for the Pluriverse*, 87.

CHAPTER THREE. SUBMERGED CAPTIVITIES

Portions of earlier versions of this chapter appeared in "The Waiting Arms of Gold Street: Manuel Muñoz's *Faith Healer of Olive Avenue* and the Problem of the Scaffold Imaginary," in *Queering the Countryside*, ed. Mary Gray and Colin Johnson (New York: New York University Press, 2016), 106–25; and "Metaphors to Love By," in *Rebozos de Palabras: An Helena María Viramontes Critical Reader*, ed. Gabriela Gutiérrez y Muhs (Tucson: University of Arizona Press, 2013), 167–91. My thanks to the editors of these volumes for their generous guidance.

1 See Jesús Carrillo Castillo's "'The World Is Only One and Not Many'" for a contextual discussion of Juan Maldonado and Francisco López de Gómara.
2 For a splendid discussion of Chicana literature and militarism, see Rincón, *Bodies at War*.

3   J. Montoya, *In Formation*, 52.
4   See especially Dorr, *On Site, in Sound*; and L. Muñoz, "Agency, Choice, and Restrictions."
5   For helpful discussions of lowrider aesthetics, see Chappell, *Lowrider Space*; and Monte Madrigal, "Lentos."
6   My thanks to Mari Carmen Ramírez for suggesting the relevance of Romero's art to this project.
7   Pérez, "Teaching the Hacienda"; and Weber, *Mexican Frontier*.
8   M. López, "Feeling Mexican," 172.
9   According to David Brodsly, "Henry Huntington retained control of a consolidated inner-city streetcar system, the Los Angles Railway Company. Operating over 1,110 miles of track and providing about 700 miles of service by 1925, the Pacific Electric gave the Los Angeles metropolitan area the largest electric interurban railway in the world. . . . Of the 42 cities incorporated in the area by the mid-thirties, 39 owed their early growth to the electric railway." Brodsly, *L.A. Freeway*, 69.
10 See also Avila, *Popular Culture*; Hutchinson, *Imagining Transit*; and Villa, *Barrio-Logos*, on the impact of freeway construction.
11 Brodsly, *L.A. Freeway*, 61.
12 Raúl Villa's *Barrio-Logos* offers a crucial companion to this novel as it brilliantly engages with the spatial/social transformation of Los Angeles and examines Chicana/o ruminations on and critiques of that multipart scalar battle. See also Franco, "Metaphors Happen"; Pattison, "Trauma and the 710"; S. Wald, "Refusing to Halt"; and Cuevas, *Post-Borderlandia*, for discussions of mobility, freeway construction, and queer shifts.
13 This is the claim of Michael Ballard, drawing on California highway transit data. See Ballard, "East Los Angeles Interchange Complex," Southern California Regional Rocks and Roads, accessed May 18, 2021, https://socalregion.com/highways/la_highways/east_los_angeles_interchange/.
14 A phrase apparently coined by a Los Angeles city planner, Gordon Whitnall, in 1924. See Foster, *From Streetcar to Superhighway*, 71.
15 P. Wald, *Contagious*, 114.
16 Shah, *Contagious Divides*, 3.
17 Brodsly, *L.A. Freeway*, 71.
18 Viramontes, *Their Dogs*, 6.
19 Viramontes, *Their Dogs*, 12, 146, 134, 303.
20 Viramontes was not the first to link freeway construction to Spain's colonial projects. Writing for *California Highways and Public Works*, Alice Fisher Simpson celebrated the freeway construction initiative with a review of California's colonial history, including discussions of Junipero Serra and Juan Bautista de Anza. Simpson also notes that contemporary California arteries follow the paths traveled by Spanish soldiers. See Simpson, "Historic Trails."
21 Viramontes, *Their Dogs*, 59.
22 Viramontes, *Their Dogs*, 12.
23 Viramontes, *Their Dogs*, 32–33.

24 Viramontes, *Their Dogs*, 146.
25 As the novel also makes clear, the intrusion of television, particularly news of urban uprisings and Vietnam deaths, further unsettles her. For a splendid discussion of television and cultural transformation, see Ontiveros, *In the Spirit*.
26 Viramontes, *Their Dogs*, 147.
27 Viramontes, *Their Dogs*, 146.
28 Viramontes, *Their Dogs*, 176–77.
29 Viramontes, *Their Dogs*, 125.
30 John Alba Cutler perceptively reads this passage as a suggestion that "literature here seeks to impel action." Cutler, "On Recent Chicano Literature," 166.
31 Viramontes, *Their Dogs*, vii.
32 Neel Ahuja links the QA to the history of the border patrol and its practices of quarantining immigrants. See Ahuja, "Postcolonial Critique."
33 Viramontes, *Their Dogs*, 12.
34 N. Smith, "Scale Bending," 209.
35 Viramontes, *Their Dogs*, 54–55.
36 Viramontes, *Their Dogs*, 62.
37 Viramontes, *Their Dogs*, 75.
38 Viramontes, *Their Dogs*, 179–83.
39 For further discussions of love in Latinx literature, see Mah y Bush, "Lovingly"; and Figueredo, "Tender Struggles."
40 For a history of this region, see McWilliams, *Factory in the Fields*.
41 J. Montoya, *In Formation*, 52. My thanks to Amber Vasquez for suggesting this poem to me.
42 Rose, "Thanksgiving," 313.
43 J. Montoya, *In Formation*, 52.
44 M. Muñoz, *Faith Healer*, 19, 3, 28.
45 M. Muñoz, *Faith Healer*, 136, 101.
46 M. Muñoz, *Faith Healer*, 28.
47 M. Muñoz, *Faith Healer*, 117–18.
48 M. Muñoz, *Faith Healer*, 105.
49 Woodward, Jones, and Marston, "Of Eagles and Flies," 273.
50 M. Muñoz, *Faith Healer*, 105.
51 M. Muñoz, *Faith Healer*, 161.
52 M. Muñoz, *Faith Healer*, 69.
53 M. Muñoz, *Faith Healer*, 144.
54 M. Muñoz, *Faith Healer*, 169, 147.
55 M. Muñoz, *Faith Healer*, 102.
56 M. Muñoz, *Faith Healer*, 136, 95, 192, 227.
57 M. Muñoz, *Faith Healer*, 208.
58 Sedgwick, *Epistemology of the Closet*, 72.
59 L. Romero, "When Something Goes Queer," 121–42.
60 M. Muñoz, *Faith Healer*, 1.
61 M. Muñoz, *Faith Healer*, 19, 7.
62 M. Muñoz, *Faith Healer*, 20–21.

63 M. Muñoz, *Faith Healer*, 5.
64 M. Muñoz, *Faith Healer*, 22–23.
65 M. Muñoz, *Faith Healer*, 105.
66 M. Muñoz, *Faith Healer*, 128–29.
67 M. Muñoz, *Faith Healer*, 125–26.
68 M. Muñoz, *Faith Healer*, 150–51.
69 Woodward, Jones, and Marston, "Of Eagles and Flies," 273.
70 Gray, *Out in the Country*, 169.
71 Gray, *Out in the Country*, 24.
72 Gray, *Out in the Country*, 92.
73 M. Muñoz, *Faith Healer*, 30.
74 M. Muñoz, *Faith Healer*, 28.
75 M. Muñoz, *Faith Healer*, 46.
76 M. Muñoz, *Faith Healer*, 103.
77 M. Muñoz, *Faith Healer*, 105.
78 M. Muñoz, *Faith Healer*, 93, 15.

CHAPTER FOUR. N + 1

Parts of this chapter previously appeared in "The Homoerotics of Immigration Control," *Scholar and Feminist Online* 6, no. 3 (2008), http://sfonline.barnard.edu/immigration/print_brady.htm.

1 With her pillorying of New England "family values," Ruiz de Burton lays bare some of the substructure undergirding both immigration policy and family-values campaigns.
2 K. Chávez, *Queer Migration Politics*, 10.
3 Quoted in K. Chávez, *Queer Migration Politics*, 10.
4 K. Chávez, *Queer Migration Politics*, 10.
5 See Canaday, *Straight State*.
6 The film's title plays on *Fear and Loathing in Las Vegas*, Hunter Thompson's fictionalized encounter with civil rights attorney Oscar Zeta Acosta. Acosta's own efforts to support improved access to education for young Latinx in Los Angeles is thereby invoked but not named.
7 Barone, "Challenging the Educational Imaginary," 210.
8 For a helpful history of the battles to legislate against discrimination based on sexuality, see Turk, "'Our Militancy.'"
9 Given how enduring this gap between frameworks has been, it's useful to study the reverberations of AB101, not least because they reveal how state-managed sexuality, with its explicit enactment through public policies governing social reproduction, functions as the most intense connection between social values campaigns and anti-immigration campaigns. Of course, the traditional-values campaigns initiated after AB101 were not the first to hook together queers and migrants as threats to the heterosexual white family, although their strategy of scapegoating migrants and queers (and queer migrants) publicly, at the same time, with direct voter initiatives was perhaps new to the 1990s.

10 Marc Lifsher, "Wilson Was like a Magnet for Trouble," *Orange County Register*, January 2, 1992.
11 Marc Lifsher, "Gov. Wilson Will Veto Gay-Rights Bill," *Orange County Register*, September 30, 1991.
12 Kenney, *Mapping Gay L.A.*, 153–57.
13 Kenney, *Mapping Gay L.A.*, 160.
14 Scott Harris and George Ramos, "Gay Activists Vent Rage," *Los Angeles Times*, October 1, 1991.
15 M. Smith and Tarallo, "Proposition 187," 665.
16 Wilson hoped to win a redistricting battle, as well as a proposition that would increase the governor's budgetary authority, and sought to elect more moderate Republicans to state office.
17 Jean Pasco, "GOP Rift Apparent as Conclave Nears," *Orange County Register*, September 17, 1992.
18 Greg Lucas and David Tuller, "Wilson Signs New Gay Rights Bill," *San Francisco Chronicle*, September 26, 1992.
19 For helpful analysis, see Robin Podolsky, "Stretching the World," *LA Weekly*, November 15, 1991; Doug Sadownick, "The Center Moves West," *LA Weekly*, November 15, 1991; and Leef Smith, "California Gov. Wilson Signs Gay-Rights Bill," *Washington Post*, September 30, 1992.
20 Marc Lifsher, "Wilson Mandate and GOP Unity Left Shaky," *Orange County Register*, November 5, 1992.
21 Lifsher, "Wilson Was like a Magnet."
22 Mookas, "Fault Lines," 14. See also Herrell, "Sin, Sickness and Crime."
23 Alexander, *Pedagogies of Crossing*, 199. It should also be noted that films like *Gay Rights, Special Rights* became a successful model for other homophobic films, including films targeting parent-teacher associations which rallied parents against school diversity and inclusivity curricula. See Lugg, "Religious Right," 267–69.
24 "A Challenge to Wilson," *Orange County Register*, April 6, 1994; Jerry Roberts and Robert Gunnson, "Wilson Wants Truce with Right Wing," *San Francisco Chronicle*, February 26, 1993.
25 Almost from the start of his governorship, Wilson had complained about the impact of immigration on state coffers and fed anti-immigration fever. See, for example, Robert Reinhold, "In California, New Talk of Limits on Immigrants," *New York Times*, December 3, 1991. My point, however, is that it was not until Wilson seemed to have no way out politically that he made anti-immigrant policies the focus of his governorship. See Jerry Roberts, "Wilson Given a Lift by GOP Convention," *San Francisco Chronicle*, March 6, 1993; John Jacobs, "Pete Wilson's Picture-Perfect Campaign," *Orange County Register*, November 22, 1994; and Scott Thrum, "Immigration, Crime Keys to Brown's Defeat," *San Jose Mercury News*, November 9, 1994. Wilson's turnaround, however, is all the more significant because in having supported the Immigration Reform and Control Act of 1986, he had also expanded the logic by which people were persuaded to seek dangerous, exploitative employment in the United States. Armbruster, Geron, and Bonacich, "Assault," 660.

26 Phillip Maiter and Andrew Ross, "Ripples of Controversy around 'Catch of the Day,'" *San Francisco Chronicle*, August 11, 1993; Pete Wilson, "Crack Down on Illegals," *USA Today*, August 20, 1993; Associated Press, "Seeking to Deny Citizenship to Some," *New York Times*, August 11, 1993; Rogert Reinhold, "California's Wish for Immigrants," *Vancouver Sun*, August 26, 1993; and "Governor's Cry: Curb Illegal Immigrants," *Atlanta Journal and Constitution*, August 11, 1993.

27 Until the 1990s, immigration policy was considered the purview of the federal government. More important, a series of Supreme Court cases had declared that once a person entered the United States, they had to be treated the same as a person born in the United States. These "standing" laws were overturned by the Supreme Court in a series of decisions that paved the way for draconian policies such as Arizona's SB1070. Wilson's campaign staff claimed they had nothing to do with the proposition; nevertheless, by relentlessly campaigning against immigration, Wilson helped mobilize anti-immigrant sentiment, at the very least. See Wroe, *Republican Party*.

28 Diamond, "Right-Wing Politics," 154–58.

29 Wilson may have inadvertently signaled the connection between AB101 and Proposition 187 when he complained, in a major public statement, that immigrants came to the United States because of its "perverse incentives" (i.e., social welfare programs). Quoted in Calavita, "New Politics," 289. For discussions of Proposition 187, see Ono and Sloop, *Shifting Borders*; Jacobson, *New Nativism*; and Santa Ana, *Brown Tide Rising*.

30 The ground for this effort was more than paved by the anti-Black labor of Ronald Reagan and other conservatives who utilized the welfare-queen trope mercilessly. See also Cohen, "Punks, Bulldaggers"; and Jakobsen, *Sex Obsession*.

31 M. Smith and Tarallo, "Proposition 187," 665.

32 A political adviser to Wilson's democratic opponent, Kathleen Brown, marked the twenty-year anniversary of Proposition 187 by noting its ongoing importance in national politics. See William Bradley, "How Prop 187 Became the Pivot for the Immigration Issue and Future of Democratic Politics," *Huffington Post*, September 17, 2013.

33 For further discussion, see Bluestone and Harrison, *Deindustrialization of America*; and Bello, Cunningham, and Rau, *Dark Victory*.

34 Calavita, "New Politics," 286. She notes that they were seen variously as strikebreakers, socialists, and anarchists.

35 Calavita, "New Politics."

36 Calavita, "New Politics," 292.

37 Calavita, "New Politics," 298.

38 For more on Bryant's campaign, see Lugg, "Religious Right," 270.

39 Despite the estimate that nearly half of all immigrants (both authorized and informal) are women, as Pierrette Hondagneu-Sotelo notes, international immigration scholarship up through the first decade of the twenty-first century paid little attention to gender. For this reason it is not surprising that scholarship on Proposition 187 would have paid little attention to broader issues that emerge out of battles over sexual freedom. See Hondagneu-Sotelo, "New Directions," 234–35.

40 G. Sánchez, "Face the Nation," 1009–10.
41 In *The Republican Party and Immigration Politics*, Andrew Wroe also argues that historians and sociologists have failed to adequately account for the importance of Republican Party politics in mobilizing anti-immigrant fervor and that Wilson's focus on illegal immigration and support for Proposition 187 raised the initiative's profile.
42 George Sánchez makes the point that a significant aspect of new nativism has been the rhetoric that "focuses on the drain of public resources by immigrants, both legal and illegal, particularly their utilization of welfare, education and health care services." G. Sánchez, "Face the Nation," 1020. For a terrific discussion of ongoing engagement with media, see Vigil, *Public Negotiations*.
43 K. Chávez, *Queer Migration Politics*, 10.
44 Bosniak, *Citizen and the Alien*, 2.
45 Bosniak, *Citizen and the Alien*, 2.
46 Bosniak, *Citizen and the Alien*, 2.
47 Bosniak, *Citizen and the Alien*, 136.
48 Bosniak, *Citizen and the Alien*, 4.
49 This is one reason a growing movement of activists and scholars has begun advocating the elimination of citizenship (akin to the radical prison abolition movement). For a moving discussion of a world without borders, see Mbembe, "Idea of a Borderless World."
50 Bosniak, *Citizen and the Alien*, 5.
51 While the fight over protection from discrimination embodied in the AB101 protests cannot be said to have caused California voters to approve Proposition 187 or to have ensured that Bill Clinton would champion and expand Operation Gatekeeper, they must be understood as related and engaged with each other in significant ways.
52 Frank Rich, "How Hispanics Became the New Gays," *New York Times*, January 11, 2006.
53 See also Rifkin, *When Did Indians Become Straight?*
54 Luibhéid, "Heteronormativity, Responsibility, and Neo-liberal Governance in US Immigration Control," 69. For robust discussions of sexuality and migration, see Luibhéid, "Queer/Migration"; Cantú, *The Sexuality of Migration*; J. M. Rodriguez, *Queer Latinidad*; and H. Ramírez, "Introduction."
55 Stern, "Nationalism on the Line," 300.
56 Stern, "Nationalism on the Line," 300, 318.
57 For a careful discussion of sexual violence and border crossing, see Vogt, *Lives in Transit*.
58 Alexander, *Pedagogies of Crossing*, 226.
59 L. Chávez, *Latino Threat*, 16.
60 M. Romero, "'Go after the Women,'" 1375–76; and Tukachinsky, Mastro, and Yarchi, "Documenting Portrayals of Race/Ethnicity."
61 David Brooks, "Two Steps toward a Sensible Immigration Policy," *New York Times*, August 14, 2005.
62 For an examination of this process, see Shah, *Contagious Divides*.

63 Sedef Arat-Koç quoted in Silvey, "Development and Geography," 511.
64 The homophobia/anti-immigration relay helps explain the persuasive power that coagulates through migrants' mobilization under banners such as "undocumented and unafraid."
65 Sonsini began his career painting backdrops for photographers and classical male physiques based on the work of the famous beefcake photographer Bob Mizer and later became well known for his portraits of male nudes. For more on Mizer's work, see Waugh, *Hard to Imagine*; Hooven, *Beefcake*; and Auricchio, "Lifting the Veil."
66 Priscilla Frank, "Artist Pays Latino Day Workers Hourly Wage," *Huffington Post*, February 11, 2016.
67 See Theodore, Valenzuela, and Melendez, "Esquina"; and Melendez et al., "Worker Centers."
68 Melendez et al., "Worker Centers," 837–38.
69 $N+1$ describes the mathematical concept of iteration as a massing that eliminates specificity and suggests the absence of a temporal end point.
70 Ken Johnson, "John Sonsini," *New York Times*, March 25, 2005.
71 Grover, "John Sonsini," n.p.
72 Artist Ramiro Gomez offers a very different approach. See Chung, "Defiant Worker."
73 Sonsini, *John Sonsini*. This is the clear supposition of the show's catalog.
74 J. Montoya, *In Formation*, 16–18.
75 Corral, *Slow Lightning*, 61.
76 Corral, *Slow Lightning*, 61.
77 Corral, *Slow Lightning*, 62.
78 Corral is signaling the casta system with terms such as *Castizo* and *Zambo*. For an authoritative discussion of the casta system, see Vinson, *Before Mestizaje*.
79 Corral, *Slow Lightning*, 17.
80 For a superb discussion, see Richard Rodríguez, *Next of Kin*.
81 See Archambault, "Women Left Behind?"
82 See Reuters, "Reno Initiative Aims to Control Immigration," *New York Times*, September 18, 1994.
83 Operation Gatekeeper has been well studied, but its relationship to homophobia less so. See Jardine, "Operation Gatekeeper"; Nevins, *Operation Gatekeeper and Beyond*; and Schmidt Camacho, *Migrant Imaginaries*.
84 Evelyn Nieves, "Illegal Immigrant Death Rate Rises Sharply in Barren Areas," *New York Times*, August 6, 2002. During the fifteen-year period from 1998 to 2012, at least 5,595 people died attempting to enter the United States. Half of that number were in Arizona.
85 Grande, *Across a Hundred Mountains*, 20.
86 Grande, *Across a Hundred Mountains*, 29.
87 Grande, *Across a Hundred Mountains*, 21.
88 Grande, *Across a Hundred Mountains*, 27.
89 Grande, *Across a Hundred Mountains*, 29.
90 Grande, *Across a Hundred Mountains*, 49.

91 Grande, *Across a Hundred Mountains*, 24.
92 Grande, *Across a Hundred Mountains*, 6.
93 Grande, *Across a Hundred Mountains*, 143.
94 See Plambech, "Sex, Deportation and Rescue," 135–40.
95 In sending remittances, Nora's father participates in an economy that sent more than $20 billion per year to Mexico between 2005 and 2013. Waddell, "Remitting Democracy?"
96 Restrepo, *Illegal*, 130.
97 Restrepo, *Illegal*, 114–15.
98 Restrepo, *Illegal*, 46.
99 Manuel Orozco, "Remittances to Latin America and the Caribbean in 2016," *Report to the Leadership for the Americas*, February 10, 2017; Corona and Orraca, "Remittances in Mexico," 1048.
100 Caminero-Santangelo, "Lost Ones," 308.
101 Puga, "Migrant Melodrama and Elvira Arellano," 359.
102 Puga, "Migrant Melodrama and the Political Economy of Suffering," 73.
103 Puga, "Migrant Melodrama and the Political Economy of Suffering," 74.
104 Duane, *Suffering*, 6.
105 See especially Schmidt Camacho, "Hailing the Twelve Million."
106 See also Beltrán, "Undocumented, Unafraid, and Unapologetic."

CHAPTER FIVE. MISPLACED

1 See Menjívar and Abrego, "Legal Violence," 1380–81.
2 The border I described as an abjection machine in 2002 is far more treacherous now. Brady, *Extinct Lands*.
3 De León, "Efficacy and Impact," 10–11. See also Slack and Martínez, "Postremoval Geographies."
4 See, for example, Macías-Rojas, *From Deportation to Prison*; Abrego et al., "Making Immigrants into Criminals"; Reiter and Coutin, "Crossing Borders"; Buff, "Deportation Terror"; Walters, "Flight of the Deported"; Coleman and Stuesse, "Disappearing State"; and Slack, "Captive Bodies."
5 See, for typical examples, Luke Mogelson, "Deported," *New York Times*, December 9, 2015; Levi Bridges, "One Deportee Confronts Violence, Isolation in El Salvador," KQED, February 9, 2018; Sarah Stillman, "When Deportation Is a Death Sentence," *New Yorker*, January 15, 2018; Kate Linthicum, "Back to Malinalco," *Los Angeles Times*, July 3, 2017; Antonio Olivo, "After Decades in America, the Newly Deported Return to a Mexico They Barely Recognize," *Washington Post*, March 3, 2017; and Laura Weiss, "No One Talks about Life after Deportation," *Nation*, April 28, 2017.
6 In "The Diachronics of Difference," Jesse Alemán also considers Ruiz de Burton and the politics of deportation.
7 For more on Hobbes see Kotef, *Movement*.
8 For more discussions of movement and freedom, see Mbembe, "Idea of a Borderless World"; and Kotef, *Movement*.

9   See especially Kotef, *Movement*, 61–86.
10 Cavarero, *Inclinations*.
11 Consider also the nineteenth-century efforts of white abolitionists to expel all African-heritage peoples from the United States by relocating them to Panama or Liberia.
12 Linebaugh and Rediker, *Many-Headed Hydra*, 40.
13 Linebaugh and Rediker, *Many-Headed Hydra*, 18.
14 Silva, *Toward a Global Idea*; Du Bois, *Souls of Black Folk*; and Muñoz, "'Chico.'"
15 Quoted in Linebaugh and Rediker, *Many-Headed Hydra*, 59.
16 Linebaugh and Rediker, *Many-Headed Hydra*, 16.
17 Quoted in Linebaugh and Rediker, *Many-Headed Hydra*, 16.
18 Linebaugh and Rediker, *Many-Headed Hydra*, 110.
19 Kanstroom, *Deportation Nation*, 26.
20 Quoted in Kanstroom, *Deportation Nation*, 34.
21 Kanstroom, *Deportation Nation*, 34.
22 Quoted in Kanstroom, *Deportation Nation*, 26.
23 Kanstroom, *Deportation Nation*, 74.
24 Kanstroom, *Deportation Nation*, 36.
25 Kanstroom, *Deportation Nation*, 49–50.
26 Kanstroom, *Deportation Nation*, 60–70.
27 Kanstroom, *Deportation Nation*, 67.
28 Kanstroom, *Deportation Nation*, 74.
29 Quoted in Kanstroom, *Deportation Nation*, 118.
30 Blue, "Strange Passages."
31 For a terrific study of the Border Patrol, see K. Hernández, *Migra!*
32 For a detailed history, see Gurman, "Collapsing Division."
33 Reiter and Coutin, "Crossing Borders," 572.
34 Abrego et al., "Making Immigrants into Criminals," 696.
35 See Chacón, "Overcriminalizing Immigration"; and Chacón, "Unsecured Borders." See also Kanstroom, "Criminalizing the Undocumented."
36 Macías-Rojas, "Immigration," 2.
37 Abrego et al., "Making Immigrants into Criminals," 695.
38 De León, "Efficacy and Impact," 15. For a discussion of the way immigrant policing appears and disappears, see Coleman and Stuesse, "Disappearing State."
39 "US-Mexico Border Migrant Deaths Rose," *Guardian*, February 6, 2018.
40 Deborah Boehm and others argue that statistics fail to count those who leave the United States to accompany deported loved ones as well as those who travel to their birth countries and then cannot find an easy way to return to the United States. See Boehm, *Returned*.
41 Cristina Rivera Garza, "*2501 Migrantes*," 49.
42 Anthropologist and filmmaker Yolanda Cruz completed a film about his project, *2501 Migrantes: A Journey* (2009). In the years after the first exhibit in Oaxaca City, Santiago continued to build his sculptures, working closely with the youth of his home village. The film culminates with a massive exhibit of all of the migrantes in Monterrey, Mexico. Sadly, Santiago died in July 2013.

43 Fojas, *Zombies, Migrants, and Queers*, 61.
44 Boehm, *Returned*, 76.
45 See Boehm, *Returned*; and De León, "Efficacy and Impact," for discussions of the dangerous informal economies seeking to exploit those abandoned by the United States.
46 Boehm, *Returned*, 36–38.
47 Martone et al., "Impact of Remittances."
48 M. Montoya, *Deportation of Wopper Barraza*, 3.
49 M. Montoya, *Deportation of Wopper Barraza*, vii.
50 Boehm, *Returned*, 81–82.
51 M. Montoya, *Deportation of Wopper Barraza*, 18.
52 M. Montoya, *Deportation of Wopper Barraza*, 40.
53 M. Montoya, *Deportation of Wopper Barraza*, 41, 42.
54 M. Montoya, *Deportation of Wopper Barraza*, 129, 172.
55 M. Montoya, *Deportation of Wopper Barraza*, 23.
56 M. Montoya, *Deportation of Wopper Barraza*, 63.
57 M. Montoya, *Deportation of Wopper Barraza*, 127.
58 M. Montoya, *Deportation of Wopper Barraza*, 98.
59 M. Montoya, *Deportation of Wopper Barraza*, 204.
60 M. Montoya, *Deportation of Wopper Barraza*, 185.
61 M. Montoya, *Deportation of Wopper Barraza*, 72.
62 M. Montoya, *Deportation of Wopper Barraza*, 211.
63 M. Montoya, *Deportation of Wopper Barraza*, 39–40. For a thoughtful discussion of homes built through remittances, see S. Lopez, *Remittance Landscape*.
64 M. Montoya, *Deportation of Wopper Barraza*, 32.
65 M. Montoya, *Deportation of Wopper Barraza*, 56.
66 M. Montoya, *Deportation of Wopper Barraza*, 36.
67 M. Montoya, *Deportation of Wopper Barraza*, 132.
68 For a helpful discussion of this new genre, see Hedrick, *Chica Lit*.
69 Alegría, *Sofi Mendoza's Guide*, 5–6.
70 Alegría, *Sofi Mendoza's Guide*, 13.
71 Alegría, *Sofi Mendoza's Guide*, 57.
72 Alegría, *Sofi Mendoza's Guide*, 92, 110.
73 Alegría, *Sofi Mendoza's Guide*, 143.
74 Alegría, *Sofi Mendoza's Guide*, 80.
75 Alegría, *Sofi Mendoza's Guide*, 57.
76 Alegría, *Sofi Mendoza's Guide*, 188.
77 Alegría, *Sofi Mendoza's Guide*, 151–52.
78 Alegría, *Sofi Mendoza's Guide*, 153–54.
79 Alegría, *Sofi Mendoza's Guide*, 125.
80 Alegría, *Sofi Mendoza's Guide*, 157.
81 Alegría, *Sofi Mendoza's Guide*, 221.
82 For example, see Reyna Grande, *Dancing with Butterflies* (2009).
83 Peña, *Bang*, 1.
84 Peña, *Bang*, 77.

85 Rosaldo, "Imperialist Nostalgia," 110.
86 Peña, *Bang*, 78.
87 Peña, *Bang*, 172.
88 Peña, *Bang*, 230.
89 Boehm argues for the term *de facto citizen* to describe long-term residents in the United States who do not hold formal residency. Boehm, *Returned*, 17, 100.
90 Peña, *Bang*, 239.

CONCLUSION

1 Glissant, *Poetics*, 190; Moten in conversation with Hanif Abdurraqib, "Building a Stairway to Get Us Closer to Something beyond This Place," *Millennials Are Killing Capitalism*, accessed June 7, 2021, https://millennialsarekillingcapitalism.libsyn.com/hanif-abdurraqib-fred-moten-building-a-stairway-to-get-us-closer-to-something-beyond-this-place; and Hogan, *Dwellings*, 46.
2 See Sánchez and Pita, *Conflicts of Interest*, 281.
3 For a helpful discussion of impersonation in another context, see Chen, *Double Agency*.
4 Escobar, *Designs for the Pluriverse*, 87.
5 Adeyemi, "Beyond 90°," 9.
6 Massey, *For Space*, 149.
7 Anzaldúa, "Haciendo caras," xv.
8 Mbembe, "Idea of a Borderless World." See also Mbembe, "Tanner Lectures."
9 Mbembe, "Idea of a Borderless World."
10 Harney and Moten, *Undercommons*, 61.
11 See Jakobsen, *Sex Obsession*; and Grabel, *When Things Don't Fall Apart*.
12 At every turn María Lugones taught this point, and I am deeply indebted to her patient unfolding of this argument across her written work and during our fleeting encounters. I am also grateful to a set of writers who got there way ahead of me but still had the grace to stand still and say hello. See the work of Yomaira Figueroa, Deborah Vargas, Fred Moten, Amy Sara Carroll, Laura Harris, Richard T. Rodríguez, Alexandra Vazquez, Juana María Rodríguez, Sonnet Retman, Daphne Brooks, and Kirstie Dorr.
13 See Jasmine Aguilera, "'Family Separation 2.0': Parents in ICE Detention Have to Decide Whether to Keep Their Children or Release Them to Sponsors," *Time*, July 27, 2020; Amnesty International, "Family Separation 2.0: 'You Aren't Going to Separate Me from My Only Child,'" Amnesty International, May 21, 2020, https://www.amnestyusa.org/wp-content/uploads/2020/04/Amnesty-International-USA-Family-Separation-2.0_May-21-2020-.pdf; and Nomaan Merchant, "Migrant Kids Held in US Hotels, Then Expelled," *AP News*, July 22, 2020.

Bibliography

Abrego, Leisy, Mat Coleman, Daniel E. Martínez, Cecilia Menjívar, and Jeremy Slack. "Making Immigrants into Criminals: Legal Processes of Criminalization in the Post-IIRIRA Era." *Journal on Migration and Human Security* 5, no. 3 (2017): 694–715.

Adeyemi, Kemi. "Beyond 90°: The Angluarities of Black/Queer/Women/Lean." *Women and Performance* 29, no. 1 (2019): 9–24.

Agard-Jones, Vanessa. "Bodies in the System." *Small Axe* 17, no. 3 (2013): 182–92.

Aguirre, Robert. *Informal Empire: Mexico and Central America in Victorian Culture*. Minneapolis: University of Minnesota Press, 2005.

Ahuja, Neel. "Postcolonial Critique in a Multispecies World." *PMLA* 124, no. 2 (2009): 556–63.

Alcott, Louisa May. *Little Women*. New York: Penguin, 2004.

Aldama, Frederick. *Latino/a Children's and Young Adult Writers on the Art of Storytelling*. Pittsburgh: University of Pittsburgh Press, 2018.

Aldama, Frederick. *The Routledge Concise History of Latino/a Literature*. New York: Routledge, 2013.

Alegría, Malín. *Sofi Mendoza's Guide to Getting Lost in Mexico*. New York: Simon and Schuster, 2007.

Alemán, Jesse. "The Diachronics of Difference: Chicano Narrative Then, Now and before Chicanidad." In *Bridges, Borders, and Breaks*, edited by William Orchard and Yolanda Padilla, 25–39. Pittsburgh: University of Pittsburgh Press, 2016.

Alemán, Jesse. "'Thank God, Lolita Is Away from Those Horrid Savages': The Politics of Whiteness in *Who Would Have Thought It?*" In *María Amparo Ruiz de Burton: Critical and Pedagogical Perspectives*, edited by Amelia María de la Luz Montes and Anne Goldman, 95–111. Lincoln: University of Nebraska Press, 2004.

Alexander, Jacqui. *Pedagogies of Crossing: Meditations on Feminism, Sexual Politics, Memory, and the Sacred*. Durham, NC: Duke University Press, 2005.

Allen, Chadwick. *Trans-Indigenous: Methodologies for Global Native Literary Studies*. Minneapolis: University of Minnesota Press, 2012.

Allen, Robert Clyde. *Horrible Prettiness: Burlesque and American Culture*. Chapel Hill: University of North Carolina Press, 1991.

Alonzo, Armando. *Tejano Legacy: Rancheros and Settlers in South Texas, 1734–1900.* Albuquerque: University of New Mexico Press, 1998.

Alryyes, Ala A. *Original Subjects: The Child, the Novel, and the Nation.* Cambridge, MA: Harvard University Press, 2001.

Alvarez, Julia. *How the García Girls Lost Their Accents.* New York: Plume, 1992.

Alvord, Daniel, Cecilia Menjívar, and Andrea Gómez Cervantes. "The Legal Violence in the 2017 Executive Orders: The Expansion of Immigrant Criminalization in Kansas." *Social Currents* 5, no. 5 (2018): 411–20.

Anzaldúa, Gloria. "Haciendo caras, una entrada: An Introduction." In *Making Face, Making Soul; Haciendo Caras: Creative and Critical Perspectives by Feminists of Color,* edited by Gloria Anzaldúa, xv–xxviii. San Francisco, Aunt Lute, 1990.

Aranda, José F., Jr. "Contradictory Impulses: María Amparo Ruiz de Burton, Resistance Theory, and the Politics of Chicano/a Studies." *American Literature* 70, no. 3 (1998): 551–79.

Archambault, Caroline S. "Women Left Behind? Migration, Spousal Separation, and the Autonomy of Rural Women in Ugweno, Tanzania." *Signs: Journal of Women in Culture and Society* 35, no. 4 (2010): 919–42.

Ardao, Arturo. *Génesis de la idea y el nombre de América Latina.* Caracas, Venezuela: Centro de Estudios Latinoamericanos Rómulo Gallegos, 1980.

Armbruster, Ralph, Kim Geron, and Edna Bonacich. "The Assault on California's Latino Immigrants: The Politics of Proposition 187." *International Journal of Urban and Regional Research* 19, no. 4 (1995): 655–63.

Arrizón-Palomera, Esmeralda. "The Trope of the Papers: The Coloniality of Citizenship and the Turn to the Undocumented in Black and Chicana Feminist Thought." PhD diss., Cornell University, 2020.

Atiya, P. S. *The Rise and Fall of Freedom of Contract.* New York: Oxford University Press, 1979.

Auricchio, Laura. "Lifting the Veil: Robert Rauschenberg's Thirty-Four Drawings for Dante's Inferno and the Commercial Homoerotic Imagery of 1950s America." In *The Gay '90s: Disciplinary and Interdisciplinary Formations in Queer Studies,* edited by Thomas Foster, Carol Siegel, and Ellen Berry, 119–54. New York: NYU Press, 1997.

Avila, Eric. *Popular Culture in the Age of White Flight: Fear and Fantasy in Suburban Los Angeles.* Berkeley: University of California Press, 2004.

Barone, Tom. "Challenging the Educational Imaginary: Issues of Form, Substance, and Quality in Film-Based Research." *Qualitative Inquiry* 9, no. 2 (2003): 202–17.

Barr, Juliana. *Peace Came in the Form of a Woman: Indians and Spaniards in the Texas Borderlands.* Chapel Hill: University of North Carolina Press, 2007.

Baudrillard, Jean. *America.* New York: Verso, 2010.

Bebout, Lee. "The First Generation: Queer Temporality, Heteropatriarchy, and Cultural Reproduction in Jovita González and Eve Raleigh's *Caballero.*" *Western American Literature* 49, no. 4 (2015): 351–74.

Bello, Walden, Shea Cunningham, and Bill Rau. *Dark Victory: The United States and Global Poverty.* San Francisco: Food First, 1994.

Beltrán, Cristina. "Undocumented, Unafraid, and Unapologetic: DREAM Activists, Immigrant Politics, and the Queering of Democracy." In *Radical Future Pasts: Untimely*

Essays in Political Theory, edited by Romand Coles, Mark Reinhardt, and George Shulman, 217-48. Lexington: University of Kentucky Press, 2014.

Bernstein, Robin. *Racial Innocence: Performing American Childhood from Slavery to Civil Rights*. New York: NYU Press, 2011.

Bishop, Rudine Sims. *Free within Ourselves: The Development of African American Children's Literature*. Westport, CT: Greenwood, 2007.

Blackhawk, Ned. *Violence over the Land: Indians and Empires in the Early American West*. Cambridge, MA: Harvard University Press, 2006.

Blackwell, Maylei, Floridalma Boj Lopez, and Luis Urrieta. "Critical Latinx Indigeneities." *Latino Studies* 15, no. 2 (2017): 126-37.

Blanchard, Pascal, Nicolas Bancel, Gilles Boëtsch, Eric Deroo, Sandrine Lemaire, and Charles Forsdick. *Human Zoos: Science and Spectacle in the Age of Empire*. Liverpool: University of Liverpool Press, 2008.

Blue, Ethan. "Strange Passages: Carceral Mobility and the Liminal in the Catastrophic History of American Deportation." *National Identities* 17, no. 2 (2015): 175-94.

Bluestone, Barry, and Bennett Harrison. *The Deindustrialization of America: Plant Closings, Community Abandonment and the Dismantling of Basic Industry*. New York: Basic Books, 1982.

Boehm, Deborah. *Returned: Going and Coming in an Age of Deportation*. Berkeley: University of California Press, 2016.

Bogdan, Robert. *Freak Show: Presenting Human Oddities for Amusement and Profit*. Chicago: University of Chicago Press, 1988.

Bosniak, Linda. *The Citizen and the Alien: Dilemmas of Contemporary Membership*. Princeton, NJ: Princeton University Press, 2008.

Brady, Mary Pat. *Extinct Lands, Temporal Geographies: Chicana Literature and the Urgency of Space*. Durham, NC: Duke University Press, 2002.

Brady, Mary Pat. "The Fungibility of Borders." *Nepantla: Views from South* 1, no. 1 (2000): 171-90.

Brady, Mary Pat. "The Homoerotics of Immigration Control." *Scholar and Feminist Online* 6, no. 3 (2008). http://sfonline.barnard.edu/immigration/print_brady.htm.

Brady, Mary Pat. "Metaphors to Love By: Toward a Chicana Aesthetics in *Their Dogs Came with Them*." In *Rebozos de Palabras: An Helena María Viramontes Critical Reader*, edited by Gabriella Gutiérrez y Muhs, 167-91. Tucson: University of Arizona Press, 2013.

Brady, Mary Pat. "The Waiting Arms of Gold Street: Manuel Muñoz's *Faith Healer of Olive Avenue* and the Problem of the Scaffold Imaginary." In *Queering the Countryside: New Frontiers in Rural Queer Studies*, edited by Mary L. Gray, Colin R. Johnson, and Brian J. Gilley, 109-125. New York: NYU Press, 2016.

Brewer, Holly. *By Birth or Consent: Children, Law, and the Anglo-American Revolution in Authority*. Chapel Hill: University of North Carolina Press, 2005.

Briggs, Laura. *Taking Children: A History of American Terror*. Oakland: University of California Press, 2020.

Brodsly, David. *L.A. Freeway: An Appreciative Essay*. Berkeley: University of California Press, 1981.

Brody, Jennifer DeVere. *Impossible Purities: Blackness, Femininity, and Victorian Culture*. Durham, NC: Duke University Press, 1998.

Brooks, Daphne. *Bodies in Dissent: Spectacular Performances of Race and Freedom, 1850-1910*. Durham, NC: Duke University Press, 2006.

Brooks, James F. *Captives and Cousins: Slavery, Kinship, and Community in the Southwest Borderlands*. Chapel Hill: University of North Carolina Press, 2011.

Brooks, Lisa Tanya. *Our Beloved Kin: A New History of King Philip's War*. New Haven, CT: Yale University Press, 2018.

Brown, Gillian. *The Consent of the Governed: The Lockean Legacy in Early American Culture*. Cambridge, MA: Harvard University Press, 2001.

Buff, Rachel Ida. "The Deportation Terror." *American Quarterly* 60, no. 3 (2008): 523-51.

Byrd, Jodi. "Souths as Prologues: Indigeneity, Race, and the Temporalities of Land; or, Why I Can't Read William Faulkner." In *Faulkner and the Native South*, edited by Jay Watson, Annette Trefzer, and James Thomas, 15-32. Jackson: University Press of Mississippi, 2019.

Byrd, Jodi. *The Transit of Empire: Indigenous Critiques of Colonialism*. Minneapolis: University of Minnesota Press, 2011.

Calavita, Kitty. "The New Politics of Immigration: 'Balanced-Budget Conservatism' and the Symbolism of Proposition 187." *Social Problems* 43, no. 3 (1996): 284-305.

Caminero-Santangelo, Marta. "The Lost Ones: Post-Gatekeeper Border Fictions and the Construction of Cultural Trauma." *Latino Studies* 8, no. 3 (2010): 304-27.

Canaday, Margot. *The Straight State: Sexuality and Citizenship in Twentieth-Century America*. Princeton, NJ: Princeton University Press, 2009.

Cantú, Lionel. *The Sexuality of Migration: Border Crossings and Mexican Immigrant Men*. New York: NYU Press, 2009.

Carrera, Magali M. *Imagining Identity in New Spain: Race, Lineage, and the Colonial Body in Portraiture and Casta Paintings*. Austin: University of Texas Press, 2003.

Carrillo Castillo, Jesús. "'The World Is Only One and Not Many': Representation of the Natural World in Imperial Spain." In *Spain in the Age of Exploration*, edited by Chiyo Ishikawa, 139-57. Lincoln: University of Nebraska Press, 2004.

Carroll, Amy Sara. *Remex: Toward an Art History of the NAFTA Era*. Austin: University of Texas Press, 2017.

Carroll, Lorrayne. "Captivity Literature." In *The Oxford Handbook of Early American Literature*, edited by Kevin J. Hayes, 144-68. New York: Oxford University Press, 2008.

Casares, Oscar. *Amigoland: A Novel*. New York: Back Bay Books, 2009.

Castiglia, Christopher. *Bound and Determined: Captivity, Culture-Crossing, and White Womanhood from Mary Rowlandson to Patty Hearst*. Chicago: University of Chicago Press, 1996.

Cavarero, Adriana. *Inclinations: A Critique of Rectitude*. Stanford, CA: Stanford University Press, 2016.

Chacón, Jennifer M. "Overcriminalizing Immigration." *Journal of Criminal Law and Criminology* 102, no. 3 (2012): 613-52.

Chacón, Jennifer. "Unsecured Borders: Immigration Restrictions, Crime Control and National Security." *Connecticut Law Review* 39, no. 5 (2006): 1827-32.

Chandler, Nahum Dimitri. *Toward an African Future—of the Limit of World*. London: Living Commons Press, 2013.

Chappell, Ben. *Lowrider Space: Aesthetics and Politics of Mexican American Custom Cars*. Austin: University of Texas Press, 2012.

Chávez, Karma R. *Queer Migration Politics: Activist Rhetoric and Coalitional Possibilities*. Champaign: University of Illinois Press, 2013.

Chávez, Leo. *The Latino Threat: Constructing Immigrants, Citizens, and the Nation*. Stanford, CA: Stanford University Press, 2008.

Chen, Tina. *Double Agency: Acts of Impersonation in Asian American Literature and Culture*. Palo Alto, CA: Stanford University Press, 2005.

Chung, Kelly I. "The Defiant Still Worker: Ramiro Gomez and the Expressionism of Abstract Labor." *Women and Performance: A Journal of Feminist Theory* 29, no. 1 (2019): 62–76.

Citizens United for the Preservation of Civil Rights. *Gay Rights, Special Rights: Inside the Homosexual Agenda*. Hermet, CA: Jeremiah Films, 1993.

Clinton, DeWitt. "Opening Speech to Forty Second Session of New York State Legislature, January 1819." In *Messages from the Governors*, vol. 2, edited by Charles Z. Lincoln, 960–87. Albany, NY: J. B. Lyon, 1909.

Cohen, Cathy. "Punks, Bulldaggers, and Welfare Queens: The Radical Potential of Queer Politics?" *GLQ: A Journal of Gay and Lesbian Studies* 3, no. 4 (1997): 437–65.

Coleman, Mat, and Angela Stuesse. "The Disappearing State and the Quasi-Event of Immigration Control." *Antipode* 48, no. 3 (2016): 524–43.

Corona, Francisco, and Pedro Orraca. "Remittances in Mexico and Their Unobserved Components." *Journal of International Trade and Economic Development* 28, no. 8 (2019): 1047–66.

Corral, Eduardo. *Slow Lightning*. New Haven, CT: Yale University Press, 2012.

Cotera, María Eugenia. *Native Speakers: Ella Deloria, Zora Neale Hurston, Jovita González, and the Poetics of Culture*. Austin: University of Texas Press, 2008.

Cox, Aimee Meredith. *Shapeshifters: Black Girls and the Choreography of Citizenship*. Durham, NC: Duke University Press, 2013.

Cruz, Angie. *Let It Rain Coffee*. New York: Simon and Schuster, 2005.

Cruz, Yolanda, dir. *2501 Migrants: A Journey*. Los Angeles: Petate Productions, 2010.

Cuevas, T. Jackie. *Post-Borderlandia: Chicana Literature and Gender-Variant Critique*. New Brunswick, NJ: Rutgers University Press, 2018.

Cutler, John Alba. *Ends of Assimilation: The Formation of Chicano Literature*. New York: Oxford University Press, 2015.

Cutler, John Alba. "On Recent Chicano Literature." *Western American Literature* 44, no. 2 (2009): 158–67.

Dávila, Arlene. *Latinos, Inc.: The Marketing and Making of a People*. Berkeley: University of California Press, 2012.

DeLay, Brian. *War of a Thousand Deserts: Indian Raids and the U.S.-Mexico War*. New Haven, CT: Yale University Press, 2008.

De León, Jason. "The Efficacy and Impact of the Alien Transfer Exit Program: Migrant Perspectives from Nogales, Sonora, Mexico." *International Migration* 51, no. 2 (2013): 10–23.

De León, Jason. *The Land of Open Graves: Living and Dying on the Migrant Trail*. Oakland: University of California Press, 2015.

Diamond, Sara. "Right-Wing Politics and the Anti-immigration Cause." *Social Justice* 23, no. 3 (1996): 154–68.

Didion, Joan. *Play It as It Lays*. New York: Farrar, Straus and Giroux, 1970.
Dietrich, Lucas. "On Commission: María Amparo Ruiz de Burton and the J. B. Lippincott and Co. Job Printing Department." *Papers of the Bibliographical Society of America* 113, no. 4 (2019): 395–408.
Dorr, Kirstie A. *On Site, in Sound: Performance Geographies in América Latina*. Durham, NC: Duke University Press, 2018.
Douglass, Frederick. *Narrative of the Life of Frederick Douglass*. New Haven, CT: Yale University Press, 2001.
Duane, Anna Mae. *Suffering Childhood in Early America: Violence, Race, and the Making of the Child Victim*. Athens: University of Georgia Press, 2010.
Du Bois, W. E. B. *The Souls of Black Folk*. New York: Oxford University Press, 2008.
Durbach, Nadja. *Spectacle of Deformity: Freak Shows and Modern British Culture*. Oakland: University of California Press, 2009.
Earle, Rebecca. "The Pleasures of Taxonomy: Casta Paintings, Classification, and Colonialism." *William and Mary Quarterly* 73, no. 3 (2016): 427–66.
Equiano, Olaudah. *The Interesting Narrative and Other Writings*. New York: Penguin, 1995.
Escobar, Arturo. *Designs for the Pluriverse: Radical Interdependence, Autonomy, and the Making of Worlds*. Durham, NC: Duke University Press, 2018.
Escobar, Arturo. "The 'Ontological Turn' in Social Theory: A Commentary on 'Human Geography without Scale' by Sallie Marston, John Paul Jones II, and Keith Woodward." *Transactions of the Institute of British Geographers* 32, no. 1 (2007): 106–11.
"Examination of Mrs. Anne Hutchinson at the Court at Newtown." In *The Antinomian Controversy, 1636–1638: A Documentary History*, edited by David Hall, 311–48. Durham, NC: Duke University Press, 1990.
Fahs, Alice. *The Imagined Civil War: Popular Literature of the North and South, 1861–1865*. Chapel Hill: University of North Carolina Press, 2010.
Ferreira da Silva, Denise. "Notes for a Critique of the 'Metaphysics of Race.'" *Theory, Culture and Society* 28, no. 1 (2011): 138–48.
Ferreira da Silva, Denise. "On Difference without Separability." In *32 Bienal de São Paulo—Incerteza Viva*, edited by Jochen Volz and Júlia Rebouças, 57–65. São Paulo: Fundação Bienal de São Paulo, 2016.
Ferreira da Silva, Denise. *Toward a Global Idea of Race*. Minneapolis: University of Minnesota Press, 2007.
Figueredo, Oscar Omar. "Tender Struggles: Geography, Affect, and Modes of Politics in Contemporary US Latina/o Fiction." PhD diss., Cornell University, 2016.
Figueroa, Yomaira. "Faithful Witnessing as Practice: Decolonial Readings of *Shadows of Your Black Memory* and *The Brief Wondrous Life of Oscar Wao*." *Hypatia* 30, no. 4 (2015): 641–56.
Fisher, Beth. "Precarious Performances: Ruiz de Burton's Theatrical Vision of the Gilded Age Female Consumer." In *María Amparo Ruiz de Burton: Critical and Pedagogical Perspectives*, edited by Amelia María de la Luz Montes and Anne Goldman, 187–205. Lincoln: University of Nebraska Press, 2004.
Fojas, Camilla. *Zombies, Migrants, and Queers: Race and Crisis Capitalism in Pop Culture*. Urbana: University of Illinois Press, 2017.
Foster, Mark. *From Streetcar to Superhighway: American City Planners and Urban Transportation, 1900–1940*. Philadelphia: Temple University Press, 1981.

Franco, Dean. "Metaphors Happen: Miracle and Metaphor in Helena María Viramontes's *Their Dogs Came with Them*." *Novel: A Forum on Fiction* 48, no. 3 (2015): 344–62.
Frost, Linda. *Never One Nation: Freaks, Savages, and Whiteness in U.S. Popular Culture, 1850–1877*. Minneapolis: University of Minnesota Press, 2005.
Galarza, Ernesto. *Barrio Boy*. Notre Dame: University of Notre Dame Press, 1971.
García, Cristina. *Dreaming in Cuban: A Novel*. New York: Ballantine Books, 2004.
Garza-Falcón, Leticia. *Gente Decente: A Borderlands Response to the Rhetoric of Dominance*. Austin: University of Texas Press, 1998.
Gill-Peterson, Julian. *Histories of the Transgender Child*. Minneapolis: University of Minnesota Press, 2018.
González, John. "Terms of Engagement: Nation or Patriarchy in Jovita González's and Eve Raleigh's *Caballero*." In *Recovering the U.S. Hispanic Literary Heritage*, vol. 4, edited by José Aranda and Silvio Torres-Saillant, 264–76. Houston: Arte Público, 2002.
González, Jovita, and Eve Raleigh. *Caballero: A Historical Novel*. Edited by José E. Limón and María Eugenia Cotera. College Station: Texas A&M University Press, 1996.
González-Torres, Félix. *Félix González-Torres: Catalogue Raisonne und Katalogredaktion*. Edited by Dietmar Elger. New York: Distributed Art, 1997.
Grabel, Ilene. *When Things Don't Fall Apart: Global Finance and Governance*. Cambridge, MA: MIT Press, 2017.
Grande, Reyna. *Across a Hundred Mountains: A Novel*. New York: Washington Square, 2006.
Grande, Reyna. *Dancing with Butterflies: A Novel*. New York: Simon and Schuster, 2009.
Gray, Mary. *Out in the Country*. New York: NYU Press, 2009.
Grise, Virginia. *Your Healing Is Killing Me*. Pittsburgh: Plays Inverse Press, 2017.
Grover, Jeffrey. "John Sonsini." In *John Sonsini*. New York: Cheim and Read, 2007.
Guidotti-Hernández, Nicole. *Unspeakable Violence: Remapping U.S. and Mexican National Imaginaries*. Durham, NC: Duke University Press, 2011.
Gurman, Hannah. "A Collapsing Division: Border and Interior Enforcement in the U.S. Deportation System." *American Quarterly* 69, no. 2 (2017): 371–95.
Haley, Sarah. *No Mercy Here: Gender, Punishment, and the Making of Jim Crow Modernity*. Chapel Hill: University of North Carolina Press, 2016.
Hämäläinen, Pekka. *The Comanche Empire*. New Haven, CT: Yale University Press, 2009.
Hamer, Fannie Lou. "'Until I Am Free, You Are Not Free Either': Speech Delivered at the University of Wisconsin, Madison, Wisconsin, January 1971." In *The Speeches of Fannie Lou Hamer: To Tell It like It Is*, edited by Maegan Parker Brooks and Davis W. Houck, 121–30. Jackson: University Press of Mississippi, 2011.
Harney, Stefano, and Fred Moten. *The Undercommons: Fugitive Planning and Black Study*. Brooklyn: Autonomedia, 2013.
Harris, Cheryl I. "Whiteness as Property." *Harvard Law Review* 106, no. 8 (1993): 1707–91.
Hatch, Reilly Ben. "'Lords of New Mexico': Raiding Culture in Pre-reservation Navajo Society." *Journal of the Southwest* 58, no. 2 (2016): 311–34.
Haywood, Chanta. "Constructing Childhood: The 'Christian Recorder' and Literature for Black Children, 1854–1865." *African American Review* 36, no. 3 (2002): 417–28.
Hedrick, Tace. *Chica Lit: Popular Latina Fiction and Americanization in the Twenty-First Century*. Pittsburgh: University of Pittsburgh Press, 2015.

Hernández, Bernadine. "Rewriting Space in Ruiz de Burton's *Who Would Have Thought It?*" CLC Web: Comparative Literature and Culture 11, no. 2 (2009).
Hernández, Kelly Lytle. *Migra! A History of the U.S. Border Patrol*. Oakland: University of California Press, 2010.
Herrell, Richard K. "Sin, Sickness and Crime: Queer Desire and the American State." *Identities: Global Studies in Culture and Power* 2, no. 3 (1996): 273–300.
Herrera-Sobek, María. *The Mexican Corrido: A Feminist Analysis*. Bloomington: Indiana University Press, 1990.
Higginson, Kate. "Caught Up: Indigenous Re/Presentations of Colonial Captivity." PhD diss., McMaster University, 2007.
Himes, Chester. *If He Hollers Let Him Go*. New York: Thunder's Mouth, 1986.
Hogan, Linda. *Dwellings: A Spiritual History of the Living World*. New York: Norton, 1995.
Hondagneu-Sotelo, Pierrette. "New Directions in Gender and Immigration Research." In *The International Handbook on Gender, Migration, and Transnationalism*, edited by Laura Oso and Natalia Ribas Mateos, 233–45. Northampton, MA: Edward Elgar, 2013.
hooks, bell. "Subversive Beauty: New Modes of Contestation." In *Felix Gonzalez-Torres*, edited by Amanda Cruz, 45–49. Washington, DC: Hirshorn Museum Press, 1994.
Hooven, F. Valentine. *Beefcake: The Muscle Magazines of America, 1950–1970*. London: Taschen, 1995.
Hutchinson, Sikivu. *Imagining Transit: Race, Gender, and Transportation Politics in Los Angeles*. New York: Peter Lang, 2003.
Hyde, Carrie. *Civic Longing: The Speculative Origins of U.S. Citizenship*. Cambridge, MA: Harvard University Press, 2018.
Jacobson, Robin Dale. *The New Nativism: Proposition 187 and the Debate over Immigration*. Minneapolis: University of Minnesota Press, 2008.
Jakobsen, Janet. *The Sex Obsession: Perversity and Possibility in American Politics*. New York: NYU Press, 2020.
Jardine, Matthew. "Operation Gatekeeper." *Peace Review* 10, no. 3 (1998): 329–35.
Jiménez Garcia, Marilisa. "En(countering) YA: Young Lords, Shadowshapers, and the Longings and Possibilities of Latinx Young Adult Literature." *Latino Studies* 16, no. 2 (2018): 230–49.
Jiménez García, Marilisa. "The Lens of Latinx Literature." *Children's Literature* 47, no. 1 (2019): 1–18.
Jiménez García, Marilisa. "Pura Belpré Lights the Storyteller's Candle: Reframing the Legacy of a Legend and What It Means for Children's Literature and Latino/a Studies." *Centro* 26, no. 1 (2014): 110–47.
Jiménez García, Marilisa. "Side-by-Side: At the Intersections of Latinx Studies and ChYALit." *Lion and the Unicorn* 41, no. 1 (2017): 122–33.
Johnson, Sara E. *The Fear of French Negroes: Transcolonial Collaboration in the Revolutionary Americas*. Berkeley: University of California Press, 2012.
Jones, John Paul, III, Helga Leitner, Sallie A. Marston, and Eric Sheppard. "Neil Smith's Scale." *Antipode: A Journal of Radical Geography* 49, no. S1 (2017): 138–52.
John, John Paul, III, Keith Woodward, and Sallie Marston. "Situating Flatness." *Transactions of the Institute of British Geographers* 32, no. 2 (2007): 264–76.

Jones, Lindsey E. "'The Most Unprotected of All Human Beings': Black Girls, State Violence, and the Limits of Protection in Jim Crow Virginia." *Souls* 20, no. 1 (2018): 14–37.

Jordan, Don, and Michael Walsh. *White Cargo: The Forgotten History of Britain's White Slaves in America*. Edinburgh: Mainstream, 2007.

Juffer, Jane. *Intimacy across Borders: Race, Religion, and Migration in the U.S. Midwest*. Philadelphia: Temple University Press, 2013.

Justice, Daniel Heath. *Why Indigenous Literatures Matter*. Waterloo: Wilfrid Laurier University Press, 2018.

Kanstroom, Daniel. "Criminalizing the Undocumented: Ironic Boundaries of the Post-September 11th 'Pale of Law.'" *North Carolina Journal of International Law and Commercial Regulation* 29, no. 4 (2004): 639–70.

Kanstroom, Daniel. *Deportation Nation: Outsiders in American History*. Cambridge, MA: Harvard University Press, 2007.

Kanstroom, Daniel, and M. Brinton Lykes, eds. *The New Deportations Delirium: Interdisciplinary Responses*. New York: NYU Press, 2015.

Katzew, Ilona. *Casta Painting: Images of Race in Eighteenth-Century Mexico*. New Haven, CT: Yale University Press, 2004.

Kelen, Kit, and Björn Sundmark. *The Nation in Children's Literature: Nations of Childhood*. New York: Routledge, 2013.

Kenney, Moira Rachel. *Mapping Gay L.A.: The Intersection of Place and Politics*. Philadelphia: Temple University Press, 2001.

Kotef, Hagar. *Movement and the Ordering of Freedom: On Liberal Governances of Mobility*. Durham, NC: Duke University Press, 2015.

Kotef, Hagar. "Violent Attachments." *Political Theory* 48, no. 1 (2020): 4–29.

Kreneck, Thomas. Foreword to *Caballero*, by Jovita González and Eve Raleigh, edited by José E. Limón and María Eugenia Cotera, ix–x. College Station: Texas A&M University Press, 1996.

Lazo, Rodrigo. *Letters from Filadelfia: Early Latino Literature and the Trans-American Elite*. Charlottesville: University of Virginia Press, 2020.

Lazo, Rodrigo, and Jesse Alemán. *The Latino Nineteenth Century*. New York: NYU Press, 2016.

Levander, Carolyn. *Cradle of Liberty: Race, the Child, and National Belonging from Thomas Jefferson to W. E. B. Du Bois*. Durham, NC: Duke University Press, 2006.

Linebaugh, Peter, and Marcus Rediker. *The Many-Headed Hydra: The Hidden History of the Revolutionary Atlantic*. London: Verso, 2000.

Ling, Jinqui. "Reading for Historical Specificities: Gender Negotiations in Louis Chu's *Eat a Bowl of Tea*." *MELUS* 20, no. 1 (1995): 35–51.

Lipsitz, George. "The Possessive Investment in Whiteness: Racialized Social Democracy and the 'White' Problem in American Studies." *American Quarterly* 47, no. 3 (1995): 369–87.

López, Lorraine. *The Gifted Gabaldón Sisters*. New York: Grand Central, 2008.

López, Marissa. *Chicano Nations: Hemispheric Origins of Mexican American Literature*. New York: NYU Press, 2011.

López, Marissa. "Feeling Mexican: Ruiz de Burton's Sentimental Railroad Fiction." In *The Latino Nineteenth Century*, edited by Rodrigo Lazo and Jesse Alemán, 168–90. New York: NYU Press, 2016.

López, Marissa. *Racial Immanence: Chicanx Bodies beyond Representation*. New York: NYU Press, 2019.

López, Sarah Lynn. *The Remittance Landscape: Spaces of Migration in Rural Mexico and Urban USA*. Chicago: University of Chicago Press, 2005.

López de Gómara, Francisco. *Historia general de las Indias*. Madrid: Calpe, 1922.

Lowell, James Russell. *The Biglow Papers*. Edited by Thomas Wortham. DeKalb: Northern Illinois University Press, 1977.

Lugg, Catherine. "The Religious Right and Public Education: The Paranoid Politics of Homophobia." *Educational Policy* 12, no. 3 (1998): 267–83.

Lugones, María. *Pilgrimages/Peregrinajes: Theorizing Coalition against Multiple Oppressions*. Lanham, MD: Rowman and Littlefield, 2003.

Luibhéid, Eithne. "Heteronormativity, Responsibility, and Neo-liberal Governance in U.S. Immigration Control." In *Passing Lines: Immigration and Sexuality*, edited by Brad Epps, Keja Valens, and Bill Johnson González, 69–101. Cambridge, MA: Harvard University Press, 2005.

Luibhéid, Eithne. "Queer/Migration: An Unruly Body of Scholarship." *GLQ: A Journal of Lesbian and Gay Studies* 14, nos. 2–3 (2008): 169–90.

MacCann, Donnarae. *White Supremacy in Children's Literature: Characterizations of African Americans, 1830–1900*. New York: Garland, 1998.

MacDonald, Ruth K. *Literature for Children in England and America from 1646 to 1774*. Troy, NY: Whitson, 1982.

Macías-Rojas, Patrisia. *From Deportation to Prison: The Politics of Immigration Enforcement in Post-Civil Rights America*. New York: NYU Press, 2016.

Macías-Rojas, Patrisia. "Immigration and the War on Crime: Law and Order Politics and the Illegal Immigration Reform and Immigrant Responsibility Act of 1996." *Journal on Migration and Human Security* 6, no. 1 (2018): 1–25.

Mah y Busch, Juan. "Lovingly: Ethics in Viramontes' Short Stories." In *Rebozos de Palabras: An Helena María Viramontes Critical Reader*, edited by Gabriella Gutiérrez y Muhs, 147–66. Tucson: University of Arizona Press, 2013.

Marez, Curtis. *Drug Wars: The Political Economy of Narcotics*. Minneapolis: University of Minnesota Press, 2004.

Marston, Sallie A., John Paul Jones III, and Keith Woodward. "Flattening Ontologies of Globalization: The Nollywood Case." *Globalizations* 4, no. 1 (2007): 45–63.

Marston, Sallie A., John Paul Jones III, and Keith Woodward. "Human Geography without Scale." *Transactions of the Institute of British Geographers* 30, no. 4 (2005): 416–32.

Martin, Michelle H. *Brown Gold: Milestones of African American Children's Picture Books*. New York: Routledge, 2004.

Martinez, Monica. *The Injustice Never Leaves You: Anti-Mexican Violence in Texas*. Cambridge, MA: Harvard University Press, 2018.

Martone, Jessica, Lina Muñoz, Rebecca Lahey, Leah Yoder, and Stephanie Gurewitz. "The Impact of Remittances on Transnational Families." *Journal of Poverty* 15, no. 4 (2011): 444–64.

Massey, Doreen B. *For Space*. London: Sage, 2005.

Mbembe, Achille. "The Idea of a Borderless World." Africa Is a Country, November 11, 2018. https://africasacountry.com/2018/11/the-idea-of-a-borderless-world.

Mbembe, Achille. "Tanner Lectures on Human Values: 'The Idea of a Borderless World.'" Yale University, March 28, 2018. https://www.youtube.com/watch?v=NKm6HPCSXDY.

McCullough, Kate. "'The Complexity of Loss Itself': The Comics Form and *Fun Home*'s Queer Reparative Temporality." *American Literature* 90 no. 2 (2018): 377-405.

McCullough, Kate. *Regions of Identity: The Construction of America in Women's Fiction, 1885-1914*. Palo Alto, CA: Stanford University Press, 1999.

McMahon, Marci. *Domestic Negotiations: Gender, Nation, and Self-Fashioning in U.S. Mexicana and Chicana Literature and Art*. New Brunswick, NJ: Rutgers University Press, 2013.

McWilliams, Carrie. *Factory in the Fields*. Boston: Little, Brown, 1939.

Melendez, Edwin J., M. Anne Visser, Nik Theodore, and Abel Valenzuela Jr. "Worker Centers and Day Laborers' Wages." *Social Science Quarterly* 95, no. 3 (2014): 835-51.

Menjívar, Cecilia, and Leisy J. Abrego. "Legal Violence: Immigration Law and the Lives of Central American Immigrants." *American Journal of Sociology* 117, no. 5 (2012): 1380-421.

Menjívar, Cecilia, and Daniel Kanstroom, eds. *Constructing Immigrant "Illegality": Critiques, Experiences, and Responses*. New York: Cambridge University Press, 2013.

Mifflin, Margot. *The Blue Tattoo: The Life of Olive Oatman*. Lincoln: University of Nebraska Press, 2009.

Miller, D. Quentin, ed. *Prose and Cons: Essays on Prison Literature in the United States*. Jefferson, NC: McFarland, 2005.

Mills, Charles. *The Racial Contract*. Ithaca, NY: Cornell University Press, 1997.

Mitchell, Mary Niall. *Raising Freedom's Child: Black Children and Visions of the Future after Slavery*. New York: NYU Press, 2008.

Mitchell, Nick. "The View from Nowhere: On Frank Wilderson's Afropessimism." *Spectre*, no. 2 (Fall 2020): 110-22.

Mohr, Nicholasa. *Nilda*. Houston: Arte Público, 1986.

Monaghan, E. Jennifer. *Learning to Read and Write in Colonial America*. Amherst: University of Massachusetts Press, 2005.

Monte Madrigal, Juan Antonio del. "Lentos, estéticos y memoriosos: Las automovilidades *lowriders* y las estéticas de la nostalgia en Tijuana." *Desacatos*, no. 45 (2014): 113-27.

Montoya, José. *In Formation: 20 Years of Joda*. San Jose: Chusma House, 1992.

Montoya, Maceo. *The Deportation of Wopper Barraza*. Albuquerque: University of New Mexico Press, 2014.

Mookas, Ioannis. "Fault Lines: Homophobic Innovation in *Gay Rights, Special Rights*." *Afterimage* 22, nos. 7-8 (1995): 14-18.

Moten, Fred. *Black and Blur*. Durham, NC: Duke University Press, 2017.

Muñoz, José Esteban. "The Brown Commons: The Sense of Wildness." Lecture, JNT Dialogue 2013: "The Queer Commons," Eastern Michigan University Student Center Auditorium, Ypsilanti, Michigan, March 25, 2013. https://www.youtube.com/watch?v=F-YInUlXgO4.

Muñoz, José Esteban. "'Chico, What Does It Feel Like to Be a Problem?' The Transmission of Brownness." In *A Companion to Latina/o Studies*, edited by Juan Flores and Renato Rosaldo, 441-51. New York: Wiley, 2007.

Muñoz, José Esteban. "Feeling Brown, Feeling Down: Latina Affect, the Performativity of Race, and the Depressive Position." *Signs: Journal of Women in Culture and Society* 31, no. 3 (2006): 675–88.

Muñoz, José Esteban. *The Sense of Brown*. Edited by Joshua Chambers Letson and Navia Nyong'o. Durham, NC: Duke University Press, 2020.

Muñoz, José Esteban. "Theorizing Queer Inhumanisms: The Sense of Brownness." *GLQ: A Journal of Lesbian and Gay Studies* 21, no. 2–3 (2015): 209–10.

Muñoz, Lorena. "Agency, Choice and Restrictions in Producing Latina/o Street Vending Landscapes in Los Angeles." *Area* 48, no. 3 (2016): 339–45.

Muñoz, Manuel. *The Faith Healer of Olive Avenue*. Chapel Hill: Algonquin, 2007.

Murray, Gail Schmunk. *American Children's Literature and the Construction of Childhood*. New York: Twayne, 1998.

Namias, June. *White Captives: Gender and Ethnicity on the American Frontier*. Chapel Hill: University of North Carolina Press, 1995.

Nevins, Joseph. *Operation Gatekeeper and Beyond: The War on "Illegals" and the Remaking of the U.S.-Mexico Boundary*. 2nd ed. New York: Routledge, 2010.

Ngai, Mae M. *Impossible Subjects: Illegal Aliens and the Making of Modern America*. Princeton, NJ: Princeton University Press, 2004.

Nixon, Cheryl L. *The Orphan in Eighteenth-Century Law and Literature: Estate, Blood, and Body*. Burlington, VT: Ashgate, 2011.

Norris, Frank. *The Octopus*. Garden City, NY: Doubleday, 1936.

Nyers, Peter. "Abject Cosmopolitanism: The Politics of Protection in the Anti-deportation Movement." In *The Deportation Regime: Sovereignty, Space, and the Freedom of Movement*, edited by Nicholas de Genova and Nathalie Peutz, 413–41. Durham, NC: Duke University Press, 2010.

Olguín, B. V. "Caballeros and Indians: Mexican American Whiteness, Hegemonic Mestizaje, and Ambivalent Indigeneity in Proto-Chicana/o Autobiographical Discourses, 1858–2008." *MELUS* 38, no. 1 (2013): 30–49.

O'Neill, Daniel I., Mary Lyndon Shanley, and Iris Marion Young, eds. *Illusion of Consent: Engaging with Carole Pateman*. University Park: Pennsylvania State University Press, 2008.

Ono, Kent A., and John M. Sloop. *Shifting Borders: Rhetoric, Immigration, and California's Proposition 187*. Philadelphia: Temple University Press 2002.

Ontiveros, Randy. *In the Spirit of a New People: The Cultural Politics of the Chicano Movement*. New York: NYU Press, 2013.

Orellana, Marjorie Faulstich. *Translating Childhoods: Immigrant Youth, Language, and Culture*. New Brunswick, NJ: Rutgers University Press, 2009.

Ortiz, Ricardo. *Latinx Literature Now: Between Evanescence and Event*. New York: Palgrave Macmillan, 2019.

Paredes, Américo. *George Washington Gómez: A Mexicotexan Novel*. Houston: Arte Público, 1990.

Paredes, Américo. *With His Pistol in His Hand*. Austin: University of Texas Press, 1958.

Pateman, Carole. *The Disorder of Women: Democracy, Feminism and Political Theory*. Cambridge: Polity, 1989.

Pattison, Dale. "Trauma and the 710: The New Metropolis in Helena María Viramontes's *Their Dogs Came with Them*." *Arizona Quarterly* 70, no. 2 (2014): 115–42.

Peña, Daniel. *Bang: A Novel*. Houston: Arte Público, 2017.
Pérez, Vincent. "Remembering the Hacienda: History and Memory in Jovita González and Eve Raleigh's *Caballero: A Historical Novel*." In *Look Away! The U.S. South in New World Studies*, edited by Jon Smith and Deborah Cohn, 471-94. Durham, NC: Duke University Press, 2004.
Pérez, Vincent. "Teaching the Hacienda: Juan Rulfo and Mexican American Cultural Memory." *Western American Literature* 35, no. 1 (2000): 33-44.
Pexa, Christopher J. "Futurity Foreclosed: Jonestown, Settler Colonialism, and the Ending of Time in Fred D'Aguiar's *Bill of Rights*." MELUS 43, no. 1 (2018): 2-20.
Pexa, Christopher J. *Translated Nation: Rewriting the Dakhóta Oyáte*. Minneapolis: University of Minnesota Press, 2019.
Pike, Mary Hayden Green. *Ida May: A Story of Things Actual and Possible*. Leipzig: B. Tauchnitz, 1855.
Plambech, Sine. "Sex, Deportation and Rescue: Economies of Migration among Nigerian Sex Workers." *Feminist Economics* 23, no. 3 (2017): 134-59.
Poovey, Mary. "Trollope's Barsetshire Series." In *The Cambridge Companion to Anthony Trollope*, edited by Carolyn Dever and Lisa Niles, 31-43. Cambridge: Cambridge University Press, 2011.
Portillo, Annette. *Sovereign Stories and Blood Memories: Native American Women's Autobiography*. Albuquerque: University of New Mexico Press, 2018.
Proyect, Louis. "The Political Economy of Comanche Violence." *Capitalism, Nature, Socialism* 24, no. 3 (2013): 217-31.
Puga, Ana Elena. "Migrant Melodrama and Elvira Arellano." *Latino Studies* 10, no. 3 (2012): 355-84.
Puga, Ana Elena. "Migrant Melodrama and the Political Economy of Suffering." *Women and Performance: A Journal of Feminist Theory* 26, no. 1 (2016): 72-93.
Pynchon, Thomas. *The Crying of Lot 49*. Philadelphia: Lippincott, 1966.
Qureshi, Sadiah. *Peoples on Parade: Exhibitions, Empire, and Anthropology in Nineteenth-Century Britain*. Chicago: University of Chicago Press, 2011.
Ramírez, Horacio Roque. "Introduction: Homoerotic Lesbian and Gay Immigrant Histories." *Journal of American Ethnic History* 29, no. 4 (2010): 5-21.
Ramírez, Pablo. "Conquest's Child: Gold, Contracts, and American Imperialism in María Amparo Ruiz de Burton's *Who Would Have Thought It*." *Arizona Quarterly: A Journal of American Literature, Culture, and Theory* 70, no. 4 (2014): 143-65.
Ramírez, Pablo. "Resignifying Preservation: A Borderlands Response to American Eugenics in Jovita González and Eve Raleigh's *Caballero*." *Canadian Review of American Studies/Revue Canadienne d'Etudes Américaines* 39, no. 3 (2009): 21-39.
Reiter, Keramet, and Susan Bibler Coutin. "Crossing Borders and Criminalizing Identity: The Disintegrated Subjects of Administrative Sanctions." *Law and Society Review* 51, no. 3 (2017): 567-600.
Reséndez, Andrés. *The Other Slavery: The Uncovered Story of Indian Enslavement in America*. Boston: Houghton Mifflin Harcourt, 2016.
Restrepo, Bettina. *Illegal*. New York: Harper Collins, 2011.
Retman, Sonnet. *Reel Folks: Race and Genre in the Great Depression*. Durham, NC: Duke University Press, 2011.

Rifkin, Mark. *When Did Indians Become Straight? Kingship, the History of Sexuality, and Native Sovereignty*. New York: Oxford University Press, 2011.

Rincón, Belinda. *Bodies at War: Genealogies of Militarism in Chicana Literature and Culture*. Tucson: University of Arizona Press, 2017.

Rivera, John-Michael. *The Emergence of Mexican America: Recovering Stories of Mexican Peoplehood in US Culture*. New York: NYU Press, 2006.

Rivera, Tomás. *... Y no se lo tragó la tierra / ... And the Earth Did Not Devour Him*. 1971. Houston: Arte Público, 2015.

Rivera Garza, Cristina. "2501 Migrantes de Alejandro Santiago." In *Dolerse: Textos desde un país herido*, 2nd ed., 45–59. Mexico City: Surplus Ediciones, 2015.

Robinson, Cedric. *Black Marxism: The Making of the Black Radical Tradition*. London: Zed, 1983.

Rodríguez, Jaime Javier. *The Literatures of the U.S.-Mexican War: Narrative, Time, and Identity*. Austin: University of Texas Press, 2010.

Rodríguez, Juana María. *Queer Latinidad: Identity Practices, Discursive Spaces*. New York: New York University Press, 2003.

Rodriguez, Ralph. *Latinx Literature Unbound: Undoing Ethnic Expectations*. New York: Fordham University Press, 2018.

Rodríguez, Richard T. *Next of Kin: The Family in Chicano/a Cultural Politics*. Durham, NC: Duke University Press, 2009.

Rodríguez, Richard T. "What Lies Beneath: The Deep Practice of Historical Thinking." *Aztlán: A Journal of Chicano Studies* 45, no. 2 (2020): 213–20.

Romero, Betsabeé. *Betsabeé Romero: Cars and Traces*. Amsterdam: KIT, 2010.

Romero, Lora. "'When Something Goes Queer': Familiarity, Formalism, and Minority Intellectuals in the 1980s." *Yale Journal of Criticism: Interpretation in the Humanities* 6, no. 1 (1993): 121–42.

Romero, Mary. "'Go after the Women': Mothers against Illegal Aliens' Campaign against Mexican Immigrant Women and Their Children." *Indiana Law Journal* 83 (2008): 1355–90.

Rooks, Noliwe. *Cutting School: Privatization, Segregation, and the End of Public Education*. New York: New Press, 2017.

Rosaldo, Renato. "Imperialist Nostalgia." *Representations* 26, no. 1 (1989): 107–22.

Rose, Wendy. "Thanksgiving on the San Joaquin Daily between Fresno and Martinez." In *Highway 99: A Literary Journey through California's Great Central Valley*, edited by Stan Yogi, 312–13. Berkeley, CA: Heyday Books, 1996.

Ross, Marlon. "Trans-Atlantic Parochialism." *Callaloo* 39, no. 4 (2017): 887–97.

Rowlandson, Mary. "A True History of the Captivity and Restoration of Mrs. Mary Rowlandson." In *Women's Indian Captivity Narratives*, edited by Kathryn Zabelle Derounian-Stodola, 7–51. New York: Penguin, 1998.

Roybal, Karen. *Archives of Dispossession: Recovering the Testimonios of Mexican American Herederas, 1848–1960*. Chapel Hill: University of North Carolina Press, 2017.

Ruiz de Burton, María Amparo. *The Squatter and the Don*. San Francisco: S. Carson, 1885.

Ruiz de Burton, María Amparo. *Who Would Have Thought It?* Edited by Rosaura Sánchez and Beatrice Pita. Houston: Arte Público, 1995.

Saccamano, Neil. "'Le plus fort lien': Sentimental Fixation and Spectacles of Suffering in *Les Liaisons dangereuses*." *Studies in Eighteenth-Century Culture* 33 (2004): 1–22.

Saldaña-Portillo, María Josefina. *Indian Given: Racial Geographies across Mexico and the United States*. Durham, NC: Duke University Press, 2016.

Saldívar, José David. *Border Matters: Remapping American Cultural Studies*. Oakland: University of California Press, 1997.

Saldívar, José David. *Trans-Americanity: Subaltern Modernities, Global Coloniality, and the Cultures of Greater Mexico*. Durham, NC: Duke University Press, 2012.

Sánchez, George J. "Face the Nation: Race, Immigration and the Rise of Nativism in Late Twentieth Century America." *International Migration Review* 31, no. 4 (1997): 1009–30.

Sánchez, Rosaura, and Beatrice Pita, ed. *Conflicts of Interest: The Letters of María Amparo Ruiz de Burton*. Houston, Arte Público Press, 2001.

Sánchez, Rosaura, and Beatrice Pita. Introduction to *Who Would Have Thought It?*, by María Amparo Ruiz de Burton, vii–lxv. Houston: Arte Público, 1995.

Sánchez-Eppler, Karen. *Dependent States: The Child's Part in Nineteenth-Century American Culture*. Chicago: University of Chicago Press, 2005.

Santa Ana, Otto. *Brown Tide Rising: Metaphors of Latinos in Contemporary American Public Discourse*. Austin: University of Texas Press, 2002.

Santiago, Alejandro. *Alejandro Santiago: 2501 Migrantes*. Oaxaca: Museo de Arte Contemporaneo de Oaxaca, 2006.

Schmidt Camacho, Alicia. "Hailing the Twelve Million." *Social Text* 28, no. 4 (2010): 1–24.

Schmidt Camacho, Alicia. *Migrant Imaginaries: Latino Cultural Politics in the US-Mexico Borderlands*. New York: New York University Press, 2008.

Sedgwick, Eve Kosofsky. *Epistemology of the Closet*. Berkeley: University of California Press, 2008.

Sedgwick, Eve Kosofsky. *Touching Feeling*. Durham, NC: Duke University Press, 2002.

Shah, Nayan. *Contagious Divides: Epidemics and Race in San Francisco's Chinatown*. Berkeley: University of California Press, 2001.

Shepperson, Archibald. *Novel in Motley: A History of the Burlesque Novel in English*. Cambridge, MA: Harvard University Press, 1936.

Sheriff, Carol. *The Artificial River: The Erie Canal and the Paradox of Progress, 1817–1862*. New York: Hill and Wang, 1996.

Silvey, Rachel. "Development and Geography: Anxious Times, Anemic Geographies, and Migration." *Progress in Human Geography* 33, no. 4 (209): 507–15.

Simón, Laura Angélica, dir. *Fear and Learning at Hoover Elementary*. San Francisco: Kanopy, 1997.

Simpson, Alice Fisher. "Historic Trails of the Padres." *California Highways and Public Works* 29–30 (1950): 3–20.

Slack, Jeremy. "Captive Bodies: Migrant Kidnapping and Deportation in Mexico." *Area* 48, no. 3 (2016): 271–77.

Slack, Jeremy, and Daniel E. Martínez. "Postremoval Geographies: Immigration Enforcement and Organized Crime on the U.S.-Mexico Border." *Annals of the American Association of Geographers* 111, no. 4 (2021): 1062–78.

Slotkin, Richard. *Regeneration through Violence: The Mythology of the American Frontier, 1600–1860*. Middletown, CT: Wesleyan University Press, 1973.

Smith, Caleb. *The Prison and the American Imagination*. New Haven, CT: Yale University Press, 2010.

Smith, Michael Peter, and Bernadette Tarallo. "Proposition 187: Global Trend or Local Narrative? Explaining Anti-immigrant Politics in California, Arizona and Texas." *International Journal of Urban and Regional Research* 19, no. 4 (1995): 664–76.

Smith, Neil. "Scale Bending and the Fate of the National." In *Scale and Geographic Inquiry: Nature, Society, and Method*, edited by Eric Sheppard and Robert B. McMaster, 192–212. London: Blackwell, 2004.

Soares, Kristie. "From Canary Birds to Suffrage: Lavinia's Feminist Role in *Who Would Have Thought It?*" *Letras Femeninas* 35, no. 2 (2009): 211–29.

Sonsini, John. *John Sonsini Exhibition Catalog*. New York: Cheim and Read, 2007.

Steinbeck, John. *The Grapes of Wrath*. New York: Penguin, 1976.

Stephens, Sharon, ed. *Children and the Politics of Culture*. Princeton, NJ: Princeton University Press, 1995.

Stern, Alexandra Minna. "Nationalism on the Line: Masculinity, Race, and the Creation of the U.S. Border Patrol, 1910–1940." In *Continental Crossroads: Remapping U.S.-Mexico Borderlands History*, edited by Sam Truett and Elliott Young, 299–323. Durham, NC: Duke University Press, 2004.

Stockton, Kathryn Bond. *The Queer Child, or Growing Sideways in the Twentieth Century*. Durham, NC: Duke University Press, 2009.

Stratton, Royal. *Captivity of the Oatman Girls: Being an Interesting Narrative of Life among the Apache and Mohave Indians*. San Francisco: Whitton, Towne and Co., 1887.

Szeghi, Tereza M. "The Vanishing Mexicana/o: (Dis)Locating the Native in Ruiz de Burton's *Who Would Have Thought It?* and *The Squatter and the Don*." *Aztlán: A Journal of Chicano Studies* 36, no. 2 (2011): 89–120.

Theodore, Nik, Abel Valenzuela, and Edwin Melendez. "La Esquina (The Corner): Day Laborers on the Margins of New York's Formal Economy." *Working USA: The Journal of Labor and Society* 9 (2006): 407–23.

Thomas, Brook. *The Literature of Reconstruction: Not in Plain Black and White*. Baltimore: Johns Hopkins University Press, 2017.

Thomas, Ebony E. *The Dark Fantastic: Race and the Imagination from Harry Potter to the Hunger Games*. New York: NYU Press, 2019.

Thomas, Piri. *Down These Mean Streets*. New York: Knopf, 1967.

Thompson, Hunter S. *Fear and Loathing on the Campaign Trail '72*. New York: Warner, 1973.

Tinnemeyer, Andrea. *Identity Politcs of the Captivity Narrative after 1848*. Lincoln: University of Nebraska Press, 2006.

Torpey, John. *The Invention of the Passport*. Cambridge: Cambridge University Press, 2000.

Trollope, Anthony. *Can You Forgive Her?* New York: Oxford University Press, 2012.

Trujillo, Simón Ventura. *Land Uprising: Native Story Power and the Insurgent Horizons of Latinx Indigeneity*. Tucson: University of Arizona Press, 2020.

Tukachinsky, Riva, Dana Mastro, and Moran Yarchi. "Documenting Portrayals of Race/Ethnicity on Primetime Television over a 20-Year Span and Their Association with National-Level Racial/Ethnic Attitudes." *Journal of Social Issues* 71, no. 1 (2015): 17–38.

Turk, Katherine. "'Our Militancy Is in Our Openness': Gay Employment Rights Activism in California and the Question of Sexual Orientation in Sex Equality Law." *Law and History Review* 31, no. 2 (2013): 423–70.

Twain, Mark. *The Prince and the Pauper*. New York: Oxford University Press, 1996.

US Commission on Civil Rights. *Trauma at the Border: The Human Cost of Inhumane Immigration Policies*. Washington, DC: US Commission on Civil Rights, 2019.

Vazquez, Alexandra T. *Listening in Detail: Performances of Cuban Music*. Durham, NC: Duke University Press, 2013.

Vigil, Ariana. *Public Negotiations: Gender and Journalism in Contemporary U.S. Latina/o Literature*. Columbus: Ohio State University Press, 2019.

Villa, Raúl. *Barrio-Logos: Space and Place in Urban Chicano Literature and Culture*. Austin: University of Texas Press, 2000.

Vinson, Ben, III. *Before Mestizaje: The Frontiers of Race and Caste in Colonial Mexico*. New York: Cambridge University Press, 2018.

Viramontes, Helena María. *Their Dogs Came with Them*. New York: Simon and Schuster, 2007.

Vizcaíno-Alemán, Melina. "Rethinking Jovita González's Work: Bio-ethnography and Her South Texas Regionalism." *Southwestern American Literature* 37, no. 2 (2012): 38–47.

Vogt, Wendy. *Lives in Transit: Violence and Intimacy on the Migrant Journey*. Oakland: University of California Press, 2018.

Waddell, Benjamin James. "Remitting Democracy? The Role of Migrant Remittances in Promoting Social and Political Change in Guanajuato, Mexico." *Journal of Community Positive Practices* 14, no. 1 (2014): 116–30.

Wald, Priscilla. *Contagious: Cultures, Carriers, and the Outbreak Narrative*. Durham, NC: Duke University Press, 2008.

Wald, Sarah. "Refusing to Halt: Mobility and the Quest for Spatial Justice in Helena María Viramontes's *Their Dogs Came with Them* and Karen Tei Yamashita's *Tropic of Orange*." *Western American Literature* 48, nos. 1–2 (2013): 70–89.

Walters, William. "The Flight of the Deported: Aircraft, Deportation, and Politics." *Geopolitics* 21, no. 2 (2016): 435–58.

Waugh, Thomas. *Hard to Imagine: Gay Male Eroticism in Photography and Film from Their Beginnings to Stonewall*. New York: Columbia University Press, 1996.

Weber, David J. *Barbaros: Spaniards and Their Savages in the Age of Enlightenment*. New Haven, CT: Yale University Press, 2005.

Weber, David J. *The Mexican Frontier, 1821–1846: The American Southwest under Mexico*. Albuquerque: University of New Mexico Press, 1982.

Weber, Max. *Politics as a Vocation*. Translated by H. H. Gerth and C. Wright Mills. Philadelphia: Fortress Press, 1965.

Wheatley, Phillis. *The Writings of Phillis Wheatley*. New York: Oxford University Press, 2019.

Williams, Danielle Terrazas. "'My Conscience Is Free and Clear': African-Descended Women, Status, and Slave Owning in Mid-Colonial Mexico." *Americas* 75, no. 3 (2018): 525–54.

Wilson, Bernard, and Sharmani Gabriel. *Asian Children's Literature and Film in a Global Age: Local, National, and Transnational Trajectories*. New York: Palgrave Macmillan, 2020.

Woodward, Keith, John Paul Jones III, and Sallie A. Marston. "Of Eagles and Flies: Orientations toward the Site." *Area* 42, no. 3 (2010): 270–80.

Woodward, Keith, John Paul Jones III, and Sallie A. Marston. "The Politics of Autonomous Spaces." *Progress in Human Geography* 36, no. 1 (2012): 204–24.

Wroe, Andrew. *The Republican Party and Immigration Politics: From Proposition 187 to George W. Bush*. New York: Springer, 2008.

Wynter, Sylvia. "Sambos and Minstrels." *Social Text* 1 (1979): 149–56.

Wynter, Sylvia. "Unsettling the Coloniality of Being/Power/Truth/Freedom: Towards the Human, after Man, Its Overrepresentation—An Argument." *CR: The New Centennial Review* 3, no. 3 (2003): 257–337.

Yava, Albert. *Big Falling Snow: A Tewa-Hopi Indian's Life and Times and the History and Traditions of His People*. Edited and annotated by Harold Courlander. Albuquerque: University of New Mexico Press, 1982.

Ybarra, Patricia A. *Latinx Theater in the Times of Neoliberalism*. Evanston, IL: Northwestern University Press, 2017.

Ybarra, Priscilla Solis. *Writing the Goodlife: Mexican American Literature and the Environment*. Tucson: University of Arizona Press, 2016.

Zaitchik, Alexander. "Who Would Jesus Deport?" *SPLC Intelligence Report*. February 1, 2007.

Index

AB101, 158-166, 195-6, 265n9, 267n29, 268n51
Abrego, Leisy, 206-7
Across a Hundred Mountains (Grande), 35, 181-90, 193, 242
Adams, John, 6-7, 16
Adeyemi, Kemi, 243
Agard-Jones, Vanessa, 26-27
Alcott, Louisa May, 62
Aldama, Frederick, 251n3
Alegría, Malín, 36, 200, 224-32, 244-46.
  See also *Sofi Mendoza's Guide to Getting Lost in Mexico*
Alexander, Jacqui, 162
Allen, Chadwick, 253n76
Allen, Robert, 64, 74
Alvarez, Julia, 181
Amigoland (Casares), 32-33, 81, 83, 87-95, 108, 115-16, 242, 260n35
Anzaldúa, Gloria, 245
Archambault, Caroline, 181

Bacon, Francis, 203
Bang (Peña), 36, 200, 232-36, 244
Baudrillard, Jean, 127
Beecher, Henry Ward, 50
Bernstein, Robin, 7, 54, 250n24
Bieber, Justin, 77
bildungsroman, 10, 213, 216, 221-22, 240-41, 243
Boehm, Debra, 212-13, 216, 271n40, 272n44, 273n89
border patrol, 1, 3, 156, 168, 183, 205, 207, 229, 249n2, 264n32

borders, 182-86, 197; abolition of, 196, 237; captivity and, 232; civil rights and, 30, 193, 201, 226; death and, 75, 77, 208, 229, 249n2; globalization and, 10, 27; racialization and, 202; scalar imaginary and, 29, 236; sexuality and, 159-60, 167-70, 177
Bosniak, Linda, 158, 166-67
Bowers v. Hardwick, 194
Bracero program, 170
Brewer, Holly, 6, 193, 197
Briggs, Laura, 250n28
Brodsly, David, 126, 263n9
Brooks, Daphne, 70
Brooks, David, 170-71, 179-80
burlesque, 4, 31-32, 38-39, 40, 44, 62-82, 240-43, 256n59, 257n78, 258n84
Bush, George H. W., 160
Bush, George W., 183
Byrd, Jodi, 28, 251n3

Caballero (González and Raleigh), 32, 82-83, 84-87, 112-16, 124, 259n8
Calavita, Kitty, 164, 267n29
Caminero-Santangelo, Marta, 191
Canaday, Margot, 168
captivity: consent and, 60, 101; economics of, 82-84, 236; forced removal and, 156-58, 210-34; forms of, 2, 3, 93-94, 136, 246; labor management and, 81, 88, 90, 94; living curiosities as, 45-53, 218; racialization and, 60; scale and, 32, 83-86, 120, 155 241; witnessing and, 11, 87-95, 96, 113

captivity narratives, 31, 35, 56–61, 81, 83, 92–95, 108, 132, 138, 216, 230, 252n41. *See also* Oatman, Olive; López, Lorraine; Rowlandson, Mary; Ruiz de Burton, María Amparo

Carrillo Castillo, Jesús, 18, 262n1

Carroll, Amy Sara, 251n3

Casares, Oscar, 32, 81–83, 91, 246. See also *Amigoland*

casta system, 20–23, 84, 169, 177, 252n60, 269n78

castagory, 18–23; consent, 60; racialization and, 39, 71, 74, 78; scalar imaginary and, 27, 53, 120, 169, 240, 247

Castiglia, Christopher, 59, 61, 256n53, 256n64, 256n66

Cavarero, Adriana, 29, 202, 243

Cervantes, Lorna Dee, 176

Chandler, Nahum, 77

Chávez, Karma, 154, 166

Chávez, Leo, 169

Chicanx studies, 26, 251n31, 259n8

child (children): captives, 1–14, 17, 25, 34, 83, 112–13, 220–26; education of, 9, 29, 70, 120–35, 235–40, 250n27; forced removal of, 36, 201–5, 208–10; racialization of, 3, 7–8, 20–23, 31–35, 52–53, 85, 112, 249n10; rectitude and, 5–6, 13, 244; representations of, 9–10; scale and, 5–6, 29–31

childhood: captivity and, 17, 30–31, 81, 130, 138 199; consent and, 5–12, 75–76; innocence and, 76, 195–96; privilege and, 2, 4, 7, 8, 12, 53, 55; racialization of, 11, 40, 54, 157, 190; rectitude and, 14, 36, 75, 81; scale and, 10, 13, 18, 27, 188; temporality and, 29, 238

Chinese Exclusion Act, 170, 179

citizenship: abolition of, 196; captivity and, 10, 38, 44, 197; figure of the child and, 5–9, 13, 200; forced removal and, 204–8; homophobia and, 154–159; modes of study of, 30, 166–67; racialization and, 16, 35, 54–56, 153; temporality of, 29, 240

Civil War: burlesque and, 63–66; Mexican American War and, 38; popular literature of, 53, 61–63; resource extraction and, 32, 42, 66–67; scale and, 44, 50 120; *Who Would Have Thought It?* and, 71–74

Clinton, Bill, 182–83, 194, 206, 208

Clinton, DeWitt, 23–25, 45, 137

coloniality: captivity and, 115, 135, 137; gender and, 83, 105; legacies of, 28 127, 133, 234, 244; racialization and, 101, 111–12, 175, 177; scale and, 3–4, 19, 31–33, 60, 121, 130, 152

Corral, Eduardo, 35, 155, 159, 176–80, 182, 245–46, 269n78

Coutin, Susan Bibler, 205

Cutler, John Alba, 264n30

Dávila, Arlene, 251n3

de Hoyos, Angela, 178

Deferred Action for Childhood Arrivals (DACA), 75–76, 195

DeLay, Brian, 90

De León, Jason, 249n2

density, 3, 4, 11, 83, 27, 151, 253n78; captivity and, 200; queer horizontality and, 144, 244; relationality and, 17, 29, 123, 141, 211, 246–47; scale versus, 115–16, 119, 239, 245–46

deportation. *See* forced removal

Deportation of Wopper Barraza, The (Montoya), 36, 200, 213–24, 231, 234–36, 242, 244

detention centers, 3, 184, 195, 198, 207–8, 245–46

Didion, Joan, 127

dis/objectification, 28, 99–100, 138, 177, 188, 240–47

Donne, John, 203–4

Douglass, Frederick, 5, 8

Down These Mean Streets (Thomas), 9

DREAMers, 40, 75–77, 193, 195, 219

Duane, Ana Mae, 193

Du Bois, W. E. B., 5, 8, 77

Emancipation Proclamation, 71

Equiano, Olaudah, 5, 8

Erie Canal, 23, 126, 137

Escobar, Arturo, 22, 243

Fahs, Alice, 61–62, 256 n.44

Faith Healer of Olive Avenue (Muñoz), 34, 121, 140–52, 242, 244

family separation, 1, 2, 17, 35, 170–71, 249n1

Fear and Learning at Hoover Elementary (Simón), 156–58

Figueroa, Yomaira, 113, 251n32

Fisher, Beth, 257n76

Fojas, Camilla, 211

forced removal, 3, 35–36, 88, 156; history of, 202–8; impact of, 156–58, 209–13, 215, 224–38; racialization and, 204–5, 223, 271n11; temporality and, 201, 211–13, 216–18, 226

Galarza, Ernesto, 181
García, Cristina, 181
Gay Rights Special Rights, 161, 165, 266n23
George Washington Gómez (Paredes), 9
Gifted Gabaldón Sisters, The (López) 32–33, 81, 83, 95–105, 110–17, 124, 242
Glissant, Édouard, 239
globalization, 23, 25, 166, 200, 210
González, Jovita, 32, 43, 81. See also *Caballero*
González-Torres, Félix, 79–80, 83
Grabel, Ilene, 253n79
Grande, Reyna, 35, 155, 159, 181, 187–92, 244–46. See also *Across a Hundred Mountains*
Grant, Ulysses S., 38, 41
Gray, Mary, 147–48
Grise, Virginia, 251n3

hacienda system, 57, 80–86, 124
Hakluyt, Richard, 203
Hamer, Fannie Lou, 30
Harney, Stefano, 245
Hernández, Bernadine, 255n3
Hernández, Esthér, 176
Higginson, Kate, 15
Himes, Chester, 127
Hobbes, Thomas, 5, 12, 16, 201
Hogan, Linda, 239
hooks, bell, 80
Hurston, Zora Neale, 43

Illegal, 35, 181–84, 188, 190–93
Illegal Immigration Reform and Immigrant Responsibility Act, 206–7
immigrant deterrence, 2, 183, 208–10, 249n2
Immigration and Customs Enforcement (ICE), 1–3, 176, 207, 213, 246
immigration: captivity and, 3–4, 10, 17, 82, 94, 122; civil rights and, 158–59, 166–70, 210–11; gender and, 35, 180–88, 267n39; sexuality and, 154–56, 171–78; racialization and, 35, 207

Immigration Reform and Control Act (IRCA), 205–6
impersonation, 4, 31, 40, 64–5, 241–44, 273n3. See also burlesque
Indigenous studies, 29, 253n76
infrastructure, 2, 157, 202; canals, 23–24; haciendas, 83–86; highways, 125–33, 139, 144–46; finance, 34, railroads, 120, 124–25; slavery as, 256n50. See also scale

Jefferson, Thomas, 7, 16, 204
Justice, Daniel Heath, 253n76, 254n82

Kanstroom, Daniel, 203–4
Kenney, Moira, 160
Kotef, Hagar, 12–13, 16, 83, 201, 270n8

Lazo, Rodrigo, 254n1
Lefebvre, Henri, 25
legal violence, 2, 45, 193, 197, 199, 201, 213, 224, 236–37
León-Portilla, Miguel, 127
Levander, Carolyn, 6–7
liberalism: constraint and, 12–16, 74–75, 120, 156, 201, 232; contract theory and, 5, 40–45, 56, 81; education and, 218–24; enmity and, 41, 60, 153, 194; figure of the child within, 4–11, 193, 240; racialization and, 17, 61–62, 193, 199; rectitude and, 71, 180, 219, 222; scale and, 34–36
Linebaugh, Peter, 202, 258n104
Locke, John, 5, 12, 16
López de Gómara, Francisco, 18, 19, 25, 28
López, Lorraine, 10, 17, 32–33, 81–83, 95–117, 246, 261n67. See also *The Gifted Gabaldón Sisters*
López, Marissa, 251n3
Lowell, James Russell, 42
lowriders, 121–22, 139
Luibhéid, Eithne, 154, 168, 268n54
Lugones, María, 113

Macías-Rojas, Patrisia, 206
Maldonado, Juan, 18–20, 27, 119
Marston, Sallie, 25–7, 252n57
mass incarceration, 2, 17
Massey, Doreen, 244
Mbembe, Achille, 197, 245, 268n49, 270n8

Index 295

Mexican-American War, 37–38, 82, 120
Mexican Revolution, 91
Mifflin, Margot, 58, 256n59
Mills, Charles, 45, 52
Mitchell, Mary Niall, 50, 250n24
Mookas, Ioannis, 161
Montoya, José, 34, 20, 123, 139–40, 152, 176
Montoya, Maceo, 36, 200, 213–24, 231, 246. See also *The Deportation of Wopper Barraza*
Morris, Robert Hunter, 6
Moten, Fred, 28, 239, 245
Muñoz, José Esteban, 28, 251n31
Muñoz, Manuel, 10, 34, 121, 123, 140–45, 151–52, 244–46. See also *The Faith Healer of Olive Avenue*

nativism, 164, 166, 168, 171, 194–95, 268n42
Nilda (Mohr), 9
Norris, Frank, 139
North American Free Trade Agreement (NAFTA), 10, 34 155, 183–85, 188, 190–92, 200, 210

Oatman, Olive, 17, 56, 58, 108, 114–15, 256n54, 261n83
Obama, Barak, 75–76, 195, 207
Operation Gatekeeper, 183–85, 207–8, 268n51, 269n83
Operation Wetback, 205, 231, 260n18
Ortiz, Ricardo, 251n3

Paine, Thomas, 6
Paredes, Américo, 89, 178
Pateman, Carole, 45, 52
Peña, Daniel, 36, 200, 232–34, 246. See also *Bang*
Pexa, Christopher, 90, 253n76
phallic verticality, 25, 29–33, 119, 121–27, 136–41, 144, 237, 244
Pike, Mary Hayden Green, 50
Proposition 187, 156–58, 161–67, 161, 182, 195, 266n16, 267n29, 267n31
Puga, Ana Elena, 192
Pynchon, Thomas, 127

queer horizontality, 4, 27, 29, 33–36, 121–23, 140, 144, 152, 202, 244–46
Quijano, Aníbal, 28

Raleigh, Eve, 32. See also *Caballero*
racialization: casta system and, 20, 68, 71; capitalism and, 20, 24, 38, 102, 192, 235, 246–47, 252n61, 256n61; children and, 4, 6–11, 22, 40, 50, 55, 190; Latinidad and, 21; nationalism and, 39, 44, 199, 202; white supremacy and, 3, 10, 43, 255n3, 262n74
Reconstruction, 16, 37, 38, 44, 120, 254n2, 255n3
reciprocity, 17, 36, 123, 218, 240
rectitude, 5, 22; child and, 22, 29, 33, 176, 190, 256n48; education, and, 157, 219–21, 240; forced removal and, 202–3, 241; freedom and, 30; masquerade and, 41, 141, 157, 244; scalar imaginary and, 138, 141, 193, 242; sovereignty and, 11. See also *respectability*
Rediker, Marcus, 202, 258n104
Reiter, Keramet, 205
relationality, 18, 27, 28–29, 114, 152, 179, 231, 242–43
remittances, 184, 191, 213, 270n95
Reséndez, Andrés, 57, 259n4
respectability, 70, 75, 117, 199, 223
Restrepo, Bettina, 35, 155, 159, 181, 246
Retman, Sonnet, 40
Rich, Frank, 167, 175
Rincón, Belinda, 262n2
Rivera Garza, Cristina, 208
Robinson, Cedric, 252n61
Rodriguez, Ralph, 251n3
Rodríguez, Richard T., 251n3
Rowlandson, Mary, 14–17, 252n42
Romero, Betsabé, 122–23, 139
Romero, Mary, 169
Rousseau, Jean-Jacques, 5, 7
Ruiz de Burton, María Amparo, 5, 8, 17, 31, 37–78, 81, 92, 120, 138, 153–56, 199, 224, 240; See also *Who Would Have Thought It?*; *The Squatter and the Don*

Saldívar, José David, 28
Sánchez, George, 268
Sánchez-Epppler, Karen, 250n14
Santiago, Alejandro, 200, 209–12, 222, 234, 236, 271n42
scalar imaginary, 2, 19, 30–33, 79, 146, 138, 211; captivity and, 11, 25, 138, 155; child and, 3, 6, 8, 10, 29, 53; coloniality of, 12, 18, 25, 124–30, 224; forced removal and, 24–27, 36; infra-

structure and, 126–28, 137; literary criticism and, 25, 253n76; nested hierarchies within, 19, 29–31, 66, 89, 116, 123, 239; naturalization of, 27, 119–21, 146, 241–43; racialization and, 18, 20, 24, 81, 246; sovereignty and, 23; spatial rationalization and, 120, 129, 132; temporality and, 26, 80, 122, 136–39, 149–50; witnessing within, 11, 33, 83. *See also* density; phallic verticality

Sedgwick, Eve Kosofsky, 114, 144

Shah, Nayan, 126, 268n62

Simón, Laura Angélica, 35, 155–58

slavery, 14, 17, 28, 43, 50, 56–60, 99, 106, 169–70, 202–4, 256n50, 261n48

Smith, Caleb, 16

Smith, Michael Peter, 163

Smith, Neil, 135

Sofi Mendoza's Guide to Getting Lost in Mexico (Alegría), 36, 200, 224–36, 244

Sonsini, John, 155, 171–80, 269n65

sovereignty: captivity and, 114, 201; child and, 10, 17, 36, 156, 200; coloniality and, 84, 115, 261n48; forced removal and, 14, 35, 197–98, 202, 214; movement and, 113, 236–37; property and, 12

Squatter and the Don, The (Ruiz de Burton), 124, 126

Steinbeck, John, 108, 139

Stephens, Sharon, 5

Stern, Alexandra Minna, 168

Stockton, Kathryn Bond, 54

Stowe, Harriet Beecher, 63

Stratton, Royal, 58

Sumner, Charles, 50

Szeghi, Theresa, 43

Tarallo, Bernadette, 163

temporality, 8, 32, 48, 137, 142, 149, 189, 192

Their Dogs Came with Them (Viramontes), 33, 120, 125–40, 152, 242, 244

Thompson, Lydia, 65, 258n84

Torpey, John, 13

Treaty of Guadalupe Hidalgo, 16, 44, 54, 57, 95

Trollope, Anthony, 63

2501 Migrantes (Santiago), 200, 209–12, 234, 236

Vazquez, Alexandra, 47 253n78

Vietnam, 120, 134, 264n25

Vigil, Ariana, 268n42

Villa, Raúl, 263n12

Viramontes, Helena María, 10, 33, 120, 123–37, 140, 152, 246, 263n20, 264n25. See also *Their Dogs Came with Them*

Wald, Priscilla, 126

Weber, David, 261n48

Weber, Max, 13

Wheatley, Phillis, 5, 8

White, Richard Grant, 64

Who Would Have Thought It? (Ruiz de Burton), 9, 31–2, 37–77, 87; burlesque, 63–74, 241; captivity and, 38, 56–61, 81–84, 116; child and, 53–61, 112, 138, 240; consent and, 39–45; enmity, and, 78, 153–5; forced removal, 199–200, 240; hacienda system and, 124; living curiosities and, 49–53; parody and, 66–68; racialization and, 39, 65–71; scale and, 120

Wilson, Pete, 160–66, 182, 266n16

witness: captivity and, 11, 33, 36, 39, 51, 56, 216, 247, 251n32; coloniality and, 179, 199, 201, 236; reparative, 34, 79, 83, 95–96, 114, 242; relationality and, 34, 79, 83, 95–96, 114, 242

Works Progress Administration (WPA), 96, 98–99, 106–8

Wynter, Sylvia, 15

Y no se lo tragó la tierra (Rivera), 9

Yava, Albert, 261n66

Ybarra, Patricia, 251n3, 257n76, 261n70

Zaitchik, Alexander, 153–54, 158, 187

www.ingramcontent.com/pod-product-compliance
Lightning Source LLC
Chambersburg PA
CBHW051049230426
43666CB00012B/2622